Asif Rahman

Flynt Leverett served at the National Security Council, State Department, and CIA and is currently a professor of international affairs at Penn State. Hillary Mann Leverett served at the National Security Council and State Department and negotiated for the U.S. government with Iranian officials; she is now senior professorial lecturer at American University. They blog at www.goingtotehran .com. Their writing has also appeared in *The New York Times, Politico, Foreign Policy,* and *Washington Monthly,* among other publications. They live in northern Virginia.

Praise for *Going to Tehran*

"A reasoned, methodical critique of the ideological folklore that prevents Washington from setting up normal diplomatic relations with Tehran . . . *Going to Tehran* is likely the most important book on U.S. foreign policy in 2013."   —*The Washington Spectator*

"This book sheds dramatic light on the central foreign policy of the Iranian government. The Leveretts superbly outline the true intentions of Iran and the way it is using international alliances and soft power to get there."   —Patricia DeGennaro, *The Huffington Post*

"An unorthodox analysis of Iran and a scathing criticism of the U.S.'s foreign policy . . . U.S. policy makers need to hear criticisms like these."
—*Veterans Today*

"A sharply different deconstruction of the prevailing orthodoxy, worthy of attention."   —*Kirkus Reviews*

"One needn't agree with every word in *Going to Tehran* to grasp its basic truth: U.S. Iran policy is delusional. To shatter this 'sorry Scheme of Things,' as the Persian poet describes it, will require . . . a plan not too different from what the Leveretts lay out."
—Lawrence B. Wilkerson, former chief of staff to
Secretary of State Colin Powell

"This courageous and important book contains the three elements that are necessary for a rethinking of U.S. policy toward Iran: a rigorous critique of the intellectual foundations of present strategy; a devastating exposé of misreporting of Iran in the Western media; and a set of bold ideas for how the present dangerous impasse in relations can be broken. It should be essential reading for policy makers and journalists alike."   —Anatol Lieven, author of
Pakistan: A Hard Country

GOING TO TEHRAN

Why America Must Accept the Islamic Republic of Iran

FLYNT LEVERETT AND

HILLARY MANN LEVERETT

PICADOR

A METROPOLITAN BOOK
HENRY HOLT AND COMPANY
NEW YORK

GOING TO TEHRAN. Copyright © 2013 by Flynt Leverett and Hillary Mann Leverett. All rights reserved. Printed in the United States of America. For information, address Picador, 175 Fifth Avenue, New York, N.Y. 10010.

www.picadorusa.com
www.twitter.com/picadorusa • www.facebook.com/picadorusa
picadorbookroom.tumblr.com

Picador® is a U.S. registered trademark and is used by Henry Holt and Company under license from Pan Books Limited.

For book club information, please visit www.facebook.com/ picadorbookclub or e-mail marketing@picadorusa.com.

Designed by Kelly S. Too

The Library of Congress has cataloged the Henry Holt edition as follows:

Leverett, Flynt Lawrence.
   Going to Tehran : why the United States must come to terms with the Islamic Republic of Iran / Flynt Leverett and Hillary Mann Leverett.
      p. cm.
   Includes index.
   ISBN 978-0-8050-9419-0 (hardcover)
   ISBN 978-1-4299-7334-2 (e-book)
   1. United States—Foreign relations—Iran.   2. Iran—Foreign relations—United States.   3. United States—Foreign relations—2001–   I. Title.
   E183.8.I55.L47 2013
   327.73055—dc23

                                                                      2012036700

Picador ISBN 978-1-250-04353-5

Picador books may be purchased for educational, business, or promotional use. For information on bulk purchases, please contact Macmillan Corporate and Premium Sales Department at 1-800-221-7945, extension 5442, or write specialmarkets@macmillan.com.

First published in the United States by Metropolitan Books, an imprint of Henry Holt and Company

First Picador Edition: January 2014

10 9 8 7 6 5 4 3 2 1

To our children

For if we should perish, the ruthlessness of the foe would be only the secondary cause of the disaster. The primary cause would be that the strength of a giant nation was directed by eyes too blind to see all the hazards of the struggle; and the blindness would be induced not by some accident of nature or history but by hatred and vainglory.

—Reinhold Niebuhr,
The Irony of American History, 1952

CONTENTS

WILL THE UNITED STATES LOSE THE MIDDLE EAST . . . OR COME TO TERMS WITH THE ISLAMIC REPUBLIC OF IRAN?

More than thirty years after a revolutionary movement inspired and guided by Grand Ayatollah Seyed Ruhollah Khomeini forced the last shah from Iran's Peacock Throne and assumed power, most of what even well-educated Americans think they know about the political order that Khomeini and his followers established—the Islamic Republic of Iran—is wrong. In this case, ignorance is not bliss but a source of grave danger, for the United States is courting strategic disaster by persisting in a fundamentally hostile posture toward the Islamic Republic.

From the earliest days of the Islamic Republic, many Americans have believed that their country has legitimate grievances against it. Such belief conditions an attitude in which it is incumbent on Tehran to address these grievances and accede to American preferences about the Middle East and its future before U.S.-Iranian relations can improve. But in reality the United States needs, for its own interest, to come to terms with the Islamic Republic. To some, this statement may seem unduly apologetic with regard to postrevolutionary Iran, and perhaps even anti-American. It is neither. To let grievances (imagined or real) and hegemonic pretension prevent the United States from doing what its interests manifestly require is the truly anti-American position.

Since World War II, and especially since the end of the Cold War, America's status as the preeminent power in the Middle East has been crucial to its global primacy. Its capability, alone among the world's major powers, to project conventional military force into the Middle East has enabled it to assume responsibility for the physical security of the oil and gas flow from the Persian Gulf on which the global economy depends, and to become the presumptive enforcer of order across the Middle East. This muscle has given the United States extraordinary economic and political influence in the region, and it has reinforced American dominance in other important parts of the world. (As a senior Japanese diplomat told us, if the United States did not guarantee the flow of Persian Gulf hydrocarbons to Asian markets, it would lose its Asian allies.) In the post–Cold War period, preeminence in the Middle East has buttressed America's claim to leadership in international economic affairs—even as the country continues losing ground to foreign competitors and setting records as the greatest debtor nation in history.

But the order in the Middle East that Washington has worked over decades to consolidate is eroding. To be sure, the United States will, for the foreseeable future, retain its unique ability to project military force into the region; no other power is capable of playing its enforcer role, or will be for years to come. But military capacity is less and less relevant to the challenges America faces there.

For our part, the two of us have been arguing since 9/11, inside and outside American administrations, that the United States' strategic position in the Middle East is at serious risk, in large measure because of U.S. policy mistakes, and that these mistakes stem from the same source: a post–Cold War temptation to act as an imperial power in this vital part of the world. Instead of dealing soberly and effectively with the region's complex political and security dynamics, the United States has tried to remake the Middle East in accordance with American preferences and with scant regard for Middle Eastern realities.[1]

For the past twenty years, America has not been content simply to maintain its military primacy in the Middle East, defend its interests there, and legitimize its leadership with political and strategic benefits to its regional partners. Instead, during the administrations of George H. W. Bush, Bill Clinton, George W. Bush, and Barack Obama, it has tried to coerce political outcomes with the goal of consolidating a pro-American regional order—by retaining military forces on the ground in Saudi Arabia and other Arab states after the first Gulf War (something it did not do, to any significant degree, during the Cold War); by leveling sanctions against Saddam Husayn's regime that led to the deaths of more than a million Iraqis, including half a million children (a policy that then United Nations ambassador Madeleine Albright defended with the notorious statement, "I think this is a very hard choice, but the price—we think the price is worth it"); and by invading Afghanistan and Iraq after 9/11 and pursuing prolonged occupations that, by the Defense Department's own figures, together have killed over 112,000 civilians (by other credible estimates, many more).[2] There is also Washington's perpetual insistence that everyone in the region not just accept Israel but tolerate virtually any definition of its security requirements and territorial needs put forward by the Israeli government. This agenda has pushed pro-Western regimes to line up against their own populations' most deeply held values, interests, and political preferences. In effect, the United States has forced its partners to be soft on Israel but hard on local Islamists—in the long run, an untenable position.

This imperial turn in Middle East policy has proven not just quixotic but deeply damaging to American standing and interests, in the region and globally. In particular, it ignores a lesson that balance-of-power theorists, foreign policy realists, and astute students of international history all know: while hegemony seems nice in theory, in the real world it is unattainable; not even a state as powerful as the United States coming out of the Cold War can achieve it. Indeed, pursuing hegemony has made the United States weaker. Of course, the temptations of empire have lured great powers before it into what the historian Paul Kennedy has called "imperial overstretch."[3] But America's drive to remake the Middle East has arguably set a new record for the largest amount of influence and wealth squandered by a great power in the shortest period of time.

As part of this imperial turn, the United States has systematically demonized would-be challengers to its primacy in the region, a practice whose most significant strategic consequence, in our view, has been a persistent refusal to come to terms with Iran's postrevolutionary order. Besides working to isolate the Islamic Republic diplomatically, press it economically, and foment its collapse, Washington has sought to exclude it from the mainstream of regional affairs. It clearly signaled this approach at the beginning of the post–Cold War period, as American power seemed at its height, when the George H. W. Bush administration organized the October 1991 Madrid conference. Convened ostensibly to relaunch the so-called Middle East peace process, the conference was really meant to convince Arab states to buy into a new, highly militarized and U.S.-led regional political and security order in return for vague promises of American leadership in Arab-Israeli peacemaking. The George H. W. Bush administration made a point of excluding Iran from Madrid; from its perspective, there was no place in the new order for the Islamic Republic. That exclusion became the template for Washington's post–Cold War Middle East diplomacy. Every subsequent administration has used the Arab-Israeli peace process to marginalize the Islamic Republic.

Successive administrations have developed three major complaints to justify their antagonism toward the Islamic Republic: its drive to produce weapons of mass destruction, its support for movements that Washington considers terrorist organizations, and its violations of human rights—the same trifecta of alarms the United States used to justify regime change in Iraq. But not only has the Islamic Republic survived; following the end of the Cold War, it emerged as the de facto leader of challengers to American ambitions to consolidate, in partnership with Israel, a dominant position in the Middle East. Thus the United States and Iran have become the leading antagonists in a struggle over American primacy, a new Cold War in which America's approach to Iran has grown ever less receptive to serious, strategically grounded engagement and ever more oriented toward coercive options that, despite the sterile vocabulary of "containment," nuclear "prevention," and "regime change," ultimately mean war.[4]

Over the years, Washington has sporadically engaged Tehran in various ways on various issues, but these diplomatic efforts have been hampered by the severely negative aspects of America's Iran policy, especially the perennial hope that a discontented Iranian populace will bring down the Islamic Republic and transform the nation into a Western-style secular democracy. No American president—not even Barack Obama—has pursued rapprochement with the Islamic Republic by dealing with it as a legitimate political entity and addressing its central interests. Instead, the United States has settled into a strategically incoherent approach (formalized and branded as the "dual track" strategy) in which it periodically offers to negotiate about issues on terms that could not possibly be attractive to Tehran, while simultaneously ratcheting up "pressure" via unilateral and multilateral sanctions and other punitive means.

Although this approach has consistently failed to produce any progress, the Obama administration clings to it as tightly as its predecessors did. It has even upped the ante, effectively adopting militarized prevention of Iranian nuclearization and the assertive rollback of Iranian influence as the core of its strategy and, especially since the Islamic Republic's June 2009 presidential election, moving steadily toward formal endorsement of regime change as the declared goal of American policy—just as President Bill Clinton did with Iraq in the late 1990s, paving the way for the American invasion in 2003. Along the way, Obama and his team have so reduced the options for negotiations that the diplomatic agenda now consists solely of small-bore proposals to limit specific aspects of Iran's civilian nuclear program—even as Washington continues to demand that Tehran give up its efforts to master the nuclear fuel cycle, the very heart of its program. Even if nuclear talks produce a narrowly drawn agreement, there is no indication that Washington intends to use such a deal to realign relations with Iran. Rather, it hopes that such discussions might contribute, in the words of one high official, to "buying time and continuing to move this problem into the future" while it waits for the Islamic Republic to collapse.[5] This is a recipe for strategic failure.

America's determination to keep Iran in a subordinate position has become the biggest single risk to the secure and adequate flow of oil and gas exports from the Persian Gulf, calling into question its claims to be the provider of global energy security. Moreover, in refusing to come to terms with the Islamic Republic, Washington has crippled its ability to accomplish important goals both in the region and globally and undermined its status as an international leader. As the United States has floundered in the two decades since the Madrid conference, the Islamic Republic has stepped up as a central player in the region's major political and strategic dramas: the Arab-Israeli conflict, the fate of Afghanistan and Iraq, the spread of nuclear weapons, and the fight against jihadi extremists. Iran has become, in effect, the most critical country in the world's most critical region, and by now the United States cannot achieve any of its high-priority objectives there without it. Contrary to the wishful thinking of many American analysts and the Obama administration, developments in the Middle East since the outbreak of the Arab awakening at the end of 2010 have made the Islamic Republic even more essential to shaping the Middle East's future. In Syria, Iranian mediation is a necessary condition for a negotiated resolution to what has become an increasingly bloody civil war. Yet the Obama administration has taken America's self-damaging animus against Iran to a new level: instead of engaging Tehran, it prefers to bet on the eventual overthrow of President Bashar al-Assad's government by armed forces increasingly dominated by Saudi-backed jihadis and other Al-Qa'ida-like elements.

By rejecting the Islamic Republic as a strategic partner, Washington has also sabotaged its ability to deal with politically engaged Islamist forces in the Middle East. In discussing political Islamism, it is critical to distinguish between groups like Al-Qa'ida, which define themselves almost exclusively through violent action, and movements such as HAMAS, Hizballah, and Egypt's Muslim Brotherhood, which have robust political agendas and, if they resort to armed resistance, do so instrumentally to advance those agendas. This second category includes some of the region's most authentic social forces, with political agendas stressing better governance and foreign policy independence and with track records of real service to their constituents. With the Arab awakening, they are now emerging as the most consequential political actors in countries that the United States has long considered parts of its regional sphere of influence. Some of the most important groups, like HAMAS and Hizballah, have long been closely linked to Tehran; others, like Egypt's Muslim Brotherhood, are now establishing cooperative ties. Meanwhile, the United States' unwillingness to deal with most of these movements only ensures that its regional influence will decline further. Rather than confront the inherent dysfunctionality of this approach, Washington embraces the logic-defying proposition that the same drivers of political change that are empowering Islamists in Arab countries will somehow transform the Islamic Republic into a secular liberal state.[6]

The United States is on the verge of losing its strategic position in the Middle East, with potentially disastrous consequences for its global standing as well. And the only way for it to forestall such an outcome is rapprochement with the Islamic Republic. In 1969, the newly inaugurated president, Richard Nixon, understood that the only way to rescue America's position in Asia and restore its global standing was to abandon twenty years of U.S. policy aimed at containing, demonizing, and undermining the People's Republic of China and, instead, to come to terms with it. Four decades later, Barack Obama shocked Washington's foreign policy elite during his first presidential campaign by signaling a similar understanding of the need for better relations with the Islamic Republic. But from virtually the beginning of his presidency, entrenched domestic antagonism toward the Islamic Republic, his own willful inability to understand Tehran's national security strategy, and his administration's colossal misreading of Iran's domestic political dynamics (especially after its 2009 presidential election) combined to derail his impulse toward engagement. More than any of his predecessors, in fact, Obama has given engagement a bad name, by claiming to have reached out to Tehran and failed when the truth is he never really tried.

Coming to terms with the Islamic Republic of Iran means dealing with it as it is, not as some might wish it to be. It is difficult for Americans to look objectively at a state like the Islamic Republic, which bases its political system on concepts of Islamic governance at odds with Western liberal paradigms. Decades ago, the eminent scholar Louis Hartz recognized a "deep and unwritten tyrannical compulsion" in America's liberal tradition, a "colossal liberal absolutism" that "hampers creative action abroad by identifying the alien with the unintelligible."[7] In recent years, this American predilection has been particularly evident in relation to the Middle East—and nowhere more so than in Iran.

As a result, America's Iran debate has been dominated by uninformed and agenda-driven views that have hardened into a powerful mythology about the Islamic Republic—its foreign policy, its domestic politics, and the way the United States ought to deal with it. This mythology has three main elements:

- *The irrationality myth*: the Islamic Republic is an immature, ideologically driven polity incapable of thinking about its foreign policy in terms of material national interests.
- *The illegitimacy myth*: the Islamic Republic is an illegitimate and deeply unstable political order at serious risk of implosion.
- *The isolation myth*: through concerted diplomatic action, economic pressure, and military measures, the United States can isolate the Islamic Republic, both regionally and internationally, and facilitate its demise.

In 1962, President John Kennedy warned that "the great enemy of truth is very often not the lie—deliberate, contrived, and dishonest—but the myth—persistent, persuasive, and unrealistic. Too often we hold fast to the clichés of our forebears. We subject all facts to a prefabricated set of interpretations. We enjoy the comfort of opinion without the discomfort of thought." Half a century later, this captures well the pernicious impact of America's Iran mythology. Not only do its constituent elements assure the continuing dysfunctionality of

Washington's Iran strategy, they make engagement with Tehran seem like a fool's errand—politically, morally, and strategically. More ominously, they are conditioning the political climate in the United States for an eventual war against Iran—just as in the late 1990s and early 2000s the political climate was conditioned for war against Iraq by falsehoods about Saddam's weapons of mass destruction, his links to Al-Qa'ida, and the Shangri-La of post-Saddam Iraqi politics.

The prevailing Iran mythology is rarely challenged in mainstream discourse, for that requires a willingness to question not just America's role in the Middle East but also basic precepts of American political culture. Many intellectuals and journalists in the United States have internalized the "liberal absolutism" described by Hartz, predisposing them to see foreigners resisting American hegemony not as rational actors with real interests but as irrational and illegitimate. Self-interest reinforces this proclivity: while artfully applying a hegemonic perspective to the perceived threat du jour can dramatically boost a career in policy analysis or journalism, an unwillingness to do so can damage one's prospects. Before the Chinese Revolution and for twenty years after, the press and a critical mass of America's Asia experts crafted an image of China's communist leaders as rabid ideologues with whom no accommodation was possible. Before the 2003 invasion of Iraq, policy analysts and reporters partnered to demonize Saddam's regime, hype the threat posed by his WMD and terrorist ties, and understate the negative consequences of removing him by U.S. military action. In both cases, those who played the game (for example, the Alsop brothers on China and Ken Pollack on Iraq) were rewarded; those who dissented were marginalized, if not—as with the so-called China hands—persecuted.

As Tehran challenges America's hegemonic ambitions in the Middle East, think tank and university specialists have given quasi-professional legitimation to the prevailing Iran mythology, helping to make it conventional wisdom among American elites. It is telling that the most detailed chronicle of U.S.-Iranian relations since the revolution was written by a historian whose day job is with U.S. Central Command (and whose father is a former CENTCOM commander) and is framed in terms of the "twilight war" between Washington and Tehran—a work that draws on virtually no Iranian sources (other than defectors and expatriates) to depict the Islamic Republic as the clear provocateur and the United States as "largely the good guy."[8] Western media routinely accept and elaborate on myths of the Islamic Republic's irrationality and illegitimacy. In a particularly outlandish case, Amir Taheri, an expatriate Iranian journalist and a darling of American neoconservatives (he appears regularly on Fox News and in *National Review*, the *New York Post*, and the *Wall Street Journal*), published an article in Canada's *National Post* in 2006 claiming that the Iranian parliament had passed a law requiring Jews to wear strips of yellow cloth pinned to their clothing.[9] Before publishing the article, the *National Post* checked with the Simon Wiesenthal Center, which vouched for it. But Taheri's claim was entirely manufactured; in a rare bit of journalistic accountability on an Iran-related story in the Western media, the *National Post* retracted Taheri's story with a public apology.[10] This was not the first time that Taheri had invented claims about the Islamic Republic or Iranian officials.[11] When asked about Taheri's penchant for falsehood, his publicist replied that accuracy is "a luxury" where Iran is concerned: "As much as being accurate is important, in the end what's important is to side with what's right. What's wrong is siding with the terrorists."[12] After the Iraq War debacle, accuracy is anything but a luxury where Iran is concerned. Yet neoconservative venues like the *National Post* and the *Wall Street Journal* are not the only media outlets that let the Iran mythology distort their coverage and commentary; as we will see, "mainstream" venues like the *New York Times* and the *Washington Post* do, too.

Given all that is at stake in the Middle East, we offer this book as a challenge to our fellow Americans and others to reconsider what they think they know about the Islamic Republic. It is especially critical to understand the Islamic Republic's international strategy and its internal politics. To that end, we present what we believe is an empathetic but objective account of how the Islamic Republic sees itself and its place in the world, acts to protect its interests, and legitimizes itself to the Iranian people. We also deconstruct the mythology that surrounds

Iran, demonstrating the extent of its persuasive power and its fallacies and identifying some of the individuals, organizations, and informal networks that perpetuate its hold over our public discourse. Finally, we outline a better way forward for the United States with Iran and the Middle East more broadly. For the alternatives to rapprochement— militarized containment, coercive regime change, and war—are far too damaging, to American interests and to the people of the Middle East, to bear serious strategic or moral consideration.

PART ONE

THE ISLAMIC REPUBLIC AS RATIONAL ACTOR

PROLOGUE

In the more than thirty years since the Iranian Revolution, Western analysts have routinely depicted the Islamic Republic as an immature, ideologically driven polity incapable of thinking about its foreign policy in terms of national interests. From this Western—and, especially, American—perspective, the Islamic Republic displayed its fanatical character early on, first in the hostage crisis of 1979–81 and shortly afterward with the deployment of teenage soldiers in "human wave" attacks against Iraqi forces during the 1980s. Supposedly the same Shi'a "cult of martyrdom" and indifference to casualties that fueled those tactics persist in a deep attachment to suicide terrorism and would, if the Islamic Republic acquired nuclear weapons, render it "undeterrable" by Western standards of rational cost-benefit calculation.[1] Allegations of the government's "irrationality" are inevitably linked to assertions that it is out to export its revolution across the Middle East by force, is hell-bent on the destruction of Israel, and is too dependent on anti-Americanism for its domestic legitimacy to contemplate improving relations with the United States.

Images of the Islamic Republic as the epitome of an irrationally radical state are often conveyed through analogies with the twentieth-century's most criminal regimes. Some—including former British prime minister Tony Blair, former Speaker of the U.S. House of Representatives Newt Gingrich, and a host of current and former Israeli officials, among them Prime Minister Binyamin Netanyahu—have compared the Islamic Republic to Nazi Germany, arguing that "it's 1938 and Iran is Germany" and "what Iran is trying to do right now is not far away at all from what Hitler did to the Jewish people just 65 years ago." According to Walter Russell Mead, a prominent historian of American foreign policy who ought to be above misplaced incendiary analogies, "It's a legitimate argument and subject for discussion about whether the Iranians are jerks like Franco who will settle down to peacefully hang homosexuals and torture dissidents at home if left to themselves, or whether they are megalomaniacal nutcases who will interpret our forbearance as weakness—if we let them have Czechoslovakia they will start reaching for Poland." The *Wall Street Journal*'s Bret Stephens has compared the Islamic Republic to "Japan of the 1930s and World War II—another martyrdom-obsessed, non-Western culture with global ambitions." Karim Sadjadpour of the Carnegie Endowment for International Peace has looked to the Soviet Union for parallels, arguing that "the Islamic Republic is a corrupt, inefficient, authoritarian regime" with a "bankrupt ideology," whose leaders, "like the men who once ruled Moscow . . . derive their internal legitimacy from thumbing their noses at Uncle Sam."[2]

Even more extreme is the racially tinged rhetoric about "mad mullahs" conspiratorially "chuckling behind their beards" as they work to acquire nuclear weapons, which they and/or Mahmoud Ahmadinejad, Iran's millenarian lay president, will use to attack Israel, the United States, and other enemies of Islam. Bernard Lewis and his neoconservative acolytes have asserted that Ahmadinejad and/or the mullahs would launch such an attack—making the Islamic Republic, in effect, history's first "suicide nation"—to hasten the reappearance of the *mahdi*, or Twelfth Imam, thus setting the stage for God's final

judgment and a more conclusive "end of history" than Francis Fukuyama ever imagined.[3] In 2006, Lewis even identified a religiously
significant date (August 22, which that year corresponded to the twenty-
seventh day of the Islamic month of Rajab, when Muslims commemorate *laylat al-mab'ath*, "the night of appointment," when the Prophet
Muhammad was launched on his prophetic mission) as the time Iran
might detonate its first nuclear weapons.[4] As Ahmadinejad himself has
mockingly noted, many Americans seem to think that Iranians are all
"sitting in the desert, turned toward Mecca, and waiting to die."

The veteran diplomat Chas Freeman points out that "to dismiss a
foreign government, policy, or circumstance as 'irrational' is to con-
fess that one does not understand its motivations, causes, or calculus,
has no idea how to deal with it short of the use of force, and has no
intention of making the effort to discover how to do so."[5] If American
political and policy elites were to make such an effort, they would discover that the Islamic Republic has shown itself to be a highly rational
actor in the conduct of its foreign policy. The Iranian government did
not launch an ideologically motivated holy war against Iraq in the
1980s; rather, it struggled to defend the Iranian people against a brutal
Iraqi invasion that was directly supported by many of Iran's neighbors
as well as by Western powers, including the United States. When in
the course of that war Iran was subjected to years of chemical attacks,
Grand Ayatollah Khomeini—the Islamic Republic's founding father—
and his associates chose not to weaponize Iran's stockpiles of chemical
agents, a move that would have enabled it to respond in kind. And for
years now the Islamic Republic's highest political and religious authorities have rejected the acquisition and use of nuclear weapons, both on
strategic grounds and because, in their view, nuclear weapons violate
Islamic morality.

Tehran's support for terrorism is another essential theme in Western narratives. Yet the most comprehensive, data-based study of suicide terrorism carried out to date determined that there has never been
an Iranian suicide bomber.[6] Iranian support for paramilitary groups
that the United States considers terrorist organizations or threats to

American forces—Hizballah, HAMAS, Shi'a militias in Iraq—has been focused in theaters where the United States, Israel, or Sunni states allied to Washington are seeking to undermine important Iranian interests. For years after 9/11, some neoconservatives claimed that Osama bin Laden was "living in luxury" in Iran, an assertion elaborated in a 2010 "documentary" that was extensively touted on Fox News.[7] The allegation was picked up by more centrist journalists like ABC's George Stephanopoulos, who pushed Ahmadinejad in an interview to say whether the Islamic Republic was, in fact, harboring bin Laden.[8] (Ahmadinejad retorted, "I heard that he was in Washington, D.C.") Beyond the demonstrated absurdity of the claim, public statements by Al-Qa'ida leaders as well as documents captured by American special forces from Osama bin Laden's compound in Abbottabad, Pakistan, in May 2011 show that the relationship between Al-Qa'ida and the Islamic Republic has been deeply antagonistic.[9]

If Westerners looked soberly at the record, they would discover that Iran is not aggressively exporting its revolution. It is true that in the years immediately following the shah's overthrow, *sudur-e enqelab*—"exporting the revolution"—was proclaimed as a principle of Iranian foreign policy by Khomeini himself. But what did this principle mean? Should the Islamic Republic actively work to replicate its revolution elsewhere, disregarding international norms of sovereignty and noninterference in other states' internal affairs? Or should it concentrate on making itself an exemplary model of Islamic governance from which other states might draw inspiration? In the decade between the revolution and his death, Khomeini made statements that seemed to support both positions. But the postrevolutionary constitution—in which the phrase "exporting the revolution" never appears—notes that the Islamic Republic must "scrupulously refrain from all forms of aggressive intervention in the internal affairs of other nations."[10] Moreover, all the major figures in the first generation of Iran's post-Khomeini leadership—including Ayatollah Seyed Ali Khamenei, who succeeded Khomeini as supreme leader, and Ali Akbar Hashemi Rafsanjani, the first president elected after Khomeini's death—were clearly committed to the exemplarist approach. Early in his tenure as supreme leader, Khamenei declared that "the Islamic Revolution of Iran has taken place and was simultaneously exported throughout the world. The revolution was exported once, and that is the end of the story."[11] Throughout his more than two decades in power, this has been a firm precept guiding Iranian policy.

Likewise, the Islamic Republic is not out to destroy Israel. One of the more pernicious legends about Ahmadinejad is that he threatened to do so—a claim now so entrenched in mainstream Western discourse as to be a social fact. But the claim is false, as Israel's intelligence minister later admitted.[12] It is based on a poor translation of a speech Ahmadinejad delivered in October 2005, shortly after he became president, and was given international currency by journalistically irresponsible articles in the *New York Times* and other outlets.[13] These accounts depict Ahmadinejad declaring that Israel must be "wiped off the map," evoking a Nazi-like campaign to exterminate the Jewish state and its people. Consider, though, what Ahmadinejad actually said in Farsi: he cited Khomeini's statement that *"een rezhim-e ishghalgar-e qods bayad az safheh-ye ruzgar mahv shavad"*—literally, that "this regime occupying Jerusalem must disappear from the page of time."[14] For those who insist on conflating anti-Zionism with anti-Semitism, this may seem a distinction without a difference. But there is no threat to destroy Israel in that sentence or anywhere else in the speech. Later, Ahmadinejad analogizes the eventual disappearance from the page of time of "the regime" in Israel to the collapse of the Soviet system—a result of internal failures, not external aggression.

Tehran's objective is to contain what Iranian leaders since Khomeini have seen as Israel's ambitions to weaken and subordinate its Muslim neighbors. Iranian policy makers take a long view of their standoff with Israel, expecting that the unsustainability of apartheidlike political arrangements in the twenty-first century will lead to the fall of Israel's current political structure—not the annihilation of its Jewish population. Such a scenario is disturbing to Israelis and Israel's supporters, but it does not entail an Iranian threat to liquidate the

Jewish state or its Jewish inhabitants. Recently, Ahmadinejad has attracted additional rounds of Western criticism over his description of Israel as an "insult to humanity." However, the phrase—which has been used by other Iranian leaders as well—is taken word for word from innumerable statements by U.N. bodies, dating back to the 1960s, criticizing South Africa's apartheid system.[15] It is language of moral condemnation, not of physical threat.

In evaluating statements about Israel from Ahmadinejad, Ayatollah Khamenei, or any other Iranian official, Westerners would do well to consider that, from Tehran's perspective, Israel is effectively at war with the Islamic Republic. Israeli officials regularly threaten to use military force against Iran, and Iranians know that Israel is sponsoring a wide range of covert actions against their country, including assassinations of its scientists and lethal terrorist bombings.[16] Westerners might also recall that, before Anwar Sadat was hailed as a "man of peace" by Israel and the United States, he made not only anti-Zionist statements but also more clearly and virulently anti-Semitic statements than anything Ahmadinejad or other Iranian officials have uttered and that he launched a war that killed thousands of Israelis. Before Israel and the United States enshrined Palestinian president Mahmoud Abbas as a "partner for peace," he published a book on "the secret relationship between Nazism and Zionism," in which he described the Holocaust as "the Zionist fantasy, the fantastic lie that six million Jews were killed." After Israel and the PLO signed the Oslo Accords in 1993, he said, regarding his book, "When I wrote [it], we were at war with Israel. Today I would not have made such remarks."[17]

The record also shows that the Islamic Republic has not been irrevocably antagonistic toward the United States. Over the past two decades Tehran has consistently cooperated on issues when Washington has requested its assistance, and it has frequently explored the possibilities for improved American-Iranian relations. It is the United States that has repeatedly terminated these episodes of bilateral cooperation and rebuffed Iranian overtures, reinforcing Iranian leaders' suspicion that Washington will never accept the Islamic Republic.

The Islamic Republic continues to frame its foreign policy with reference to principles reflecting its religious and revolutionary roots. But for many years it has defined its diplomatic and national security strategies in largely nonideological terms, on the basis of national interests that are perfectly legitimate: to be free from the threat of attack and from interference in its internal affairs; to be accepted by neighbors and the world's most militarily powerful state as Iran's legitimate government. And for more than twenty years the Islamic Republic has shown itself capable of acting rationally to defend and advance these interests. Americans may not like Tehran's strategic and tactical choices—its links to political factions and their associated militias in Afghanistan and Iraq, its support for HAMAS and Hizballah, its pursuit of nuclear fuel cycle capabilities that would also give it a nuclear weapons option. But these choices are far from irrational, particularly in the face of continuing animosity from Washington and a number of regional states.

Stereotypes depicting the Islamic Republic as an aggressively radical state are not merely wrong but, worse, dangerous, because they skew Western thinking toward the inevitability of confrontation. In January 2011, Tony Blair told a British government inquiry into the Iraq War that the Islamic Republic was a "looming challenge," "negative and destabilizing," that had "to be confronted and changed." In his call for regime change in Iran—as in his earlier call for regime change in Iraq—Blair has been backed by a chorus of neoconservative leaders in the United States, a rising number of U.S. senators and representatives on both sides of the aisle, and a growing body of European elites.

Hence the importance of understanding accurately the Islamic Republic's foreign policy and national security strategy. As an astute Iranian strategist wrote:

If the Iranian leadership's actions are perceived as offensive and expansionist, then the rational choice for the United States is to maintain robust deterrence. In contrast, if Iran's policies are defensive, then the rational choice for the United States is to seek cooperation with Iran and eventually to help integrate Iran into the regional political-security architecture. Such integration is certainly inseparable from settling the ongoing nuclear dispute and reaching a broader and much anticipated *détente* with the United States. It is essential that Washington not misinterpret Iran's actions.[18]

It is indeed essential. For if the myth of the Islamic Republic's irrationality is not dispelled, Western perceptions that war with Iran is inevitable will eventually turn into a self-fulfilling prophecy.

1

A REVOLUTIONARY STATE IN
A DANGEROUS WORLD

The position of a state in the world depends on the degree of independence it has attained.

—Leopold von Ranke, 1833

In a surprise assault beginning on September 22, 1980, more than half of Saddam Husayn's army poured into the nascent Islamic Republic of Iran, seizing significant chunks of its territory. Defying the Iraqi president's expectations of quick victory, the new government in Tehran mounted a tenacious defense of its homeland. Over eight bloody years, Iran recaptured all the territory the Iraqis had taken, paying a horrible price in the process.

In 1982, the Iraqi forces began using chemical weapons—initially, tear gas—on the battlefield; from 1983 on, they unleashed more potent chemical weapons, mainly mustard gas and nerve agents, against Iranian forces as well as against civilian targets. Iraqi officials later told United Nations inspectors that their military had used approximately 100,000 munitions filled with chemical weapons against Iran.[1] To raise the cost of resistance even more, in 1984 Iraq made population centers its primary target, opening the so-called war of the cities, with air and missile strikes that continued until the fighting ended, in 1988. By then, more than 200,000 Iranians had been killed and almost

400,000 injured. More than 10,000 Iranian victims of Iraqi chemical weapons attacks died; 60,000 to 90,000 continue to suffer—in many cases, acutely—from the effects of their exposure.[2] Beyond the human cost, the war inflicted extensive damage on Iran's economy and infrastructure.[3]

What Iranians to this day call the Imposed War and the Holy Defense had a profound effect on the way they see their country's strategic situation. It drove home how severely the Islamic Republic, as a revolutionary state, is threatened in a dangerous world. For it was not launched solely by a power-mad tyrant seeking more territory. Throughout his war of aggression, Saddam had the financial, logistical, political, and intelligence support of the United States, other Western powers, and the Arab world's richest states. In September 1987, as the war still raged, Ayatollah Seyed Ali Khamenei, then Iran's president, told the United Nations General Assembly that "no revolution is safe from the counterstrikes of the power system dominating our world, but the variety, the depth, and the enormity of the enmities and the wild anger unleashed against us . . . constitute an exceptionally interesting story."[4] This view remains widely shared by his compatriots.

Western students of international affairs have long divided states into two categories. Those that accept the formal and informal rules of international interactions and the distribution of power underlying them are said to pursue "status quo" foreign policies; those that do not accept the prevailing international order and want to change it in fundamental ways are deemed to have "revisionist" or even "revolutionary" foreign policies.[5] The distinction is problematic; it overlooks the fact that consequential states (including, for most of its history, the United States) usually seek to increase their power relative to others even as they work within prevailing frameworks of international order.[6] Nevertheless, it continues to influence the way in which Westerners, and especially Americans, think and talk about international relations.

For all that the United States is the product of a revolution, it has generally not liked revolutions in other countries and has certainly not approved of states with what it considers revolutionary foreign policies.[7] Many analysts argue that revolutionary states are, almost by definition, more likely than others to initiate conflict, either because their ideologies compel them to export their revolutions (even in violation of international norms of sovereignty and nonintervention) or because their internally fractious nature creates a need to divert public attention from domestic problems by creating external enemies.[8] In Western discourse, the Islamic Republic is commonly tagged with this image of the revolutionary state as an ideologically driven aggressor.

The historical record shows that postrevolutionary Iran has been—and, Iranians say, desires to be—a fundamentally defensive state. In contrast to other Middle Eastern powers, it has never attacked another state or even threatened to attack one. In fact, since the revolution it has grown less and less capable of projecting conventional military force beyond its borders. The Iranians who forced the shah from his throne in 1979 inherited the powerful U.S.-armed military he had built up during the last quarter century of his reign. But in the revolution's wake, most of the officers who had commanded the shah's military either fled or were executed. Washington cut off logistical and technical support immediately after the revolution, a debilitating measure that was exacerbated by an embargo on military shipments from most other countries during the Iran-Iraq War. Once the war ended, the Iranian government shifted budgetary resources away from the military and toward reconstruction and economic development, reducing the nation's conventional military capability to marginal levels. Today, the United States spends almost seventy times more on defense than Iran does, Saudi Arabia more than quadruple, and Israel nearly double.[9] Assertions that the Islamic Republic poses an offensive threat are baseless; to borrow a phrase from the U.S. Army, it won't be parking its tanks in anybody's front yard anytime soon.

While some revolutionary states have been aggressors, they are not inevitably so; history shows that a revolutionary order can just as easily become the target of aggression by states that, fearful of destabilizing contagion, calculate that its internal upheaval makes it more vulnerable to defeat.[10] This was precisely the Islamic Republic's experience. It had to fight off a devastating Iraqi invasion launched less than eighteen months after its creation—an invasion prompted by Saddam's confidence that the fledgling state could not defend itself.[11] Coming out of this war, Iranian policy makers understood that a stable region was crucial—for postwar reconstruction, for longer-term economic development, and for the growth of the Islamic Republic's regional influence. As one Iranian academic points out, his nation's "interest in a stable Middle East is arguably greater than that of the United States—after all, this is Iran's neighborhood."[12]

The essence of sound strategic calculation—whether by a diplomat, general, CEO, or coach—is what game theorists and business school professors call "interdependent decision"—the recognition that determining your best course of action depends in considerable measure on understanding the agendas of your competitors and assessing accurately how they will react to your decisions.[13] But American myths badly distort the discussion of Iran's strategic concerns, perceptions, and goals. The irrationality myth, especially, insulates Americans against having to face their real problem with the Islamic Republic: its unwillingness to accede to American domination. As a result, the record of U.S. policy toward Iran since the 1979 revolution reflects an extraordinary and ever worsening obtuseness about Iran's national security and foreign policy agenda and its evolving role in the Middle East's balance of power.

How should Americans understand the Islamic Republic's international behavior? Its national security policies are shaped, like everyone else's, by a mix of factors. Material realities—geography, demographics, military and economic capabilities (what political scientists call "structure")—play a large role. But softer factors—shared identities and aspirations, principled beliefs about right and wrong, subjective assessments of other states' intentions (what scholars call "strategic culture")—bear an influence as well.[14] These and other factors embedded in domestic politics function as a prism through which policy makers, in Iran and elsewhere, interpret the international environment, identify strategic options, and choose among them.

Iran's national security strategy cannot be properly understood without grasping the way Iranians see their country and its place in the world. In particular, their sense of being part of a profound political experiment—an Islamic Republic—conditions their responses both to their history and to lived experiences like the Iran-Iraq War. Those responses, in turn, shape their relationships to other actors in their strategic environment. More specifically, they shape the way Iranians perceive the threats emanating from others.

THE HISTORICAL LEGACY

For Iranians, questions of national identity are inextricably bound up with their country's history of domination by great powers from outside the Middle East.[15] Iran's location in the heart of the Persian Gulf and at the crossroads of the Middle East, Central Asia, and South Asia has long made it a focus for ambitious states seeking influence over a critical part of the Eurasian landmass. Since the advent of the oil age, its enormous hydrocarbon resources—the world's third-largest proven reserves of conventional crude oil and second-largest proven reserves of natural gas—have reinforced its strategic importance. Between its natural gas reserves and its oil reserves, the country's hydrocarbon resources are effectively equal to those of Saudi Arabia and significantly greater than those of Russia.[16]

Western powers—especially Britain and Russia—began asserting influence over Iran in a serious and sustained way in the early 1800s. Their "great game" for regional primacy in Central Asia culminated in the Anglo-Russian Convention (or Entente) of 1907, which formally divided Iran into British and Russian spheres of influence.[17] For most of the twentieth century, Britain and Russia, and then the United States, exercised strategic control over Iran's foreign policy and domestic politics, including the creation and maintenance of the Pahlavi dynasty. British machinations facilitated Reza Pahlavi's ascension to the Peacock

Throne in 1926. In 1941, after he had cultivated relations with Nazi Germany as a hedge against British and Soviet influence, collaborative maneuvering and armed intervention by Britain and the Soviet Union led to his replacement by his son, Mohammad Reza.[18] The perception that the new shah had been installed by Iran's two long-standing foreign masters doomed any prospect of indigenous support he might have had, and opposition to his reign mounted over the next decade. In 1953, popular pressure forced his departure from Iran. But later that year, a CIA-instigated coup brought down Mohammad Mossadeq's democratically elected government and reinstated the shah.[19]

For Khomeini and those who shared his quest to overthrow the Pahlavi dynasty, restoring Iran's sovereignty after a century and a half of rule by puppet regimes was an essential element of the revolutionary agenda. In his earliest writing about politics—*Revelation of Secrets (Kashf-e Asrar)*, a book written shortly after Reza Shah's forced abdication—Khomeini decried Iran's domination by the West and the Pahlavis' collaboration in it:

> The day everyone was forced to wear a Pahlavi cap, it was said, "We need to have a national symbol. Independence in matters of dress is proof and guarantee of the independence of a nation." Then a few years later, everyone was forced to put on European hats, and suddenly the justification changed: "We have dealings with foreigners and must dress the same way they do in order to enjoy greatness in the world." If a country's greatness depended on its hat, it would be a thing very easily lost! While all this was going on, the foreigners, who wished to implement their plans and rob you of one hat while putting another on your head, watched you in amusement from afar and laughed at your infantile games. . . . Meanwhile, the historic patrimony of the country was being plundered from one end to the other, all its sources of wealth were being carried off, and you yourselves were being reduced to a pitiful state.[20]

Two decades later, in one of his first high-profile challenges to Pahlavi rule, Khomeini charged that the shah and his government had "nothing to do with the people" and had treasonously surrendered Iran's freedom and independence to "our masters" in Washington. Iran, Khomeini said, was effectively "occupied by America," while the shah's deputies and ministers were "all agents of America, for if they were not, they would rise up in protest."[21]

Those words cost Khomeini dearly. He spent the next fifteen years in forced exile—first in Turkey, then in Iraq, and finally in France. During this period, his scathing indictment that the shah was an American puppet resonated across Iranian society. Ever since Britain and Russia had subverted Iran's 1906 Constitutional Revolution—when Iranians created both their first written constitution and their first elected parliament—Iranian elites had chafed at foreign powers' using the country as a pawn in their strategic games while undermining its political development. The unpopularity of the shah's partnership with the United States helps to explain why, in 1978, as the Iranian Revolution reached its climax on the streets, one of the slogans demonstrators most frequently chanted was "*esteqlal, azadi: jomhouri eslami*" ("independence, freedom: Islamic republic"). Once the shah was gone, Khomeini promised, an Iranian state no longer beholden to outside powers would look to the true interests of the Iranian nation and its people.

Protecting Iran's independence and sovereignty, de facto and de jure, became the primary goal of the Islamic Republic's foreign policy; it remains so today. As Khomeini put it, "Our policy is always based upon the preservation of freedom, independence, and interest of the people. We will not sacrifice this principle for the sake of something else." Similarly, the Islamic Republic's constitution declares that

the freedom, independence, unity, and territorial integrity of the country are inseparable from one another, and their preservation is the duty of the government and all individual citizens. No individual, group, or authority has the right to infringe in the slightest way upon the political, cultural, economic, and military independence or the territorial integrity of Iran under the pretext of exercising freedom.[22]

(That is why the mere perception of American support for opposition movements in Iran dooms them to failure.)

This historical legacy has important consequences for the Islamic Republic. International relations scholars explain that a nation confronted by a more powerful state chooses between two basic options: it either "bandwagons" with the powerful state or "balances" against it.[23] For the Islamic Republic, bandwagoning is simply not possible. Such an alignment, with the compromises to sovereignty it necessarily entails, was a key aspect of what Iranians rejected when they revolted against Pahlavi rule. During the Cold War, Khomeini took as the motto for Iran's new foreign policy "neither East nor West"—words that are literally carved in stone at the entrance to the country's Ministry of Foreign Affairs. From its outset, the Islamic Republic has been irrevocably committed to balancing.

Many Western and expatriate Iranian analysts either refuse to accept or simply ignore this point. Some of them argue that "neither East nor West" might have made sense during the Cold War but that, in a post–Cold War world, "getting ahead" requires compromising on foreign policy independence to cultivate better relations with the United States and avoid being left out of the prosperity generated by globalization.[24] Others, like Ray Takeyh, one of Washington's mainstream Iran analysts, argue that the Islamic Republic, "by virtue of its size and historical achievements," believes it has "the right to emerge as the local hegemon"; the key strategic questions for Iran, according to Takeyh, are "how it should consolidate its sphere of influence and whether it can emerge as a regional hegemon in defiance of or accommodation with the United States."[25]

Such a reading of the Islamic Republic's strategic orientation is doubly flawed. First, the Islamic Republic does not seek to replace American aspirations to regional dominance with its own hegemonic ambitions. As a matter of policy, it aspires to become the Middle East's leading nation, economically, scientifically, and technologically.[26] But as we will see, its foreign policy and national security strategy are defensive, with the overarching goal of ensuring its security and safety, defined in terms of national independence and territorial and political integrity. Second, and more immediately relevant, there is no way the Islamic Republic could pursue regional hegemony in "accommodation with the United States." That was the shah's strategy. He did not bandwagon with Washington to neutralize an American threat to the security of an Iranian regime that the CIA had returned to power; rather, he was willing to trade off aspects of Iran's autonomy and partner with America because he calculated that this was the best way to realize his ambitions for Iran to become a regional hegemon.[27] (In this sense, his strategy was far more revisionist than any course the Islamic Republic has even considered.) Seeking regional dominance in accommodation with Washington has also been Israel's strategy. It could not be Khomeini's strategy or the strategy of those who, since his death, have guided the political order he founded.

RELIGIOUS AND REVOLUTIONARY IDENTITIES

The Islamic Republic's commitment to defending its independence and sovereignty is reinforced by its religious and revolutionary principles. More than twenty years after his death, Khomeini is still regarded in the West as a dogmatic authoritarian, the quintessential fundamentalist. But in the Muslim world even his detractors acknowledge him as one of the most innovative figures in modern Islamic thought.

As with many other Iranians, Khomeini's full name—Seyed Ruhollah Mustafavi Mousavi Hindi Khomeini—conveys a great deal of information about his background.[28] Seyed, from the Arabic *sayyid*, or "lord," is an honorific, indicating that its bearer is a lineal descendant of the Prophet Muhammad, an important status in Shi'a culture and tradition. Ruhollah, really his first name, comes from Arabic and means "God's spirit," suggesting that his parents were deeply religious. Mustafavi refers to Ruhollah's father, Mustafa, who was a Shi'a cleric. Mousavi conveys that Seyed Ruhollah Mustafavi was descended from the Prophet through Musa al-Kazim, the seventh of the 12 imams. (In Shi'a belief, the imams are those descendants of the Prophet Muhammad—twelve over the course of human history, the last being the *mahdi*, or "hidden Imam"—singled out by God to lead the Muslim community. This is the reason mainstream Shi'a are frequently referred to as "Twelvers"; some minority Shi'a sects do not accept all twelve of the imams.) Hindi shows that part of Khomeini's family had ties to India; in the eighteenth century, some of his ancestors migrated from their original homeland in northeastern Iran to India (long home to the world's second-largest Shi'a population), settling in Lucknow and, later, in Kashmir, where they served local Shi'a communities as clerics.

Khomeini, commonly treated as Seyed Ruhollah's surname, signifies that his family had settled in the village of Khomein, in central Iran between Tehran and Esfahan, where the future religious and political leader was born in 1902. (His grandfather, Seyed Ahmad, also a cleric, had come to Iran from Kashmir in the nineteenth century.) Most Iranians did not have surnames, as Westerners understand the practice, until 1924, when Reza Shah ordered all his countrymen to take one. Just a few years earlier, the young Seyed Ruhollah had left his birthplace to study theology in the venerable pilgrimage center of Qom, 160 miles northeast of Khomein. When the decree about surnames was issued, he did what many Iranians (especially clerics) did and took his from the name of his hometown.

By the 1930s Seyed Ruhollah Khomeini had been recognized as an ayatollah (literally "sign of God"), a significant clerical rank, and given a teaching position in Qom's *hawza*, or seminary; he quickly emerged as one of the city's most charismatic scholars and began to attract a public following. Over the course of his life, he produced an enormous body of writings, on many aspects of theology, philosophy, and religious law; he also composed more than two hundred mystical poems, many of arresting quality, that belie the dour puritanical image he continues to hold in the West. But the most intellectually and historically consequential part of his work focused on the intersection of religion and politics.

Khomeini believed that religion and politics are inseparable and that political engagement is a sacred responsibility. He rejected a quietist conception of Islam that "concerns itself only with rules of ritual purity after menstruation and parturition" but "has nothing to say about human life in general and the ordering of society." Islam could only be properly understood as "a comprehensive religion providing for every aspect of human life"—including, specifically and especially, politics and government.[29] And in Khomeini's simultaneously religious and political vision, politics was not just about the distribution of power and the nature of the state; it was also about the eternal struggle between *haq va batel*, which can mean both "right and wrong" and "truth and falsehood." By the early 1960s, he had been recognized as a grand ayatollah (*ayatollah al-ozma*), the highest clerical rank in Shi'a Islam; this gave him the standing to begin articulating a sharp and religiously grounded public critique of Pahlavi rule.

Khomeini's approach made him one of the intellectual architects of "political Shi'ism," as some have come to call the body of ideas developed by prominent scholars at the hawza in Najaf, the shrine city and citadel of Shi'a learning in Iraq, during the 1960s and 1970s.[30] Khomeini spent thirteen of his fifteen years in exile there, addressing the social implications of religious principles. In essence, these ideas make it a religious duty for Muslims to oppose corrupt and illegitimate rulers and to confront injustice. As Khomeini's standing and authority grew, during the revolution and afterward, he would come increasingly to be referred to not by his clerical title, Grand Ayatollah, but as Imam—an extraordinary acknowledgment that, as an associate put it, "his authority has gone far beyond the traditional bounds" of religious guidance to encompass political leadership as well.[31]

For Khomeini, the revolutionary commitment to restore Iran's sovereignty and defend its independence was grounded in the underlying principles of justice, equality among peoples and nations, and unity of the *umma* (the community of Muslim believers). These principles are themselves grounded in Islam; in Khomeini's reading, they imply staunch opposition to hegemony and domination in all forms. In the most systematic exposition of his thinking on the integration of religion and politics before the Iranian Revolution—a series of lectures delivered in Najaf in early 1970 and subsequently published in book form as *Islamic Government (Hukumat-e Eslami)*—Khomeini defined Islam as "the religion of militant individuals who are committed to truth and justice. It is the religion of those who desire freedom and independence. It is the school of those who struggle against imperialism."[32]

Khomeini's revolutionary agenda emphasized the *mostazafin*, the "dispossessed." Domestically, a focus on the mostazafin meant prioritizing the problems of the poor. Internationally, Khomeini used the term to designate countries that lack power and are exploited, juxtaposing them with the *mostakbarin*, states that have power and use it to dominate others. Iran's subjugation, he argued, was not an isolated episode of injustice; the Western conspiracies against the Islamic world were of long standing, driven by imperialist ambitions to control the Middle East's strategic territory and resources. By throwing out the puppet regime that governed Iran for the benefit of outside powers, Khomeini and his followers were not merely defending Iranian interests but also standing up for the umma—the whole Muslim world—and for all mostazafin.

That is why, for Khomeini, it was critically important to recover the political and social dimensions of true Islam:

> If you pay no attention to the policies of the imperialists, and consider Islam to be simply the few topics you are always studying, and never go beyond them, then the imperialists will leave you alone. Pray as much as you like; it is your oil they are after—why should they worry about your prayers? They are after our minerals, and want to turn our country into a market for their goods. That is the reason the puppet governments they have installed prevent us from industrializing, and instead, establish only assembly plants and industry that is dependent on the outside world. They do not want us to be true human beings, for they are afraid of true human beings. Even if only one true human being appears, they fear him, because others will follow him and he will have an impact that can destroy the whole foundation of tyranny, imperialism, and government by puppets.[33]

In the years since the Islamic Republic's founding, opposition to hegemony has been a far more prominent feature of Iranian thinking about international affairs than dreams of exporting the revolution. In the first-ever address by a president of the Islamic Republic to the United Nations General Assembly, Ayatollah Seyed Ali Khamenei observed in 1987 that "despite earfuls of adverse propaganda, the awakening of Muslims in many Islamic countries is not an offspring of Iran's Islamic revolution; it is its brother-in-Islam." The Islamic Republic is not out to impose its revolution on others, he continued; it is prepared to cooperate with "all nations and governments that wish to remain independent and ignore the wishes of the big powers." He added that "the message of our revolution remains as it was: the rejection of the doctrine of domination." Peace, he said, "is, without doubt, a beautiful and attractive word. . . . But, in our opinion, justice, a word that the powerful and the oppressors regard with fearful caution, is even more important and more beautiful." In the international sphere justice requires, first of all, working to ensure "our own defense and the prevention of the usurpation of our legitimate rights" by the U.S.-led "system of world domination."[34]

More than two decades later, opposition to domination and the defense of legitimate rights remain defining themes in Iranian discourse about global affairs. Khamenei, who succeeded Khomeini as supreme leader in 1989, has continued to emphasize them. Since becoming president of the Islamic Republic in 2005, Mahmoud Ahmadinejad has also regularly spoken out against governments that have "taken the place of God" by seeking to "impose their values and wishes on others." These "bullying powers" have, in his words, created a system in which "deception in interactions is called foresight and statesmanship, looting the wealth of other nations is called development efforts, occupation is introduced as a gift toward promoting freedom and democracy, and defenseless nations are subjected to repression in the name of defending human rights."[35]

For Iranians moved by Khomeini's vision, the Islamic Republic is a state unique in world history and contemporary affairs that many other states find threatening simply by virtue of its nature and location. Being part of a unique project carries special responsibilities, of which the most important is to resist external domination and hegemony. As Ahmadinejad told his countrymen in 2010,

> The influence of the people of Iran, the role of the people of Iran in regional relations and interactions is quite clear to hegemonic powers. . . . They oppose us because they want to dominate the Middle East and the whole world. A free Iran, an advanced and powerful Iran, is considered an impediment to this objective. This is the secret behind the opposition to the Iranian nation in the past thirty-one years. They want us to be kept weak and under the domination of dictators, to make us dependent on others and to eliminate the freedom and independence of Iran. . . . We will never allow them to dominate this region.[36]

These ideas look back to ones deeply imbedded in Iranian and Shi'a religious culture and evoked every year on the tenth day of the sacred month of Muharram, the holy day of *Ashura* ("ten" in Arabic), when Shi'a Muslims around the world commemorate the death of Imam Husayn in AD 680 at the battle of Karbala.

Husayn was the younger son of Ali, the Prophet Muhammad's cousin and husband to his daughter, Fatima. Shi'a Muslims believe that Ali, as Muhammad's blood relative, should have been the first caliph (from the Arabic *khalifa*, "successor") chosen to lead the Muslim community after Muhammad's death in 632; they continue to recognize him as the First Imam, or rightful heir to the Prophet. (The Shi'a were first known, in Arabic, as *shi'at 'Ali*, or "followers of Ali," subsequently shortened to *shi'a*, the name by which this branch of Islam became known around the world.) Shi'a Muslims also believe that Ali's elder son, Hasan, the Second Imam, should have succeeded him and that all leaders of the umma should be descendants of the Prophet through Fatima and Ali. However, because of disagreements within the umma, Ali was only the fourth caliph and ruled for a brief four years from his capital in Kufa, in what is now southern Iraq. After his murder in 661, the caliphate passed not to Hasan but to Muawiya, the head of the Damascus-based Umayyad dynasty. Muawiya agreed to leave the selection of the next caliph to the umma; Hasan was confident that the community would return the caliphate to the Prophet's family. But in 669 Muawiya arranged for Hasan to be killed and designated his own son, Yazid, to succeed him. When Muawiya died in 680, Yazid demanded that all leading figures in the umma declare allegiance to him. Ali's younger son, Husayn—recognized by Shi'a as the Third Imam—refused. After seeking sanctuary in Mecca, he decided to flee with his family and a few dozen followers to his father's old capital of Kufa. Before they could get there, he and his party were tracked down at Karbala by thousands of soldiers loyal to Yazid. After valiant resistance, Husayn and most of his family were martyred there, on the tenth day of Muharram.

For devout Shi'a, the message of Husayn's death and the holy day that commemorates it is that the truth must never be betrayed, even at the cost of great sacrifice. For supporters of Khomeini's vision, that means that the Islamic Republic must never surrender to external aggression or pressure. In Khamenei's words, the religious quality of Iran's revolution "stops the people, the leader of the revolution, and its administrators from any retreat, defeat, fear, or weakness. When you fight for God there is no defeat, let alone fear, weakness or retreat."[37] Likewise, the Islamic Republic can never trade away its independence or sovereignty to outsiders—not even for substantial strategic or economic benefits. As an articulate defender of the revolution said to an expatriate critic in the West, "When push comes to shove, we will choose martyrdom and you will choose a green card."

THE LESSONS OF THE IMPOSED WAR

Ever since the revolution, delivering on the promise to defend Iran's independence (*esteqlal*) and freedom (*azadi*) has been the most critical test of the Islamic Republic's legitimacy. Meeting it has not been easy, for, in the language of diplomats and military planners, the Islamic Republic has little "strategic depth." Strictly defined, strategic depth is the distance between a state's enemies and its core population centers and economic areas. A lack of it increases a nation's vulnerability to attack—a vulnerability that, in the Islamic Republic's case, was underscored shortly after its founding by the Iraqi invasion of September 1980.

In Iran, the war with Iraq feels very recent; the entire society was deeply affected by it, in ways that persist to this day. Travelers to the Islamic Republic frequently encounter war veterans and, even more frequently, people whose families lost fathers, sons, uncles, and brothers. Visitors to the part of the enormous Behesht-e Zahra cemetery in southern Tehran reserved for those who fell in the Holy Defense can witness the war's legacy. More than 36,000 servicemen from Tehran province are buried there. A steady stream of relatives and friends still visit the well-tended graves, many marked with pictures and other mementos of the fallen, flags of the Islamic Republic, and religious texts. Spending time at the cemetery gives outsiders a sense of the bonds that the war created between the fledgling revolutionary state and the wider society. As Khamenei explained, "Our preoccupation with innumerable internal problems relating to the revolution and our lack of sufficient experience made the invasion possible, but the particular characteristics of this revolution came to our rescue."[38] Put differently, the war marked the moment when a critical mass of Iranians invested themselves in the Islamic Republic's survival and success. Their investment has carried across generations.

Certainly the Imposed War was *the* formative experience of the generation that bore the brunt of combat, a generation that today is assuming top-level positions in politics, academia, and other important sectors and will lead the nation for the next quarter century. For Iranians, this group—not the exiles and expatriates held up by the West—is Iran's "greatest generation." And its wartime experience is closely bound up with the rise of two interrelated organizations as leading actors in the Islamic Republic's security apparatus and political system: the Revolutionary Guards (*Sepah-e Pasdaran-e Enqelab-e Eslami*, literally the "army of guardians of the Islamic Revolution") and the *Basij* ("mobilization") paramilitary citizen militia. The Revolutionary Guards were founded barely a month after the establishment of the Islamic Republic as an ideologically committed alternative to the suspect remnants of the shah's military; the Basij was formed less than a year later.[39] Both organizations played important roles in the Holy Defense against Saddam's invasion and bore a disproportionate share of the casualties.[40]

As noted, when Saddam's armies invaded, Iranian leaders had to come to grips with the disquieting situation that the threats facing their country were not issuing solely from a predatory dictator. Iraq's war of aggression was funded by Saudi Arabia and other Gulf Arab states—which together contributed roughly $100 billion in cash, oil sold on Iraq's behalf, and concessional loans—and endorsed by most of the rest of the Arab world.[41] More disturbing, it was supported in multiple ways by the United States and other Western powers, who, with other aid, exported hundreds of billions of dollars' worth of "dual-use" goods and technologies to build up Iraq's military industries, including its chemical and nuclear weapons programs. At the outset of the war, according to an authoritative study, Iraqi chemical munitions capabilities "consisted of limited research and production of nerve and blister agents" with no corresponding ability to "produce indigenously most of its CW precursors"—that is, the compounds required to produce chemical weapons agents.[42] But by taking advantage of the technology and materials imported from Western countries, as United Nations weapons inspectors subsequently documented, the Iraqi CW program was soon in a position to manufacture large quantities of both nerve and blister agents, to fabricate sophisticated (and lethal) chemical munitions, and to produce large stocks of CW precursors indigenously.

That is why, in Iranian eyes, those governments shared complicity in the gassing of more than 100,000 Iranian soldiers and civilians—complicity compounded by Western silence on the topic. In 1982, almost immediately after Iraq started attacking Iranian targets with chemical weapons, the Islamic Republic began seeking help from the United Nations Security Council, but to no avail. Between 1984 and 1988, Secretary-General Javier Pérez de Cuéllar—acting on his own,

Iranian soldiers gassed by Saddam Husayn's military in 1988. *AP/Greg English*

because the Security Council would not support him—dispatched six fact-finding missions to investigate Iraq's use of chemical weapons. Their reports consistently confirmed Iran's charges; just as consistently, the council declined to act. It would take four years and the Iraqi military's being caught red-handed in a chemical weapons attack on the Iraqi Kurdish town of Halabja in March 1988 for the council to take formal notice.[43] Even when it finally adopted Resolution 612 the following May, the council merely condemned "the continued use of chemical weapons in the conflict between the Islamic Republic of Iran and Iraq," without specifying who had been using them, and exhorted "both sides to refrain from the future use of chemical weapons," though no credible charges that Iran used chemical weapons have ever been advanced.

This broad support for Saddam reinforced Iranians' sense that the Islamic Republic is not only a unique state but one that other powers would like to eliminate and led them to conclude that they could not rely on outsiders for their security, certainly not on an amorphous and Western-dominated "international community." As President

Khamenei told the General Assembly in 1987, the Security Council had been pushed into an "indecent" and "condemnable" position by the United States. Its refusal to punish Saddam's aggression and his use of chemical weapons had left Iranians "quite alone in restoring our legitimate rights" and underscored that "the security provided by such a Security Council [is] nothing but a nice-looking house of cards."[44]

A generation later, Iranians retain their resentment—something that Ahmadinejad, himself a war veteran, has used effectively with domestic audiences. During his first presidential campaign, in 2005, he contemptuously dismissed expressions of international concern about Iran's nuclear program; where was the international community, he asked, when Iranians were being gassed? In another piece of campaign rhetoric, he charged: "The Germans supplied the chemicals, the French supplied the missiles, and the Americans provided the intelligence" to Saddam.

Throughout the Holy Defense, Iran was able to buy some arms and equipment from China and the Soviet Union—though both sold larger quantities to Iraq—and even from Israel. (Although Iranian officials deny that Tehran ever procured supplies directly from Israel, items of Israeli origin were among the black market matériel that made its way into the Islamic Republic's military inventories.) But for the most part the Islamic Republic was on its own. Thousands upon thousands of Iranian men volunteered for service on the front, knowing that, in many situations, they would not have adequate equipment (at times, some Iranian soldiers did not even have rifles) or protective gear. Hence the periodic use of tactics that Western commentators called "human wave" attacks—stories of which are commonly embellished with colorful but unsubstantiated accounts of plastic "keys to heaven" being distributed to soldiers and actors dressed as Imam Husayn appearing on horseback to inspire frontline units. To be sure, the war produced its share of extraordinary self-sacrifice by Iranian troops, but the demand for such self-sacrifice was greatly exacerbated by shortages of weapons and equipment.

These experiences convinced Iranians that they must never again be dependent on outsiders for anything critical to the nation's defense.

Since then, the Islamic Republic has become largely self-sufficient in the production of ordinary weapons and military equipment, including tanks, armored personnel carriers, guided missiles, radar systems, surface ships, and submarines, and it is developing its capacity to manufacture more advanced weapons systems. Though Iran's products do not always match the best available on the global arms market, Iranian policy makers believe that indigenous military industries must be supported in order to guarantee the Islamic Republic's security and independence. So, for example, when Russia succumbed to American pressure and reneged on a contract to supply antiaircraft missile batteries to defend Iran from an American or Israeli attack, Tehran was able to proceed with its own program. It may take longer to bear fruit than buying directly from Russia would, but it gives the Islamic Republic options for self-defense that less independent states do not have. Similarly, the Islamic Republic has made achieving self-sufficiency in food a high priority, so that external powers cannot use control over its food supplies as a source of strategic leverage.

The war revealed the Islamic Republic's vulnerability not only to external threats but also to externally supported campaigns of internal subversion like the CIA-instigated coup that undermined Mossadeq in 1953. Iraq had supplemented its military campaign by trying to mobilize both ethnic Arabs in Khozestan province, along Iran's western border, and Iranian Kurds against Tehran's postrevolutionary government. But the biggest threat came from Iraq's support for the *mojahedin-e khalq* (the "people's holy warriors," widely known by the Farsi acronym, MEK), an armed political movement dedicated to synthesizing Islam and Marxism that had fought against the shah's regime in the 1960s and 1970s.

In the years immediately following the revolution, Iran was torn by a bitter contest over its future course, which its wartime adversaries sought to exploit to their advantage. One side, organized mostly under the banner of the Islamic Republic Party (IRP), was fundamentally loyal to Khomeini and his vision of an Islamic Republic. The other side wanted the new political order to move in a more secular direction; this camp included the MEK. The conflict between the two camps intensified during the first half of 1981, less than a year after the Iraqi invasion. As it came to a head, the MEK—with support from Saddam and perhaps the United States—launched a campaign of terrorist bombings intended to "decapitate" the IRP; well over a hundred leading figures in the fledgling Islamic Republic were killed. At Behesht-e Zahra, a mausoleum on the fringes of the section devoted to the Iran-Iraq War dead holds the remains of more than thirty of these victims, including prominent politicians, military commanders, and religious leaders. Ayatollah Khamenei, the current supreme leader, was the target of one of these attacks on June 27, 1981, after speaking at a mosque near Tehran's main bazaar; his right hand was permanently damaged.

The personal impact—both emotional and physical—of MEK terrorism on the Islamic Republic's political elite comes through in Khamenei's subsequent account of the 1981 terror campaign:

> By stealing arms and ammunition and explosive matériel—not a difficult job in those chaotic days of revolution—and through the assistance of certain foreign governments, terrorist groups who lacked any form of popular base established a vast network in Iran. Individual and group assassinations, colossal bomb explosions, the hijacking of aircraft, kidnapping, horrible incidents of torture, indiscriminate shootings, and the deliberate slaughtering of people were among the measures carried out with the support and encouragement of our Iranian society's infamous enemies. Their victims included important leaders and authorities of the revolution, as well as ordinary men and women and, of course, innocent children and passersby. . . . In one act alone, some seventy-two leading figures of the revolution, including several cabinet ministers, a score of parliamentarians, and other irreplaceable personalities . . . died inhuman deaths. In another incident the president and the prime minister were both killed in a bomb attack.[45]

Ever since the MEK's terror campaign, Iranian officials and many ordinary Iranians have referred to the group, in a play on the Farsi word *mojahedin*, as the *monafeqin*—hypocrites. The MEK fought alongside Iraqi military units against the Islamic Republic during the Iran-Iraq War. It has continued to carry out terrorist attacks inside Iran, in collaboration with foreign powers. American law enforcement officials say that the MEK "made a pact" with Al-Qa'ida's Ramzi Youssef a year after he masterminded the first terrorist strike on the World Trade Center in 1993; according to them, Youssef built a bomb that MEK agents placed and detonated inside one of Shi'a Islam's greatest shrines, the tomb of Imam Reza (the Eighth Imam) in the Iranian city of Mashhad, on June 20, 1994, killing at least twenty-six people (mostly women and children) and wounding more than two hundred.[46] In 2012, U.S. intelligence officials said that the MEK is cooperating with Israel to assassinate Iranian nuclear scientists.[47] The disclosure is ironic given that the United States has itself provided clandestine military training and support to the MEK—even after Washington designated it as a foreign terrorist organization in 1997.[48]

While the MEK is beloved in some parts of Paris, Washington, and Beverly Hills, it remains widely detested in Iran. Iranian leaders have repeatedly condemned Western support for the MEK during and after the Iran-Iraq War as a perfidious attempt to undermine the Islamic Republic. Khamenei observed: "Today, the leaders of these terrorist groups, who have often claimed responsibility for criminal actions, are given security and protection, provided with a comfortable life in the United States, France, and other Western countries, and euphemistically called 'opposition to the revolution'—and the countries that patronize these terrorists accuse the Islamic Republic of 'terrorism!' "[49] During the political controversy following the Islamic Republic's 2009 presidential election, Ahmadinejad's principal challenger, Mir-Hossein Mousavi, derided the MEK in his public statements as a way of forestalling suggestions that he might be associated with it.

While the Imposed War taught Iranians that the revolutionary order must always be vigilant against a wide range of security threats, it also promoted the belief that the Islamic Republic can resist—and eventually weather—whatever its adversaries hurl at it. The war with Iraq was the first war in more than two centuries in which an Iranian government successfully defended all the territory under its control.

Through eight years of fighting, Iran suffered under a nearly comprehensive arms and economic embargo while it was both under attack by an Iraqi military supported by major regional and international powers and pressed from within by an externally backed domestic terror campaign. But the Islamic Republic came through with a determination that should give pause to anyone who still thinks that sanctions will force changes in Iranian decision making.

KNOWING THE ENEMY

As retired U.S. Army general Stanley McChrystal told us, you can learn a lot about a country's national security agenda by looking at a map. You can see from a map that Iran today shares boundaries— land, water, and coast—with fifteen states.[50] From Iran's vantage, not one of these states is a natural ally, and several have been used as platforms for hostile actions against it. Since the war with Iraq, the Islamic Republic has had to cope with failing states, ethnic and sectarian conflict, and mounting instability in Afghanistan and Pakistan on its eastern border; with the breakup of the Soviet Union and the rise of potentially unstable post-Soviet states in Central Asia and the South Caucasus on its northern border; and with American military interventions in Afghanistan and Iraq on both its eastern and western borders. Even to its south, on the other side of the Persian Gulf, it has had to deal with what it has called "authoritarian and security dependent" Arab regimes chronically at risk of political and social disruption and of American penetration.[51]

In this dangerous environment, the experience of war with Iraq crystallized the nation's biggest security problem: that virtually any of its neighbors as well as several other regional states could be used as launching pads to attack the Islamic Republic or to otherwise undermine its interests. It regards those most inclined to exploit this vulnerability as the United States, Israel, and those Sunni states, especially Saudi Arabia and Pakistan, aligned with Washington.

Tehran has long believed that the United States—which has established a presence in many of Iran's neighbors in multiple ways and

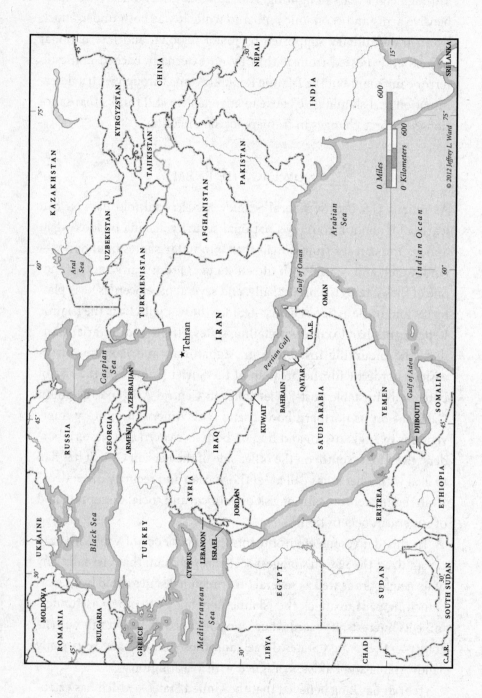

whose military can strike it directly from aerial and maritime platforms—poses by far the most serious threat.[52] The revolutionaries who toppled the shah were bound to be distrustful of the Americans. After all, a quarter of a century earlier the CIA had organized the coup that brought down the Mossadeq government and restored Shah Mohammad Reza Pahlavi to the Peacock Throne. Between 1953 and 1979, Washington worked with the shah to turn Iran into one of its most important strategic partners. After British forces withdrew from the Persian Gulf in 1971 as part of a pullback from all imperial positions "east of Suez," the Nixon administration turned to the shah to take Britain's place as America's "regional policeman" in the Persian Gulf. In this role, Iran purchased enormous amounts of weapons systems and other military equipment from the United States, and the shah used them to secure the Gulf in accordance with American preferences.[53]

In return, the United States strongly backed the shah, virtually until the very end of his reign. Notwithstanding the increasing incongruity between his agenda and the interests of Iranians—an incongruity highlighted by the growing popular receptivity to Khomeini's message—successive American administrations embraced him as a critical ally. Even as the revolution gained momentum on the streets of Iranian cities over the course of 1978, national security adviser Zbigniew Brzezinski and other senior officials in the Carter administration were arguing that the United States should encourage the shah, as a State Department official later recounted, "to send [his] troops out and shoot down as many people as necessary and bring an end to the rebellion once and for all."[54] Increasingly concerned that the shah might not be able to hold back the rising tide of opposition, in January 1979 President Carter dispatched a U.S. Air Force general who had served previously in Iran to Tehran to determine, as one American official later put it, "if the Iranian military had the stomach to attempt a coup and suppress the revolution."[55] The administration was divided over the wisdom of a military crackdown and Carter ultimately demurred, but that fit of scrupulousness could not reverse the impact of a twenty-five-year record that convinced Iran's new rulers the United States had been "on the side of the Shah and against them."[56]

This conviction influenced decision making in Tehran both before and after students seized the U.S. embassy on November 4, 1979, in reaction to Carter's decision to allow the deposed shah into the United States for medical treatment. American support for the shah and the close ties between the CIA and SAVAK, the shah's intelligence organization, had made the embassy in Tehran an inevitable focus of concern for a new political order fearful that Washington was out to undermine it; Carter's decision to admit the shah was virtually guaranteed to provoke a backlash. As John Limbert, a student of Iranian culture and history who as a young foreign service officer was one of the hostages, later wrote:

> In October 1979 the American administration thought it could some-how placate Iranian public opinion by announcing that the United States was admitting the deposed Shah for medical treatment and for purely humanitarian reasons. The American people may have accepted such a statement. Given the history of Iranian-American relations, however, no Iranian cognizant of that history would have believed it. The statement, rather than reassure its Iranian audience, insulted its intelligence and seemed to confirm what many, in the highly charged atmosphere of late 1979, already suspected: that the United States was plotting against the revolution and was looking to restage the events of 1953.[57]

It has become a commonplace of Western commentary that the hostages became a tactical lever for Khomeini and his supporters to use against their domestic opponents. But their actions were driven by much deeper strategic concerns. The overlap of the shah's departure with the Soviet invasion of Afghanistan—widely perceived in American policy circles as the start of a push by Moscow to expand its influence in the Persian Gulf—persuaded the United States that its position in the region was under unprecedented challenge. In Washington, a consensus developed that the U.S. military should assume direct military responsibility for the security of Gulf oil flows. Consequently, Carter declared in his January 1980 State of the Union address that "an attempt by any outside force to gain control of the Persian Gulf region will be regarded as an assault on the vital interests of the United States of America, and such an assault will be repelled by any means necessary, including military force." The United States began building up a robust naval presence in the Gulf, while also prepositioning equipment and arranging for bases so that it could send ground and tactical air forces into the region in the event of a crisis.

Faced with this buildup, Limbert notes, "the Islamic Republic felt that possession of the American embassy staff gave it an advantage over a U.S. government determined to destroy the revolutionary regime and replace it with either a restored monarchy or something else more friendly to American interests."[58] Iranian leaders thus used the hostages as bargaining chips to trade for an American commitment not to attack or subvert the Islamic Republic. And that is what they got, enshrined in the very first article of the Algiers Accord, which ended the hostage crisis in January 1981, after 444 days: "The United States pledges that it is and from now on will be the policy of the United States not to intervene, directly or indirectly, politically or militarily, in Iran's internal affairs."[59]

Even as the accord was being negotiated, the United States was betraying its spirit. The CIA knew in advance of Saddam's plans to attack Iran. As the agency's Iran desk officer later recounted, "In the first week of September 1980, I went to New York for a meeting with a senior Iranian general, a man who had been known during the revolution as the 'butcher of Tehran.' And he told me in his suite at the Waldorf that he had just been in Iraq, where he had been meeting with Saddam Husayn and his senior Iraqi generals, and that the Iraqis were going to invade Iran." Washington did not try to stop the Iraqis because, then vice president Walter Mondale explained, "We believed that this war would put further pressure on the Iranian government."[60] In fact, in the months before the invasion the Carter administration explored possibilities for closer ties to Saddam's government. After Ronald Reagan became president in 1981, American support for Saddam intensified. Washington did not have diplomatic relations with Baghdad when Iraq invaded Iran. Reagan, however, appointed former and future secretary of defense Donald Rumsfeld as his special envoy to Saddam and, by 1984, the U.S. government had removed Iraq from its list of state sponsors of terrorism and restored diplomatic relations. Reagan also signed a classified directive authorizing U.S. military and intelligence support for Saddam's forces.[61] And, for four years, the United States took the lead in blocking any meaningful action by the Security Council to stop Iraq's use of chemical weapons against Iranian military and civilian targets. Washington was fully aware of what Iraq was doing; during one of Rumsfeld's visits to Baghdad, Saddam's foreign minister, Tariq Aziz, gave the American visitor videotapes showing tens of thousands of Iranian soldiers killed by Iraqi chemical weapons, to underscore what "civilized Iraqis have to do in order to stop the barbarian Iranians." But, former secretary of state George Shultz subsequently (and rather cold-bloodedly) explained, "It was a very hard balance. They're using chemical weapons. So you want them to stop using chemical weapons. At the same time, you don't want Iran to win the war."[62]

As the war ground on, the United States became more directly involved in the fighting, effectively on Iraq's side. In 1984 Saddam ordered his military to attack tankers transporting Iranian oil exports. After Iranian forces responded in kind, by harassing tankers carrying oil shipments from Iraq and Gulf Arab states supporting it, Kuwait requested American protection for its tankers; in March 1987 Washington agreed, bringing American and Iranian naval forces into regular head-to-head confrontation.[63]

This aiding and abetting of Iraq reinforced an already strong Iranian inclination to see virtually any American initiative as threatening. This outlook was further validated when, sixteen months into the so-called tanker war, on July 3, 1988, an American guided missile cruiser, the USS *Vincennes*, shot down an Iranian civilian airliner, Iran Air 655, over the Strait of Hormuz, killing all 290 civilians (including 66 children) aboard. The flight had originated in Tehran, had stopped in the southern Iranian port city of Bandar-e Abbas on the Persian Gulf to pick up more passengers, and, after taking off again, had headed out over the Strait of Hormuz en route to Dubai, its final destination; it was attacked seven minutes after taking off from Bandar-e Abbas.

In Washington, the Reagan administration blamed the incident on Iran. It initially charged that the *Vincennes* had been under attack by Iranian surface vessels in international waters; that Iran Air 655's crew had not used the plane's transponders to identify it, in internationally recognized fashion, as a civilian airliner; that the plane was not following its normal flight path and had been descending, which made it look like a hostile military aircraft on the *Vincennes*'s radar; and that Iranian military aircraft may have been using it as a cover for attacks against U.S. warships in the Persian Gulf. All these claims played on unfounded assumptions about Iranian intentions and capabilities, and every one of them was subsequently proven false. A year after the incident, the commanding officer of another U.S. Navy warship that had also tracked the plane, having reached a point at which he "could not bear to read yet another apologia for the *Vincennes* incident without commenting," wrote publicly:

> When the decision was made to shoot down [Iran Air 655], the airliner was climbing, not diving; it was showing the proper identification friend or foe—IFF (Mode III); and it was in the correct flight corridor from Bandar Abbas to Dubai. The *Vincennes* was never under attack by Iranian aircraft. There was no targeting being done by the Iranian P-3. There was no coordinated attack involving the Iranian Revolutionary Guard Corps (IRGC) boats and Iranian military forces. Iranian Air Flight 655, also known as track number (TN) 4131, was mistakenly classified by the *Vincennes* as an Iranian F-14 diving at the ship. . . . Captain Will Rogers III [commander of the USS *Vincennes*], no doubt, did what he *thought* he had to do, but he was wrong.[64]

Washington was not interested in the truth. Two days after the incident, Vice President George H. W. Bush, who led the American delegation in the United Nations Security Council deliberations on the incident, stated, "I'll never apologize for the United States of America. Ever. I don't care what the facts are." And indeed, the U.S. government has never admitted wrongdoing in the incident, although media investigations found substantial evidence that the commander and crew of the *Vincennes* had sufficient information to know that the plane was a civilian airliner.[65] Instead, the commander and several of his officers were commended for their performance.

Whether the commander and crew of the *Vincennes* were criminally negligent—in other words, whether they could have and should have correctly identified their target, as the naval officer quoted above suggests—remains an open question. The evidence that they knew what they were doing is significant but circumstantial. Nevertheless, most Iranians believed (and believe to this day) that the destruction of Iran Air 655 was deliberate. The prevailing Iranian assessment was that the United States had committed a war crime in order to punish and intimidate the Islamic Republic for repelling Saddam's invasion and even, for a time, forcing Iraq to cede strategic territory along the Persian Gulf—a new tilt in the regional balance of power that the United States found highly unattractive. This assessment had both short- and long-term consequences. In the short term, it helped convince Khomeini to accept the August 1988 cease-fire ending the Iran-Iraq War. Though he found it "more deadly than drinking from a poisoned chalice," by that point Iran had recaptured all its territory. Faced with fighting the United States as well as Iraq, Khomeini said that he "submitted myself to God's will and took this drink to His satisfaction."[66]

In the longer term, the perception that the United States was willing to use its military to kill Iranian civilians compounded Iranians' worst fears. The belief that Washington would never accept the Islamic Republic was further buttressed by the post–Cold War imperial turn in America's Middle East policy. Today many Americans may still be inclined, as President Carter was in 1979, to dismiss the 1953 coup as "ancient history," but that is not how Iranians see it. For supporters of the Iranian government, Washington's backing for the opposition Green movement that emerged with Iran's 2009 presidential election and its ongoing connections to movements seeking regime change in Tehran—including the MEK—and, in some cases, the partition of Iran along ethnic lines, prove that the American threat to the Islamic Republic remains very much alive. The United States has pushed international sanctions to "cripple" Iran's economy, and it regularly reiterates that "all options are on the table"—code for the potential use of military force. In April 2010 the Obama administration, as part of its Nuclear Posture Review, declared that it even reserved the right to use nuclear weapons first, at its discretion, against the Islamic Republic. In 2012, the same administration lifted the MEK's terrorist designation, paving the way for it to receive open U.S. government support. Defenders of American policy dismiss Iranian leaders' "paranoid self-delusion" that the United States is intent on dismantling the Islamic Republic.[67] But, as Henry Kissinger noted, "Even paranoids can have enemies." Dealing with American threats has, for sound reasons, become a priority for the Islamic Republic's national security strategy.

After the United States, Tehran views Israel as the most serious threat to its security and strategic position. In his earliest challenges to Pahlavi rule, Khomeini made Tehran's relations with Israel part of his bill of particulars against the shah. His messages also contain numerous references to Israel as an integral part of the West's imperial strategy toward the Middle East. In a 1972 "message in support of Palestine," he warned that "everyone must know that the goal of the great powers in creating Israel does not end with the occupation of Palestine. They are planning to make all Arab countries share in Palestine's fate, God forbid."[68] A year later, he cautioned Muslim governments that Israel

> has not been put there merely to suppress the Arab nation; rather it is dangerous and harmful to the Middle East as a whole. The plan is for the domination and supremacy of Zionism over the Islamic world and the further colonization of the rich lands and abundant resources of the Islamic countries.[69]

During the first decade of the Islamic Republic's existence, Israel tried to preserve as much as it could of the cooperative relationship it had enjoyed with the shah. When Iraq, a nation hostile to Israel, invaded Iran, Israeli officials worried that an Iranian defeat would position Iraq—with the largest Arab army and vast oil reserves of its own—to become the leading Arab power. So Israel began providing weapons to Iran indirectly, via the black market, even though the United States had cut off all military and dual-use sales to Tehran and was pressing others to do the same. Throughout the 1980s, the American Israel Public Affairs Committee (AIPAC, the heart of the pro-Israel lobby in Washington) argued against imposing sanctions on the Islamic Republic. Israel even sought to use its arms transfers to Iran as a channel to facilitate American-Iranian rapprochement.[70]

But from their earliest days in power, the Islamic Republic's leaders were wary of Israel's long-term intentions. They were particularly disturbed by the Israeli invasion of Lebanon in 1982, which they saw first of all as an assault on southern Lebanon's largely Shi'a population. Beyond Shi'a solidarity, they correctly judged that the invasion was intended to install a pro-Western government in Beirut that would make a separate peace with Israel—allowing the United States as well as Israel to apply greater pressure on Syria and thus gradually turn the Levant into a Western platform that could be used to back Iraq in its war against Iran. After Israel, with U.S. backing, installed the Maronite-dominated Gemayel government and concluded a peace agreement with it in 1983, Khomeini denounced "this American-Zionist-Lebanese accord which strengthens American dominance in the region and will allow Israel to conquer the Islamic country of Lebanon and, subsequently, the other Arab and Islamic countries"; he warned his fellow Muslims that "America, from the other side of the world," was aiming to "govern their destinies through the usurping infidel, Israel."[71] Later that year, he excoriated Prime Minister Yitzhak Shamir's vision of "Greater Israel," whose ambition, he declared, was for Palestine to be completely destroyed and all the territories in Israel's hands to become an integral part of Israel and whose ultimate goal was "an Israel stretching from the Nile to the Euphrates."[72]

The Israeli threat to Iranian interests increased significantly in the early 1990s, with the end of the Cold War, Iraq's invasion of Kuwait, and the first Gulf War. Saddam's defeat by the United States and the loss of his Soviet backing removed Iraq as a major factor in the regional balance and thus emboldened Israel, since there was no longer an Arab military force that could constrain it—and no longer a superpower that could constrain the United States. Under these circumstances, most Arab states focused on developing their relations with Washington, giving Israel yet more space to pursue an ambitious regional agenda. For many years Israel had followed a national security doctrine—misleadingly labeled "deterrence" in Israeli military circles—emphasizing the first use of force.[73] Conditions in the early 1990s offered Israel an opening to consolidate a near-absolute freedom of military initiative that would enable it not just to "preempt" perceived threats but to "prevent" them from arising in the first place—by striking first, with overwhelming force, whenever and wherever it deemed necessary.

Israel's post–Cold War drive for regional dominance means that it cannot countenance another state with the determination and the material potential to inhibit its freedom of military action. After the first Gulf War and the end of the Cold War, Iran was the only such state in the Middle East. So, in the early 1990s, Israel dropped the idea of maintaining any sort of strategic cooperation with Tehran, and for the past twenty years it has done everything possible to undermine the Islamic Republic's regional position—dramatically heightening Tehran's perception of a serious Israeli threat to its interests.[74] In recent years, this perception has been further aggravated by Western media stories about American-Israeli collaboration to sabotage Iran's nuclear program.[75] As noted above, U.S. intelligence officials report that Israel has been collaborating with the MEK to assassinate Iranian nuclear scientists. Israeli journalists report that it also supports Iranian separatist groups carrying out terrorist attacks inside Iran.[76] Now high-level Israeli officials, claiming their prerogative to launch preventive wars, say publicly that they may attack civilian, internationally safeguarded nuclear facilities inside the Islamic Republic if the international community does not stop Iran's nuclear development by other means.

Israeli hegemony is unacceptable to the Islamic Republic. But Tehran's response, despite erroneous press reports to the contrary, has not been to threaten Israel's destruction. It has been, instead, to look for ways to contain, delegitimize, and ultimately roll back Israel's expansionist ambitions by mostly political means.

Of course, given Israel's close ties to Washington, the threat Iran faces from Israel is tightly linked to the threat posed by the United States. Demonization of the Islamic Republic as an "existential threat" to the Jewish state has become a constant in Israeli representations to U.S. administrations and to Congress. Because of America's "special relationship" with Israel—and the Israel lobby's influence in Washington—these representations have deeply distorted the Iran debate in the United States, with corresponding effects on policy. Israel and the Israel lobby have been major players in the campaign to expand American sanctions against Iran. AIPAC rewrote its talking points in the 1990s to put expanding anti-Iranian sanctions at the top of its agenda (virtually on a par with protecting U.S. aid to Israel), where it remains to this day.[77] Washington's acceptance of Israel's insistence that its survival depends on its unchallenged ability to strike first (notwithstanding the enormous damage this position inflicts on American interests) has led to surreal assessments of the Iranian-Israeli military balance—as when Iran's potential acquisition of purely defensive capabilities such as antiaircraft missiles and radar systems is described by U.S. administrations as "provocative" and "threatening." By accepting Israel's hegemonic view of its security requirements, the United States has—both in Iranian perceptions and in reality—incorporated Israeli aspirations to military dominance in the Middle East into its own imperial agenda for the region.

Similarly, Iranian policy makers believe that Saudi Arabia, the quintessential Sunni Muslim state, has used its long-standing strategic partnership with the United States as a cover to advance its own intensely anti-Iranian agenda. As previously noted, Saudi Arabia and other Gulf Arab states allied with the United States helped finance

Saddam's war against Iran. For many years Saudi money has also funded the promotion of a severe form of Sunni Islam that regards Shi'a as the foremost enemy for pious believers—ahead of both Zionists (Israel) and modern-day crusaders (the United States).

In the West, this form of Islam is often called Wahhabi, after Muhammad Ibn 'Abd Al-Wahhab, the eighteenth-century religious revivalist whose program for a return to what he defined as pure Islam provided the ideological justification for the efforts of the Al-Saud—the family that would subsequently found and lead the modern Saudi state—to assert control over the Arabian peninsula. However, Saudis themselves—and Iranians—generally use the term *salafi* to describe the type of Islam promoted today by Saudi Arabia.* In Tehran's view, the spread of Salafi Islam—particularly when linked to support for armed movements targeting Iranian interests—significantly expands its security challenges. Even before the Iranian Revolution, Saudi Arabia had begun promoting a strict version of Salafi Islam, using part of its oil wealth to build mosques, distribute Qur'ans and religious tracts, and provide clerics to Muslim communities around the world; after the revolution, Saudi leaders intensified this campaign as a way of pushing back against the threat an Islamic Republic posed to both their legitimacy and their role in global Islam.[78] At times, the campaign has gotten away from their control, as with the emergence of Al-Qa'ida out of the jihad against the Soviet occupation of Afghanistan in the 1980s.

From Tehran's vantage, the Saudi campaign has played out with greatest force in Afghanistan, where for three decades the kingdom's intelligence service, the General Intelligence Directorate (GID), has

---

* The adjective *salafi* comes from the Arabic *salaf*, meaning "predecessors"; in a religious context, it refers to the first three generations of Muslims—the "companions" of the Prophet Muhammad, the "followers" of the Prophet, and the "followers of the followers"—which Salafi believers consider the eternally correct model of Islamic practice. The Salafi Islam sponsored by Saudi Arabia may more accurately be described as *takfeeri* Islam—from the Arabic *takfeer*, referring to the practice of declaring those Muslims who do not subscribe to a particular view of Islam unbelievers (a key aspect of Muhammad Ibn 'Abd Al-Wahhab's original program). This aspect of Saudi religious ideology is certainly the most problematic—indeed, threatening—to Iranians and other Shi'a Muslims, for movements like the Taliban and Al-Qa'ida use it to justify the violent suppression of Shi'a believers.

collaborated with Pakistan's Inter-Services Intelligence (ISI) Directorate to build up armed Pashtun factions, partly as anti-Iranian forces.[79]
With the Soviet invasion of Afghanistan in 1979, Riyadh saw support
for anti-Soviet Pashtun mujahideen—which it coordinated with
Washington as well as with Islamabad—as a way to press Iran from the
east while Iraq, also with Saudi backing, was simultaneously attacking
it from the west.[80] Even after the Soviets withdrew from Afghanistan
in 1989, the GID and the ISI continued constructing a Pashtun-based
anti-Iranian "Sunni wall" in Pakistan and Afghanistan, an effort that
in the early 1990s gave rise to a Salafi military and political movement
calling itself the Taliban.[81] Once the Taliban captured Kabul in 1996
and proclaimed the Islamic Emirate of Afghanistan, they acted aggressively against Iranian interests. Strategically, the rise of the Taliban—
which, of course, made an alliance with Osama bin Laden and
Al-Qa'ida—constituted a dangerous expansion in the ability of Saudi
Arabia and Pakistan to use Afghanistan as an anti-Iranian platform.

Saudi backing for anti-Iranian militias has not been limited to
Afghanistan. Riyadh financed anti-Shi'a Sunni insurgents in post-
Saddam Iraq, who killed thousands of Iraqi Shi'a and destroyed Shi'a
holy sites. Today, Saudi Arabia (along with Qatar and Turkey) is backing anti-Shi'a Sunni fighters in Syria. Closer to home, Tehran thinks
that Riyadh and Islamabad are colluding to support Jundallah (Arabic
for "soldiers of God")—a violent group claiming to fight for the rights
of Sunni Muslims in Iran—and other active terrorists. (The CIA and
the U.S. military may also have ties to Jundallah, a topic to which we
will return.) Based in Pakistani Baluchistan—part of a dangerous tri-
angle encompassing Baluchi areas in Pakistan and Taliban strong-
holds in southern Afghanistan as well—Jundallah operates mainly in
Sistan-Balochistan, Iran's only Sunni-majority province, where it has
carried out a number of high-casualty attacks.[82]

This, then, is the view of the world from inside the Islamic Republic—a
view shaped by structural realities and historical experience along
with notions of national identity and religious and revolutionary prin-

ciples. In line with this view, political and policy elites in Tehran have identified a range of threats and strategic challenges facing the Islamic Republic—antagonistic and/or unstable neighbors, American hostility, U.S.-backed Israeli ambitions to regional dominance, and the sponsorship of anti-Iranian militias and terrorist groups by Sunni states allied to Washington—all of which are exacerbated by Iran's lack of strategic depth, a consequence of the absence of natural allies among its fifteen neighbors.

Under these conditions, it is not easy being an Iranian strategist. Certainly, Iranian decision makers have not had the luxury of indulging in flights of ideological fancy where their country's security is concerned. While they continue to frame the Islamic Republic's foreign and military policy around such principles as Shi'a solidarity, support for the umma, and opposition to domination, they derive their foreign policy and national security goals—protecting Iran's independence, preserving its territorial integrity, and guarding the political integrity of the Islamic Republic as the authentic expression of Iranian self-determination—from standard international law and practice.[83] In the next chapter, we consider how these leaders have sought to defend the Islamic Republic against perceived threats, deal with its strategic challenges, and advance its regional and international position.

2

RATIONALITY, REALISM, AND IRANIAN GRAND STRATEGY

Strategy without tactics is the slowest route to victory. Tactics without strategy is the noise before defeat.

—*Chinese proverb (apocryphally attributed to Sun Tzu)*

In August 1998, Taliban forces captured the city of Mazar-e-Sharif in northern Afghanistan. They summarily executed hundreds of Hazara (Afghan Shi'a) men and boys, ostensibly to prevent them from mounting resistance to Taliban rule. In addition, what the Taliban later claimed were "renegade" forces stormed the Iranian consulate in Mazar-e Sharif, killing eight diplomats and an Iranian journalist. This action brought the Islamic Republic to the brink of war with the Taliban; in the weeks that followed, the Revolutionary Guards and Basij deployed more than 70,000 additional troops to Iran's border with Afghanistan.

But the Islamic Republic did not go to war. As the then deputy foreign minister Mohsen Aminzadeh later explained, Supreme Leader Ayatollah Seyed Ali Khamenei's "opinion was that 'Afghanistan is like a swamp; anyone who has entered has not been able to exit gracefully.' He believed that showing a reaction is essential, but we should consciously consider all the conditions of any armed reaction." In the end, Iranian policy makers concluded that armed intervention "could become a long and permanent problem for Iran. . . . [It] was senseless and should not happen."

At the same time, they recognized that "the attack on the Iranian consulate in Mazar-e Sharif, at the international level, could bring a new and different opportunity for Iran." Aminzadeh well recalled that the international community "had shown a negligible reaction" to the 1994 attack on the tomb of Imam Reza in Mashhad by the MEK and Al-Qa'ida, but he and his colleagues suspected that the incident at Mazar-e Sharif would "attract more attention" and offer Iran a chance "to initiate collaboration with the international community to confront such incidents in Afghanistan."[1] And that, in fact, was what happened: the Islamic Republic worked diplomatically, within the United Nations, to help launch the so-called 6+2 framework, which brought Afghanistan's six neighbors—China, Iran, Pakistan, Tajikistan, Turkmenistan, and Uzbekistan—together with the United States and Russia to coordinate policies for dealing with the security problems its internal turmoil created.

Many Americans have invested so much energy and political capital in demonizing the Islamic Republic for its ideologically driven "irrationality" that they cannot take it seriously as a strategic actor. But Aminzadeh's account suggests that postrevolutionary Iran has a strategy, which it pursues even in the face of extreme provocations like the murder of its diplomats and coreligionists. As the current supreme leader, Ayatollah Khamenei, has noted, "regarding our vital issues, we are not sentimental. We do not make decisions based on emotion. We make decisions through calculation."[2]

One of the most important concepts that Imam Khomeini introduced into the Islamic Republic's political discourse was *maslahat*, well translated as "interests" or, more abstractly, "expediency." In 1988, not long before his death, Khomeini even created a special commission— the Council for Discerning the Interests of the System, usually rendered as the Expediency Council—to cut through ideological controversies over policy and identify sound, practical solutions.[3] For Khomeini as well as for his successor, maslahat does not imply abandonment of the Islamic Republic's principles; rather, it underscores the imperative of choosing the most suitable path to realize them. As Khamenei put it to senior Foreign Ministry officials not long after succeeding Khomeini, the Islamic Republic's foreign policy must always balance between expediency and honor ('*izzat*); the key to striking that balance is wisdom (*hikmat*), applied through "logical calculations, the establishing of strong foundations, taking steps on a level playing field, and refraining from imprudence, ignorance, and arrogance."[4]

As it has worked to strike this balance, the Islamic Republic has developed what might even be called a grand strategy—a framework for marshaling all elements of national power (diplomatic, economic, and political, as well as military) to defend itself and achieve important long-term objectives.[5] Protecting vital interests is the first order of business for any country's grand strategy. In Iran's case, this has been a severe challenge. Traditionally, states can address external threats in two ways: by mobilizing their own defense resources and by forging alliances with other states.[6] But Tehran's options for the former are circumscribed by its deficiencies in conventional military capabilities and its unwillingness to divert spending from domestic needs to correct them. Its options for the latter are complicated by long-standing American efforts to build and lead a political and security order covering most of the Middle East—and excluding the Islamic Republic.

Within these demanding parameters, Iranian policy makers have worked to compensate for their country's conventional military weaknesses and lack of strategic depth. Over the years, Tehran has come to rely especially on two sets of policy tools. First, it has cultivated relations with an array of "proxies"—sympathetic constituencies in other regional states that are open to strategic cooperation with Iran. Second, it has established an increasingly robust capacity for "asymmetric" defense and deterrence, developing an ever-expanding array of unconventional military capabilities that it can credibly threaten to use in response to aggression. In the West, these tools are simultaneously dismissed and condemned as support for terrorism and pursuit of WMD. But they are critical elements of a fundamentally defensive Iranian posture—as even the Pentagon's 2012 report on Iran's military power acknowledged.[7]

Beyond the protection of vital interests, grand strategies also try to improve states' positions relative to others. The Islamic Republic's grand strategy seeks to advance its regional and international position not through armed aggression but by using diplomacy and other non-coercive means to reset a regional balance of power that Tehran has long seen as tilted against it. Key to this aspect of its strategy is what might be called the Islamic Republic's soft power offensive. Twenty years ago, Harvard University's Joseph Nye defined soft power as the ability to get others to "want what you want," which he contrasted with the ability to compel others via "hard" military and economic assets.[8] Iran's increased influence in the Middle East over the past decade has far less to do with hard power than with the growth of its soft power—its power to attract rather than coerce through force or payment.

The cultivation of proxy allies, asymmetric military capabilities, and soft power have been part of Iranian security policy from the Islamic Republic's early years. But they were only integrated into a coherent strategic framework in the late 1980s and early 1990s, in the wake of the Iran-Iraq War and under the influence of Ali Akhbar Hashemi Rafsanjani and Seyed Ali Khamenei.[9]

Rafsanjani—a former student of Khomeini's and one of the Imam's closest associates during the revolution—played a major role in formulating the Islamic Republic's international policies for most of its first two decades. In the 1980s, while serving as speaker of the first postrevolutionary Majles—the Iranian parliament—he was Tehran's point man in reviving relations with a number of countries. During his two presidential terms (1989–97), he strove to put Iranian foreign policy on a sustainable, interest-based foundation, using the newly created Supreme National Security Council to build consensus on basic questions of strategy.[10] After leaving the presidency, he remained a major figure in public life as chairman of the Expediency Council; he also headed the Assembly of Experts, a clerical body that selects and oversees the leader, from 2007 to 2011.

Khamenei—another former student of Khomeini's—contributed at least as much, over an even longer period, to his country's national security strategy. Before succeeding Khomeini as supreme leader in

1989, Khamenei served in the assembly that drafted the Islamic Republic's constitution, was named by Khomeini as the leader of Friday prayers in Tehran, and was elected to the first Majles formed under the new constitution. Following the Iraqi invasion, he was the Majles's representative to the frontline military, the Defense Ministry, and the new Islamic Revolutionary Guard Corps; he then served as president from 1981 to 1989. Thus, he came to the position of supreme leader with experience in state affairs that no other candidate could match.

Although the president formally chairs the Supreme National Security Council, the leader has greater influence over its decision making. Since succeeding Khomeini, Khamenei has used this leverage to gain ultimate control over important foreign policy matters, opening the way to a more fundamentally interest-based grand strategy. Khamenei's ongoing support for the strategic framework he helped codify during Rafsanjani's presidency has ensured its continued force through the presidencies of Mohammad Khatami (1997–2005) and Mahmoud Ahmadinejad (2005–13, when he is constitutionally bound to leave office). Khamenei allows presidents a measure of tactical flexibility in implementing this strategy, but while there is genuine internal debate about foreign policy tactics, there is also broad agreement about the framework's main elements. This strategy will almost certainly continue to shape the Islamic Republic's foreign and national security policies under its next president.[11]

TIES THAT BIND

To understand the Islamic Republic's unique approach to balancing external threats, it is necessary to look more deeply at Iran's geographic, historical, and cultural setting. As noted, Iran's location and hydrocarbon endowments make it an object of strategic attention from states in and outside the Middle East. But that location also offers it a wide range of cultural connections with peoples and states in its immediate neighborhood and beyond. Over the past three decades, the Islamic Republic has made these connections an important part of its foreign policy and national security strategy, translating them into effective partnerships with political movements (often with associated para-military capabilities). Strengthened by shared religious and revolution-ary principles, these partnerships have enabled Iran to influence outcomes in key regional arenas and to prevent nearby states from being used as platforms to undermine its independence and standing.

Even a cursory review of Iran's regional environment reveals the striking breadth and depth of the religious, ethnic, and linguistic links between Iranians and their neighbors. First, there are its links to Shi'a Muslims outside Iran. While Shi'a represent only 15 percent of the world's Muslims, they are a sizable transnational community, roughly 140 million strong; furthermore, they are strategically located, spanning the heart of the Middle East as well as Central and South Asia and straddling the world's most important concentration of hydrocarbon reserves. There are extensive ties between Iran and Iraq's Shi'a majority, reflected in the large number of Iranians with familial connections to Iraq. For example, four of the five Larijani brothers, all of whom play prominent roles in the Islamic Republic's public life, were born in the Iraqi shrine city of Najaf, where their father, Grand Ayatollah Haj Mirza Hashem Amoli, one of the twentieth century's most prominent Shi'a clerics, spent thirty years. Iraq's most highly regarded Shi'a cleric, Grand Ayatollah Ali Sistani, is ethnically Per-sian and was born in Iran. In Afghanistan, Iran has religious links to the Hazara (Afghan Shi'a) and linguistic ties to Dari- and Tajik-speaking communities that extend into Tajikistan and other parts of Central Asia. Iran also has connections to Shi'a communities in Leba-non (where Shi'a are the largest sect), Azerbaijan (with a large Shi'a majority), Bahrain (also with a Shi'a majority), Kuwait (close to a fifty-fifty Sunni-Shi'a mix), Yemen (just over 40 percent), Pakistan (roughly 20 percent), and Saudi Arabia (roughly 10 percent, concentrated in the oil-rich Eastern Province).[12]

While the Islamic Republic's enemies have regularly tried to mobi-lize the nation's purportedly disaffected ethnic minorities against it, the diversity of Iranian society also fosters the country's connections to other peoples and states. Only about half of Iran's 74 million people are Persian. Almost a quarter—including Ayatollah Khamenei—are

Azeri, giving Iran cultural and linguistic inroads to Azerbaijan and Turkey. Other significant minorities include Kurds (7 percent of the population), Arabs (3 percent), Baloch (2 percent), and Turcomen (2 percent), bolstering Iran's ties to Afghanistan, Azerbaijan, Pakistan, Turkey, Turkmenistan, and the Arab and Kurdish areas of Iraq.

Under virtually any political order, these connections would give Iran a measure of "natural" influence in its regional environment. But some regimes are more able to take advantage of it than others. Thus, while the last shah was nominally Shi'a, he laid no claim to leadership in the Shi'a world. (Indeed, in Iran he was widely seen as hostile not just to the clergy but to religion itself.) Since his rule had no ideological or principled basis, there was no reason for his ties to regional constituencies to be guided by anything other than tactical expediency. So, in the 1970s, when he sought to use local proxies as a lever against Iraq in a border dispute, he turned not to Iraqi Shi'a but to Iraqi Kurds, backing a Kurdish rebellion against Saddam's rule. Once this tactic succeeded in pressing Saddam to sign a border agreement at least slightly favorable to Iran, he quickly dropped his erstwhile allies. (In classified testimony to Congress, Secretary of State Henry Kissinger defended the Kurds' abandonment with the observation that "covert operations should not be confused with missionary work.")[13]

In contrast, the Islamic Republic's religious and revolutionary identity has enabled it to cultivate more profound ties with proxy allies, giving Iran leverage it did not have under Pahlavi rule. The United States and Israel typically anathematize these proxies as terrorists. But whether in Lebanon, Palestine, or elsewhere, Iran's allies see themselves—and are widely seen in their local and regional environments—as resisting foreign occupation; helping them in their struggle has appreciably boosted the Islamic Republic's regional standing. In many cases Tehran has magnified the payoffs from its proxy strategy by picking political winners as its partners. This is especially true in the case of Hizballah and HAMAS, movements that win elections for the right reasons—because they speak for important but marginalized constituencies with legitimate grievances. Iranian support has enabled both groups not only to increase their strength as paramilitary forces but also to break into political processes from which they and those they represent had heretofore been barred by Western-backed local authorities.

EMPOWERING SHI'A

Khomeini's revolutionary vision stressed the importance of nurturing and protecting the unity of the umma, with a special emphasis on solidarity with Shi'a Muslims everywhere. And, in fact, the Islamic Republic has maintained a clear commitment to Shi'a solidarity. For historically repressed Shi'a communities, this support is critical, above all, because it is reliable. At its most basic level, Iranian influence is not a function of how many guns, bombs, rockets, or even dollars Tehran supplies; rather, it reflects that, while others—especially the United States—can always cut deals with Sunni players, the Islamic Republic is the only major regional actor that will virtually always support Shi'a populations.

Shi'a solidarity has been indispensable in keeping Iraq and Lebanon, two strategically critical countries with significant Shi'a populations, from becoming anti-Iranian platforms. Moreover, by supporting greater inclusion of previously disenfranchised Shi'a communities in local politics, the Islamic Republic has been able to influence the evolution of the Iraqi and Lebanese political orders to its advantage.

Iraq has long been a major security concern for Iran. The Iraqi invasion in September 1980 was arguably the most serious threat that the Islamic Republic has ever faced. And even though Iraq was one of Iran's most dangerous enemies, the American invasion two decades later posed multiple challenges for Tehran. In response, the Islamic Republic has relied heavily on local proxies to defend its interests in Iraq.

Tehran began supporting Shi'a Islamists seeking Saddam's overthrow during the Iran-Iraq War—a clear case, for Iran's new order, of Shi'a solidarity overlapping with geopolitical imperatives. It also continued the shah's policy of supporting Iraqi Kurdish oppositionists, proving, over three decades, to be a far more reliable partner.[14] After the Iran-Iraq War ended in 1988, Tehran continued backing various anti-Saddam Shi'a and Kurdish parties. In the process, Iran took in thousands of high-profile as well as ordinary Iraqi Shi'a, housed, clothed, fed, and educated them, and helped train and equip many of them for anti-Saddam militias.

After 9/11, the stakes became even greater. As the Bush administration set its sights on regime change in Baghdad, all of the Iranian-supported parties received permission from Tehran to cooperate in an American-forged Iraqi opposition front. But the Bush administration rebuffed Iranian offers to coordinate policies on Iraq, leaving Iran more concerned than ever that, after Saddam's removal, American forces would try to turn Iraq into an anti-Iranian staging ground. Rafsanjani outlined Iran's apprehensions at the time of the U.S. invasion in 2003:

> There are two options in Iraq. The best option is to have a unified and popular government. The worst option is an American puppet government. This is worse than Saddam, and may repeat the mischief committed by Saddam. It is easy for America to cause us trouble and endanger our security and oil sources through their agent in Iraq. They would also take the side of Israel *vis-à-vis* Palestine. If an American puppet government is established in Iraq, states such as Qatar and Bahrain would be regarded as provinces of Iraq and have to obey the latter's orders, OPEC would be disturbed, and oil prices would be determined by the US and its oil cartels to suit their interests. Our desire to take revenge against Iraq should not induce us to aggravate the situation.[15]

After Saddam's defeat, all the Shi'a Islamist and Kurdish parties that Iran had sheltered for twenty years returned home to Iraq with their militias, giving Tehran multiple options to forestall developments there that threatened its interests. But its goals have been moderate: it supports Iraq's territorial integrity and democratization, and it has participated in almost all of the regional meetings on Iraqi security held since 2004. Defenders of the U.S. invasion continue to fume against an Iranian "counterinvasion" that challenged American forces occupying Iraq and usurped the Bush administration's ostensible plans to create a secular, pro-Western democracy there.[16] In fact, Tehran was relatively restrained in exercising its considerable capacity to inflict damage on the American position in Iraq—even in the face of significant provocations, such as the storming of the Iranian consulate in the northern Iraqi city of Irbil and the seizure of Iranian diplomats there by American troops in 2007.[17]

Tehran's proxy allies have also shored up its confidence that any "unified and popular government" in Iraq would be pro-Iranian. American occupation authorities initially tried to promote secular politicians like Iyad Allawi and the discredited Ahmad Chalabi (to whom Washington gave hundreds of millions of dollars in the 1990s) as Iraq's post-Saddam leaders. But as Iraq moved from American-appointed governments to elected ones, ethnic and sectarian identity became the biggest impetus of its politics. In every election since 2005, Iran's Shi'a and Kurdish allies have proved themselves Iraq's most important political players. Every government formed out of these elections has been grounded in a coalition of Shi'a Islamists and Kurdish parties—and every one of them has had solid ties to Iran that Tehran has reinforced with economic links (including trade, investment, and infrastructure expansion) to sustain burgeoning cross-border flows of goods and people.

The Islamic Republic's proxy strategy has made it the most influential external force in post-Saddam Iraq, ensuring that Iraq will no longer pose a serious threat. The Iranians are clearly in Iraq for the long term. As an intelligence officer who had served with British forces in Iraq observed in 2006, "The Iranians were there before we arrived; I have no doubt they will be there when we leave."[18] Iran's influence was vividly on display in March 2008, when Ahmadinejad traveled to Baghdad on a landmark visit. Unlike Bush and Obama—whose visits were never announced in advance and who landed in the dead of night and kept largely to the Green Zone and tightly secured U.S. military installations—Ahmadinejad arrived in broad daylight, amid much ceremony, and traveled freely. The strength of Iran's influence was even more apparent when Iraqi prime minister Nouri al-Maliki's government—which owed its existence to the American invasion—stuck to the terms of the 2008 Status of Forces Agreement governing the deployment of U.S. soldiers and demanded that all American military units leave by the end of 2011. On their own, Maliki and some of his coalition partners would have preferred Americans to stay; for its part, the Obama administration wanted to keep as many as 20,000 troops, on an open-ended basis. But Maliki's government depends on the support of Shi'a Islamist parties with close ties to Tehran, including the Sadrists (who follow the Iranian-trained and -supported Shi'a cleric Muqtada al-Sadr). And the Sadrists, like Tehran, were adamantly opposed to Americans remaining at all, much less in an open-ended arrangement. In strategic terms, the United States lost the Iraq War and the Islamic Republic won it.

Iran's use of proxies to resist Israeli expansionism began in Lebanon, drawing on that country's long-disadvantaged Shi'a community. When Israel invaded Lebanon in 1982, Iranian leaders dispatched Revolutionary Guard cadres to help organize Shi'a resistance to Israel Defense Forces (IDF) occupying Shi'a-majority areas in south Lebanon and to American military forces and intelligence personnel supporting Israel and its Maronite Christian clients.[19] American commentators who attribute the bombing of the U.S. embassy in Beirut—where the CIA maintained a large station—in April 1983 and of the U.S. Marine barracks at Beirut International Airport in October 1983 to Iranian instigation never bother to explain why Tehran should have looked tolerantly on the insertion of a significant number of American troops and intelligence officers into a highly contested Middle Eastern arena, without U.N. or other valid international authorization, to impose an anti-Iranian government on Lebanon (and, if Washington had had the chance, on Syria).

In this charged environment, Hizballah (an Arabic compound meaning "party of God") took shape, over the course of the 1980s and with considerable Iranian input, as Lebanon's leading Shi'a Islamist resistance movement. The intensification of Iranian-Israeli geopolitical rivalry in the 1990s made Hizballah an ever more important ally for Tehran. The group's increasingly effective resistance campaign forced Israel to pay a steep price for occupying south Lebanon, culminating in the IDF's withdrawal from its declared "security zone" in 2000—an outcome that boosted Hizballah's popularity in Lebanon and across the region.

Hizballah's subsequent conduct punctures the conventional wisdom that it and other Iranian proxies are irrationally committed to terrorizing Israelis. Since the IDF's withdrawal, Hizballah has not carried out a single suicide terror attack against Israel or Israeli interests abroad.[20] But it has, with Iran's support, continued expanding and improving its military capabilities, preparing for what the movement's leaders anticipated would be periodic large-scale Israeli military operations in Lebanon.[21] In the summer of 2006, Israel—with the Bush administration's backing—undertook a thirty-three-day campaign to destroy Hizballah's military infrastructure and undermine its popular standing. But with Tehran's backing, Hizballah emerged triumphant once again, and more popular than ever. Today its military wing has larger rocket and missile arsenals, with longer ranges, than before the 2006 war. Israeli military planners must now take seriously the risk that strikes against Iranian targets could prompt retaliation not only by Iran but also by Hizballah, on their own doorstep.

Under the leadership of its secretary-general, Sayyid Hassan Nasrallah, Hizballah has, with Iranian encouragement, matched its military gains with political achievements. Following the IDF withdrawal, Nasrallah adroitly mined the popular support that the movement's resistance activities and social service programs accrued to produce strong performances in Lebanon's 2001, 2005, and 2009 parliamentary elections. The United States, major European powers, Israel, and so-called moderate Arab states such as Saudi Arabia have all been discomfited by Hizballah's political ascendancy and the concomitant increase in Iranian influence in Lebanon. All have tried in recent years to counter these trends. But Hizballah has consolidated its standing as the region's most successful resistance force, Lebanon's most popular and effective political party, and a potent check on Israeli ambitions to dominate the Levant. As in Iraq, these developments have boosted

Lebanese poured into the streets of Beirut to welcome President Ahmadinejad in 2010, highlighting the Islamic Republic's appeal on the Arab street. *AP*

Iran's local standing. When Ahmadinejad traveled to Beirut in October 2010, he received what even an anti-Hizballah reporter admitted was a "rapturous" welcome from tens of thousands of Lebanese; he enjoyed even warmer receptions in southern Lebanon and Dahiya, a predominantly Shi'a suburb just south of Beirut.[22]

SUPPORTING CROSS-SECTARIAN RESISTANCE

While Shi'a solidarity is an important part of Iran's proxy strategy, the Islamic Republic's capacity to exert regional influence through its proxy allies transcends sectarian bounds. Along with "neither East nor West," Khomeini's other great foreign policy slogan was "neither do injustice nor accept it"—an injunction that has both enabled and legitimized Iranian support for non-Shi'a groups engaged in resistance. But the Islamic Republic has not used proxy allies to export its revolution—and neither Shi'a solidarity nor a commitment to resistance has prompted Tehran to seek such allies where it judges that Iranian interests are not seriously threatened or would be better served by other approaches.[23] Instead, it has sought to match ideological commitments to geopolitical needs, supporting local proxies as instruments of influence where that influence is needed to keep neighboring states from being used as platforms for attacking Iran and to push back against the United States and Israel.[24]

From its creation, the Islamic Republic has had a strong interest in gaining greater influence over the disposition of Palestine, obviously a critical arena for containing what Iranians see as Israeli ambitions to regional hegemony. But early efforts to forge an alliance with the secular, Arabist Palestine Liberation Organization (PLO) and its long-time chairman, Yasir Arafat, met with scant success. Although Arafat was the first foreign dignitary Iran's new political order welcomed in 1979, his endorsement of Iraq's invasion of the Islamic Republic badly damaged this relationship. And Arafat's repeated attempts to curry favor with Washington by recognizing Israel, renouncing violence, and calling for peace talks while getting little in return later prompted Khamenei to denounce him as "a traitor and stupid, too."[25]

Deepening dissatisfaction among Palestinians with Arafat, his Fatah party, and the PLO created openings for Iran to explore alternative, explicitly Islamist connections to the Palestinian cause. As Palestinians are overwhelmingly Sunni Muslims (with a small Christian minority), ties to Sunni Islamist organizations became the critical channel through which the Islamic Republic built up its involvement in Palestinian affairs. It turned first to Islamic Jihad, a resistance movement that had taken shape in the early 1980s, inspired by Khomeini's revolutionary model. After the outbreak of the first Palestinian intifada, in 1987, a new party emerged out of the Muslim Brotherhood's Gaza branch, dedicated to integrating the provision of social services with armed resistance to Israeli occupation. This movement called itself HAMAS—simultaneously an acronym for the group's full name in Arabic, *Harakat Al-Muqawama al-Islamiyya* (Movement of the Islamic Resistance), and the Arabic word for zeal.

In contrast to Islamic Jihad, HAMAS did not initially try to establish a relationship with Iran; it sought support instead from Saudi Arabia and other Sunni Arab countries. But President George H. W. Bush determined to exclude both the Islamic Republic and HAMAS from the "new world order" he planned to create in the Middle East after the first Gulf War, hoping that both would somehow disappear. Instead, HAMAS sent a high-level delegation to Tehran in 1992 and opened an office there the following year, establishing a relationship reinforced by the Clinton administration's efforts to marginalize so-called rogue actors in the Middle East. To bolster Israeli prime minister Yitzhak Rabin's interest in negotiating with "acceptable" Palestinians, Washington pressed Saudi Arabia to cut off funding to HAMAS. A senior HAMAS official who has been intimately involved in the group's relationship with Iran told us that, but for this U.S. action, Saudi Arabia might have been the movement's biggest supporter. Instead, the Islamic Republic became a willing replacement.

With the collapse of the peace process at the end of the 1990s, HAMAS began positioning itself to reap the gains from its record of social service, resistance to occupation, and strategic perspicacity. In January 2006, HAMAS capitalized on its credibility—helped by its role in forcing Israelis' withdrawal from Gaza in 2005 and its reputation for incorruptibility—to enter mainstream politics, winning a striking victory in Palestinian legislative elections. Just as Iran had supported Hizballah's entry into Lebanese politics, it backed HAMAS's political debut. Since then, the organization's popular standing and electorally endorsed control of Gaza have made it an indispensable factor in Palestinian politics. At this point, there is no plausible way to reach a sustainable Israeli-Palestinian agreement without HAMAS's involvement—and, therefore, without Iran's buy-in as well, a situation that has given Tehran an indirect but decisive influence over the Palestinian issue. Contrary to the wishful thinking of many Western analysts and reporters, differences between Tehran and HAMAS over internal unrest in Syria since March 2011 have not fundamentally altered their relationship. While HAMAS has distanced itself from the Assad government, senior figures from the movement continue to travel to Tehran, where they extol the Islamic Republic's "limitless support" for the Palestinian Islamic resistance.[26]

A cross-sectarian approach has also been critical to the Islamic Republic's proxy strategy in Afghanistan. The Iranian Revolution came less than a year before the Soviet Union invaded Afghanistan in December 1979; like Iraq, Afghanistan has been a major security concern for almost the Islamic Republic's entire history. For more than thirty years, it has been an arena where Sunni states allied to Washington—and, after 9/11, Washington itself—have sought power and influence in ways that threaten Iran.

From its inception, the Islamic Republic has supported the Hazara (Afghan Shi'a) against anti-Shi'a forces. In keeping with the principles of resistance and Muslim solidarity, it condemned the Soviet invasion. But while Tehran was concerned about the presence of Soviet troops in Afghanistan, it was even more concerned about American and Saudi cultivation of Afghan factions, especially Pashtuns, to fight the Soviet occupation—proxies that could also be turned against Iran. Iranian policy makers understood that Soviet withdrawal, which finally took place in 1989, would result in a high-stakes proxy war in Afghanistan, with Saudi Arabia, Pakistan, and their local Pashtun allies on one side and the Islamic Republic and whatever local partners it could muster on the other. As fighting continued against the Soviet-installed government in Kabul, Tehran strove to beef up its roster of local proxies, expanding beyond the Hazara to deepen its ties to a range of disenfranchised, non-Pashtun Sunni factions—Tajiks, Uzbeks, and others. (Over the years, the Islamic Republic took in over 2 million Afghan refugees.) With the Taliban's rise, Tehran worked to join the Hazara and these non-Pashtun Sunni groups (together forming about 45 percent of Afghanistan's population) to counter pro-Pakistani, pro-Saudi Pashtun elements (the roughly 42 percent of the population from which the Taliban come). After the Taliban took Kabul in 1996, Iran played a key role in uniting Tajik, Uzbek, and Hazara militias into the so-called Northern Alliance.[27] For the next five years, Iran collaborated with Russia and India to improve the alliance's military capabilities and keep it fighting the Taliban on the ground, making it the only viable anti-Taliban force in Afghanistan on the eve of 9/11.

With 9/11, Iranian leaders concluded almost immediately that the United States would go to war in Afghanistan, and they promptly offered to cooperate in deposing the Taliban and creating a post-Taliban political order. Tehran and Washington used the United Nations' 6+2 framework as cover to open a bilateral channel for coordinating strategy toward Afghanistan and Al-Qa'ida; Hillary Mann Leverett, first as part of the U.S. delegation to the U.N. Security Council and then at the White House, was one of a small number of American officials engaged in these discussions.[28]

The Islamic Republic contributed substantially to the post-9/11 campaign against Al-Qa'ida and the Taliban. Most important, Tehran put its Afghan proxy allies at Washington's disposal. When the United States and its allies launched Operation Enduring Freedom in October 2001, the Northern Alliance provided the bulk of the troops fighting the Taliban on the ground and generated essential intelligence and targeting information for American air operations. Iran gave permission (as it had during the first Gulf War) for the U.S. military to conduct search-and-rescue missions on Iranian territory and provided information on Al-Qa'ida and Taliban targets to U.S. forces. Tehran also opened a humanitarian corridor for the flow of relief supplies into Afghanistan—a significant contribution because it forestalled international demands that the American military pause its air operations to allow relief supplies to enter the country.[29]

Furthermore, Iranian officials pledged to cooperate in Afghanistan's political reconstruction. To parry American assumptions that Iran would skew assessments of Afghanistan's ethnic and sectarian composition to favor its allies, Tehran offered to accept whatever demographic data Washington proffered—including, as one senior Iranian diplomat said, the figures in the CIA's *World Factbook*. Iranian support was crucial in establishing the Afghan Interim Authority (AIA), Afghanistan's first post-Taliban government, at the December 2001

Bonn conference: Tehran delivered its Afghan allies to the table to endorse the AIA, overrode their objections to the naming of Pashtun Hamid Karzai as president, and sidelined actors who might play spoiler roles. It provided similar backing to the *loya jirga*, or grand assembly, convened in June 2002 to legitimize the Karzai government, and it directed the *Sepah-e Mohammad*—an anti-Taliban militia made up of Afghan Shi'a refugees that had been founded, armed, and funded by the Islamic Republic—to join the U.S.-sponsored Afghan military. It also delivered over $500 million in economic aid, more than any other country, and became one of Afghanistan's most important economic partners, with expanding trade, investment flows, and initiatives to build roads and other vital infrastructure, especially in the country's north and west.[30]

Hillary's experience and our subsequent discussions with Iranian officials indicated that two principal considerations motivated Tehran's cooperation. First, Iranian policy makers calculated that helping the United States respond to the 9/11 attacks would prompt it to reconsider its attitude toward the Islamic Republic. Second—and of greater relevance here—Iran warily accepted Washington's representations that it wanted an independent, stable Afghanistan free from the sway of the Taliban and their Pakistani and Saudi backers. However, by the first Afghan elections—for president in 2004 and parliament in 2005—U.S.-Iranian cooperation had collapsed, largely as a result of different approaches to postconflict stabilization.

For Tehran, the ideal approach would have involved a coordinated effort at political reconstruction based on power sharing among Iran's Tajik, Uzbek, and Hazara allies and non-Taliban Pashtuns, followed by the speedy withdrawal of U.S. and other foreign troops. Iranian policy makers suspected that Washington wanted a longer-term option to use Afghan bases—most worrisomely in Herat province on Iran's eastern border—to project military power into other parts of the region, and the 2005 U.S.-Afghan Declaration for Strategic Partnership, which made it clear that American forces would not be leaving in the foreseeable future, confirmed their fears.

Besides perceiving a prolonged military presence in Afghanistan as a direct threat to Iranian interests, Tehran also anticipated that local populations would see a prolonged American military presence as occupation—a judgment borne out by events, as greater geographic penetration by U.S. forces since 2006 and the deployment of additional U.S. troops since 2009 correlated directly with escalating violence.[31] That instability enabled the Taliban to make a comeback, forcing Karzai and Washington to negotiate with them, largely on the Taliban's terms. This led Iranian policy makers to question not only U.S. intentions in Afghanistan but also U.S. competence. As an Iranian Supreme National Security Council official asked us in 2010, with no small amount of sarcasm, "If America wants to make a deal with the Taliban, why did it invade Afghanistan to overthrow the Taliban in the first place?" Tehran is dismayed that the Obama administration never developed a strategy for a political settlement. At this point, any settlement will have to include the Taliban—a worrying prospect for Iran.

No longer able to rely on the United States to suppress the Taliban, the Islamic Republic has itself reached out in recent years to elements in the Taliban. But contrary to some Western claims, it is hardly collaborating with the Taliban and Al-Qa'ida against the United States. Tehran continues to oppose the Taliban's unchecked participation in the Afghan government. It also continues to advocate a genuinely regional approach to postconflict stabilization—and to underscore that no lasting solution is possible without its involvement. Our Iranian interlocutors say that, while Iran will not "provoke" the Taliban, it will take steps "as necessary," working with local allies, to "defend Iranian interests."[32] In this regard, moves by the United States to engage the Taliban unilaterally and unconditionally have generated deep unease among Afghanistan's Tajik, Uzbek, and Hazara communities, who dominate the Afghan military's upper echelons and are organizing to resist power sharing with the Taliban. If Washington continues ignoring Iranian interests, it risks triggering another full-blown civil war, pitting non-Pashtun factions supported by Iran, India, and Russia against the Saudi- and Pakistani-backed Taliban—a situation disturbingly similar to the one on the eve of 9/11.

THE POLITICS OF MILITARY ASYMMETRY

Policy makers in Tehran do not regard proxy allies alone as sufficient to deter American or Israeli military action against the Islamic Republic. So, Iran has also developed increasingly robust capabilities for asymmetric defense and deterrence. Contrary to Western assertions, it is not resorting to nuclear, chemical, or biological weapons for this purpose. Rather, it is relying on ballistic missiles armed with conventional explosives and a range of interrelated systems to disrupt shipping in the Persian Gulf. Though portrayed in the West as highly provocative, this posture reflects a fundamentally defensive logic, described by an Iranian strategist as "an interconnected security and concomitant domino effect"—that is, Tehran's asymmetric capabilities are designed to create a situation where "Iran's security is equivalent to regional security and, conversely, Iran's insecurity will produce regional insecurity."[33] This is the classical logic of deterrence as understood by every Western student of national security affairs.

Iran's development of asymmetric assets has gone furthest in its ballistic missile programs. Since the 1990s, it has steadily moved toward missile-based deterrence; today, it possesses the Middle East's largest number of ballistic missiles.[34] Although the last shah invested heavily in advanced weaponry, at the time of the revolution Iran's missile arsenal was limited to artillery rockets. During the Iran-Iraq War, Tehran determined it needed ballistic missiles to strike targets deep inside Iraq; it obtained Soviet-designed short-range ballistic missiles, launchers, and technology from Libya, North Korea, and Syria, and in the late 1980s it began building its own versions of these systems. Today the Islamic Republic's arsenal of Shahab ("meteor") 1 and Shahab 2 missiles—adaptations of the Scud B and Scud C, respectively—allows it to threaten targets throughout the Persian Gulf. Iranian officials believe this capacity helps deter U.S. military action, both by complicating the prospective use of American forces deployed in the region and by discouraging Gulf Arab states from cooperating in an American attack.

Besides ballistic missiles, the Islamic Republic is now developing unmanned drones capable of bombing ground targets at high speeds; it has also shocked Washington by electronically commandeering an American drone launched from Afghanistan to spy on Iran in December 2011. It has several types of antiship missiles, along with submarines, "fast attack" boats, and mine-laying capabilities—assets that enable it to threaten Persian Gulf shipping, including American warships and vessels transporting oil, in response to military strikes against it. Iranian officials have suggested publicly that they might also use these assets in response to a blockade or to sanctions so severe as to constitute a blockade—again, a posture reflecting the logic of deterrence through "interconnected security."

There is considerable controversy among military and security analysts as to whether Iran could shut down Persian Gulf oil exports for a sustained period.[35] Iranian officials and analysts profess confidence that the Islamic Republic, as one told us, has built up "a sophisticated network of military hardware and software" to defend Iranian interests in the Gulf. In 2002, the largest war-game exercise ever conducted by the U.S. military, code-named Millennium Challenge and focused on a confrontation between "Blue" (American) and "Red" (not formally specified but clearly Iranian) forces in the Persian Gulf, suggested that Tehran's capability to wreak havoc on American forces is indeed highly developed. On the first day of the exercise, the Red team used missile and fast-boat "swarm" attacks to sink an American aircraft carrier and fifteen other ships in its battle group; in a real battle, at least 20,000 American military personnel could have died.[36] What is less clear is whether American officials have learned any lessons from this exercise. A senior U.S. military officer told us in 2012 that when, in response to threats of escalating sanctions and military attack, Iranian officials heralded Iran's capability to threaten free passage through the Strait of Hormuz, the Obama administration was taken by surprise; it seemed not to have seriously considered the possibility before.

Iranian policy makers believe that a fully elaborated deterrent posture requires the ability to strike Israel as well. Since the 1990s, Tehran has used imported missiles and technology to produce an adaptation of North Korea's medium-range No-dong missile, labeled the Shahab

3, and an extended-range model, the Ghadr ("powerful") 1. In recent years, Iran has tested an indigenously developed medium-range solid-fuel missile known in different versions as the Sajjil ("baked clay") or the Ashura.

As noted earlier, Iran has an established capacity to produce chemical agents but opted not to weaponize them during its war with Iraq. Citing its experience as a target of chemical attack, it has taken a strong public position against the possession and use of chemical weapons. In ratifying the Chemical Weapons Convention (CWC) in 1997, it acknowledged that it had developed chemical weapons capabilities during the war but declared that, "following the establishment of [the] cease-fire, the decision to develop chemical weapons capabilities was reversed and the process was terminated." Of course, Iran retains at least a basic capability to manufacture and weaponize chemical agents. But over the past decade U.S. intelligence has backed away from earlier claims that the Islamic Republic has stockpiles of chemical agents and munitions. Moreover, the most comprehensive open-source assessment of Iran's missile programs, published by the International Institute for Strategic Studies in 2010, concludes that "there is no evidence in the public domain indicating that Iran has developed or tested a chemical or biological warhead for its ballistic missiles."[37]

THE NUCLEAR PROGRAM AND IRANIAN STRATEGY

One of the more inflammatory pieces of Western conventional wisdom about the Islamic Republic is that it is actively working to develop nuclear weapons. On the surface, there seem to be many authoritative sources for this assessment. American, Israeli, and other Western intelligence services have claimed since the early 1990s that Iran is three to five years away from acquiring nuclear weapons; at times, Israel has offered even more alarmist figures. But twenty years into this constantly resetting forecast, no Western agency has come remotely close to producing hard evidence that Iran is trying to fabricate nuclear weapons. In Russia, which has its own extensive intelligence and nuclear weapons communities and close contacts with the Iranian nuclear program, high-level officials say publicly that Iran is not seeking to build nuclear weapons—a judgment echoed privately by Russian officials knowledgeable about both nuclear weapons and Iran's nuclear program. Mohamed ElBaradei, the Nobel laureate who served as director general of the International Atomic Energy Agency (IAEA) from 1997 to 2009—and under whose leadership the IAEA correctly assessed Iraq's lack of WMD when every Western intelligence agency got it wrong—has said on multiple occasions that there is no evidence the Islamic Republic is trying to build nuclear weapons. If these assessments are correct, how does the nuclear program fit into the Islamic Republic's grand strategy? Answering that question requires understanding of some historical, technical, and political realities.

A lot of Western commentary makes it seem as though Iran's nuclear program was launched under the Islamic Republic. But this is not the case. Iran's nuclear program began during the 1950s under the shah, with major American input. At their most elaborate, U.S. plans for Iran's nuclear development envisioned twenty-three power plants. A Ford administration strategy paper, prepared in 1976 while Dick Cheney was White House chief of staff and Donald Rumsfeld secretary of defense, noted that the "introduction of nuclear power will both provide for the growing needs of Iran's economy and free remaining oil reserves for export or conversion to petrochemicals"—a rationale that Cheney later dismissed when he was George W. Bush's vice president.[38]

Even though Iran had signed the Treaty on the Non-Proliferation of Nuclear Weapons (NPT) as a nonweapons state, the shah publicly declared his intent to acquire nuclear weapons, and Washington was ready to provide him with everything he needed, starting with the Tehran Research Reactor (TRR, recently at the center of diplomatic discussions about Iran's nuclear activities) in 1965. Originally, the TRR operated only on uranium so highly enriched it was close to the quality required for nuclear weapons. More tellingly, in 1976 Washington offered the shah the technology to extract bomb-grade plutonium from spent reactor fuel, which would have given Iran a complete nuclear fuel cycle—something Washington regards as unacceptable for the Islamic Republic—and a ready source of weapons-grade fissile material. The then secretary of state Henry Kissinger later said that when he and his colleagues discussed the deal, "I don't think the issue of proliferation came up."[39]

Those commentators who acknowledge the Iranian nuclear program's prerevolutionary origins almost universally project the shah's strategic logic for seeking nuclear weapons onto the Islamic Republic, without taking into account the different factors motivating Iran's postrevolutionary order. Just as Khomeini opposed the development and use of chemical weapons on moral grounds, so he opposed nuclear weapons acquisition. After the revolution the Islamic Republic abandoned the potentially weapons-related aspects of the nuclear program; it also reconfigured the TRR to work on uranium enriched to just below 20 percent, dramatically reducing the proliferation risks. A former Iranian nuclear negotiator noted that "if the Shah had not been overthrown by the Islamic Revolution in 1979, and were in power today, Iran would have a large nuclear arsenal. The West thus owes a debt of gratitude to the Islamic Republic because Iran has neither produced a nuclear bomb nor diverted its nuclear program toward military purposes."[40]

The Islamic Republic did, however, proceed to establish a civil nuclear energy program, including indigenous capabilities for uranium enrichment—a part of the fuel cycle that could also be part of a weapons program but that NPT signatories are allowed to pursue under IAEA monitoring. In the 1980s, it experimented with converting uranium into gas and began importing centrifuges—which process uranium gas to generate material with higher percentages of fissionable uranium isotopes—from Pakistan. In the 1990s, it started building facilities at Esfahan for producing uranium gas and, in 2000, at Natanz for processing the gas through centrifuges.[41] In 2002, a Washington-based affiliate of the MEK publicly announced these facilities' existence, before the IAEA was informed about them. Some commentators charged that Iran was concealing its nuclear work, but under the arrangements then in force for implementing Iran's IAEA safeguards agreement, Iran was not required either to declare new nuclear sites or to allow access to them until six months prior to the introduction of nuclear materials and thus had not breached its safeguards agreement. Following the MEK's "revelations," the IAEA sought and was granted access to the facilities.

Today the Islamic Republic is using its own adaptations of Pakistani-designed centrifuges to enrich uranium; besides Natanz, it has opened a second enrichment site at Fordo, near the city of Qom. Iran's facilities for making uranium gas feedstock and processing it through centrifuges operate under full IAEA safeguards; agency officials have told us they have better access to these facilities than to analogous sites in some Western countries. The IAEA reports that Iran is enriching uranium at the 3–4 percent level needed to make fuel for power reactors. More recently, it has started enriching to the near–20 percent level needed to make fuel for the TRR. But even at this level Iran is below both the NPT threshold for "high enriched" uranium and the 90+ percent level needed for bomb-grade material.

American, Israeli, and other Western intelligence services claim Iran has done at least theoretical work on engineering problems relating to the design and construction of nuclear weapons. For years during the tenure of Mohamed ElBaradei as the IAEA's chief, the United States and some of its allies pushed him to include these claims in the agency's reports on Iran's nuclear activities. Baradei refused, because he could neither corroborate them nor be confident about their provenance and quality. His successor, Yukiya Amano— who has told American officials he is "solidly in the U.S. court"— reversed Baradei's decision and, since November 2011, the IAEA has put the claims in its reports.[42] How different analysts interpret these claims correlates strongly with their assessments of Iran's nuclear intentions (to which we turn below). None of the claims, though, are substantiated by hard evidence, and none contradict the IAEA's ongoing affirmation of Iran's nondiversion of nuclear material.[43] Even if some or all of the claims were accurate, the NPT does not prohibit the research Iran has been accused of conducting.[44]

What does the possibility that the Islamic Republic has worked on aspects of nuclear weapons design signify about its nuclear intent? Some analysts simply assume that Tehran is working to acquire nuclear arms. One does not have to be a neoconservative to think along these lines; the dean of foreign policy realism in American academia, Kenneth Waltz, has attracted considerable attention with his argument that Iran's nuclearization would actually stabilize the Middle East.[45] In a manner reminiscent of their inaccurate and unprofessional coverage of WMD issues in the run-up to the Iraq war, the *New York Times*, the *Washington Post*, major broadcast networks, and other high-profile media outlets have regularly run poorly sourced and reported stories referencing the Islamic Republic's "quest for nuclear weapons," its "nuclear weapons program," and how Tehran "refused" IAEA inspectors access to sensitive facilities.[46]

But all of this begs the question of whether Tehran really seeks nuclear weapons. As noted, Iran has signed on to the NPT and allows the inspections of its nuclear sites that the NPT requires. Both the American and Israeli intelligence communities concede that the Islamic Republic has not made nuclear weapons and that its leaders have not taken a decision to make them. Indeed, former U.S. national security adviser Zbigniew Brzezinski points out that, in contrast to Chinese and North Korean leaders, who said publicly that they were determined for their states to acquire nuclear arms, the most senior Iranian officials have consistently stated over many years that the Islamic Republic does not want and is not seeking them.[47] Ali Asghar Soltanieh, Tehran's IAEA ambassador, has said that it would be a "strategic mistake" for Iran to build nuclear weapons, as it "cannot compete in terms of the numbers of warheads possessed by the nuclear-armed powers, so if it seeks to produce nuclear weapons, it will be in a disadvantageous position compared with these countries."[48] Even after the Obama administration's 2010 Nuclear Posture Review singled out Iran as a potential target for the first use of nuclear weapons, Khamenei told an audience of Iranian military commanders that, while "in recent years the Americans made many efforts to show that the Islamic Republic of Iran is unreliable on the nuclear issue," American nuclear strategy clearly showed "that the governments that possess atomic bombs and shamelessly threaten to bomb others are the unreliable ones."[49]

There are other reasons to challenge the assumption that the Islamic Republic's nuclear intentions are focused on weaponization. Iranian officials calculate (perhaps correctly, perhaps not) that neither the United States nor Israel would attack Iran if it did not cross the "red line" of weaponization but that crossing this line would provoke a military confrontation that Tehran does not want. The countries most supportive of Tehran on the nuclear issue—Russia, China, Turkey, Brazil, South Africa—strongly oppose Iranian weaponization; political support for Iran's position would evaporate if Iran weaponized.[50]

Beyond strategic considerations, there is the argument that nuclear weapons, like chemical weapons, violate Islamic precepts—that they are, to use the religious term, *haraam* ("forbidden by God"). This argument, first laid down by Khomeini, has been reiterated by Khamenei throughout his tenure as supreme leader and is regularly echoed by other officials. Ahmadinejad has described nuclear weapons as a "fire against humanity," charging that "to have a nuclear bomb is not only a dishonor; it's obscene and shameful. Threatening to use it and using it is even more shameful." While serving as head of the Atomic Energy Organization of Iran, Ali Akbar Salehi (now the Islamic Republic's foreign minister) stressed that Iran was not trying to manufacture nuclear weapons: "It's against our tenets. It's against our religion." When asked what he would do if the policy changed and he were requested to begin working on weaponization, he replied bluntly, "Of course I wouldn't accept it. . . . Because this is against my religion. And this is what my supreme leader has said. The supreme leader is not only a political leader. He is a religious leader as well. How can he change his words so easily?"[51] As recently as 2012, Khamenei reiterated his stance that, "from an ideological and *fiqhi* [Islamic jurisprudence] perspective, we consider developing nuclear weapons as unlawful. We consider using such weapons as a big sin."[52]

This moral constraint on weaponization is more substantial than most Western analysts appreciate. There is the precedent that the Islamic Republic decided—even as Iraq was attacking it with chemical weapons—not to weaponize its stockpiles of chemical agents in order to retaliate in kind. Today, to be sure, some Iranian officials support nuclear weapons acquisition; according to opinion polls, so does roughly a third of the public.[53] But senior reformist and conservative figures, as well as the national security adviser to a foreign head of state, who have met with the supreme leader, say that Khamenei remains steadfastly opposed to weaponization; he acknowledges some pressure to push ahead with building weapons but has given clear instructions not to take the program in that direction.

Against this record of official and religious rejection of nuclear weapons, for Khamenei or any future supreme leader to shift course would mean having to explain—to Iranians and to the entire Shi'a world—how Iran's strategic circumstances had changed to such an extent that manufacturing nuclear arms was now both necessary and legitimate. That, of course, is not an absolute constraint on Iranian weaponization. But it would require, at a minimum, a widely perceived and substantial deterioration in the Islamic Republic's strategic environment—most plausibly effected by an Israeli and/or U.S. attack on Iran. It is far from certain that Tehran would opt for weapons acquisition even then. But those urging military action to block the Islamic Republic's nuclear advancement advocate a course that would raise the risk of Iranian weaponization, not reduce it.

The purposes of Iran's current nuclear program are more multifaceted and subtle than standard Western models of nuclear development and proliferation allow. Iranian officials say, with considerable plausibility, that the program serves a variety of economic and technological interests. Soltanieh, an American-trained nuclear physicist, told us that it acts as a kind of industrial policy for the Islamic Republic, much as the space program did for the American economy in the 1960s and 1970s. It allows Iranian scientists, engineers, and technicians to develop expertise (for example, in centrifuge technology) that can be applied beyond the nuclear arena and to establish new sectors (for example, producing medical isotopes) for the Iranian economy. To an even greater extent than was the case when the Ford administration prepared its 1976 strategy paper on nuclear cooperation with the shah's Iran, generating nuclear power prospectively allows the Islamic Republic to devote more of its oil to export or to high-value-added processes like oil-based petrochemicals; likewise, nuclear energy frees up natural gas for injection into aging oil fields and for the cultivation of petrochemicals and other gas-based industries. Iran already exports electricity to Afghanistan, Iraq, Pakistan, and Turkey, and wants to expand such exports in the future.

From a security perspective, Iranian leaders have reportedly confided to officials from other states that the program is intended to give Tehran a "threshold" or "break out" capability.[54] The way that the program has been conducted suggests it is partly aimed at creating a nuclear weapons option—going to the very edge of Iran's nonproliferation obligations to foster the perception that the Islamic Republic is mastering the competency to fabricate nuclear weapons without actually fabricating them. In other words, it is meant to give Iran the same standing as Japan, Canada, and other nations that joined the NPT as nonweapons states but are widely seen as able to produce nuclear weapons in short order should they ever choose to do so. As Baradei points out, for a state to attain nuclear weapons capability—not weapons but the capacity to build them—is "kosher" under the NPT.[55]

There is consensus across the Islamic Republic's political spectrum that a nuclear weapons option holds deterrent value even without overt weaponization. But the main strategic purposes of the program are political rather than military. Domestically, the enrichment issue has prompted officials to make a highly resonant public case that, in pressing for a halt, the United States and other major powers are trying to deny Iran one of its sovereign rights. Among Iran's elite, there is broad support for the nuclear program, including enrichment. Likewise, polls by both Iranian and Western organizations have regularly shown that an overwhelming majority of Iranians support continuing enrichment.[56] (The same polls also indicate that most Iranians oppose weapons acquisition.) Even as the economic impact of sanctions has intensified, no methodologically rigorous survey has suggested the emergence of a significant constituency for giving up enrichment in exchange for sanctions relief and other material incentives.[57]

Strategically, the nuclear program is a powerful asset for Iranian foreign policy. The Islamic Republic has been able to position itself as a defender of all developing countries' nuclear rights under a global nuclear regime dominated by the interests and preferences of the United States and other nuclear weapons states. For years Washington has worked to close or at least narrow what many American officials and nonproliferation experts see as a loophole in the NPT that permits nonweapons states to develop fuel cycle capabilities, including uranium enrichment. Several emerging powers—including Brazil and South Africa, which became nonproliferation heroes for giving up their weapons programs following their democratization—strongly oppose this move, arguing that it amounts to rewriting the treaty after the fact. Against this backdrop, Iran has been able to parlay its defiance of Security Council resolutions calling for it to suspend enrichment—resolutions that Tehran denounces as illegitimate attempts to take away a sovereign right—into an exercise of resistance to American bullying of non-Western states over the development of indigenous fuel cycle capabilities. Ahmadinejad has played on the theme very effectively, accusing the Western powers of using the issue as "a pretext" for keeping Iran down while "their warehouses are filled with nuclear weapons and, in fact, they have been equipping certain individual nations in this region with nuclear weapons. They have monopolized the technology and want to hamper the Iranian nation from getting such technologies."

Closer to home, the Islamic Republic has used its defiance of the West regarding its nuclear activities to boost its regional standing. As Ayatollah Khamenei recently commented:

Western powers have stressed that, through sanctions, they want to force Iran to back down on its nuclear program. Well, when we do not back down—and we will not back down—what happens? In the eyes of the people in the region . . . the West and their threats will no longer be perceived as credible, and Iran's power will become more admired. And that is in our interest.[58]

Similarly, the Islamic Republic has exploited Western criticism of its nuclear activities to draw greater attention to Israel's status as an undeclared nuclear weapons state that has never submitted to the NPT, taking the lead from other regional states—especially Egypt and Saudi Arabia—that have been working futilely for years to bring world attention to Israel's nuclear arsenal.[59]

Most important, the nuclear program gives Tehran the leverage to compel Washington to come to terms with it. This makes the nuclear issue an attractive point of entry for dealing with the United States and other major powers on larger strategic questions.[60] Baradei says that Iranian officials have told him many times they have no problem with the United States as a global power but that they want it to recognize Iran's status as a regional power; in his view, Iran wants a nuclear weapons capability in order to force America to take it seriously as a regional force.[61]

CULTIVATING A SOFT-POWER EDGE

One of the primary purposes of the Islamic Republic's grand strategy is to improve its position in the regional and international balance of power. The proxy component of Iranian strategy contributes to this goal by elevating the standing of political forces that are inclined to cooperate with Tehran. Iran's asymmetric military capabilities contribute by raising the cost of using force against it, while the nuclear program subtly reinforces Iran's deterrent posture and boosts its diplomatic leverage. Iranian decision makers have also sought to integrate these strands of foreign and national security policy to cultivate greater soft power.

Joseph Nye, in his 2004 book on the subject, argues that a country's soft power can come from three sources: its culture, its political values, and its foreign policy (when that policy is seen as having legitimacy and moral authority).[62] Abbas Maleki, a former Iranian deputy foreign minister who has become one of the Islamic Republic's leading commentators on international affairs, posits that America's soft power has been generated by "Hollywood, Harvard, Microsoft, and Michael Jordan"—formidable cultural assets, certainly, but probably not enough to offset the damage done to the moral authority of its foreign policy by the misuse of its hard power. Iran's soft power, by contrast, derives from all three of Nye's sources.[63]

On the cultural front, we have already noted the wide range of ethnic, linguistic, and religious ties linking Iran to nations and groups beyond its borders. With regard to political values, the Islamic Republic has worked to present itself both at home and abroad as an authentically indigenous political project aiming to integrate Islamic principles with democratic institutions and processes. Western critics claim that no major constituency outside Iran, Shi'a or Sunni, is clamoring for the Islamic Republic's specific constitutional arrangements. But this barb misses the point, that most Middle Eastern populations want for themselves what Iranians have been attempting since 1979: to build indigenous and independent political systems that they can own, warts and all.

Iran's foreign policy is even more central to its accumulation and application of soft power. Iranian decision makers understand that the Islamic Republic's opposition to American hegemony in the Middle East, its support for resistance to Israeli occupation, and its defiance of the West over the nuclear issue are more closely aligned with regional public opinion than are the policies of regimes that cooperate with Washington. Tehran has used this boost to its soft power to pursue what, in American foreign policy circles, is called "public diplomacy"—the strategic cultivation of public opinion in other countries.[64] Washington's public diplomacy in the Middle East has amounted to a succession of ham-fisted initiatives intended to persuade regional publics to support American policies that are antithetical to their interests and values. Examples include trips to the region by the likes of Karen Hughes (President George W. Bush's public relations expert), appearances by Secretary of State Hillary Clinton on Oprah-esque women's TV shows, and Radio Free Europe–style broadcasting initiatives aimed at Iran and other states "of concern." By contrast, the Islamic Republic has achieved soft-power gains, on a scale that strategists in Washington can only dream of, by pursuing policies that actually address Middle Easterners' grievances and affirm their values.

This is a dynamic that Ahmadinejad, an exceptionally adept populist politician, has understood very well. Many in the West have dismissed Ahmadinejad's rhetorical themes of justice and redressing grievances as the unsophisticated propaganda of a crude demagogue. In fact, they are key to the Islamic Republic's soft-power edge. Ahmadinejad has regularly spoken out against all forms of hegemony in international affairs; focusing on the Middle East, he has sharply criticized the United States for trying to dominate the region, for launching military campaigns that have killed hundreds of thousands of civilians and displaced millions, and for enabling Israel's ongoing occupation of Arab and Muslim populations. When Ahmadinejad questions what really happened on 9/11 and in the Holocaust, many Westerners are horrified. But to regional audiences he is challenging the foundational premises of wildly unpopular American and Israeli policies—and those audiences applaud him for it. While careful not to deny that thousands of innocent people died on 9/11 or millions in the Holocaust, he has confronted what people in the region see as America and Israel's assertion of an exclusive prerogative to draft the reigning narratives about these episodes, assign blame for them, and define remedies that have had massive repercussions for innocent Muslims. By implication (and, on occasion, directly), he has also rebuked those regional governments that aid and abet American and Israeli misdeeds. Local audiences applaud him for that, too.

Israel and Iran are, as noted, in a virtual state of war. Israel prosecutes this war through multifaceted covert attacks; it also threatens large-scale conventional strikes. The Islamic Republic fights this war not only by supporting anti-Israel proxies around the region but also through a robust soft-power strategy. This is the context in which Ahmadinejad's rhetoric about Israel and the Holocaust needs to be understood. When he holds forth on these subjects in ways that offend Israelis and many Westerners, he is tapping into a deep anger throughout the Middle East and in much of the rest of the Muslim world about Israeli and American policies—which are seen in these settings as one and the same. In contrast to most established Arab leaders, who criticize only specific Israeli and/or American policies (as if the only problem with them were their "excessiveness"), Ahmadinejad has questioned what is widely seen as the most fundamental rationale for these policies. In doing so, he has adroitly used hot-button historical episodes to hold up the Islamic Republic to Muslim audiences as the most principled defender of resistance to Israeli policies of occupation, unilateral resort to disproportionate force, and hegemony.

Ahmadinejad has been able to do this, in no small part, because the Islamic Republic, while anti-Zionist, is not anti-Semitic, as manifested in its treatment of Iran's Jewish community (the Middle East's largest outside Israel, estimated at 9,000–22,000). As two Iranian scholars point out,

> Anti-Semitism, scientific racism per se, is a particularly European phenomenon; that race theory developed out of the ideological laboratories of European modernity. There is no Iranian or Islamic theory of anti-Semitism. There may be anti-Semitic sentiments of course, but these have never really morphed into a fascist ideology or a cod science such as "phrenology" that identified Jews as sub-humans. Opposition to Israel is a political stance and has nothing to do with scientific racism which fed into Nazi ideology, especially in Germany. Being opposed to the policies of the state of Israel is not the same as being anti-Jewish. . . . There are Stars of David publicly displayed in Tehran, for instance on the walls and signs of the Beheshtieh Jewish cemetery where dozens of Holocaust victims are buried.[65]

Today, Jews in the Islamic Republic vote like other Iranians for president and for deputies to represent their cities and towns in parliament. But the Jewish community is also constitutionally guaranteed a seat of its own in the Majles, even though it is much smaller than a normal parliamentary district. There are at least two dozen functioning synagogues (some with Hebrew schools), 21 kosher restaurants, and a Jewish newspaper in Iran; in Tehran, there is a 20,000-volume Jewish library and a Jewish hospital. Jews are conscripted into the army (many fought in the Iran-Iraq War). In 2006, the head of the community

criticized—with impunity—Ahmadinejad's rhetoric about the Holocaust in an open letter distributed to Iranian and international media.
(Where the government draws a line is with regard to support for
Israel. There has been at least one high-profile case, in 2000, in which a
number of Iranian Jews were arrested and convicted of spying on
Israel's behalf.) In 2009, some Jews participating in postelection protests were arrested and released like virtually all other demonstrators
detained by the authorities. Although a sizable portion of Iran's Jewish community left the country immediately after the revolution,
Iranian Jews have in recent years overwhelmingly rejected financial
incentives—almost $10,000 per person, just over $30,000 per family,
offered by diaspora groups on top of Israeli government incentives—to
emigrate to Israel.[66] All of this helps make anti-Zionism an important
part of the Islamic Republic's soft-power strategy.

The Islamic Republic's soft-power gains surface clearly in public
opinion polls conducted in the Middle East. Since the beginning of
Ahmadinejad's presidency, in 2005, surveys of (mostly Sunni) Arab
populations have consistently identified him as one of the three or
four most admired leaders in the world. Although Americans often
have a hard time understanding how a figure can become internationally popular by opposing U.S. policy, by the end of George W. Bush's
presidency a number of Western analysts were compelled, by polling
data and other evidence, to acknowledge that Iran's posture of resistance had won it approbation among Arabs.[67] But most of these
commentators soon returned to form, happily asserting—with no
supporting evidence—that international criticism of Iran's 2009 presidential election, the Iranian government's response to postelection
protests, and the outbreak of the Arab awakening at the end of 2010
had eviscerated popular support for the Islamic Republic across the
region.[68] Many also claimed that mounting concern among Arab
elites over the continued progress of Iran's nuclear program (a concern that surfaced dramatically in classified State Department cables
published by WikiLeaks in November 2010) reflected a broader and
growing antipathy toward Tehran's nuclear ambitions.[69]

In fact, though, methodologically reliable surveys of public opinion

in those same Arab states whose leaders have complained so vigorously
to Washington about Iranian influence reveal continued high regard for
Iranian foreign policy positions. More than three years after the Islamic
Republic's 2009 presidential election, Ahmadinejad remained one of the
most admired leaders in the Arab world.[70] When asked in 2010 whether
Iran's acquisition of nuclear weapons would be positive for the region, a
strong majority of respondents in a highly regarded annual survey of
Arab public opinion said that it would; in 2011, two-thirds of respondents said that Iran had a right to its nuclear program and should not be
pressured to stop it.[71] This means that, in Arab countries where the ruling authorities (aided by the United States) have devoted substantial
effort to convincing their citizens that Iran aspires to a regional hegemony contrary to their interests through the acquisition of nuclear
weapons, local populations are simply not buying the argument. It would
be hard to find a better testament to the appeal of Iranian soft power.

RESHAPING THE BALANCE

Western commentators are prone to dismiss the significance of soft
power in the coldly competitive power politics of the Middle East. Zbigniew Brzezinski has been an exception, recognizing the importance of a
"global political awakening" in which "nearly universal access to radio,
television, and the Internet is creating a community of shared resent-
ments and envy that transcends sovereign borders." Brzezinski believes
that, in the Middle East and other regions "scarred by memories of
colonial or imperial domination," a "yearning for human dignity" and
"cultural respect" is developing among populations that, "disliking the
status quo, are susceptible to being mobilized against those whom they
perceive as self-interestedly preserving it."[72]

Iranian policy makers long ago grasped the potential for this kind
of mobilization to challenge existing regimes, a regional order dominated by the United States, and a regional balance of power tilted
against Iran. Tehran is using the political awakening in the Middle
East to alter the very nature of power politics in the region. More specifically, it is working to transform the region's traditional balance of

power, defined by conventional military capabilities and other hard-power assets in which the Islamic Republic is relatively deficient, into a balance of influence, defined by aspects of soft power in which it enjoys unique advantages. This transformation is bolstering Tehran's ability to shape strategic outcomes.

Most immediately, the Islamic Republic's popular standing across the region imposes meaningful constraints on its neighbors' ability to act against Iranian interests. This aspect of Iranian soft power was made clear during the 2006 Lebanon war. After the fighting broke out, senior Saudi leaders, including the foreign minister, Prince Saud al-Faisal, made public statements sharply critical of Hizballah and its Iranian backers for sparking the conflict. In Washington, these Saudi statements were hailed as evidence of the potential for a U.S.-led "moderate" Arab-Israeli coalition to counter Iran and its allies. But after ten days of nonstop regional media coverage of Israel's military campaign in Lebanon, Saudi leaders retreated and began criticizing the inhumanity of Israeli actions and American support. They did this for a simple reason: the kingdom's Interior Ministry had polls showing that the Saudi public was siding with Hizballah and Iran.[73] Since then the growth of Iranian soft power has only reinforced these constraints. However much some Sunni Arab elites may want to see the Islamic Republic cut down to size, there is little overall Arab support for confrontation with it. Reputable international polls show that, by orders of magnitude, Arabs are concerned more about the threat posed to them by Israel and the United States than about that posed by Iran.[74]

Under these circumstances, the idea (pushed by policy makers and pundits through the Clinton, George W. Bush, and Obama administrations) that Washington can exploit the Iranian "threat" to unite Arab states and Israel in a grand alliance under American leadership is nothing short of delusional. The prospect of Arab state cooperation with Israel against the Islamic Republic remains profoundly unpopular with Arab publics; even the most moderate Arab regimes would not be (and have not been) able to sustain such cooperation. Likewise, there is little support among Arab populations for American and/or Israeli military action against Iran, even over the nuclear issue.

The Islamic Republic is using its soft-power edge to encourage neighboring states to better represent their populations. Tehran calculates that democratization ends up empowering its allies—for example, Shi'a communities and other constituencies that have been systematically marginalized. Iranian policy makers are confident that any regional government that grows more representative of its people's values, concerns, preferences, and interests will grow, in turn, less enthusiastic about strategic cooperation with the United States and Israel and more receptive to Iran's message of resistance.

This perspective on regional politics is what made the Islamic Republic the nation least surprised by the Arab awakening and certainly the one most pleased by it. Writing at the beginning of 2011, on the eve of the outbreak of the anti-Mubarak protests in Egypt, Seyed Mohammad Marandi—a scholar well connected with Iranian foreign policy circles—offered a clear account of Iran's view:

> In Tehran, there is a strong belief that the region is changing dramatically in favor of Hizballah, the Palestinians, and the Resistance. The rise of an independent Turkey, whose government has a worldview very different from that of the U.S., German, British, and French governments, along with the relative decline of Saudi and Egyptian [under Mubarak] regional influence, signals a major shift in the regional balance of power. Saudi military incompetence during the fighting with Yemeni tribes along the border between the two countries, the general decline of the Egyptian regime in all respects, and the almost universal contempt among Arabs as a whole for the leaders of these two countries and other pro-Western Arab regimes and their corrupt elites are seen as signs that the center cannot hold. The fact that the Iranian president and the Turkish prime minister are so popular in Arab countries, while most Arab leaders are deeply unpopular, is a sign that the region is changing.[75]

Since Marandi wrote those words, the trend toward the more participatory politics that has empowered Iranian allies in Iraq, Lebanon, and Palestine has brought down pro-Western regimes in Tunisia and

Egypt, forced a leadership change in Yemen (a key U.S. ally in the war on terror), and spread to several other Arab states.

Thus, the Islamic Republic is pushing real and enduring changes in the Middle East's balance of power. Conventional wisdom in Washington holds that Iran is one of the biggest losers from the Arab awakening.[76] But consider the regional scene from Tehran's perspective: Iraq and Lebanon are hardly turning into paragons of pro-American "stability"; it seems more likely that both will grow more aligned with Iran's axis of influence. HAMAS's standing in Palestinian politics means that the American vision of an Israeli hegemonic peace is not tenable as the basis for an Israeli-Palestinian settlement. In Tehran's view, even if the pro-American regime in Bahrain (home of the U.S. Fifth Fleet) persists in the face of massive popular opposition, it cannot hold on forever.

And now the strategic orientation of Egypt—an anchor of the Middle Eastern political and security order that the United States has been trying to build for thirty years—is up for grabs, and Iranian policy makers see an opening. Since Mubarak stepped down, the Muslim Brotherhood has strongly endorsed closer relations. Just two weeks after Mubarak's ouster, a senior Brotherhood official told a University of Tehran audience that, "given the recent developments in the region, we need unity among the Muslim countries and Iran can play an important role in this regard." He also declared that Ahmadinejad "is the bravest man in the Muslim world and we [in Egypt] need innocent, honest, and brave leaders like him."[77] In fact, all the major political forces in post-Mubarak Egypt have identified closer ties to the Islamic Republic as a foreign policy priority.

In August 2012, the newly elected president of Egypt, Mohamed Morsi, defied the Obama administration by going to Tehran to attend the Nonaligned Movement (NAM) summit before his inaugural trip to the United States; Morsi was the first Egyptian leader to travel to Iran in almost forty years. In Washington, neoconservatives and liberal internationalists flailed at the Egyptian's lack of deference. Michael Mandelbaum of Johns Hopkins University's School of Advanced International Studies asserted that, without a communist bloc, "the main division in the world is between democratic and undemocratic countries." Picking up on the theme, Thomas Friedman of the *New York Times* found it "disturbing" that Morsi could be "nonaligned when it comes to choosing between democracies and dictatorships—especially the Iranian one." Drawing on the flawed analysis of Abbas Milani and Karim Sadjadpour, Friedman charged that the Egyptian president was "lending his legitimacy to an Iranian regime that brutally crushed" a democracy movement at home—"the exact same kind of democracy movement that brought you, Mr. Morsi, to power in Egypt." Morsi, Friedman intoned, "should be ashamed of himself."[78] But Mandelbaum, Friedman, and others with outlooks like theirs are oblivious to reality in the Middle East. Most Middle Easterners do not think that the Islamist features of Iran's political system make it undemocratic. And, however much the Islamic Republic may have benefited from Morsi's visit, Morsi needed it more than Tehran did. For most Egyptians and other Middle Easterners, the "main division in the world" is not between democracies and dictatorships but between countries whose strategic autonomy is subordinated to the United States and countries who exercise genuine independence in policymaking. For most people in the Middle East, the Islamic Republic is on the right side of that divide.

There are, of course, countervailing pressures working to constrain post-Mubarak Egypt's assertion of strategic autonomy. The Egyptian military wants to preserve its lucrative relationship with the United States, and Saudi Arabia is spending furiously to maintain its influence. But even with these pressures, Egypt is going to have a more independent foreign policy—and Iran is confident that the change will work to its advantage.

Not surprisingly, the West and its Sunni allies have looked for ways to reverse Iranian gains. Since March 2011, they have focused on unrest in Syria—the Islamic Republic's oldest Arab ally—as their most promising opportunity. The emergence of armed opposition groups in Syria has called the Assad government's longevity into doubt for many Western observers, raising questions about the future of the Iranian-Syrian alliance and Iran's ability to supply Hizballah through Syria. Ankara's decision to break with Tehran and support the Syrian opposition is also seen as having created an opening to weaken the Islamic Republic's regional position.[79]

Iranian policy makers believe that unrest in Syria, while reflecting genuine discontent, is also a proxy channel for U.S., Saudi, and perhaps Israeli efforts to bring down President Bashar al-Assad—partly by turning it into a crassly sectarian anti-Shi'a campaign.[80] Tehran recognizes that many Syrians want reforms (and regularly urges Assad to pursue them); at the same time Iranian officials calculate that, absent Western intervention, the Assad government is unlikely to fall, as a narrow majority of Syrians still supports it. Iranian leaders have called for negotiations between Assad and his opposition and for the holding of open elections to resolve what has become a civil war in Syria. They seem confident that Iranian participation is essential to any serious discussion of conflict resolution and political transition in Syria. Tehran has encouraged international efforts to mediate Syria's internal conflict—even as the United States and its European partners have worked to block Iran's involvement—and welcomed Egyptian President Morsi's call in August 2012 for a regional contact group on Syria, including the Islamic Republic along with Egypt, Saudi Arabia, and Turkey.

Iranian policy makers recognize that, as Syria's internal conflict continues, Iranian support for the Assad government and its constituencies is not popular among many Arabs outside Syria. Nevertheless, they also calculate that Saudi Arabia's partnership with Washington (and tacit cooperation with Israel) will slowly but surely discredit the kingdom's support for anti-Assad rebels. As Ahmadinejad noted at a summit meeting of Muslim countries convened in Mecca in August 2012 by King Abdallah to discuss the Syrian situation, "Who is killing whom in our region? Who have aligned themselves against whom in Afghanistan, Iraq, Syria, Sudan, Bahrain, Yemen, Libya, and other countries?" In Syria, especially, this is "providing the enemy the best opportunities for free." Similarly, Tehran calculates that Turkey is playing a losing hand by collaborating with Saudi Arabia and the United States to support Syrian oppositionists—and that Ankara will ultimately have to come back into closer alignment with its neighbors, including the Islamic Republic.

Iran no longer has to rely on Syria to supply Hizballah; it can now do so through other routes—precisely because of favorable shifts in the regional balance. One of the first significant policy decisions by post-Mubarak Egypt was to open the Suez Canal to Iranian military vessels, giving Iran direct access to Lebanese ports—all of which are effectively under Hizballah control. Furthermore, it is wrong to assume that Tehran would be undermined if the current Syrian government were replaced. The opposition takes issue with Assad's internal policies, not his strategic orientation, especially toward Israel and the United States. A post-Assad government, if even minimally representative, would pursue a foreign policy perhaps even less interested in strategic cooperation with the United States and less inclined to keep Syria's southern border with Israel quiet.

Iranian officials believe that, taken together, developments are steering the regional balance in Tehran's favor.

As the relative power of the United States decreases, the strategic impact of the Islamic Republic's soft power increases. Well before the advent of the Arab awakening, policy elites in Tehran had concluded that, as a declining power in the Middle East, the United States was no longer able to dictate strategic outcomes and was becoming less and less capable of achieving its stated policy goals in the region. Even in the purely military sphere, where the relative power differential remains greater than in any other category, the United States appears less able to use force without inflicting more damage on its already strained position.

As Tehran watches—and tries to accelerate—this decline, it still understands that the United States, by its choice of policies, can either seriously exacerbate or substantially improve the myriad security challenges facing the Islamic Republic. So even while it works to balance against the United States, its grand strategy also encompasses the possibility of rapprochement. In the next chapter, we consider the Islamic Republic's approach to diplomacy with what remains, even in its decline, the world's only superpower.

3

ENGAGING AMERICA

If they [the United States] do not resort to bullying and step down from the ladder of imperialism . . . we will not have problems with negotiations. But negotiations are impossible as long as they behave like this.

—*Ayatollah Seyed Ali Khamenei, August 20, 2010*

In April 2010, Ali Akbar Salehi, then head of the Atomic Energy Organization of Iran (AEOI), did something that managers of the Islamic Republic's nuclear program rarely do: he gave an interview to a Western news organization, CBS News. Salehi—who in December 2010 would become his country's foreign minister—is a genuinely impressive figure. Like the Larijani brothers, he was born in Iraq (in Karbala), where his father, a distinguished Shi'a cleric, spent several years. A religious man, he earned a Ph.D. in nuclear engineering at MIT. The first sentence in his doctoral dissertation quotes, in Arabic, the opening line of the Qur'an: *bism illah ir-rahman ir-rahim*—"in the name of God, the merciful, the compassionate." (The rest, in English, discusses "Resonance Region Neutronics of Unit Cells in Fast and Thermal Reactors.") After completing his doctorate, Salehi returned to Iran to pursue a career that encompassed teaching and administration at the Sharif University of Technology (frequently described as Iran's MIT), high-level diplomatic assignments on nuclear issues, and a stint in Saudi Arabia, as deputy secretary-general of the Organization of the

Islamic Conference (now the Organization of Islamic Cooperation). He became director of the AEOI in July 2009.

In the interview with CBS News, Salehi spoke about his years at MIT and his feelings about the United States:

> I have a lot of respect for the US . . . for the people of the US. And I've always said this: I do not consider the US as a country. I think the US belongs to the whole human kind. It's a human heritage. I don't think history will be able to produce another country like the US. Because it's a country that has served humanity so much, in terms of technology, in terms of science. . . . Most of my professors were from the US. Even my bachelor's degree is from the American University of Beirut. Again I had a lot of US professors there. I feel indebted to them. This is part of my religion. You know, whoever teaches you something, you are indebted to them for your life. So my respect goes for the entire US people. But you see this is different when it comes to the actions of their government.[1]

Salehi's praise for the United States may cause cognitive dissonance in American readers, for whom conventional wisdom about the Islamic Republic is that its political order is irrevocably anti-American. How then could the man appointed by Ahmadinejad and Ayatollah Khamenei to run Iran's nuclear program and serve as its foreign minister have such favorable things to say about the United States?

The proposition that the Islamic Republic is implacably and unreasoningly hostile to the United States is, of course, a staple of neoconservatism.[2] A related argument—that the Iranian government is too dependent on anti-Americanism for its domestic legitimacy ever to contemplate improved relations with the United States—is peddled by more mainstream analysts.[3] In both versions, this conviction that the Islamic Republic is inalterably antagonistic strongly, and wrongly, conditions Western discourse about Iran, prompting the belief that when Iran does negotiate with the United States, it does so only to buy time, not to work toward a resolution of differences.

All too frequently this view degenerates into essentialist, if not racist, stereotypes of Iranian negotiators as "rug merchants" who haggle over the smallest details, seize every opportunity to deceive, and have no intention of keeping whatever commitments they might make. Over the years, ideologically driven American and Israeli think tanks have produced innumerable publications wrapping such bigotry in a pseudoscholarly veneer. For example, a 2010 monograph written by a former U.S. Defense Department official and published by the ultra-hawkish Jerusalem Center for Public Affairs asserts that "the Western concept of demanding that a leader subscribe to a moral and ethical code does not resonate with Iranians" and that "Westerners, especially Americans who place a high value on candor, straightforwardness, and honesty, are often bamboozled by Iranians who know that those in the West are easily taken in by their effusively friendly, kind, generous, and engaging behavior."[4] Michael Ledeen of the Foundation for the Defense of Democracies has offered an even more extreme take:

> The best metaphor for talking with the Iranians is that great scene from [the James Bond movie] *Goldfinger*, where Bond is splayed out on a sheet of gold, and Goldfinger is standing up on the balcony looking down at the scene, and the laser beam is slicing through the sheet of gold headed toward Bond's private parts, and Bond looks up and says, "Do you expect me to talk?" And Goldfinger looks down and says, "No, Mr. Bond, I expect you to die." For me, that's Iran. Iran expects us to die. And Iran wants us to die.[5]

Whatever else this argument is, it is politically convenient, absolving Washington of any responsibility to engage seriously with Tehran until the deus ex machina of regime change solves its Iran problem. But, like most aspects of conventional wisdom about Iran, it is wrong. The Islamic Republic is determined to be part of the modern world—on its own terms. (Recall the opening of Salehi's dissertation.) And while it is true that Khomeini defined its international orientation as "neither East nor West," the Islamic Republic has demonstrated a clear and enduring interest in better relations with the West, especially the United States.

In contrast to the shah, however, the Islamic Republic's leaders have not been willing to surrender what they consider Iran's sovereign rights or to sacrifice its strategic autonomy in order to realign with Washington. Starting with Khomeini, virtually every prominent figure in Iranian political life since the revolution has denounced the kind of client or puppet relationship Iran had with the United States under the shah. Even the reformist Mohammad Khatami sought to explain to American audiences that the revolution had been necessary "to terminate a mode of relationship between Iran and America"—a priority still reflected in the anti-American chants and slogans at public events.[6] But for most of the past three decades Tehran has been prepared to pursue rapprochement with Washington, so long as it is based on American acceptance of the Islamic Republic and the reciprocal and balanced accommodation of both sides' core interests.

KHAMENEI AND THE UNITED STATES

The Islamic Republic's interest in improving relations with the United States is rooted in a sober appreciation of America's enormous—even if now declining—power. From the mid-twentieth century on, as the United States has grown more deeply engaged in the Middle East, dealing with Washington has been a strategic imperative for any government in Tehran. In the Cold War's early days, Mohammad Mossadeq, his public advocacy of nonalignment notwithstanding, was interested in cooperating with America to counter British and Soviet penetration of Iran. Unfortunately for Mossadeq, the United States opposed the relative independence he sought and agreed with the British to overthrow him. After the 1953 CIA coup that replaced Mossadeq with the shah, Iran aligned squarely with Washington, to such a degree that the Nixon, Ford, and Carter administrations all regarded Tehran as their most important strategic partner in the Persian Gulf.

Since the revolution, the Islamic Republic has viewed the United States as by far the leading threat to its political and territorial integrity. At the same time, decision makers in Tehran have recognized that Iran has basic national security and foreign policy needs that can only be met—or at any rate only optimally met—through rapprochement with Washington. Since the Iran-Iraq War, Iranian policy makers have also understood that improved relations would advance postwar reconstruction, economic modernization, and the realization of Iran's enormous potential as an exporter of oil and natural gas. Consequently, all four men who have held Iran's presidency since 1981 have explored the possibility of normalizing ties. Ayatollah Seyed Ali Khamenei did so with the explicit backing of Khomeini, the first supreme leader; since Khomeini's death, in 1989, Ali Akbar Hashemi Rafsanjani, Seyed Mohammad Khatami, and Mahmoud Ahmadinejad have pursued it with the clear assent of Khamenei, Khomeini's successor.

Khamenei was elected president in October 1981, after his predecessor's assassination by the MEK. Starting at the end of 1982—by which point the fledgling revolutionary government had largely turned back the MEK's terror campaign and Khomeini's supporters had decisively defeated their more liberal opponents—Iranian leaders began advocating an interest-based approach to diplomacy. In 1984, Khamenei, following what he described as "the expressed wish of Imam Khomeini," defined Tehran's foreign policy as an "open door": Iran, he said, would seek "rational, sound, and healthy relations with all countries"; in subsequent statements he made it clear that "all countries" included the United States.[7]

As the Islamic Republic struggled during Khamenei's presidency to fend off the American-backed Iraqi invasion, its leadership realized that an opening to the United States was of potentially enormous value. Many Americans hazily recall the secret "arms for hostages" swap between Washington and Tehran that collapsed in the Iran-contra affair as an early indicator of Iranian perfidy; former national security adviser Robert McFarlane's presentation of a Bible and a cake shaped like a key during his May 1986 visit to Tehran is seen by them as a textbook example of American naiveté in dealing with blood-thirsty and deceitful mullahs. But at the heart of the project was a complex scheme to supply Iran with weapons in exchange for its help in securing the release of American hostages held by Lebanese militias.

On the American side, it was also intended to open channels to important figures in the Islamic Republic and to use the provision of badly needed weapons to boost the standing of Iranian leaders willing to work with Washington. The scheme collapsed in 1986 because U.S. officials tried to skirt American law by diverting proceeds from these arms sales to anticommunist rebels in Nicaragua, not because of Iranian duplicity or recalcitrance. Even after Washington became embroiled in the ensuing scandal, Tehran was ready to continue dialogue and cooperation; it was the United States that withdrew.[8]

In fact, Khamenei traveled to New York the following year to deliver the first-ever address by an Iranian president to the United Nations General Assembly. His speech cited Iran's numerous grievances against the United States and denounced the U.S.-led "system of world domination." But he also said that "this indictment is directed against the leaders of the United States regime and not against the American people who, had they been aware of what their governments have done against another nation, would certainly endorse our indictment."[9] In other words, the Islamic Republic had a problem not with the United States per se but with particular American policies; if those policies changed, there would be, from Tehran's perspective, no obstacle to normal relations. Khamenei made the point more explicit to an Iranian newspaper: "Certainly there are conditions where our ties with the United States could be normalized."[10]

A willingness to normalize relations with Washington so long as to do so does not entail "accepting domination" has grounded Tehran's posture toward the United States since Khamenei succeeded Khomeini as supreme leader more than two decades ago.[11] To be sure, Khamenei understands that the Islamic Republic cannot surrender its principles and remain the Islamic Republic; managing relations with Western powers, especially the United States, presents the hardest case of what he describes as the challenge of balancing between the imperatives of expediency and honor. But Western analysts who selectively and misleadingly read Khamenei's rhetoric to portray him and the entire Islamic Republic as dependent for their very survival on antagonism with America, are wrong. While Khamenei has grown increasingly skeptical that Washington is interested in genuine rapprochement, the historical record clearly shows that he has been a consistent backer of every Iranian president's efforts to improve relations with the United States. Claims advanced by Karim Sadjadpour, Ray Takeyh, and others that Iran's leadership is too ideologically constrained, fractious, or politically dependent on anti-Americanism to pursue a strategic opening to the United States are not just at odds with the historical record.[12] Such claims push the United States ever further in its support of coercive regime change and, ultimately, down the disastrous path toward war.

TACTICAL COOPERATION AND ITS DISCONTENTS

Arguably no figure in revolutionary Iran's public life has attached greater importance to cooperation with the United States than Ali Akbar Hashemi Rafsanjani, the archetype of the Islamic Republic's "pragmatic conservative" camp. Contrary to stereotypes about Iranian clerics' insular experience, Rafsanjani's attitude toward the United States was influenced by a tour he made of the country in 1974. While he later recalled being repelled by the loose morality of American society, he also acknowledged that there was much Iran could learn from the American commitment to political freedom, and he came away impressed with the United States' economic and strategic weight.[13]

During the Iran-Iraq War, Rafsanjani understood that, to obtain badly needed weapons, Tehran would have to leverage American interest in securing Iranian cooperation on other issues—a model he would turn to repeatedly for the next twenty years. While serving as Majles speaker, he played a major role in the tentative exchanges with the United States at the center of the Iran-contra scandal; afterward he remained convinced that the hostage issue could be the key to better relations. He even cited it as he addressed America directly in one of his parliamentary speeches, invoking Khamenei's "open door" formula: "At the moment we are your enemy and you are our enemy. If you wish us to intercede on your behalf, we have left the door open."[14]

Rafsanjani's focus on identifying areas of mutual interest between

Tehran and Washington intensified after he assumed the presidency in 1989. Taking office in the immediate aftermath of the Iran-Iraq War, Rafsanjani made postwar reconstruction and longer-term economic modernization his priority. (The official coffee-table-book history of his presidency is titled *The Age of Construction*.) Judging that Iran's economic development required a more stable international environment, he enunciated a foreign policy of détente, both with neighbors and with major powers outside the Middle East—in particular, the United States.[15] Like Khamenei, though, Rafsanjani believed that cooperation with Washington should be pursued only under appropriate conditions. Shortly after his election to the presidency in 1989, he said, "Iran will be ready to work with Western countries, but only if they approach us in the right way. That means on equal terms, and without colonial attitudes."[16]

George H. W. Bush became president of the United States that same year. In his inaugural address, Bush referred to American hostages still held captive in Lebanon with an oblique plea to Iran that could have been crafted by Rafsanjani himself: "Assistance can be shown here, and will be long remembered. Goodwill begets goodwill. Good faith can be a spiral that endlessly moves on." Based on this representation and subsequent ones from Washington, U.N. envoy Giandomenico Picco spoke directly to Rafsanjani and worked with senior Iranian officials to secure the hostages' freedom. Tehran spent several million dollars and exerted considerable pressure on Shi'a militias in Lebanon for this purpose.[17] Mohsen Rezae, then the commander of the Revolutionary Guards, has said that Iranian officers in Lebanon were attacked by some Lebanese militias over Iran's efforts to extract the hostages.[18] None of these actions would have happened without Khamenei's assent.

But Iranian cooperation did not elicit the response Rafsanjani had expected. The Bush administration excluded the Islamic Republic from the October 1991 Madrid conference intended to ratify what Bush called the "new world order" in the Middle East, including the stationing of tens of thousands of American troops in countries neighboring Iran. In April 1992, Bush's national security adviser, Brent Scowcroft, informed Rafsanjani through Picco that there would be no reciprocal steps by the United States—even though Iran had succeeded in free-ing the last American hostages—and no breakthrough in relations. Iran had been stiffed, and its leaders were furious. When Picco flew to Tehran to tell Rafsanjani personally that Washington had changed its mind about goodwill begetting goodwill, the Iranian president warned him, "I think it is best if you leave Tehran very, very quickly. The news of what you have told me will travel fast to other quarters, and they may decide not to let you go."[19]

Despite his disappointment, Rafsanjani continued looking for areas of mutual interest with the United States after President Bill Clinton was inaugurated in January 1993—notwithstanding the Clinton administration's decision to lump Iran together with Saddam Husayn's Iraq under its "dual containment" policy in the Persian Gulf. By early 1994, Rafsanjani had an opening: just as the first Bush admin-istration had needed Iran's help to free the last American hostages in Lebanon, the Clinton administration needed it to supply arms to Muslims in Bosnia.

As a presidential candidate, Clinton had pledged to aid Bosnian Muslims by lifting the arms embargo against the former Yugoslavia and ordering American air strikes against Serbian military infrastruc-ture. But upon taking office he encountered strong opposition from European states with peacekeepers in the Balkans. As a result, his administration faced a major problem: how could it get arms and other supplies to Bosnian Muslims and Croats when U.N. Security Council resolutions and U.S. law prohibited it? Legal considerations aside, Clinton worried that any direct American arming of Muslims and Croats would be detected, potentially prompting Serbian reprisals against U.S. forces, severely negative Russian reaction, and European withdrawals from the internationally mandated peacekeeping force. What Washington needed was a third party that could get arms into Bosnia with relatively low risk of detection—and that, from an Amer-ican perspective, would be expendable if discovered. So, as the Senate Select Committee on Intelligence later documented, the Clinton admin-istration decided "the Iranians could be the suppliers."[20]

The Islamic Republic was clearly eager to help the beleaguered Bosnian Muslims, in keeping with its commitment to Muslim solidarity; before the arms embargo was imposed, it had worked with Croatia to ship weapons into Bosnia. In the spring of 1994, the Clinton administration gave Croatian president Franjo Tudjman the "green light" to resume Iranian arms shipments. From the administration's perspective, the result was a success: the arms flowed in and neither the Serbs, the Russians, nor the Europeans took the actions that Washington had feared might lead to a wider and bloodier war. Instead, the creation of a more level battlefield helped bring the parties together for the negotiations that culminated in the Dayton Peace Agreement of December 1995.

At the same time, Rafsanjani sought to cultivate what he thought were obviously shared Iranian and American interests in oil and gas. Tehran put forward a pipeline proposal for marketing oil exports from the Caspian basin via Iran; as an alternative, it also offered to facilitate transport of oil exports from the Caspian basin through Iran by way of oil "swaps." But though the Clinton administration wished to develop non-Russian export routes for newly independent energy-producing states in Central Asia and the Caucasus, it adamantly insisted that Iran be excluded from efforts to bring Caspian basin hydrocarbons to international markets.

Likewise, Rafsanjani sought to draw American energy companies into the development of Iran's vast hydrocarbon reserves. At his instigation, the Majles passed a law authorizing the Oil Ministry to permit foreign companies to invest in the production of Iranian oil and gas through so-called buy-back contracts with the National Iranian Oil Company (NIOC). There were strong economic and technical arguments for boosting foreign investment in Iran's upstream energy sector, which was in need of both capital and advanced technology. But Rafsanjani also saw this step as a potentially valuable foreign policy tool. Once the law was passed, the NIOC began negotiations with international energy companies, and by early 1995 it was ready to enter into its first contract—a $600 million deal to develop two oil and gas fields off Sirri Island in the Persian Gulf. The NIOC recommended two companies: the American Conoco (now ConocoPhillips) and the French Total. As a deliberate overture to the United States, Rafsanjani authorized the NIOC to award the contract to Conoco, which it did in March 1995.[21]

Once again, the American reaction was hardly what Tehran anticipated. Within two weeks of the offer, President Clinton issued an executive order barring American companies from participating in the development of Iran's hydrocarbon resources. (The NIOC then offered the contract to Total, which happily accepted it.) Two months later, Clinton issued another order, which effectively imposed a comprehensive American economic embargo on the Islamic Republic—something the United States had not done even after Iranian students seized the U.S. embassy and took its diplomats hostage in 1979. The next year, he signed the Iran-Libya Sanctions Act, authorizing the imposition of so-called secondary sanctions against third-country entities investing in the development of Iranian hydrocarbons. The Islamic Republic, in what Rafsanjani and his associates had seen as both an exercise in economic good sense and a meaningful strategic gesture, had offered its first-ever oil production contract with a foreign company to an American firm, and Washington had not merely rebuffed the offer but reacted hostilely and punitively.

Rafsanjani's efforts to build a bridge to the United States by working together in areas of mutual interest were further damaged when the Clinton administration beat a highly public retreat from cooperation with Tehran on providing arms to the Bosnian Muslims. In April 1996, seven months before the coming American election, the *Los Angeles Times* broke the story: "President Clinton secretly gave a green light to covert Iranian arms shipments into Bosnia in 1994 despite a United Nations arms embargo that the United States was pledged to uphold and the administration's own policy of isolating Tehran globally as a supporter of terrorism."[22] Two days later, the Republican-led Senate Intelligence Committee—with Clinton's presumptive GOP challenger in the 1996 presidential election, Senator Robert Dole, weighing in—launched its inquiry. Because it was so close to the election and Iran was such a potentially devastating issue, the Clinton administration publicly condemned Tehran for trying to establish an Islamist beachhead in Europe's backyard—even though Iran had done exactly what Washington wanted and, in fact, had proven essential to its plan to bring the Bosnian conflict to an end.

To this day, Iranian officials are livid over what they describe as American perfidy in Bosnia. Not only did the Islamic Republic get no credit for cooperating with the United States, it was castigated for "taking advantage" of the conflict in the Balkans to export its revolution. One of Hillary Mann Leverett's interlocutors during the official U.S.-Iranian dialogue over Afghanistan in 2001–03 was an Iranian diplomat who had had contacts with Clinton administration officials over Bosnia between 1994 and 1996; he observed caustically that, while it was worthwhile for Iran to have done what it could to forestall further ethnic cleansing in the region, the episode showed yet again how unwilling or unable America was to sustain cooperation with Iran even when such cooperation was manifestly in its own interest. Rafsanjani's attempts to improve relations with the United States were not undermined, as Takeyh and other conventional analysts assert, by Ayatollah Khamenei and unspecified "hardliners."[23] Indeed, Rafsanjani could not have made these efforts without Khamenei's assent. Rafsanjani's initiatives were undermined by American administrations unwilling to reciprocate positive Iranian moves or even to keep their diplomatic commitments. This experience impelled mounting skepticism in Tehran about Washington's ultimate intentions toward the Islamic Republic. Such skepticism strongly influenced Iran's approach to the United States under Rafsanjani's successor.

PUTTING THE BALL IN WASHINGTON'S COURT

Seyed Mohammad Khatami, the champion of a new reformist trend in Iran's political life, campaigned for the presidency on a platform that, on foreign relations, emphasized "reduction of tensions"—effectively an extension of Rafsanjani's détente policy. Once in office, though, Khatami was less interested than his predecessor in identifying specific areas of mutual interest in which Tehran and Washington might cooperate. His signature foreign policy initiative, the "dialogue among civilizations," sought instead to improve relations with the United States and other Western countries by highlighting the shared cultural and intellectual traditions that would enable the Islamic Republic to assume a prominent role in an increasingly globalized international order.

Early in his presidency, Khatami generated wide hopes for improved American-Iranian relations, most notably in a January 1998 CNN interview with the Iranian-born Christiane Amanpour. He professed "an intellectual affinity with the essence of American civilization," cited Tocqueville to compare the United States and the Islamic Republic as religiously grounded revolutionary states seeking freedom for their peoples, and expressed "regret" that the 1979–81 hostage crisis had left Americans with negative feelings toward the Islamic Republic.[24] But behind Khatami's forward-leaning rhetoric, most Iranian decision makers, including Ayatollah Khamenei, had made a sober calculation: the days of cooperation with the United States "for free" were over. From their perspective, the onus for improving relations was now on Washington, which would have to prove its sincerity about closer ties before Tehran would engage with it again. As Foreign Minister Kamal Kharrazi explained at the beginning of Khatami's presidency:

> The U.S. cannot deny the strategic importance of Iran in the region, and the positive role that Iran can play in peace and security of the region. Therefore, it depends on the will of the U.S.—if the U.S. wants to recognize this importance or to block the role Iran can play. If they are interested to see Iran play an important and a positive role in that region, they will have to change their attitudes and policies toward Iran. The ball is in the court of the Americans. . . . They have put sanctions against us. They are making accusations against us. They are blocking us from any positive role in the region. So if they believe in what they said, they have to show that in their deeds, not only in their words.[25]

But the Clinton administration was not at all prepared to change.[26] Since Clinton left office, he and several colleagues have tried to spin the record of U.S.-Iranian diplomacy during Khatami's first term (which largely overlapped with Clinton's second term) as one of Washington reaching out to Tehran repeatedly, only to be rebuffed. But in fact his administration's one real stab at engaging the Islamic Republic was nothing more than a crude attempt to play Iranian factions against one another for the purpose of getting Tehran to give up its ties to its proxy allies.

In June 1999, the Omani foreign minister, acting at Washington's behest, brought to Tehran a "Message to President Khatami from President Clinton." He had been instructed by American officials to deliver the document when he was alone with Khatami. Its background was the 1996 bombing of Khobar Towers, a housing complex for American military personnel in eastern Saudi Arabia.

The counterterrorism community in the United States is divided over the question of Iranian complicity in this operation. Some believe that there is sufficient evidence to warrant a conclusion that Tehran was behind it; as to motive, Richard Clarke and Steven Simon, senior counterterrorism officials at the National Security Council during the Clinton administration, argue that the attack was an Iranian response to the first congressional appropriation (for $18 million, passed in 1995) supporting the Islamic Republic's overthrow.[27] But the case for Iranian involvement rests largely on information provided by Saudi authorities, not evidence obtained independently by U.S. agencies. Michael Scheuer, director of the CIA's Bin Laden unit when the attack occurred, and a host of other current and former officials say that the American government developed a substantial body of evidence indicating that Al-Qa'ida, not Iran, perpetrated the attack. This evidence was reportedly suppressed by others—including the then FBI director Louis Freeh, who would later become a paid promoter of the MEK—intent on preserving their (tightly controlled) access to the Saudi investigation.[28] The Saudis, for their part, allegedly wanted to deflect attention from the emerging (and homegrown) threat posed by Al-Qa'ida. By 1998, though, even Saudi interior minister Prince Nayif acknowledged that the bombing "was executed by Saudi hands. No foreign party had any role in it."[29] Those who believe that Tehran was involved dismiss this as motivated by Saudi interest in forestalling the potentially destabilizing consequences of a U.S. military strike against the Islamic Republic. But Warren Christopher, Clinton's secretary of state, recounted that "there was never any adequate proof" of Iranian involvement; after leaving office, Clinton's defense secretary, William Perry, said he had come to believe that "Al-Qa'ida rather than Iran was behind" the strike.[30]

Yet, with a highly uncertain case for Iranian involvement—or even a clear motive—the Clinton administration decided to use Khobar Towers to press the Islamic Republic. Thus, Clinton's missive to Khatami opened with a stark accusation: "The United States Government has received credible evidence that members of the Iranian Revolutionary Guard Corps (IRGC), along with members of Lebanese and Saudi Hizballah, were directly involved in the planning and execution of the terrorist bombing in Saudi Arabia of the Khobar Towers military residential complex." While acknowledging that "the bombing occurred prior to your election," the message nonetheless stipulated preconditions for diplomatic engagement: "We need a clear commitment from you that you will ensure an end to Iranian involvement in terrorist activity . . . and will bring those in Iran responsible for the bombing to justice either in Iran or by extraditing them to Saudi Arabia."[31]

Clinton administration officials later claimed that the Iranians failed to respond; most colorfully, the Iraq War cheerleader Kenneth Pollack described the Iranian response as "*bupkis*"—Yiddish for "nothing."[32] But declassified records show that Tehran replied promptly, denying the charges and reiterating its willingness to engage if Washington dropped its preconditions and its threats:

> No agency of or entity connected with the Islamic Republic of Iran had any part, whatsoever, in the planning, logistics or execution of the said incident. Such allegations are fabricated solely by those whose illegitimate objectives are jeopardized by stability and security in the region. The US Government—which has not only failed to prosecute or extradite the readily identifiable American citizens

responsible for the downing of an Iranian civilian airliner, but in fact has decorated them—is now seeking the trial or extradition of individuals totally unknown and without any connection whatsoever to the Islamic Republic of Iran. This behavior is unacceptable and must cease immediately. It is also imperative that the US Government prevent further support of certain official US agencies and institutions for terrorist elements and organizations with irrefutable records of crimes against Iranian people. . . . The Islamic Republic of Iran bears no hostile intentions towards America and the Iranian people not only harbor no enmity, but indeed have respect for the great American people. . . . As its irreversible and fundamental strategy, the Government of Iran . . . shall vigorously pursue the policy of détente.[33]

The Clinton administration followed up its "overture" to Khatami by continuing to appeal to particular Iranian figures whom it considered more "pragmatic" (meaning relatively pro-American) in order to marginalize Khamenei. In March 2000, Secretary of State Madeleine Albright finally offered a tangible—if utterly marginal—incentive: a modification of U.S. sanctions to permit the import of Iranian caviar, pistachios, and rugs.[34] This tiny gesture reflected a calculation that relaxing the ban on pistachio imports might appeal to an Iranian president whose family hails from Iran's largest pistachio-growing region. But that president was Rafsanjani, who had left office three years earlier, not Khatami. And by 2000, even Rafsanjani could hardly welcome the measure, which would only increase the already mounting suspicions of ordinary Iranians that his motives for rapprochement with the United States were personal and financial.[35] Predictably, Tehran dismissed Albright's offer as inadequate, insisting on the removal of all sanctions—not just those on nuts and carpets—before reopening a dialogue.

TEHRAN RECONSIDERS

The diplomatic situation changed dramatically on September 11, 2001. That morning, Hillary Mann Leverett—then a diplomat at the U.S.

Mission to the United Nations in New York—was scheduled to meet with her Iranian counterpart to discuss an upcoming meeting of the 6+2 foreign ministers. As Hillary and her colleagues were being evacuated from the U.S. Mission after the World Trade Center was hit, she received a call from this Iranian diplomat, who told her, without hesitation, that the Islamic Republic would be condemning what was surely an Al-Qa'ida attack against the United States and, indeed, the entire civilized world.

His representations proved true. Within hours of the attacks, Khatami, who had been reelected three months earlier, became one of the first foreign leaders to denounce them. Three days later, in a Friday prayer sermon broadcast to tens of millions of Iranians and others around the world, Khamenei delivered an eloquent condemnation of terrorist killings, "wherever they may happen"—New York and Washington included—"and whoever the perpetrators and the victims may be." And in the days after 9/11, thousands of Iranians poured into the streets of Tehran to hold candlelight vigils for Al-Qa'ida's victims in America.

More substantively, the Islamic Republic extended its unconditional cooperation against Al-Qa'ida and the Taliban. In contrast to its responses to Clinton's threat-draped 1999 overture and Albright's relaxation of the ban on carpet, caviar, and pistachio imports, Tehran asked for nothing from the Bush administration in return for its help, which included putting the Northern Alliance at the United States' disposal as the primary ground force component in the campaign to topple the Taliban. When the 6+2 foreign ministers—including Kharrazi and Secretary of State Colin Powell—finally met at the United Nations in November 2001, Iran's vigorous representations were critical to overcoming Pakistani opposition to a strong statement committing the parties to fight terrorism and take all necessary steps to ensure that Afghanistan would never again become a launching pad for Al-Qa'ida. When Khatami came to New York in November 2001 for the General Assembly's delayed opening, he asked to visit Ground Zero so that he might offer prayers and light a candle in memory of the 9/11 victims; Tehran also offered to send terrorism experts with his delegation to open an American-Iranian counterterrorism dialogue. The Bush administration rejected both proposals.

Tehran made these gestures in part because it saw an opening after 9/11 to strike back against Al-Qa'ida and the Taliban. But it also believed that the attacks had been such a devastating blow to the United States that help from Iran in responding to them would prompt Washington to reconsider its posture toward the Islamic Republic. Iranian policy makers calculated that it might even be possible to move the United States away from its reflexive support of Saudi Arabia and Pakistan, the two chief external supporters of the Taliban and Al-Qa'ida. The Iranian government decided, in effect, to give tactical cooperation with America another try. And Tehran would never have done so without Khamenei's approval.

Yet just six weeks after the December 2001 Bonn conference, where Iranian cooperation was indispensable in setting up Afghanistan's first post-Taliban government, President George W. Bush condemned Iran, along with North Korea and Saddam's Iraq, as part of the "axis of evil" in his January 2002 State of the Union address. Bush's rhetoric forced Tehran to consider that, even after an event as strategically jolting as 9/11, Washington was unlikely to allow bilateral cooperation over Afghanistan to transform the American-Iranian relationship.

Nevertheless, Iran continued to cooperate with the United States. Just before the Bonn conference, Hillary Mann Leverett had transferred to the White House to become the National Security Council's director for Iran and Afghanistan affairs. In this role she participated in regular meetings between American and Iranian representatives, stretching from the Taliban's defeat in the fall of 2001 to just before Saddam's overthrow in the spring of 2003, to coordinate policies on Afghanistan and related issues.[36] Iranian representatives told Hillary and her colleagues that their discussions were closely followed at the highest levels in Tehran and that there was still considerable interest in a wider opening, even after the "axis of evil" speech. Throughout, the Iranians worked hard to maintain cooperation with Washington. Besides collaborating with the United States on political and security matters in Afghanistan, Iranian authorities apprehended hundreds of Al-Qa'ida and Taliban fighters who had fled to Iran, documenting the identities of more than two hundred to the United Nations. Many were repatriated to their countries of origin; in cases where Iran did not have relations with their countries or the countries would not repatriate their nationals, Tehran expressed its willingness to try detainees in Iran or to discuss alternatives under U.N. auspices.

But over the course of 2002, as the Bush administration shifted its attention to the prospective invasion of Iraq, Tehran realized that the potential for cooperation on Afghanistan to facilitate a broader opening was diminishing. It also perceived that the invasion of Iraq would open a new front from which the United States could press Iran. Consequently, Iranian officials began making the case for American-Iranian cooperation on Iraq—directly, with Hillary and her colleagues, and publicly, as in a May 10, 2003, op-ed in the *New York Times* by the Islamic Republic's American-educated ambassador to the United Nations, Mohammad Javad Zarif.[37]

To undermine prospects for further cooperation, Bush administration hard-liners made coordination on Iraq dependent on Tehran's finding, arresting, and deporting a number of specific Al-Qa'ida figures (beyond the hundreds Tehran had already apprehended) who, Washington claimed, had fled Afghanistan into lawless areas of Iran's Sistan-Balochistan province in 2002. The Iranian government took some of these individuals into custody; others named by the United States, it reported, were either dead or not in Iran. But with the invasion of Iraq looming, the Islamic Republic was reluctant to relinquish additional Al-Qa'ida detainees without assurances that Washington would not unleash the MEK's Iraq-based cadres against it. Though Hillary and her colleagues assured their interlocutors that American forces would target the MEK as part of Saddam's military, the Iranians pointed to a stream of public statements by senior Pentagon officials indicating interest in using the MEK as a vanguard for regime change in the Islamic Republic. At the beginning of May 2003, after Baghdad had fallen, Tehran offered to exchange Al-Qa'ida figures in Iran for a small group of MEK commanders in Iraq, with treatment of the latter to be monitored by the International Committee for the

Red Cross and a commitment not to apply the death penalty to anyone prosecuted. But even though the U.S. government had designated the MEK a foreign terrorist organization in 1997—and Bush himself initially thought a deal should go forward because, as he pointed out in a White House Situation Room meeting on the subject, there was no such thing as "a good terrorist versus a bad terrorist"—his administration refused to consider an exchange.[38]

On May 12, 2003—just two days after Zarif's op-ed piece—Al-Qa'ida carried out a coordinated series of bombings in Riyadh, Saudi Arabia, and Casablanca, Morocco. Although the bombings were perpetrated by local Al-Qa'ida operatives, the Bush administration used the occasion as an excuse to cut off the American-Iranian dialogue over Afghanistan and Al-Qa'ida, citing a Defense Department claim to have a communications intercept indicating that an Al-Qa'ida figure inside Iran might have been involved. The claim was never substantiated and was disputed by much of the U.S. intelligence community; the Bush administration was eventually reduced to telling the *Washington Post* that "there are suspicions, but no proof" that Al-Qa'ida figures in Iran "may have been involved from afar in planning" the attacks.[39]

But for those in Defense Secretary Donald Rumsfeld's office and elsewhere in the administration who opposed any engagement with the Islamic Republic, the claim had served its purpose. The Iranians' wager—that helping the United States respond to 9/11 would prompt it to reconsider its posture toward Iran—was lost on an administration whose self-styled "realists" lacked the strategic vision to contest the neoconservatives' adamant opposition to any rapprochement. After Washington terminated the dialogue, the Defense Department granted MEK cadres in Iraq "protected persons" status, which legally barred the American-installed interim Iraqi government from extraditing them to Iran, despite its professed interest in doing so.

THE TURN TOWARD COMPREHENSIVE ENGAGEMENT

The failure of Khatami's efforts to reorient American-Iranian relations by working with the United States against the Taliban and Al-Qa'ida finally discouraged Iranian policy makers from a limited, issue-specific approach to cooperation. Iran had repeatedly responded to American requests for help on specific issues by doing much—not all, but much—of what was asked, and each time the United States had backed off, for reasons that had nothing to do with the issues on which the two governments were cooperating. From an Iranian perspective, it was particularly telling that the American side refused to let tactical cooperation serve as the basis for a broader opening and repeatedly broke off engagement—usually because of concerns about domestic blowback or after a terrorist attack or an arms shipment that someone argued might be linked to Iran. Over time, the failure of these approaches to bring about a fundamental and sustained transformation in relations persuaded Iranian decision makers that incremental détente was simply not workable. Washington pocketed whatever cooperation Tehran extended without offering anything in return—and sometimes turned on Iran in ways that brought the two countries closer to conflict.

From these experiences, a critical mass of Iranian political and policy elites concluded that the only way to achieve real progress was through a comprehensive realignment in relations, which would require Washington to indicate early on that it was prepared to accept the Islamic Republic. Iran continued to show up for talks about Iraq and the nuclear issue—matters on which even the Bush administration recognized that its help was needed. But, starting with Khatami's second term, comprehensive engagement has been the goal of Iranian diplomacy toward the United States. Both Khatami and his successor, Mahmoud Ahmadinejad, advanced proposals for comprehensive negotiations; under both presidents, Tehran sought to use international discussions of its nuclear activities as a gateway to a wider opening with Washington. Khamenei allowed Khatami and Ahmadinejad to pursue these policies, notwithstanding his deepening skepticism about American intentions.

The Islamic Republic's pursuit of comprehensive engagement started in the spring of 2003, when the Iranian Foreign Ministry sent the State Department, via the Swiss Foreign Ministry, a "Roadmap" for negotiations aimed at resolving the major differences between Tehran and Washington.[40] (The United States has no diplomatic representation in Iran, so Switzerland acts as its protecting power there.) The Roadmap identified a set of "US aims"—that is, issues important to the United States that Iran was open to discussing. These included weapons of mass destruction (including "full transparency for security that there are no Iranian endeavors to develop or possess WMD"), terrorism (including "decisive action against any terrorists—above all Al-Qa'ida—on Iranian territory"), Iraq (including "coordination of Iranian influence for actively supporting political stabilization and the establishment of democratic institutions and a democratic government representing all ethnic and religious groups"), and the peace process (including "acceptance of the two-states approach" and "action on Hezbollah to become an exclusively political and social organization within Lebanon"). It also identified a set of "Iranian aims": a commitment by the United States to refrain "from supporting change of the political system," the "abolishment of all sanctions" and concomitant "access to peaceful nuclear technology, biotechnology, and chemical technology," "recognition of Iran's legitimate security interests in the region," American "action against the [MEK] and affiliated organizations," and "respect for the Iranian national interests in Iraq and religious links to Najaf/Karbala." Finally, it outlined steps to get to negotiations.

Contrary to assertions by some Western observers, the Roadmap was not proffered solely or even primarily out of concern that Iran was going to be the next target in the American war on terror. Rather, it was put forward out of frustration with the failure of incremental engagement: discussions over Afghanistan had reached an impasse; the Bush administration was refusing to coordinate policy on Iraq, and it was intensifying pressure on other states to refer Iran to the United Nations Security Council over its nuclear activities. Under these challenging circumstances, the Iranian government was making a serious attempt to lay out a comprehensive agenda for rapprochement—an agenda prepared by the Foreign Ministry and vetted by both Khatami and Khamenei.

The Bush administration refused to respond to the document—technically called a "non-paper," meaning that it was not signed or transmitted on official stationery—and complained to the Swiss Foreign Ministry that the Swiss ambassador in Tehran had exceeded his brief by passing the Roadmap to Washington. Secretary of State Colin Powell and Deputy Secretary of State Richard Armitage later claimed it had not been evident that the Roadmap was genuine, partly because it had not been signed by or attributed to any Iranian official or agency. This, however, is the defining feature of non-papers, the format for most government-to-government communications between the United States and the Islamic Republic.[41] That the Roadmap, as vouched for in writing and transmitted by Swiss diplomats, was not physically identifiable as having originated within the Iranian government was hardly grounds for dismissing it. The only way to verify its seriousness was through diplomacy, which the Bush administration rejected.

Over the past few years, as we have written and spoken about the failures of the Bush administration's Iran policy, a number of neoconservative activists have asserted that the Roadmap did not actually come from the Iranian Foreign Ministry but was in fact concocted by the Swiss ambassador in Tehran.[42] The ambassador, though, made clear in his cover note accompanying the Roadmap the circumstances under which and the persons from whom he received it. Moreover, several Iranians who held senior diplomatic or political positions when the Roadmap was transmitted—including Khatami's first vice president, Mohammad Ali Abtahi, the Islamic Republic's ambassador to the United Nations at the time, Mohammad Javad Zarif, and the Roadmap's principal drafter, Sadeq Kharrazi, a senior diplomat and Foreign Minister Kharrazi's nephew—have subsequently confirmed its validity.[43] (As Iran's regional position has improved since 2003 and its president changed, officials have also said that Tehran would not offer such generous or concessionary terms today.)

After this failure, the Khatami administration worked with third parties to explore other paths to a breakthrough with the United States, focusing on the nuclear issue. Europe feared that the diplomatic breakdown between Tehran and Washington in the first half of 2003 could lead to war, with American and Israeli concern about Iran's nuclear activities as the likely casus belli. So in the summer of 2003, the "EU3"—Britain, France, and Germany, the European Union's major powers—began engaging Tehran over the nuclear issue, acting as a self-appointed stalking horse for a standoffish America, which the Europeans and Iranians alike hoped to draw into the dialogue.[44] Iran entered these discussions with a clear redline and a long-term objective: it would not accept any outcome requiring it to surrender its right to the full range of civil nuclear technology, including uranium enrichment, and it wanted to embed multilateral talks about its nuclear activities in a broader conversation about its security interests and regional role—a conversation that would, to a large extent, take place bilaterally with the United States.

To create an atmosphere conducive to productive negotiations and to help persuade the Bush administration to join, Khatami's advisers recommended what one of them later described as a policy of "confidence building" toward the IAEA and the West. This meant taking a number of concessionary steps requested by the EU3, including cooperating with the IAEA beyond the NPT's requirements and temporarily suspending fuel cycle activities. Khatami agreed, and Khamenei—despite his skepticism—allowed the president and his team to run a tightly conditioned experiment: Iran would suspend, but only temporarily, in return for substantive commitments from its interlocutors that, if fulfilled, would lead to recognition of its nuclear rights and normalization of its international status.[45]

In an October 2003 declaration with the EU3 foreign ministers in Tehran, the Islamic Republic "reaffirmed that nuclear weapons have no place in Iran's defense doctrine and that its nuclear program and activities have been exclusively in the peaceful domain." To demonstrate its "commitment to the nuclear non-proliferation regime," it agreed to sign the Additional Protocol to the NPT—which permits the IAEA to conduct more extensive and intrusive inspections—and to suspend all enrichment-related activities. (At the time, it had barely started enriching uranium in centrifuges.) In return, the Europeans promised "dialogue on a basis for longer-term cooperation," encompassing economic, technological, and security concerns.[46] But the real prize for Iran had nothing to do with the EU. Tehran expected the Europeans to bring the United States to the negotiating table.

Iran signed the Additional Protocol, submitted it to the Majles for ratification, and voluntarily observed its terms pending parliamentary approval; it also provided more information to the IAEA about its past nuclear activities and allowed agency officials to visit a nonnuclear military site where, Western intelligence services claimed, Iranian scientists might have conducted research on key nuclear weapons components. (Iran is under no obligation to allow the IAEA into such nonnuclear sites, and agency officials found nothing suspicious.) But Europe failed to follow through on its promises, as officials from the EU3 governments acknowledge. Like its post-9/11 cooperation over Afghanistan, Tehran's decision to suspend uranium enrichment was a bet—that positive action on its part could draw the United States into comprehensive talks. Khatami and his advisers thought that this time the odds were better, because the Europeans seemed willing to establish a framework for negotiations—on nuclear issues, regional security, and Iran's place in the international order—that would define clear diplomatic goals and that the United States would eventually have to accept.

Up against the Bush administration, though, Iran once again lost its bet. Over the course of 2004, it waited for the Europeans to deliver something—if not the United States, then at least a plan for resolving the standoff. To press the Europeans, Tehran began pushing the limits on its suspension of "enrichment activities," and the more conservative Majles elected in 2004 declined to ratify the Additional Protocol. The EU3—now joined by Javier Solana, the EU's foreign policy chief—worked to save the 2003 declaration by negotiating a follow-up agreement with the Islamic Republic in November 2004, spelling out both sides' commitments with greater specificity.[47] The Europeans, however, continued to drag their feet on concrete proposals while insisting on "objective guarantees" of the peaceful nature of Iran's nuclear program.[48]

In March 2005, the Iranians put forward their own proposals for resolving the dispute, offering (among other measures) to ratify and implement the Additional Protocol, to limit the number of centrifuges they would deploy and restrict their production of low-enriched uranium (LEU), to convert their enriched uranium into (proliferation-resistant) fuel rods, and to allow "continuous on-site presence of IAEA inspectors" at their fuel cycle facilities. In return, the Europeans would (among other measures) "guarantee Iran's access to EU markets and financial and public and private investment resources," to "advanced and nuclear technology," and to "fuel for Iranian nuclear power reactors to complement Iran's domestic production"; they would work with Iran to build new nuclear power plants there; and they would accept Iran's basic right to enrich uranium.[49] In May 2005, Tehran offered to accelerate the implementation of its commitments under its March proposal.[50] But the Europeans were unprepared—largely because of American pressure—to discuss expanded access for international inspectors and limits on the nature and scope of specific nuclear activities. Only suspension, for an ever-lengthening period of time, would do. Britain and France even began warning that as part of a negotiated settlement Iran might be required to suspend fuel cycle activities indefinitely—for Tehran, a wholly unacceptable outcome.

In Iran, these developments discredited the approach that Khatami and his advisers had taken—especially the decision to suspend enrichment. The perception that they had agreed to limit the Islamic Republic's exercise of an internationally recognized right and gotten nothing in return gained wide currency. As one of the country's chief nuclear negotiators at the time acknowledged later, "The Khatami administration came under fire at home from radical politicians for these concessions. This rhetoric was used to transform the nuclear issue into one of national pride and to sideline moderate political camps in election campaigns."[51] In particular, Khatami's willingness to suspend enrichment became a wedge issue that Mahmoud Ahmadinejad, a rapidly rising conservative politician, could use in his 2005 presidential campaign—especially in the runoff against former president Rafsanjani, several of whose protégés had also been among Khatami's top advisers and negotiators on nuclear matters.[52]

Following Ahmadinejad's election in June 2005, Khatami's

government—recognizing the damage it had done to the reformists' image as competent stewards of the Islamic Republic's national security and foreign policy—announced its intention to resume working on enrichment. It gave the initial orders to restart operations at the uranium conversion facility in Esfahan and informed the IAEA of its directive on August 1, 2005, just two days before Ahmadinejad took office.[53] A week later, the Europeans finally came through with a package of security, technological, and economic incentives for further talks.[54] But they were too little too late. Among other things, the package called on Iran to make "a binding commitment not to pursue fuel cycle activities other than the construction and operation of light water power and research reactors"—meaning that Iran would have to abandon uranium enrichment—for at least ten years. A month after Khatami's departure from office, Ahmadinejad's government reaffirmed the directive to resume enrichment activities.[55] In January 2006, Iran asked the IAEA to remove its seals from the enrichment facility at Natanz and recommended introducing uranium gas into the centrifuges there.[56]

The failure of nuclear talks with the EU3 led Iranian policy makers to conclude that engaging "the West without America" was not feasible. The IAEA's former director, Mohamed ElBaradei, has said that the Europeans "weren't interested in a compromise with the government in Tehran"; instead they were, like the Americans, set on "regime change—by any means necessary."[57] Diplomats from EU3 countries and the EU mothership in Brussels deny this charge. But whatever the Europeans' intentions, negotiating with the EU3 drove home to Tehran that Europe did not constitute a strategic alternative to the United States.[58]

TEHRAN GETS TOUGHER

In this setting, Ahmadinejad's victory in the Islamic Republic's 2005 presidential election was tied to a recalibration of Tehran's approach to the United States, a shift shaped by two factors in particular.[59] First, Ahmadinejad's rise marked a resurgence of conservative—or "principlist," as they have come to be called in the Islamic Republic—figures and forces in Iranian politics. By the time Ahmadinejad took office, a critical mass of Iranian principlists—including not just the new president but also his leading conservative rivals and Khamenei—judged that the Islamic Republic's bargaining power was increasing as a result of its growing influence in the post-9/11, post-Saddam Middle East.[60] The United States would eventually be compelled by the sheer force of reality to recognize that it had to come to terms with the Islamic Republic in order to avoid strategic failure in the region.

Second, by the time of Ahmadinejad's accession, the Iranian leadership knew that the nuclear issue had unique potential to draw the United States to the bargaining table with the aim of reaching a genuine strategic understanding. So, beyond the decision to move ahead with enrichment, Tehran began to take a much tougher approach in nuclear negotiations. It refused to suspend enrichment again, either as a condition for talks or as part of a negotiated outcome. It also insisted that, for a diplomatic solution to be possible, the United States and other Western powers would have to recognize the Islamic Republic's nuclear rights, including the right to enrich; acceptance of its nuclear program, it calculated, would pave the way for acceptance of its political order, place in the region, and role in world affairs. This new approach was signaled early in Ahmadinejad's tenure, in Tehran's reaction to a Russian proposal that Iran pursue its nuclear activities in collaboration with Moscow, but with actual enrichment conducted only in Russia and only by Russian scientists.[61] Tehran responded that it was willing to conduct its nuclear program in a multinational framework but maintained that the full range of fuel cycle activities—including enrichment—would have to be conducted in Iran.

This exchange provided a preview of Iran's approach to nuclear diplomacy during Ahmadinejad's presidency. The Islamic Republic was no longer interested in discussing whether and to what extent it might develop its nuclear capabilities; from Tehran's vantage, the main topic would henceforth be the extent to which the United States and other international players could participate in and monitor its nuclear activities.[62] Iranian policy makers had in mind a nuclear bargain very different from the one Washington and its European partners favored: they expected the world to accept the reality of an Iran working to master the full range of civil nuclear capabilities in exchange for meaningful—in some respects unprecedented—access to its nuclear infrastructure. Since 2006 Tehran has been prepared, under appropriate conditions, to ratify and implement the Additional Protocol and negotiate further measures to enhance confidence that the proliferation risks associated with its fuel cycle activities will be controlled. But these conditions include recognition of Iran's right to enrich as well as an even more basic acceptance of the Islamic Republic as the country's legitimate government—which Washington has remained unwilling to grant. This tougher stance has been strongly backed by Khamenei.

As a result, Iranian diplomacy toward the United States during Ahmadinejad's presidency has been focused on establishing a "comprehensive framework" in which to structure bilateral dialogue—a framework oriented toward fundamentally realigning relations by addressing the Islamic Republic's core security interests, acknowledging its regional role, and normalizing its international status.[63] A wide range of principlist figures, including Ahmadinejad and a number of his leading rivals, argue that without such a framework Iranian leaders cannot have confidence in the end goal of engagement. As then foreign minister Manouchehr Mottaki put it in 2008, "Before I go into a room, I need to know what will be in it." Mohsen Rezae—a founding commander of the Revolutionary Guards who, since stepping down from that post, has been secretary-general of the Expediency Council and a notable figure in the Islamic Republic's political life—expressed the same idea: Iran would benefit from realigning relations with the United States but could not "realign to nothing." It needed to know beforehand that Washington was serious about a more positive relationship.[64]

To advance this agenda, Ahmadinejad personally wrote twice to President George W. Bush and to President Obama—something, he told us, that "was not easy to get done" on the Iranian side. (Neither American president responded. In fact, senior officials in the Bush and the Obama administrations ridiculed the letters' length and use of flowing language as evidence of Ahmadinejad's "irrationality.") More important, the Islamic Republic has, during Ahmadinejad's presidency, advanced several proposals for comprehensive dialogue with Washington. But both the Bush and the Obama administrations dismissed them.

After the failures of the EU3 and Russian initiatives, at the beginning of 2006 the Bush administration, by then in its second term, pushed the IAEA's Board of Governors to "report" Iran's nuclear activities to the Security Council. (China and Russia balked at "referring" the issue, an action that would have implied a serious breach of the NPT.) However, Secretary of State Condoleezza Rice persuaded Bush that for Washington to obtain the requisite support for international sanctions against Iran, it needed to be actively involved in nuclear diplomacy. So in the spring of 2006 the EU3 was replaced as Tehran's nuclear interlocutor by the "P5+1": the five permanent members of the council (Britain, China, France, Russia, and the United States) plus Germany, with Javier Solana, the EU's foreign policy chief, continuing to take part.[65]

While the P5+1 finally brought the United States into the established channel for nuclear diplomacy, the Bush administration continued to insist that Iran suspend enrichment as a condition for U.S. participation in talks, which Tehran was no longer prepared to do. It also insisted that any acceptable negotiated outcome would have to put an end to Iran's fuel cycle activities, which the Islamic Republic would not countenance, either. And the Bush team rejected the notion of embedding nuclear talks in a broader process of American-Iranian rapprochement, which for Tehran was the sine qua non for serious diplomacy.

Thus, to elicit formal U.S. agreement to P5+1 proposals to Iran, the EU3 accepted a significant weakening of its already deficient (from an Iranian perspective) offer. It is instructive, in this regard, to compare the EU3's original August 2005 incentives package with the new package that the P5+1 rolled out in June 2006.[66] The proposals for economic and technological cooperation in the two documents are broadly similar—indeed, in some passages almost identical. But there is a huge difference on security issues. The 2005 EU3 package offered the Islamic Republic assurances that the Western signatories would not attack or undermine it and would even help defend it against attack; the package also contained a commitment to cooperate in establishing "confidence-building measures and regional security arrangements" as well as a regional WMD-free zone. But since the Bush administration refused to join in offering negative security guarantees, much less positive security assurances, to the Islamic Republic, there is virtually no mention of security issues in the 2006 P5+1 package endorsed by the United States. At American insistence, the fuller references to security in the earlier package had been stripped out.[67]

Iran articulated its problems with the new package as well as its desire to establish a broader framework for negotiations in its formal response to the P5+1 proposal in August 2006.[68] It refused to suspend its fuel cycle activities as a precondition for talks, even though the demand that it halt uranium enrichment had been enshrined in a Security Council resolution adopted the preceding month.[69] Further, Tehran wanted amplification of the package's meager language on security—a demand that would necessarily require discussion of a wide range of nonnuclear issues (for example, Iran's regional role, its ties to groups that Washington considers terrorist organizations, its policy toward key regional conflicts like those in Afghanistan and Iraq), as well as of the United States' ultimate intentions toward the Islamic Republic. Iran also sought explicit acknowledgment of what the NPT describes as its "inalienable right" to civil nuclear technology, including uranium enrichment.[70] Beyond these requirements, Iran wanted more information about the P5+1's offers of economic and technological cooperation—details on timing, the substance of particular items, and the willingness of the United States to lift multilateral and unilateral sanctions.

After the P5+1 package was released, the United States tried once again to play Iranian politics, attempting through Solana—the P5+1 representative dealing with the chief Iranian negotiator, Ali Larijani—to work around Ahmadinejad and draw Iran into talks on its

own terms. But there was a strong consensus in Tehran on the requirements for successful negotiations, and Western efforts to evade them
were unsuccessful.[71] Pushed by the United States, the Security Council began authorizing international sanctions against Iran at the end
of 2006; it expanded them in 2007 and reaffirmed them in 2008.[72] But
Tehran continued to hang tough. It would not suspend as a condition
for talks; on the contrary, it increased the budget for its nuclear program.

At the same time, it renewed its push for a "comprehensive framework" for negotiations—most notably in a May 2008 letter from Foreign Minister Mottaki to Ban Ki-moon, secretary-general of the United
Nations.[73] This effort, too, failed to move Washington. Under pressure
from its P5+1 partners, the Bush administration agreed in June 2008
to modify the group's earlier incentives package.[74] (It also allowed a
senior U.S. diplomat—William Burns, who had replaced Nick Burns
as undersecretary of state for political affairs—to attend the meeting
at which P5+1 representatives presented the modified package. Burns,
however, was enjoined from saying anything.) The revised package
included more language on political and security issues, but on the
specific core point of the Islamic Republic's security the document
only reaffirms states' "obligations under the U.N. Charter to refrain in
their international relations from the threat or use of force against the
integrity or political independence of any state or in any manner
inconsistent with the Charter of the United Nations." To Tehran, this
was hardly satisfactory. There had been no Security Council resolution authorizing the invasion of Iraq, yet the United States and Britain
had proceeded anyway. Unless Washington and London were prepared to acknowledge that the invasion had violated their obligations
under the U.N. Charter, the revised incentives package provided no
meaningful assurance on their future posture toward "the threat or
use of force against the integrity or political independence" of the
Islamic Republic.

By the end of George W. Bush's presidency, the experience of
nuclear dialogue with the United States had reaffirmed for Iran's leaders the importance of establishing—up front—Washington's ultimate

intentions toward the Islamic Republic before engaging in serious diplomacy. This outlook has strongly conditioned Tehran's response to the presidency of Barack Obama.

CHANGE EVEN TEHRAN WANTED TO BELIEVE IN

The Iranian reaction to Obama's election was warily optimistic. Iranians were as intrigued by Obama's background and personal history as were others around the world and speculated as to whether he might really be a different sort of American politician. Both of Obama's books were translated into Farsi and were readily available to Iranians; visiting the University of Tehran after he entered the White House, we met students who said the books were required reading in some of their courses. Even Obama's name appealed to Iranians—he shares his middle name, Hussein, with one of Shi'ism's founding figures, and his last name makes a pun in Farsi: *Ū bā mā* means "he is with us."

Iranians were also struck by Obama's initial rhetorical outreach. In his inaugural address, he spoke of engaging "the Muslim world" on the basis of "mutual interest" and "mutual respect"; although pitched broadly, these words were largely calculated to strike a positive note in Tehran.[75] In his first television interview after taking office (with the Saudi-owned, Dubai-based Al-Arabiyya network), he revived language from his campaign to underscore that "we are using all the tools of U.S. power, including diplomacy, in our relationship with Iran."[76] And in March 2009, he released a video for Nowruz (Persian New Year) directed to "the people and leaders of the Islamic Republic of Iran"—the first time that an American president had referred to the country by its official name. Declining to follow his predecessors' attempts to play the Iranian public against its leaders, he declared that "my administration is now committed to diplomacy that addresses the full range of issues before us, and to pursuing constructive ties among the United States, Iran, and the international community."[77]

Two days after Obama's Nowruz video was issued, Ayatollah Khamenei responded to it in his own annual Nowruz address in Mashhad,

Iran's holiest city (and, incidentally, his hometown). Khamenei ran through a long litany of American transgressions against Iran over many decades. He then turned to Obama's message:

> Changes in words are not adequate. . . . Change must be real. I would like to say this to U.S. officials, that this change that you talk about is a real necessity; you have no other choice, you must change. If you do not change, then divine traditions will change you, the world will change you. You must change, but this change cannot be in words only. It should not come with unhealthy intentions. You may say that you want to change policies, but not your aims, that you will change tactics. This is not change. This is deceit. There can be true change, which should be seen in action. . . . If the U.S. government continues its same behavior, method, course, policies against us, as in the past thirty years, we are the same people, the same nation that we were for the past thirty years.

Then Khamenei offered what Iranian policy makers consider the speech's money line. Noting that "we do not have any experience with the new U.S. president and government," he addressed Obama directly: *"We shall see and judge. You change, and we shall change as well."*[78] The Islamic Republic was prepared to give Obama a chance. If he demonstrated through concrete steps that he was serious, Tehran would respond.

On the day in 2009 when Khamenei spoke, we were in the Middle East meeting with former Iranian officials as part of our ongoing effort to exchange ideas with a cross-section of politically engaged Iranians. One of our interlocutors was a diplomat with considerable high-level policy making experience in the Rafsanjani and Khatami presidencies. When Flynt read, from his BlackBerry, Khamenei's pledge, our Iranian colleague's eyes grew wide and he exclaimed, "This is already very positive!"

Certainly the line was intended that way, as senior Iranian Supreme National Security Council officials later confirmed to us. Khamenei's address was not, as Karim Sadjadpour baselessly asserted, a "cynical response." Khamenei was inviting Obama to offer a substantive agenda for realigning relations. Iranian officials have told us that Khamenei's formulation—which left it up to Obama to determine the change in American behavior or policy he was prepared to make—was crafted to maximize the new president's opportunities to show his serious intent. Tehran reiterated the formulation a few weeks later, in a message to Obama made in response to a letter Obama had sent Khamenei. From Tehran's perspective, however, Obama's letter suggested that the new American president's Iran policy might be less promising than it had seemed. Contradicting his Nowruz message, Obama had made his own bid to play Iranian politics by addressing just the "right" interlocutor in Tehran. Following ill-informed advice from its political appointees and their preferred outside expert the White House decided to try dealing directly and exclusively with Khamenei while ignoring Ahmadinejad; thus Obama wrote to Khamenei without responding to the unprecedented congratulatory note Ahmadinejad had sent him in November 2008. Ahmadinejad did not take this action well—and neither did Khamenei, since it indicated a continuing disregard for the Islamic Republic's political system. More substantively, although Sadjadpour, Trita Parsi, and others extol Obama's "unprecedented and unrequited overtures to Tehran," his administration has, in fact, never made such overtures.[79]

Since then, Iran has not seen the kind of change in American policy it is looking for; we explore its disappointment in greater depth in part 3. For all that defenders of failed status quo approaches like Ken Pollack and Ray Takeyh insist on Obama's "passionate determination to emphasize carrots" in his Iran policy, his administration has never offered any carrots that might seriously interest Tehran.[80] Even as Obama was making his "unprecedented" outreach, his administration was pursuing the coercive track of the dual-track approach—in particular, economic sanctions—at least as assiduously as the George W. Bush administration had; in the process, it undermined the credibility of its own overtures. On this point, Khamenei himself said, "Negotiations that are conducted under threats and pressure are not in fact negotiations. It is not acceptable if one side of negotiations

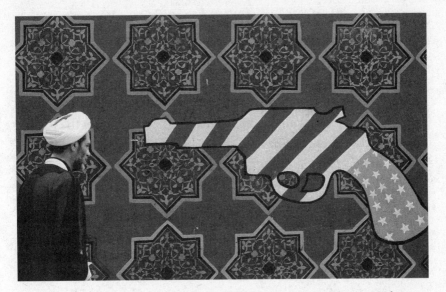

A man walks past a mural painted on the side of the former U.S. Embassy in Tehran—a reminder that, while restoring relations with America may be desirable, the Islamic Republic will not accede to Washington's demands under pressure and threats. *Getty/ Majid Saeedi*

threatens and pressures the other side like imperialists, imposes sanctions and shows an iron fist and at the same time says that the two sides should sit at a table and negotiate. This does not qualify as negotiations. We will not engage in this kind of negotiations with anyone."[81]

Despite the talk of change, the United States has still not demonstrated that it is prepared for rapprochement with the Islamic Republic based on mutual accommodation of both sides' core interests. In contrast to the Bush administration, the Obama administration allowed U.S. officials to negotiate with Iranian counterparts through the P5+1. But it has aimed only at a narrow and lopsided deal whereby Iran would stop enrichment at the 20 percent level, surrender most (if not all) of its LEU stockpiles, and close its new, IAEA-safeguarded facility near Qom—without Western recognition of its right to enrich even at the 3–4 percent level. Parroting the administration's spin, Pollack and Takeyh assert that Obama has offered Iran's "theocratic leaders a respectful path out of their predicament."[82] But this "respectful" path boils down to Tehran's surrender of what it considers its sovereign rights and acceptance of ongoing American hegemony in the Middle East. In August 2010, Ayatollah Khamenei succinctly addressed this point: "The United States of America's view of the Islamic Republic is based on the rejection of its existence.... Of course they deny this and say that they are only trying to change the behavior of the Islamic Republic. The change of behavior they are talking about—and they do not always emphasize this change of behavior—is the same as rejecting the identity of the Islamic Republic."[83]

PART TWO

THE ISLAMIC REPUBLIC AS
LEGITIMATE STATE

PROLOGUE

For more than thirty years, American analysts and policy makers have consistently misread and misinterpreted Iranian politics and, thus, consistently misled the American public. The U.S. government treated the Iranian Revolution of 1978–79 as a major surprise—but the only reason it was a surprise was official Washington's denial of the Iranian people's growing demand for an independent political order free from American domination. Notwithstanding the Islamic Republic's staying power, American political and policy elites still refuse to engage in serious, open-minded analysis of the basic forces driving Iranian political life. The clearest manifestation of this attitude is the persistent depiction of the Islamic Republic as a system despised by its own population and in imminent danger of being overthrown. David Brooks provides a succinct, representative specimen in one of his columns for the *New York Times*: "The Iranian regime is fragile at the core. Like all autocratic regimes, it has become rigid, paranoid, insular, insecure, impulsive, clumsy, and illegitimate. The people running the regime know it. . . . The Iranian on the street knows it. And the world knows it."[1]

Western "experts" on Iran have been asserting that the Islamic Republic is on the cusp of collapse virtually since its founding. Such claims were put forward during the Iran-Iraq War in the 1980s and after the death of the Islamic Republic's founding father, Imam Khomeini, in 1989. They were advanced during the 1990s, when Iran's reform movement appeared and started winning elections, and in the mid-2000s, when it stopped winning elections and largely collapsed. They were made in 1999, when students launched protests in support of the reformist president Mohammad Khatami—protests that were limited in scope and quickly suppressed—and on subsequent anniversaries of those protests, though few Iranians came out to commemorate them. As members of the National Security Council in the George W. Bush White House, we heard President Bush declare that one of the reasons for the United States to overthrow Saddam Husayn was to inspire Iranians to rise up against their political order and push for the same kind of liberal secular democracy that their next-door neighbors were going to get through the largesse of American military action.

Assessments of the Islamic Republic as an illegitimate order on the verge (if not already in the process) of implosion multiplied in the wake of Iran's June 12, 2009, presidential election, which Western analysts and media condemned as a fraud, almost universally judging former prime minister Mir-Hossein Mousavi to have defeated incumbent president Mahmoud Ahmadinejad. In the months that followed, widely held assumptions (with the strength of convictions) about the Islamic Republic's fragility were reflected in excited claims by virtually every foreign policy pundit and Middle East expert who came before the American public: Ahmadinejad had no popular support; Khamenei had lost his legitimacy; unprecedented divisions had erupted among Iranian political elites (even though such divisions had for the past thirty years been cited by every U.S. administration as one excuse for not diplomatically engaging the Islamic Republic); and the Green movement was a mass popular uprising poised to sweep away the Islamic government, perhaps within a few months. This grave misreading of

Iran's 2009 election and its aftermath entrenched the illegitimacy myth not only among neoconservatives and other traditional hawks but, even more significantly, also among liberals who had been more optimistic that internal "reform" would transform the Islamic Republic into something more palatable to Western sensibilities. More concretely, it reinforced the Obama administration's flawed policy calculations in ways that are still damaging America's long-term interests.

Reality in Iran was profoundly at odds with these confident assertions.[2] The facts were evident for anyone who chose to face them: neither Mousavi nor anyone in his campaign nor anyone connected with the Green movement ever presented hard evidence of electoral fraud. Moreover, every methodologically sound poll carried out in Iran before and after the election—fourteen in all, conducted by Western polling groups as well as by the University of Tehran—indicated that Ahmadinejad's reelection, with two-thirds of the vote (which was what the official results showed), was eminently plausible.[3] It was also evident that the Green movement which emerged with the election did not represent anything close to a majority of Iranians and that within a week of the election its social base was already contracting.

But not many were willing to face these facts. Pointing them out was treated across the American political spectrum as a kind of intellectual treachery, demonstrating how liberal internationalists and progressively minded humanitarian interventionists could come together with neoconservatives to impose conventional wisdom on the Iran debate, as they had on the Iraq debate before the 2003 invasion. The *New York Times* columnist Thomas Friedman, a champion of that invasion, sent us a note denouncing our June 15, 2012, op-ed in *Politico* (titled, not very subtly, "Ahmadinejad Won. Get Over It") as "shameful" without identifying how it was wrong. Another op-ed, which we published in the *New York Times* on January 6, 2010—the first high-profile piece to chart the decline of the Greens and to predict (accurately) that they would not be able to generate significant protests on February 11, the Iranian Revolution's anniversary—was denounced by Abbas Milani in the *New Republic* as "the most infuriating op-ed of the New Year."[4] Later, the *New Republic* itself editorialized that we "should be ashamed" of our analysis. We even received e-mail, sent to our personal accounts, declaring that we should be shot and left to die in the street as Neda Soltan had been. (Though not herself a protestor, Neda Soltan was gunned down during postelection protests on June 20, 2009. Oppositionists tried to hold up her death as emblematic of their plight.) One such message was accompanied by a photograph of the mortally wounded Neda Soltan lying in the street, blood streaming from her mouth and nose.

From this experience, we were hardly surprised that the myth of the Islamic Republic's illegitimacy and instability did not die as a result of the Green movement's failure. Indeed, it got a new lease on life in early 2011, when mass protests forced autocratic leaders from office in Tunisia and Egypt. Through the pro-Green lens that continues to shape most Western commentary on Iranian politics, it seemed inevitable that waves of popular discontent like those that took out the pro-American leaders in Tunisia and Egypt, forced a leadership change in Yemen's U.S.-allied government, and seriously threatened another U.S.-allied government in Bahrain would engulf the Iranian government, too. Most of the pundits who had jumped on the regime-change bandwagon in 2009 hopped back on for another ride. After all, hadn't the Green movement come close to bringing down the Islamic Republic in the weeks and months following the June 2009 election? On February 21, 2011, the billionaire financier George Soros, appearing before a worldwide audience on CNN's *GPS* with Fareed Zakaria (who has stated his own desire to see the end of the Islamic Republic), proffered a bet that "the Iranian regime will not be there in a year's time." Two days later, in *Foreign Policy*, we took Soros up on his wager. We even bet that not only would the Islamic Republic still be Iran's government in a year's time but that the balance of influence and power in the Middle East would be tilted further in its favor.[5] Almost two years have elapsed since Soros made his wager; we're eager to collect on it.

Still the trend continues. In the summer of 2010, Western journalists, commentators, and the Obama administration all cited a strike by *bazaaris* in Tehran, Esfahan, and Tabriz as evidence the Iranian merchant class was turning against the state to side with what was left of the Green movement. The *Los Angeles Times* reported that "all eyes in Iran are on the bazaar"—even though, while the strike was going on, Iranians seemed to be paying more attention to a double suicide bomb attack by Jundallah against a Shi'a mosque in the capital of Sistan-Balochistan province that killed twenty-one people and wounded more than a hundred. In Michael Ledeen's estimation, the bazaar strike showed that "the death spiral of the Islamic Republic" was "gathering momentum."[6] In fact, the strike—effectively a repeat of a similar episode in 2008—was a largely successful effort by a traditional business elite to resist the imposition of additional taxes (something that the International Monetary Fund had recommended to the Iranian government). It was not in any way a signal that *bazaaris* were breaking with the Islamic Republic.

In 2011, Western analysts focused on the back-and-forth between Khamenei and Ahmadinejad over the resignation and reinstatement of Intelligence Minister Heydar Moslehi (which appeared to prompt Ahmadinejad to stay away from cabinet meetings and other official duties for a few days) and other issues. Iran experts and the mainstream media gave these developments overblown, even hysterical treatment, portraying them as unprecedented signs of an insecure regime fracturing at the top.[7] These characterizations reveal, at the very least, ignorance about the Islamic Republic's history, which since the revolution has been marked by much the same kind of intense competition among elites over policy and power as in the United States. Escalating tensions between Khomeini and the Islamic Republic's first elected president, Abolhassan Bani-Sadr, resulted in Bani-Sadr's impeachment in 1981. After Khatami became president in 1997, his disagreements with Khamenei—by then the Supreme Leader—were at least as contentious as the recent jockeying between Khamenei and Ahmadinejad. Even if Ahmadinejad were to leave office before his term ended, it would not mark a systemic crisis. He would simply be replaced, pursuant to the constitution—politics as usual in a system with multiple power centers and institutionalized checks and balances.

In early 2012, Western-based Iran specialists teamed up once again with ideologically sympathetic journalists to promote a story that

Ayatollah Khamenei would abolish the presidency, perhaps before Ahmadinejad finished his term, and vest executive power in a prime minister selected by the Majles and therefore supposedly more subject to manipulation. Moreover, Khamenei had reportedly tasked his son to stage-manage the 2012 parliamentary elections to produce a Majles that would support his plan. In some versions, the story held that, after 2012, Ali Larijani would be replaced as Majles speaker by Gholam-Ali Haddad-Adel, a long-serving parliamentarian related to Khamenei by marriage. Few bothered to note that, even if Khamenei were so inclined, he could not unilaterally abolish the presidency and create a prime ministerial post; that would require amending the constitution by popular referendum.[8] (After the 2012 elections, the new Majles reelected Larijani as speaker.) Later in the year, Western pundits hyperventilated about "hyperinflation" in Iran, arguing that a sharp devaluation in the country's currency would turn the population not only against Ahmadinejad, but against the Islamic system. This assessment, too, proved fanciful.

Depictions of the Islamic Republic as an illegitimate and unstable polity are grounded not in rigorous inquiry but in what is effectively an article of faith: that Iranian politics are inexorably inclined toward a Western-style secular democracy that is, by definition, incompatible with the Islamic Republic's continued existence. In the United States, the notion that secular liberalism is ultimately universal is a cardinal tenet of liberal internationalism; on the right, Francis Fukuyama and other thinkers have made it a core neoconservative precept.[9] But as a prominent liberal intellectual admitted, it is a "statement of conviction, not prediction." The Islamic Republic challenges Westerners to consider that secular liberalism, far from being universal, grew out of specific historical and cultural settings. The idea that Iranian politics is inevitably headed in the same direction is nothing but wishful thinking dressed up as historical determinism. Yet it has distorted Western interpretations of the Iranian Revolution, the creation of the Islamic Republic, its subsequent evolution, and its future prospects. Substituting this kind of wishful thinking for serious analysis has had horrendous consequences for American policy.

Many educated Iranians who live in and support the Islamic Republic hold that the Iranian Revolution will be seen, in historical perspective, as equal in significance to the American and French revolutions, in that each gave rise to a unique form of governance. While the claim may strike American, French, and other observers as grandiose, the revolution that overthrew the shah in 1979 is the only fully successful Islamist challenge to an existing political order since the Muslim world was divided, along Western lines, into nation-states after World War I. And the political system to which that revolution gave birth is indeed an unprecedented experiment.

Instead of evaluating the results of that experiment through a secular prism—or by a Manichaean standard relegating anything other than liberal democracy to the dark realms of Oriental despotism—we examine Iranian politics, before and after the revolution, against the benchmark of the Iranian people's actual preferences. By this standard, we argue that most Iranians living in Iran do not want a political order grounded in Western-style secular democracy; as a defender of the Islamic Republic noted to an expatriate critic, "Secularism is itself a religion. That's why we fight it."[10] Rather, they want an indigenously generated political order reflecting their cultural and religious values— as President Khatami wrote in 2004, "freedom, independence, and progress within the context of both religiosity and national identity."[11] And that is what the Islamic Republic, with all its flaws, offers them the chance to pursue.

More broadly, it seems that many Muslims, in Iran and elsewhere, do not want to live in a "flat" world where cultures are driven toward a convergent sameness. Most Muslims do not come from liberal societies and are not persuaded that jettisoning their culture for a secularized foreign alternative is in their interest. Instead, they want to live in political orders that, while modern and connected to the world, retain a richly textured cultural authenticity as part of their sovereign identity. As a volunteer in Iran's Basij militia said, "Wearing the latest fashion or listening to the latest piece of shit from Britney Spears or getting publicly wasted (there's plenty of it going on privately) are nothing compared to literacy, basic needs, and independence."[12]

That many Muslims do not want to be secular liberals does not mean they are content with autocracy. But they would like to see popular participation in political decision making develop within an explicitly Islamic framework. On this point, Americans and other Westerners can draw insight from the Turkish experience. Turkey is a Muslim-majority country that has had, since the days of Kemal Atatürk, one of the most scrupulously secular political orders in the world, reinforced by decades-long membership in NATO and aspirations to membership in the European Union. Yet, over the past three decades, whenever Turks have had real electoral choices they have opted to be governed by Islamic political parties, whose leaders have often proved more respectful of democratic norms than the military and bureaucratic guardians of Atatürk's legacy and their "republican" allies. The pattern has been repeated in other places (Egypt, the Gaza Strip, Indonesia, Iraq, Tunisia) where Muslim populations, given the choice, opted to be governed by Islamists. It is now playing out in Egypt and other countries touched by the Arab Spring.

Displaying similar attitudes, Iranians have demonstrated a sustained desire for a political order integrating Islam and participatory politics. In contrast to the Turks, though, the Iranians definitively rejected the ambitions and the legacy of their secular, modernizing autocrats— Reza Shah, who took Atatürk as his model, and Reza's son, Mohammad Reza, the last shah—through revolution. This difference in historical experience has allowed Iran to embrace, more fully and openly than Turkey, the project of building a state that is simultaneously Islamic and democratic. If Americans and other Westerners made the effort to understand this project, they would come to a new assessment of the Islamic Republic's legitimacy, its stability, and the future trajectory of its politics. And that is an essential step toward thinking rationally about how to deal with today's Iran. For if the Islamic Republic is not some ephemeral way station in the Iranian people's inexorable journey toward secular liberalism but an enduring reflection of their political aspirations, this is another compelling reason for Washington policy makers and politicians to reconsider America's unremitting hostility toward it.

4

RELIGION, REVOLUTION, AND
THE ROOTS OF LEGITIMACY

Do you know the phrase that makes the Iranians sneer the most, the one that seems to them the stupidest, the shallowest? "Religion is the opium of the people" . . . Shi'ism, in the face of the established powers, arms the faithful with an unremitting restlessness. It breathes into them an ardor wherein the political and the religious lie side by side.

—*Michel Foucault*, Corriere della sera, *October 8, 1978*

Late on the evening of January 31, 1979, Grand Ayatollah Seyed Ruhollah Khomeini, accompanied by an entourage of aides and supporters, boarded a chartered Air France 747 in Paris and departed for Iran's capital city, Tehran. The revolution in his native land that he had inspired and directed was reaching a climax; after fifteen years of forced exile, the Imam was coming home.

Khomeini's representatives had agreed to the airline and its insurer's request that the plane fly only half full, so that if it was not allowed to land in Tehran there would be enough fuel to return to Paris. Fearful that enemies of the revolution might sabotage or attack the plane, the Imam's aides decided that Iranian women would not be allowed on the flight. (Khomeini's wife, daughter, daughter-in-law, and grandchildren would travel to Iran later, as would the families of his associates.) But the Imam's inner circle also decided to include among the passengers a pool of journalists from many of the world's leading media outlets—as "a kind of insurance," one of the aides later said.[1]

Years afterward, a correspondent from the *New York Times* who had been part of the press pool compared the atmosphere on board the plane to that on one of the Freedom Rides in the American South during the civil rights movement—a heady combination of a deep sense of mission with a spirit of celebration. It was both a historic moment and a triumphant one for Khomeini. When the Imam had been exiled to Iraq in 1964, he had judged that Iran was not yet ripe for an Islamic revolution. In his 1970 lectures in Najaf, he noted that "ours is a goal that will take time to achieve. . . . We must persevere in our efforts even though they may not yield their result until the next generation."[2] To hasten that day, he devoted himself to spreading his revolutionary vision among Iranian youth—directly with students who came to study with him in Najaf and indirectly through public statements and writings. Then, in October 1977, Khomeini's older son, Mostafa, died in Najaf; among Iranians, it was widely believed that he had been assassinated by SAVAK, the shah's intelligence service. Inside Iran, widespread Shi'a mourning ceremonies (which take place at three-, seven-, and forty-day intervals after a death) for Mostafa touched off the first significant mass protests against Pahlavi rule in more than a decade. Khomeini saw an opportunity and seized it. Over the next year, he orchestrated a campaign of escalating popular agitation against the shah. When the shah's security forces resorted to force, firing into crowds of demonstrators to suppress the unrest, Khomeini used the funerals and subsequent mourning rituals for the fallen to galvanize still more people to take to the streets.

After reaching a border agreement with Iran in 1975, Saddam Husayn's regime had become progressively less tolerant of Khomeini's activism against the shah. In September 1978, the Iraqi government proposed to Iranian authorities that it assassinate the Imam. The shah demurred, out of concern that such a killing would turn his longtime antagonist into a martyr and exacerbate the unrest inside Iran. He did, however, ask Iraq to expel Khomeini, hoping to cut him off from his Iranian supporters and audience. Iraq did so in October 1978; after being denied entry to Kuwait, Khomeini moved to France, where he spent almost four months in the Paris suburb of Neauphle-le-Château, during which time the revolutionary campaign intensified into what was effectively a sustained general strike across Iran. Protests reached a high point on December 11 and 12, 1978—the Shi'a holy days of Tasua and Ashura (the ninth and tenth days of Muharram)—when, following Khomeini's direction, more than a million people each day marched in the streets of Tehran to demand the shah's departure. Large rallies took place in Mashhad, Esfahan, and other cities, too.

As the revolution grew, it became not just one of the largest but also one of the broadest social explosions in history, including virtually every urban constituency in Iran: secular liberals and nationalists as well as the religious, traditional *bazaari* merchants and newer bourgeois forces—businessmen, students, civil servants, and intellectuals. Eventually, workers and villagers joined in. The key to mobilizing this coalition was Khomeini's inspirational leadership, exercised through messages smuggled into Iran, relayed over telephone lines to thousands of mosques, and disseminated even more widely on cassette tapes. Under mounting pressure from the protests, the shah fled Iran on January 16, 1979, two weeks before Khomeini boarded the chartered airliner to return home. A seventy-six-year-old Shi'a cleric living in exile and armed with nothing but the power of his beliefs, his words, and his personality had brought down the *shahanshah*, the "king of kings," who commanded the world's fifth-largest army and had the backing of one of its two superpowers. On board the plane, Peter Jennings of ABC News asked Khomeini, "What do you feel in returning back to Iran?" Famously, the Imam replied, "*Hichi. Hich ehsasi nadaram*" ("Nothing. I feel nothing").[3] But a German television crew that was allowed access to Khomeini's personal cabin captured images—rare in the West, much less so in Iran—of him smiling.

Khomeini knew his real work was just beginning. A provisional government appointed by the shah before his departure clung to power, and the military remained formally loyal to it. But this was not the biggest challenge facing the Imam and his associates. As the Air France 747 entered Iranian airspace and approached Tehran, Khomeini handed a sealed manila envelope to Sadeq Tabatabai, scion of a distinguished clerical family, who was one of his closest aides and a relative by marriage; Tabatabai, in turn, passed the envelope to the journalist Peter Scholl-Latour, then the dean of European foreign correspondents, requesting that, should he be killed or arrested after their arrival in Iran, Scholl-Latour hide the envelope. Inside was what many would surely have regarded as a dangerous document: a draft constitution for an "Islamic republic." As Khomeini arrived back home, he was focused not only on finishing a revolution but also on building a new kind of state that would combine religious principles with participatory politics.

Since the Islamic Republic of Iran was established, assumptions about its inherent illegitimacy have kept Americans and other Westerners from accurately interpreting its political dynamics. To understand how its political system is organized, why it is organized that way, and how it legitimates itself, one needs to consider first of all the character of the revolutionary struggle that brought the Imam back home at the beginning of 1979, for the system that Khomeini and his followers created is very much the product of that struggle.

(MIS)UNDERSTANDING A REVOLUTION
IN GOD'S NAME

Western assessments of the Iranian Revolution and the political order it generated have typically taken one of two approaches, both strongly negative. One sees the revolution itself as inherently regressive—for surely only the irrationally ungrateful could have rejected the modernization and development that the shah was providing. From this perspective, the Islamic Republic is the revolution's tragically predictable progeny, a repressively medieval, authoritarian nightmare. This reading, established in some of the more influential initial pieces of long-form English-language journalism about the revolution and the Islamic Republic's early days (most notably by V. S. Naipaul), continues to shape Western attitudes.[4] In his memoirs, Henry Kissinger elaborates on it in emblematic fashion:

The single most important factor in the Shah's collapse was the policy he learned from the West: the modernization of a feudal, Islamic

society. . . . Western liberal maxims caused the Shah to build a secular, modern state in the reformist mold of Kemal Atatürk and to
force-feed industrialization to a population that had barely left the
feudal age. . . . The modernizing cultural influences from the West,
flooding over the broken dam of Iran's cultural isolation, overwhelmed
Iran's religious and social traditions. The rootless, the newly powerful, the orthodox, and the spiritually dispossessed came together
with disparate, often conflicting motives and swept away the Shah's
rule in an orgy of retribution and vengefulness. But retribution for
what? To be sure, there was corruption at the Shah's court, though
not unusually so by the standards of the region or even by the standards of the regime that followed. . . . [H]is accumulated failures
were almost certainly less severe than the practices of other nations in
the Persian Gulf or among the nonaligned that have not been exposed
to opprobrium. And nothing that happened can compare with the
witch trials, executions, terrorism, and lunacy that followed, reminiscent in bloodiness and judicial hypocrisy of the worst excesses of
Robespierre.[5]

The second approach takes a more benign view of Iranians' eagerness to get rid of the shah, but it depicts Khomeini and his followers
as, in effect, a cadre of Qur'an-carrying Bolsheviks who disguised
a totalitarian ideology in religious vocabulary and deceptively
democratic-sounding references to capture what could and should
have been a liberal revolution; in the process, these critics charge, the
Khomeini camp betrayed the aspirations of those who actually carried out the campaign that deposed the shah. Over the past three
decades, this narrative has profoundly affected Western perceptions
of the Islamic Republic. In our own day, it was reflected in Secretary of
State Hillary Clinton's September 2010 remarks:

You know, I have grave disagreements with the Iranian Revolution,
but the early advocates of it said this would be a republic. It would be
an Islamic republic, but it would be a republic. . . . [A] lot of Iranians,
even those who stayed, even those who were originally sympathetic,

are starting to say, "This is not what we signed up for." And I can only hope that there will be some effort inside Iran, by responsible civil and religious leaders, to take hold of the apparatus of the state.[6]

Or, as she said even more bluntly in February 2011, "Talk about a revolution that was hijacked: Iran is Exhibit A."[7]

From either perspective, the Islamic Republic cannot be truly legitimate (or engageable) until it is transformed into a secularized Western-style "Republic of Iran." But both are deeply flawed as analytical frames and therefore dangerously misleading as guides for policy making.

How should Westerners understand the mass movement that swept the shah from power? One can certainly argue that the Iranian Revolution was, if not strictly speaking nationalist, strongly focused on restoring Iran's national dignity; as we saw in part 1, there are important insights to be gleaned from looking at the revolution in this light. While Khomeini periodically belittled the notion of the nation-state as a Western construct foisted on Muslims to divide the umma and set it up for conquest and exploitation, he was also intensely devoted to restoring the full measure of Iran's sovereign independence after a century and a half of foreign domination and rule by puppet regimes. From the Islamic Republic's establishment, the defense of the country's *esteqlal* and *azadi* (independence and freedom) has been the first task of the political order bequeathed by Khomeini's revolution. But the Iranian Revolution was also uniquely Islamist in its origins and goals—that is, it was grounded in the belief that "Islam as a body of faith has something important to say about how politics and society should be ordered in the contemporary Muslim world."[8] This point is poorly understood by Westerners yet indispensable to comprehending both the Islamic Republic's political system and the sources of its legitimacy.

Since Tocqueville and Marx launched modern social science, their scholarly descendants have generalized from a small number of cases to persuade Western (and Westernized) intellectuals that revolutions are caused by "structural" factors—for example, military defeat or other severe external pressures, inequitable distributions of wealth and power among social classes, and backward agricultural systems—that engender deep discontent, especially among workers and peasants, rooted in a sense of "relative deprivation." For that discontent to result in mass activism, there must also be a decline in the coercive capabilities of established regimes.[9] Social scientists have generally dismissed the causal significance of ideas and individual leaders; they are particularly oblivious to the revolutionary potential of religious beliefs and institutions. Some scholars allow that, once a revolution is under way, new counterelites may use socialist or nationalist ideologies to exploit ongoing turmoil and grab political power.[10] But in the reigning Western view, ideas, ideologies, and those who formulate and espouse them do not "make" revolutions; revolutions just come. This is essentially the thesis proposed by Harvard University's Theda Skocpol in *States and Social Revolutions* (1977), her influential study of the French, Russian, and Chinese revolutions.[11]

Devotion to structuralist models has prompted many Western and expatriate scholars to assess the Iranian Revolution by focusing on such factors as the social dislocation associated with the shah's modernization initiatives, the thwarting of rising economic and political expectations that those initiatives encouraged, and a downturn in oil prices during 1977 and 1978. But these assessments are misleading, if not flat-out wrong, because Iran's experience did not conform to Western stereotypes of how revolutions start and play out. The Iranian Revolution was not driven by either the proletariat or the peasantry, the classes identified by twentieth-century Marxists as most prone to revolutionary activism. By the standards that structurally oriented analysts apply, it should not have happened. As Skocpol herself subsequently admitted, the shah "had both munificent wealth and ominous repressive power at his disposal. Whatever the ups and downs of oil prices and revenues, he should have been able to ride out waves of urban social discontent, just as many other (less well-endowed) Third World rulers have been able to do."[12] As another student of the Iranian Revolution asked (and answered) more than twenty years ago, "If the Shah's regime collapsed despite the fact that his army was intact, despite the fact that there was no defeat in war, and despite the fact that the state faced no financial crisis and no peasant insurrections, where does all this leave the usual generalizations about revolutions? Mostly in the pits."[13]

But if these structural factors did not drive revolutionary activism in Iran—and keep people pouring into the streets to face an intact and capable security apparatus that did not hesitate to fire into crowds and kill thousands of Iranians between late 1977 and the beginning of 1979—what did?[14] The Islamic Republic's constitution provides the beginning of an answer, with its declaration that "the basic characteristic of the revolution, which distinguishes it from other movements that have taken place in Iran during the past hundred years, is its ideological and Islamic nature." This statement should not be dismissed as propaganda, for it reflects an important reality: fundamentally, the revolution that drove the shah from power was motivated by Islamic belief and a political ideology grounded in that belief—factors distinguishing it not only from other movements that have sought political change in modern Iran but also from other revolutions.[15] One could plausibly criticize Pahlavi rule as unjust, unrepresentative, and corrupt. But the most resonant critique—initially articulated by Khomeini in his denunciation of the shah's White Revolution (*Enqelab-e Sefid*, an authoritarian modernization program launched in the early 1960s)—was that it was un-Islamic.

Over several years, we have asked dozens of people who lived through the revolution—from Khomeini supporters who still live in Iran to officials in the shah's last government who relocated to the West— what the grievances were that ultimately brought down the Pahlavi dynasty. Virtually every one of our respondents, from the deeply religious to the wholly secular, has said that the most basic source of resentment was the shah's indifference to the religious sensibilities of Iranians. The revolution was, among other things, a challenge to Western social science's "secularization hypothesis," which posited the secularization of culture as a necessary by-product of modernization. Under the Pahlavis, modernization was correlated not with secularization but with Islamic revival; that revival, in turn, was the soil in which revolution took root. And the role of religion in Iranian politics cannot rightly be reduced to a "dependent" or "intervening" socioeconomic variable.[16] As a supporter of the Islamic Republic who participated in the revolution and later became a member of the Basij paramilitary apparatus said, "We conducted the revolution because we wanted to save Iran's Islamic identity."[17]

Of course, for a revolution to occur, grievance must be translated into collective action. In this regard, too, Iran's experience diverges from Western expectations, for those best able to articulate and channel anti-Pahlavi resentment for revolutionary ends did not come from "progressive" segments of the Iranian elite; rather, they were deeply and traditionally religious figures. Michel Foucault, the philosopher and intellectual historian who covered the revolution for several French and Italian newspapers, rightly observed that, in Shi'ism, believers are not compelled to follow a specific religious authority: "One follows only the one to whom one wants to listen. The Grand Ayatollahs of the moment, those who, in facing down the king, his police, and the army have just caused an entire people to come out into the streets, were not enthroned by anybody. They were *listened to*."[18] Khomeini and his disciples were listened to not because they peddled some "new" ideology but because they were seen by most Iranians as Islam's authentic representatives. Asked in 1992 why so many Iran experts in the West failed to predict the revolution, Rafsanjani replied, "They were unaware of our contact with, and influence over, the masses. According to their logic, we did not have a political party or an official organization. It is extremely difficult for those who do not hold religious views to comprehend how influential religion could become and what a momentous force it really is."[19]

Accounts like Secretary Clinton's, which posit a theocratic vanguard capturing already mobilized constituencies, run up against the facts of how Iran's Islamic Revolution actually happened. Khomeini did not "capture" the Iranian Revolution; there would have been no revolution without him. From exile in Iraq and, later, in a Paris suburb

Millions of Iranians crowded into every public space possible to hear Imam Khomeini, the founding father of the Islamic Republic. *AP*

2,600 miles from Iran, the Imam directed the campaign, in *Time* magazine's account, "like a company commander assaulting a hill."[20] As Skocpol has acknowledged,

> If ever there has been a revolution deliberately "made" by a mass-based social movement aiming to overthrow the old order, the Iranian Revolution against the Shah surely is it. . . . What Western socialists have long dreamt of doing (without success except where war has intervened to help), the people of urban Iran did accomplish as they mobilized in an all-inclusive movement against a "corrupt," "imperialist" monarchy. Their revolution did not just come; it was deliberately and coherently made. . . . That [the Shah] was unable to survive, that both he and his state succumbed to revolution, can be explained only by reference to the extraordinarily sustained efforts made by urban Iranians to wear down and undercut the Shah's regime. These efforts, in turn, were based in traditional centers of urban communal life and in networks of Islamic religious communication and leadership.[21]

Khomeini united what Max Weber described as charismatic authority—"resting on the exceptional sanctity, heroism, or exemplary character of an individual person, and of the normative patterns or order revealed or ordained by him"—with the traditional authority of one of the world's major religions.[22] This combination made him a unique figure among history's revolutionaries; it also put him in an unassailable position to advance the case for Islamic government as his country's rightful political orientation. To turn Clinton's phrase around, postrevolutionary Iran would be a republic, but it would be a decidedly Islamic one. And at every step along the way—from an initial referendum on the establishment of an Islamic republic, through elections for a constituent assembly to draft its constitution, to the ratification of that constitution—Khomeini would ask for and receive the Iranian public's overwhelming support.

FROM REVOLUTIONARY LEADER TO FOUNDING FATHER

When Mehdi Bazargan, the founder of the Liberation Movement of Iran, met with Khomeini in Neauphle-le-Château in October 1978, he was struck by the Imam's determination to go beyond the dismantling of monarchical rule and create an entirely new political order. That determination made Bazargan uneasy. In his long career, the seventy-one-year-old leader had played a part in many of the critical episodes in Iran's post–World War II political life that had, by the late 1970s, brought it to the brink of revolution. An ethnically Azeri French-educated technocrat, he had been the first native Iranian to head the University of Tehran's engineering faculty and, under Mossadeq's government, to serve as the National Iranian Oil Company's CEO. Originally a member of Mossadeq's secular liberal National Front, Bazargan founded the Liberation Movement in the 1960s as a more religious alternative.[23] Following the model advanced during the 1906 Constitutional Revolution (which produced Iran's first written constitution and launched its initial attempt at parliamentary government), he championed the country's transformation into a constitutional monarchy, with the shah functioning as a national figurehead and an elected parliament invested with political power.

By the time Bazargan traveled to France, in October 1978, the United States was quietly exploring options for a political transition in Iran that would entail the shah's gradual relinquishing of power; to this end, the shah had proposed holding "free and fair" parliamentary elections in the summer of 1979. Non-Islamist opponents of Pahlavi rule, including both the National Front and the Liberation Movement, wanted to accept. Reflecting their views, Bazargan warned Khomeini that if the opposition pushed too quickly to remove the shah, the United States would intervene. The concern was not wholly fanciful. That fall, Moscow announced that it considered Khomeini's call for an Islamic government in Iran "dangerous." As Foucault noted, this was a signal to the United States "that the USSR did not object to a solution, even a 'vigorous one,' that would block the way for an opposition movement under Khomeini"; it also signaled the shah that "in case of a long and violent struggle, the opposition would find no support" in Moscow.[24]

Khomeini categorically rejected Bazargan's counsel, saying that "America will not oppose us, because we speak the truth." Bazargan, by his own account, cautioned that "the world of politics and the international environment are not like the clerical circle of Najaf and Qom, where logic and truth may be sufficient. We face a thousand difficulties and problems, and they will crush [our] schemes and plans. [The Shah and his American backers] won't surrender just because we speak the truth." Implacably, the Imam responded that "when the Shah is gone and I have returned to Iran, the people will elect parliamentary representatives, and then a government." Bazargan later wrote that "Khomeini's indifference to and heedlessness of the obvious problems of politics and administration grieved me"; at the same time, Bazargan "marveled at and admired his seeing things so simply, his quiet certitude that success was near."[25]

In fact, Khomeini was neither as indifferent to nor as heedless of practical problems of politics and administration as Bazargan suggests, and Bazargan's agenda was not as innocent as he implies. A full report of their conversation shows that Khomeini had well thought-out reasons for pushing ahead with his revolutionary campaign—above all, that the moment was at hand to "make use of the opportunity to create fundamental and basic changes" in Iran's political life. The people were on the streets, mobilized as never before; momentum was with the revolution, and it could be lost if the demonstrations stopped.[26] As for Bazargan, his interest in cooperating with Khomeini was almost entirely tactical. As he had acknowledged during an interrogation by SAVAK a month before traveling to France, "We, the previous leaders, have lost the leadership of the movement and the young people; they are more affected by the ideas of Imam Khomeini, who believes in fighting and jihad."[27] Bazargan was out not to promote Khomeini's agenda but to co-opt Khomeini's standing to promote his own.

Still, Bazargan and other secular opponents of the Pahlavi regime were not prepared to accept the shah's proposal if it meant bucking Khomeini. The Imam, in turn, appointed Bazargan and some associates to work with his clerical allies in the Council of the Islamic Revolution, set up to guide the transition from monarchical rule.[28] In his statement establishing the council, issued on January 12, 1979, Khomeini cited the enormous demonstrations taking place in Iran (as well as demonstrators' public recognition of his leadership) as "a vote of confidence given me by the overwhelming majority of the Iranian people." He also declared that "the demands of the oppressed people of Iran are not restricted to the departure of the Shah and the abolition of the monarchy. Their struggle will continue until the establishment of an Islamic Republic that guarantees the freedom of the people, the independence of the country, and the attainment of social justice."[29] On this last point the Liberation Movement's cooperation with Khomeini was disingenuous, for while Bazargan accepted the formulation "Islamic Republic," he had no desire to create an Islamist government.

This posture was emblematic of non-Islamist collaboration with the Imam. Secularists calculated that while the aging ayatollah was useful for getting people into the streets, once the shah was gone they could outmaneuver him and take charge of Iran's government. Such a calculation was profoundly mistaken; control over events had passed out of their hands well before the revolution succeeded.[30] In reality, it had probably never been in their hands in the first place.

Western interpretations of postrevolutionary Iranian politics have been badly distorted by the accounts of non-Islamist players who failed in their efforts to sideline Khomeini. "As participants in the revolution will readily attest," writes a leading American scholar of contemporary Shi'a politics, "there was a negative consensus, namely toppling the Shah, but there was by no means any consensus on what should come next. Many demonstrators simply presumed that what-ever came after the Shah would be better, others expected a democ-racy of one sort or another, still others expected a socialist republic, and, of course, those who ultimately triumphed yearned for an Islamic state."[31] This is, as far as it goes, an accurate summary of secularist testi-mony about the revolution. But that testimony self-servingly glosses over the intensity of public support that the different camps actually commanded. Visiting Iran in October 1978, Foucault reported that in response to the question "What do you want?" four out of five respondents—including "religious leaders, students, intellectuals," and "former guerrilla fighters"—answered, "An Islamic government."[32] And his respondents were predominantly from Tehran and so presumably drawn from the most secular parts of Iranian society. While not a scientific sample, these responses underscore an important truth: as the anti-shah struggle reached its climax, no alternative perspective for a postmonarchical order could compete for popular backing with Khomeini's Islamist vision.

Practically speaking, those alternatives fell into two categories—liberal and socialist. There is a slightly more than 100-year-old tradi-tion of liberal advocacy among some of the more secularized parts of the Iranian intelligentsia, dating back to the 1906 Constitutional Revolution and drawing explicitly on concepts and categories expounded in Western political philosophy. Under both Reza Shah and his son, Mohammad Reza, liberal advocates worked to encourage Iran's evolution into a constitutional monarchy with an elected and empowered parliament. But liberalism has never gained much of a base in Iranian society, and the most serious attempt to consolidate meaningful parliamentary democracy before the 1979 revolution—Mossadeq's National Front government, from 1951 to 1953—was thwarted by a U.S.-instigated coup. In the years after Mossadeq's overthrow, liberal advocacy came to be divided between the National Front and the more religious Liberation Movement, but neither group was ever in a position to reshape Iran's politics. The revolution that finally broke out in the late 1970s was neither a proletarian nor a peasant revolution, but nor was it an American-style bourgeois revolution, either.

As Khomeini's campaign against the shah gained momentum, the National Front split. The head of the provisional government appointed by the shah, Shahpour Bakhtiar, was from the front, as were several of his ministers; the front's chairman, however, endorsed Khomeini's revolutionary leadership. The Liberation Movement had its own limitations. While Bazargan and other senior figures in the Liberation Movement were personally religious, they were not in any substantive sense Islamists. After the revolution, the Liberation Movement became the main locus for what is called in Iran a "nationalist-religious" approach to politics—that is, a party of religious liberals with a more progressive (in the Western sense) view of religion's role in public life than Khomeini's.[33] Its religious cast made the Liberation Movement more popular than the National Front but never popular enough to challenge Khomeini on major issues of postrevolutionary state building.

Prospects for a socialist alternative were even less promising. During the shah's reign, the communist Tudeh ("masses") party and other socialist groups made little headway in spurring mass political activism based on socioeconomic grievances. Even those Iranians whose class interests had been harmed by the shah's policies were disinclined to embrace parties espousing foreign and secular (even atheistic) ideologies and, in the Tudeh's case, tied to a major external power, the Soviet Union, that had invaded Iran and occupied half of its territory just a few decades earlier. (In a later manifestation of this dynamic, future president Mahmoud Ahmadinejad—from a working-class background and one of the more prominent prorevolutionary student leaders in Iran—opposed storming the American embassy and taking hostages there in 1979. He argued that the Soviet Union was an even greater danger to the revolution than the United States, and that if any embassy were to be seized it should be the Soviet one.)[34]

While the Liberation Movement sought to carve out a kind of liberalism with an Islamic face, a number of groups established during the 1950s and 1960s tried to do the same with Marxist ideology. The most significant of them was the MEK, launched in the mid-1960s as a radical offshoot of the Liberation Movement; it distinguished itself from its parent during the 1970s by embracing Marxism and the use of violence.[35] Just as the Liberation Movement's religious character made it more popular than the purely secular National Front, the MEK's originally religious cast gave it a bigger initial popular base than that of the Tudeh or other nonreligious socialist parties. But the MEK's ideological drift away from Islam damaged its popularity; as subsequent events would demonstrate, it had nothing close to the standing it needed to challenge Khomeini successfully.

As events played out, the shah departed Iran less than two months after Bazargan's meeting with Khomeini in Neauphle-le-Château. The Imam turned immediately—and with the same "quiet certitude of success" noted by Bazargan—to bringing down the provisional government.

After landing at Tehran's Mehrabad Airport on the morning of February 1, 1979, Khomeini was greeted by massive crowds as he traveled to Behesht-e Zahra to honor demonstrators killed by security forces. At the cemetery, he denounced the provisional government for "trying to bring back the regime of the late Shah or some other regime." Western commentators frequently point to his declaration that "I will appoint a government, and I will give this [Bakhtiar] government a punch in the mouth" as proof of his authoritarian outlook. But moments later, Khomeini elaborated "that it is our duty to continue this movement until all elements of the Shah's regime have been eliminated and we have established a Constituent Assembly, based on the votes of the people."[36]

For the next ten days—now commemorated in the Islamic Republic as "the decade of dawn"—people once again poured out en masse, this time to demand the provisional government's ouster.[37] On February 4, the Council on the Islamic Revolution proposed a new "provisional revolutionary government," based on "the vote of the overwhelming majority of the Iranian nation for leadership of the movement [as] represented in the vast gatherings and wide and numerous demonstrations across Iran." Khomeini accepted and personally named Bazargan prime minister, charging him "to perform a referendum and refer to a public vote of the nation about turning the country into an Islamic Republic," to set up "a Council of Founders from the representatives of the people to approve a constitution for the new regime," and to "hold elections for representatives to the parliament of the nation on the basis of the new constitution."[38] A week later, on February 11 (the twenty-second day of Bahman in the Persian calendar, now celebrated annually as Islamic Revolution Victory Day), the military declared its neutrality in the "political disputes" between the provisional government and its revolutionary competitor—meaning, effectively, that it would no longer protect Bakhtiar and his cabinet. Within hours, revolutionaries took control of all state facilities and announced the end of the provisional government.

The extent of popular support for an Islamist order soon became evident. On March 29 and 30, 1979, less than two months after the revolution's triumph, a referendum was held to decide whether a postrevolutionary Iranian state should be, as Khomeini had pledged, an Islamic republic. Well over 90 percent of eligible voters turned out; 98.2 percent of them voted yes. On April 1, 1979, after the referendum results were certified, the Islamic Republic of Iran came formally into being. (Today, April 1 is celebrated in Iran as Islamic Republic Day.) Given the balance of public opinion, its creation cannot be read as a betrayal of the revolution. It was the revolution's culminating—and legitimate—achievement.

IRAN AND THE ISLAMIST PROJECT

The very idea of a political order that seeks to integrate democracy with traditional notions of Islamic governance seems to many Westerners a severe oxymoron, for their civilization has developed quite a different way of thinking about the intersection of religion and politics. For the West, the critical turning point was the Peace of West-phalia in 1648, which ended the religious wars sparked by the Protestant Reformation and ratified the principles of *cuius regio, eius religio* ("whose region, his religion")—meaning the Catholic or Protestant identity of European states would henceforth be determined by the religion of the individual sovereign—and tolerance of sectarian minorities. (Not coincidentally, the settlement also marked the modern nation-state's emergence as the main organizing unit of international relations.) Since then, Western politics have come to treat religion largely as a private, personal matter, with the state constrained from interfering with religious communities. Religiously motivated citizens may bring their beliefs into the public square through their electoral choices and policy views. But the state is not defined on the basis of religious principles; indeed, to Westerners, secularism and liberal democracy have become the sine qua non of a fully legitimate political order—not just for themselves but for everyone.[39]

Khomeini explicitly rejected the Western position, and his followers reject it, too. As a matter of law and policy, postrevolutionary Iran has always accepted the reality of an international order comprising sovereign nation-states; indeed, it is committed, as noted, to vigorously defending Iranian sovereignty in all respects. But the Islamic Republic and its defenders have an approach to legitimating states and their governments very different from that of the post-Westphalian West. They do not view the American experience as a model; as an Iranian writer commented, "The United States is not universal; [its political development] is particular to a specific history, culture, and religious branch."[40] More fundamentally, the idea of separating religion and politics, which has over the past four centuries become central to Western notions of modernization, remains deeply antithetical to Islamic norms and ways of thinking.

The essence of Islam is well conveyed by the Arabic word *tawhid*—unity. In a religious context, tawhid is usually translated into Western languages as "belief in one God." And in the grand sweep of history, Islam can appropriately be seen as a reassertion of Abrahamic mono-theism, following in the footsteps—and, from an Islamic viewpoint, correcting the errors—of Judaism and Christianity. But translating tawhid as "monotheism" obscures Islam's original vision of itself as a comprehensive system uniting individual believers, society, and the state—the "three Ds" of *din* ("faith"), *dunya* ("worldly life"), and *dawla* ("state")—in an indivisible whole.[41] For the Prophet Muhammad and his followers, building a just community in which all would be treated with the respect due them as God's creatures was not a distraction from spiritual pursuits but rather an essential part of how Muslims come closer to God. Thus, Shari'a (Islamic law) is not limited to *'iba-dah* ("prayer and ritual worship"), *adab* ("morals and manners"), and *i'tiqadat* ("beliefs"). It also covers areas such as *mu'amalat* ("transactions") and *'uqubat* ("punishments"), for in Islam properly conducted worldly exchange is at least as essential to salvation as purely religious devotion.[42] For this reason, the logic of the secularization hypothesis is far removed from the way most Muslims have conducted and thought about their lives under conditions of modernization.

As the Muslim world has declined to validate the Western model, many have concluded that it is Islam, not Western expectations, that should change. Since the 1970s and especially since 9/11, a growing number of commentators, officials, and religious leaders in the United States, Europe, and Israel have argued that the only way to remedy Muslim "illiberalism" is for Islam to go through its own reformation, analogous to the experience of European Christianity. As envisioned by its mostly non-Muslim proponents—though some Muslim writers, like Reza Aslan, contribute as well—such a process would lead the Muslim world to a version of a Westphalian settlement and help it learn the same lessons about the separation of religion and politics that Westerners drew from their history.[43]

But the most politically consequential intellectual and cultural actors in the Muslim world reject arguments for an Islamic reformation, at least of the sort that Westerners advocate. (Certainly they reject Aslan's suggestion that Muslims "look to Israel"—which he acknowledges as an "apartheid state"—for "a model that combines democracy and religious belief.")[44] Muslim thinkers have been working through the challenges posed by Islam's encounter with modernity, under the pressure of extensive Western penetration of Muslim societies, for more than two centuries. No significant figure has argued that self-administered Westernization, as in Meiji Japan, is the way to repair the Muslim world's standing and autonomy. The dominant theme, instead, has been a return to Islam as practiced in the time of the Prophet and the first generations of Muslims—or, for Shi'a, a return to the doctrines of Islam as taught by the Prophet and the imams.

This reclaiming of first principles is the essence of what Westerners call "Islamism." In its more fundamentalist variants—such as the Wahhabi strain of Salafi Islam that has given rise to the Taliban—Islamism can come close to an outright rejection of modernity. But most forms of Islamism, Sunni as well as Shi'a, take a different approach, embracing modernity but rejecting what some Islamist thinkers describe as "modernism," meaning a concept of modernity that insists on secularism as one of its indispensable elements. Muslims are reminded that the West's scientific, military, and economic preeminence rests on Islamic civilization's earlier achievements and are urged to return to their own best traditions to restore their independence and position in the world.[45]

This is the project Khomeini took on as his life's work. Well before the Iranian Revolution, he rejected the separation of religion and politics as not merely a watering down of authentic Islam but a tool for helping the West subjugate Muslim populations and lands. In his 1970 Najaf lectures, Khomeini argued that once imperialist powers began to penetrate Muslim countries,

> they regarded it as necessary to work for the extirpation of Islam in order to attain their ultimate goals. It was not their aim to alienate the people from Islam in order to promote Christianity among them, for the imperialists really have no religious belief, Christian or Islamic. Rather, throughout this long historical period, and going back to the Crusades, they felt that the major obstacle in the path of their materialistic ambitions and the chief threat to their political power was nothing but Islam and its ordinances, and the belief of the people in Islam. . . . This slogan of the separation of religion from

politics and the demand that Islamic scholars should not intervene in social and political affairs have been formulated and propagated by the imperialists.[46]

Thus, for Khomeini, recovering true Islam—which he deemed essential to restoring sovereignty and independence for Iran and other Muslim lands—meant recovering it as "a comprehensive system." He warned his students, "Do not allow the true nature of Islam to remain hidden, or people will imagine that Islam is like Christianity (nominal, not true Christianity), a collection of injunctions pertaining to man's relation to God, and the mosques will be equated with the church."[47]

Throughout the struggle against the shah, Khomeini instructed his followers that Islam required political action. Commemorating students killed in protests in Qom in January 1978, he invoked the Exodus story, pointing out that "we constantly read in the Qur'an that the Pharaoh acted in a certain way and Moses in another . . . but we don't think about why the Qur'an tells us this. It tells us this so that we may act like Moses toward the Pharaoh of our age."[48] And as he told his charges in Najaf, the goal of such action was clear: "It is our duty to work toward the establishment of an Islamic government."[49] As early as his announcement of Bazargan's appointment as head of the provisional revolutionary government, the Imam noted that it would be "based on Shari'a."[50]

The Iraqi writer Ali Allawi argues that, confronted by Western liberalism, contemporary Muslim societies face a choice between two very different paths: either diminishing Islam to the point that it resembles, in functional terms, the nonestablished churches of the modern West or creating "an alternative modernity."[51] Many Western intellectuals and political leaders want the Muslim world to choose the first path; we, in contrast, argue that the Islamic Republic is the outstanding example of a Muslim society trying to navigate the second. This is clearly reflected in Khomeini's revolutionary vision for integrating Islamic governance with participatory politics. It is also reflected in the Islamic Republic's commitment to economic and social development—within Islamic parameters, to be sure, but with a more equitable distribution of the benefits of growth and modernization than Iran experienced under the shah.

It is hard for Westerners, their thinking informed by very different historical experiences and cultural references, to develop an empathetic understanding for non-Westerners who do not want secularism for themselves. But given the direction in which many Muslim societies' political dynamics are evolving, the United States needs, in its own interest, to learn to live with and deal with the Islamic Republic and other manifestations of political Islamism.

KHOMEINI'S THEORY OF ISLAMIC GOVERNMENT

By definition, Islamists, whether Sunni or Shi'a, believe that a genuinely Islamic political order must be based on religious principles, presented via divine revelation (the Qur'an) and tradition (for example, *hadith*, or authenticated sayings of the Prophet) and embodied in Shari'a. In the modern period, most have held that proper government is grounded in "justice on the part of the rulers, obedience on the part of the ruled, and *shura* ('consultation') between rulers and ruled." A ruler is just "only because he submits to the authority of God"; while the Qur'an enjoins Muslims to obey such a ruler, it also enjoins rulers to "take counsel" with the community on issues for which there is no explicit revelation.[52] This formula, while an important starting point for Islamist discourse on politics, leaves major questions unaddressed—for example, what does a truly consultative political order look like and who should hold authority in it? Khomeini devoted decades of reflection prior to the Iranian Revolution to addressing these questions; his answers did much to shape the political order the revolution generated.

He approached the task of designing a genuinely Islamic system of governance not just as a pious Muslim but as a leader thoroughly shaped by Shi'a history, experience, and ways of thinking. Early on, the experience of living as a persecuted minority under the Sunni caliphate taught Shi'a thinkers to be suspicious of absolute monarchy. Theology reinforced this attitude, for, according to the Shi'a doctrine

of *imamah* (awkwardly but usefully rendered in English as "the imamate"), wholly legitimate authority rests only with the imams, those
descendants of the Prophet chosen by God to lead the umma. Since God
placed the Twelfth Imam—Muhammad al-Mahdi, or the "hidden
Imam"—into a state of *ghaybah* (literally "hiddenness," but usually
translated into English as "occultation") in AD 874, there has not been
a fully legitimate temporal authority, embodied in an imam, on earth;
moreover, there cannot be one until the Mahdi reappears. (This is why
his followers' attribution of the title Imam to Khomeini was such an
evocative marker of the extraordinary political and religious standing
he had attained.) Until then, Shi'a Muslims are challenged to find the
best possible interim form of government.

Yet a belief that no temporal authority is fully legitimate pending
the Mahdi's return does not mean that all temporal authority is
devoid of legitimacy or that religion has no place in government.
From the time of the Iranian Revolution, a stream of politically
motivated analysts—primarily Iranian expatriates and American
neoconservatives—have argued that "true" Shi'a doctrine posits an
almost Jeffersonian wall of separation between mosque and state.[53]
This argument was even incorporated into the George W. Bush administration's case for invading Iraq. Administration officials claimed that
Saddam's overthrow would empower allegedly "quietist" Iraqi clerics,
such as (Iranian-born) Grand Ayatollah Ali Sistani, to assert Najaf's
primacy over Qom as Shi'ism's intellectual center; their assertion, in
turn, would undermine the Islamic Republic's legitimacy by challenging
Khomeini's theory of government. This notion, however, is a polemical
misreading of Shi'a thought, concocted by pulling together a discon-
nected set of arguments, advanced at widely separate historical points,
about the posture that Shi'a Muslims should assume toward hostile governments and packaging them as mainstream Shi'a political theory.

In fact, Khomeini's theory of government is well anchored in Shi'a
belief and tradition, rooted in two long-established concepts. One
is "protectorship," or "guardianship" (*velayat* in Farsi, from the Arabic
wilaya), usually associated with the exercise of authority; the other is
nezarat, or clerical supervision. In Shi'a teaching, velayat is intimately

bound up with the doctrine of the imamate and the role of the clergy during the Mahdi's occultation, or hiddenness. The earliest authoritative statements of Shi'a doctrine, elaborated over the course of the tenth and eleventh centuries, hold that, in the Mahdi's absence, a government that recognized him and ruled in his name would be entitled to obedience. It would, however, need authorization by his representatives, specifically the *Olema*, or learned clergy.

Among Shi'a olema, the *fuqaha* (clerics well schooled in *fiqh*, or religious jurisprudence) are accorded special esteem. For they are recognized as *mujtahids*, or clerical scholars trained in the practice of *ijtihad*—judicial reasoning based on independent interpretation of traditional legal sources that also may take into account factors of time and place, technological and social conditions, and other contingent circumstances. This emphasis on ijtihad is unique to Shi'a Islam. While Sunnis allow qualified clerics to practice *qiyas*—judicial reasoning by analogy from recognized sources of law—most Sunni communities have for the last several centuries not allowed ijtihad; for Shi'a, by contrast, there has never been a prohibition on its practice.[54] In the Shi'a world, the special status of those fuqaha recognized as mujtahids has major political ramifications, as important Shi'a thinkers have, since the tenth century, systematically assigned to them all the prerogatives of the imams. Besides the interpretation of religious sources, these prerogatives include powers that, in modern Western parlance, belong to the state—administering justice, collecting taxes, and organizing the defense of the community against external threats.[55]

Apart from being one of the great mujtahids of his time and a grand ayatollah, Khomeini was also a *marja'-e taqlid* ("source of imitation")—a mujtahid whose judgments were considered authoritative by a large number (today, hundreds of thousands if not millions) of followers. Every Shi'a Muslim who is not a mujtahid is supposed to choose a marja' as his or her personal reference in religious matters. As one can glean from the Web sites of currently active *maraji* like Iraq's Grand Ayatollah Sistani, a marja' may advise his followers on a wide range of subjects, from details of prayer and ritual to the sexual practices of married couples to questions of modern medical ethics. But maraji may also issue judgments dealing with social and political affairs—a prerogative that implicitly ascribes a substantial measure of political authority to the most senior and esteemed clergy. These were the traditions that gave Khomeini his unique authority in Iranian society. They also provided him with the intellectual and cultural building blocks for his concept of *velayat-e faqih* ("protectorship by a qualified scholar of religious jurisprudence"), which became the defining feature of the Islamic Republic's political order. Certainly, Khomeini did not invent the idea that the fuqaha are custodians of political authority and thus responsible for political issues; he took it from long-standing Shi'a doctrine.

The concept of clerical nezarat (supervision) was critical to Khomeini's thinking about the place of representative institutions in Islamic governance—another important dimension of the Islamic Republic's political system. Although he never employed the word "democracy," which he associated with secularism and the West, Khomeini nonetheless recognized the importance of popular participation in consultative government. His ideas on this point were informed by the history of relations between the clergy and the modern Iranian state. After the Safavid dynasty made Shi'ism the official religion of a reunified Iran in the sixteenth century, some clerics argued that rule by kings who followed Islamic ordinances as understood in Shi'ism (and who respected the interests and prerogatives of the clergy) was the best possible form of interim government; accordingly, these fuqaha delegated political authority to Safavid monarchs, lauding them as "shadows of God."[56] But the Safavids fell in the first half of the eighteenth century; after a short interregnum, the Qajars assumed dynastic authority in 1785. From then on, arrangements between "turban and crown" came under increasing stress owing to Western penetration, the Qajars' inability to defend Iran's independence, and their concomitant willingness to cut concessionary deals with foreign powers.[57]

In the second half of the nineteenth century, as Iranian clergy debated what to do when a Shi'a state is failing in its duties, some made a quietist argument for protecting clerical interests while eschewing political engagement. Such an argument, though, was based less on religious principle than on a prudential assessment that the standing and prerogatives of the clergy might be put at risk if they became too politically involved. In contrast, other olema worked to limit the shah's executive authority, especially his freedom to make deals with foreign powers, by introducing constitutional government in Iran. With the 1906 Constitutional Revolution, two schools of thought emerged among politically engaged clergy regarding the compatibility of Western-style constitutional government with consultative rule and the primacy of Shari'a. "Legalists" endorsed the institutionalization of checks and balances over the shah's exercise of executive authority (with a major role for senior mujtahids) but rejected the enactment of laws by a civil legislature as inherently contradictory to Shari'a. "Constitutionalists" argued that the investment of substantial legislative as well as executive powers in elected laymen could be consistent (or at least not inconsistent) with Islam.[58]

In his own thinking, Khomeini amalgamated legalist and constitutionalist ideas about consultative government. In his 1941 treatise, *The Revealing of Secrets*, he accepted both monarchical rule and (with greater reservation) parliamentary legislation as compatible with Islam, so long as they operated under clerical supervision: "The government can remain under the control of anyone, but he has to have the authority of the Fuqaha to dispense his authority. . . . Government must be run in accordance with God's law, for the welfare of the country and the people demand this, and it is not feasible except with the supervision of the religious leaders." To this end, he held that a clerical council, composed of "the exalted and just Fuqaha and mullahs," should have "supervision over the legislative and executive branches" of government. At this stage, Khomeini held back from arguing that the fuqaha themselves should govern: "That government and guardianship must be in this time with the fuqaha does not mean that a Faqih should be king." But if the king did not have to be a faqih, the fuqaha should nonetheless be kingmakers, empowered to "deliberate on the election of a sultan for the benefit of the country and the people, and then to choose a just sultan who will respect the laws of Islam, the laws of the land, which are based on divine law."

By the time of his Najaf lectures, thirty years later, the constitutionalist and legalist dimensions of Khomeini's political thinking had matured in ways that would profoundly influence the Islamic Republic's constitution. On the constitutionalist side, he explicitly recognized an elected legislature as one of government's branches, along with the executive and the judiciary; furthermore, he endorsed the formal separation of powers (a formula originated not by Shi'a jurists or earlier Islamic authorities but by Montesquieu, an eighteenth-century Frenchman). At the same time, Khomeini affirmed the legalist argument that "in Islam the legislative power and competence to establish laws belongs exclusively to God Almighty. No one has the right to legislate and no law may be executed except the law of the Divine legislator." Therefore, an elected Majles should be an "agenda-setting" (*barnamehrizi*) body, acting under clerical supervision, rather than a "law-enacting" (*qanungozari*) institution: "In an Islamic government, a simple planning body takes the place of the legislative assembly that is one of the three branches of government. This body draws up programs for the different ministries in the light of the ordinances of Islam and thereby determines how public services are to be provided across the country." Nevertheless, the "planning" functions he assigned to an elected Majles were substantial, including budgeting, oversight, and even the setting of administrative and legal rules on subjects not explicitly addressed by Islamic law.[59]

By the beginning of the 1970s, moreover, Khomeini had concluded that monarchical regimes violate Islam and that Muslims had a duty to end them:

Both law and reason require that we not permit governments to retain this non-Islamic or anti-Islamic character. . . . We have in reality, then, no choice but to destroy those systems of government that are corrupt in themselves and also entail the corruption of others, and to overthrow all treacherous, corrupt, oppressive, and criminal regimes. This is a duty that all Muslims must fulfill, in every one of the Muslim countries, in order to achieve the triumphant political revolution of Islam.[60]

Khomeini's public articulation of a more categorical opposition to monarchical rule was an important development in his political thinking. It set him apart from Grand Ayatollah Seyed Hossein Borourjerdi, who ran the hawza (seminary) in Qom during the decades that Khomeini had spent there and who calculated that, if he were too antagonistic toward Pahlavi rule, the shah might be prompted to act against the hawza's institutional interests. Practically speaking, Khomeini's opposition to monarchy helped justify the campaign to oust the shah. It also had important ramifications for his theory of government—for, while he stopped short of saying so in Najaf, the rejection of monarchy and the embrace of separated powers implied acceptance of an elected chief executive along with an elected parliament.

In his Najaf lectures, Khomeini extrapolated from his premise that government is ultimately in the hands of the fuqaha to argue that only they could rightfully exercise political authority:

> If the ruler adheres to Islam, he must necessarily submit to the Faqih, asking him about the laws and ordinances of Islam in order to implement them. This being the case, the true rulers are the Fuqaha themselves, and rulership ought officially to be theirs, to apply to them, not to those who are obliged to follow the guidance of the Fuqaha.[61]

This argument provides the foundation for Khomeini's concept of clerical guardianship, velayat-e faqih:

> Since Islamic government is a government of law, those acquainted with the law, or more precisely, with religion—i.e., the Fuqaha—must supervise its functioning. It is they who supervise all executive and administrative affairs of the country, together with all planning. The Fuqaha are the trustees who implement the divine ordinances in levying taxes, guarding the frontiers, and executing the penal provisions of the law.[62]

Khomeini suggested that "the highest authority" be exercised by a singularly qualified faqih possessing two essential traits—"comprehensive knowledge" of "the provisions and ordinances of Islam" and "justice," meaning "excellence in belief and morals." Such a "just Faqih" would "possess the same authority" as the Prophet "in the administration of society, and it will be the duty of all people to obey him."[63]

While Khomeini's political ideas, including clerical guardianship, have never enjoyed universal acceptance among senior Shi'a clerics, the number of maraji who have explicitly rejected them is small—and, contrary to American neoconservative legend, does not include Sistani. Since Saddam's overthrow, no Iraqi cleric of prominence has challenged the Islamic Republic's legitimacy. Though neoconservatives depict Sistani as a "steady rebuke to the Iranian establishment," the record since March 2003 suggests that if he has been a steady rebuke to anything, it is to the American occupation of Iraq.[64] Sistani has opened a large office in Qom and Iranians who have met him on pilgrimages to Najaf report that he expresses great satisfaction with Iran's development as a genuinely independent state since 1979. In Iran, Khomeini's ideas have enjoyed widespread—not unanimous but widespread—support among the clergy and have been consistently endorsed by a majority of Iranians as the basis for their political order.

FRAMING THE ISLAMIC REPUBLIC

More than any other source, Khomeini's political thought provided the raw material from which the constitution of the Islamic Republic was fashioned. However, when the Imam returned home, it was neither clear nor predetermined how a new order would embody the various elements in his theory of government. Iran was going to have a system that integrated Islamic principles and practices with popular representation, but the specific contours of that system were still to be defined. At every critical juncture in this process, Khomeini displayed caution, tactical acumen, and the ability to marshal clear majoritarian support; his adversaries, for their part, displayed the opposite qualities.

As Iran's revolutionary transition got under way, the Imam sought to embrace as many elements opposed to the shah as possible; with

Khomeini's approval, Bazargan staffed his cabinet almost entirely with figures from the Liberation Movement, the National Front, and other secular parties. The Imam judged that the new Islamic Republic needed the technocratic expertise these parties could offer. For that reason he was initially prepared to accept a constitution that did not explicitly include velayat-e faqih, even though it was a major element of his political thinking and, from the time of his return to Iran, he exercised precisely this kind of authority. The draft constitution Khomeini had brought from France had many features immediately comprehensible to anyone familiar with Western (especially French) constitutionalism, including the separation of powers across three branches of government. With regard to Islamic governance, it provided for clerical supervision (nezarat) through a supervisory council of mujtahids, but not for clerical guardianship (velayat). Once the provisional revolutionary government was in place, this document was reviewed by a panel reporting to Bazargan; following the Islamic Republic's establishment on April 1, 1979, a revised text, which still did not make any reference to velayat-e faqih, was published as the "official" draft constitution.[65]

Extending the "hijacked revolution" narrative, secularists (or their scholarly acolytes) who failed in their campaign to displace Khomeini's Islamist agenda argue that the omission of velayat-e faqih from the draft constitution was a deliberate deception, meant to deceive non-Islamists into supporting the revolution by disguising its ultimate goals.[66] Such claims do not stand up to scrutiny; in reality it was the secularists who were trying, without popular support, to hijack the constitutional process. Khomeini had been speaking and writing on politics for four decades before the revolution; his views, including his advocacy of Islamic government, were well known. Even after the March 1979 referendum confirmed strong support for an Islamic republic, he was still prepared to accept a constitution without explicit references to velayat-e faqih. In accordance with statements made during his French exile, he also barred clergy from taking posts in the interim government (though his clerical allies remained active in the Revolutionary Council). Those secularists who today bemoan velayat-e faqih could have had a constitution that did not include it. Instead, when the official draft was published, they agitated to eliminate all of its Islamist components; while the Iranian people had opted for an Islamic republic, non-Islamists remained determined to create a secular state.[67] It was only in the face of the secularists' obdurate defiance of political reality that Khomeini brought velayat-e faqih into the constitutional debate.

As secularists mounted their campaign in the spring and summer of 1979, Khomeini marshaled the clergy, urging them not to "sit back while 'foreignized' intellectuals, who have no faith in Islam, give their views and write the things they write. Pick up your pens and in the mosques, from the altars, in the streets and bazaars, speak of the things that in your view should be included in the constitution." While some prominent clerics opposed velayat-e faqih, most did not; in response to Khomeini's exhortations, clerical societies and a number of leading olema launched a public campaign to include it in the new constitution. In August 1979, Iranians turned out in huge numbers to elect delegates to the Assembly for the Final Examination of the Constitution of the Islamic Republic of Iran.[68] Of the seventy-two delegates elected, fifty-five were olema who had declared their support for "the Imam's line."[69]

After this body drafted a new text that incorporated velayat-e faqih, tensions between the Imam and religious liberals increased; the situation deteriorated further when Bazargan and several cabinet members resigned over the seizure of the American embassy in Tehran.[70] The public, though, maintained support for Khomeini—a reality that expatriate scholars either ignore or try to explain away as a liberal version of what Friedrich Engels derided as workers' "false consciousness" regarding their class interests.[71] In a referendum held on December 2 and 3, 1979, the new constitution was approved by 98 percent of participating voters. Its first article announced that "the form of government of Iran is that of an Islamic Republic, endorsed by the people of Iran on the basis of their long-standing belief in the sovereignty of truth and Qur'anic justice, after the victorious Islamic Revolution led by the eminent marja'-e taqlid Grand Ayatollah Imam Khomeini, in the referendum" of March 29 and 30, 1979.

The constitution reflects the mix of constitutionalist, legalist, and clerical elements in Khomeini's theory of Islamic government. In a quintessentially legalist declaration, it proclaims that "absolute sovereignty over the world and man" belongs to God. But the text continues, in a more constitutionalist vein, that "it is He Who has placed man in charge of his social destiny. No one can deprive man of this God-given right, nor subordinate it to the interests of a given individual or group." Stating that its purpose is to spell out "the paths" by which "the people exercise this God-given right," the document asserts that "the powers of government in the Islamic Republic consist of the legislative, the judiciary, and the executive," which are "independent of each other," and that "the affairs of the country must be administered on the basis of public opinion expressed by means of elections." From these premises, substantial legislative and executive authority is vested in elected officials, without requiring that any of them be clerics.

Citing the Qur'an to justify making "consultative bodies" the "decision-making and administrative organs of the country," the constitution sets up a Majles, or parliament—initially the National Consultative Assembly, later renamed the Islamic Consultative Assembly.[72] The Majles is empowered to "establish laws on all matters" so long as they do not violate Islamic ordinances or the constitution. It is also authorized to ratify treaties, approve ministerial appointments, exercise oversight over "all affairs of the country," remove ministers, and impeach the president. Currently, the Majles has 290 seats, elected en bloc to four-year terms. Slightly more than half the seats are from geographically defined single-seat districts. In large cities with multiple seats, residents can vote on all of them (in Tehran, for example, citizens cast their ballots for up to thirty seats). Five seats are allocated to Iran's Christian, Zoroastrian, and Jewish communities.

Regarding executive authority, the text states that "after the leader, the president is the highest official in the country. His is the responsibility for implementing the constitution and acting as the head of the executive, except in matters directly concerned with the office of the leadership." The president is elected to a four-year term; an incumbent may stand for reelection but may not serve more than two consecutive terms.

Alongside these institutions and offices, which seem familiar to Westerners, the constitution creates another set, which Westerners find more bewildering (and, in many cases, off-putting). These reflect the clerical dimensions of Khomeini's political thought, culminating in velayat-e faqih. In keeping with the Imam's advocacy of a supervisory council of mujtahids, the constitution creates the Council of Guardians, with a mandate "to protect the ordinances of Islam and the constitution by assuring that legislation passed by the Majles does not conflict with them"—meaning that the guardians are there not just to protect Shari'a but also (like the U.S. Supreme Court) to protect the constitution itself.[73] The council has twelve members, including "six just fuqaha, conscious of current needs and the issues of the day," selected by the supreme leader, and six other jurists, "specializing in different areas of the law, to be elected by the Majles from among the Muslim jurists presented to it" by the leadership of the judiciary. The council reviews "all legislation passed by the Majles" for "compatibility with the criteria of Islam and the constitution."[74] It also supervises national elections; this responsibility includes the vetting of potential candidates by evaluating their faithfulness to Islam and their loyalty to the Islamic Republic.

The constitution further states that, as long as the Mahdi remains absent, "the governance and leadership of the nation devolve upon the just and pious faqih" who is "recognized and accepted as leader (*rahbar*) by the majority of the people." The phrase "leader of the revolution" (*rahbar-e enqelab*, customarily if also somewhat inaccurately rendered in English as "supreme leader") became the official title for the "just and pious faqih" chosen to serve as *vali-ye faqih*— that is, the executor of velayat-e faqih.[75] The powers of the supreme leader are formidable, encompassing functions normally assigned to a head of state or head of government: "appointment of the [six] fuqaha on the Guardian Council"; "appointment of the supreme judicial authority"; "supreme command of the armed forces" (including the regular military and the Revolutionary Guards); "declarations of war and peace"; "dismissal of the president of the republic" following either a parliamentary vote of impeachment or a judicial judgment that an incumbent is failing to discharge his legal duties; and "pardoning or reducing the sentences of convicts."

After the constitution was ratified, Khomeini continued trying to preserve a measure of unity with non-Islamists. He prohibited clerics from running in the January 1980 presidential election, effectively barring the Islamic Republican Party from fielding any of its most popular figures as a candidate; this interdict, in turn, paved the way for the Liberation Movement's Abolhassan Bani-Sadr (a noncleric) to become the Islamic Republic's first elected president. Two months later, though, elections for the first Majles under the new constitution revealed the real balance of support between the Imam and his adversaries: out of 247 seats contested, IRP candidates captured 130; the Liberation Movement won only 20, with the National Front and other parties taking even smaller numbers. The MEK won no seats at all.

Still, secularists continued to contest the Islamic Republic's Islamist character. For most of them, this challenge took purely political, nonviolent forms; for others, including the MEK and some ethnic separatists, it came to include terrorist violence and collaboration with Iran's enemies. Either way, the opponents of velayat-e faqih had picked a fight they could only lose. Those who stuck to the political process could not marshal sufficient public support to prevail against the Imam; those, like the MEK, who resorted to violence as the Islamic Republic struggled to defend itself against the Iraqi invasion saw their popular base quickly shrink to negligible levels.

By 1982, the defeat of those who wanted to roll back the idea and reality of Iran as a velayat-e faqih state was clear. Bani-Sadr had been impeached and forced into exile.[76] Other political figures who opposed key aspects of the new constitutional framework, including some who had held high office in Bazargan's cabinet and Bani-Sadr's administration, had either left the country or been put on trial for seeking to overthrow the Islamic Republic (and, in a few cases, for plotting to assassinate Khomeini). A number of those so accused were executed, as were others caught up in the government's crackdown on the MEK.

The most prominent clerical critic of velayat-e faqih, Grand Ayatollah Seyed Mohammad Kazem Shariatmadari, was placed under house arrest and, by some accounts, stripped of his status as a marja' over his alleged support for bringing down the new order.[77] Western and expatriate detractors of the Islamic Republic point to these cases as proof of an illegitimate regime's determination to silence its internal critics; the Islamic Republic and its supporters hold that the government responded appropriately to those who (like the MEK) had gone beyond acting as dissidents to become—during wartime—enemies of the state.

As the new political order consolidated, it became more clerical in composition. When Bani-Sadr's successor, Mohammad-Ali Rajai, was assassinated by the MEK in August 1981, Khomeini dropped his opposition to clerics as presidential candidates, enabling Seyed Ali Khamenei's election to the presidency later that year.[78] Over time, clerics assumed more cabinet positions, establishing a de facto hold over several key portfolios, including intelligence and interior.

———

In the succeeding years, Khomeini realized that the constitutional framework he had done so much to shape needed revision. Six weeks before he died, he created the Assembly for the Reappraisal of the Constitution; the amendments it recommended were approved in a popular referendum on July 28, 1989, just seven weeks after his death.[79] These changes affected the constitutional order in three main ways. First, the executive branch was reorganized. Initially, executive powers had been divided, in the French manner, between a directly elected president and a prime minister named by him and approved by the Majles; with Khamenei as president and the leftist Mir-Hossein Mousavi as prime minister for much of the 1980s, this arrangement proved dysfunctional. So the revised constitution abolished the prime minister's post, unifying executive authority in the presidency. Since then, the president has been empowered to appoint, supervise, and dismiss ministers; sign treaties with foreign governments and international organizations and appoint ambassadors; and oversee "national planning and budget." The revisions further bolstered the presidency by authorizing its holder to appoint vice presidents and to chair the new Supreme National Security Council.

Second, the 1989 changes incorporated a new body—the Expediency Council—into the constitutional order. Besides chronic disputes within the executive branch, political life in the Islamic Republic's first decade was marked by frequent impasses between the Majles and the Guardian Council over legislation. So in 1988 Khomeini had created the Expediency Council to adjudicate such disputes. The revisions formalized this role; they also made the council an advisory agency for the supreme leader, directing it to "meet for consideration on any issue forwarded to it by the leader," who appoints its members.[80]

Third, the constitutional changes clarified the authority of and selection process for the supreme leader. They added to the leader's specified powers the authority "to issue decrees for national referenda" and to appoint the head of the Islamic Republic's state broadcasting network. More broadly, they spelled out, for a post-Khomeini context, the leader's responsibility for "delineation of the general policies of the Islamic Republic of Iran" and for "supervision over the proper execution of the general policies of the system."

With regard to selection, the original version of the constitution specified two "qualifications and attributes of the leader": first, "suitability with respect to learning and piety, as required for the functions of [a] marja'"; second, "political and social perspicacity, courage, strength, and the necessary administrative abilities for leadership." It further noted that when, as with Khomeini, "one of the fuqaha possessing the qualifications specified . . . is recognized and accepted as marja' and leader by a decisive majority of the people," he should be supreme leader. If no individual commanded this level of popular support, "experts elected by the people" would choose a single candidate with "outstanding capacity for leadership" or else "appoint either three or five marja's" as "members of a leadership council." In 1985, the first such Assembly of Experts named Grand Ayatollah Hossein-Ali Montazeri—a former Khomeini student who had become a marja' in his own right, supported the revolution, and been one of the most prominent clerical voices in the 1979 campaign to include velayat-e faqih in the constitution—as the Imam's deputy and heir apparent.[81]

Before his death in 1989, however, Khomeini seems to have thought more strategically about his succession. By 1988, mounting disagreements with Montazeri prompted the Imam to begin consulting with the Assembly of Experts about Montazeri's suitability to become supreme leader. Khomeini also appears to have become concerned that the next leader have exceptional political skills. During its deliberations, the Assembly for the Reappraisal of the Constitution asked for and received the Imam's blessing to drop the requirement that the leader be a marja' and to dispense with the option of a leadership council. These changes opened the way for Ayatollah Khamenei—who, as noted, had acquired considerable experience in matters of state by 1989—to succeed Khomeini. (While Khamenei was recognized as a mujtahid and there is evidence he was already acknowledged as an ayatollah in some quarters, he lacked standing as a marja'.)[82] The revisions also gave the Assembly of Experts supervisory authority over the leader, including the power to dismiss an incumbent who "becomes incapable of fulfilling his constitutional duties or loses one of the qualifications" for office. Currently, the assembly has eighty-six seats, distributed across Iran's thirty-one provinces by population. Members are elected en bloc to eight-year terms; candidates must be approved by the Guardian Council as experts in *fiqh* (religious jurisprudence).

The Islamic Republic's constitution reflects the commitment of Khomeini and those who followed him to create a genuinely independent state that would realize Iranians' aspirations for a participatory political order grounded in explicitly Islamic principles and practices. It achieves this goal by juxtaposing familiar republican institutions with institutions charged with ensuring that the government, its laws, and its policies are in line with Islamic precepts. In evaluating these arrangements, Western commentators frequently describe the Islamic Republic as a "dual polity," with elected officials competing with unelected but constitutionally privileged officials and bodies for influence over policy.

Clerics, officials, politicians, and scholars in Iran dispute this charac-
terization. While some important positions and bodies in the political
order are not directly elected, all are popularly accountable in some
fashion. Thus, the leader is not directly elected but is chosen by the
Assembly of Experts, which is directly elected to an eight-year term
and constitutionally mandated to oversee him. Likewise, the Guardian
Council is not elected, but half its members are named by the popularly elected Majles, the other half by the leader.

The constitutionalist aspects of Khomeini's theory of government
have been essential to the Islamic Republic's legitimacy. A crucial
dimension of Khomeini's vision is the balance it draws between constitutionalism and legalism, allowing the system to hold what mainstream
Iranian opinion considers extreme religious and secular views at bay
while allowing a substantial degree of political competition. To this
day, there are legalist clerics (usually described by Western media as
"ultraconservative") who disdain the constitution's republican components as deviating from purely clerical rule. They have not, however,
been able to eliminate electoral competition from the system. While that
competition takes place among candidates who accept the constitutional framework, including velayat-e faqih, it is both real and robust.
The result, as a regular commenter on our blog recently suggested, is a
democratic order "of the Shi'a, by the Shi'a, and for the Shi'a"—but
with constitutional guarantees for Jews, Christians, Zoroastrians, and
non-Shi'a Muslims.

Americans and other Westerners have criticized the Islamic Republic, virtually from its inception, as an illiberal and therefore illegitimate state. But their criticisms overlook the reality that most of its
people do not want to live in a Western-style secular democracy. However much Westerners and Iranian expatriates may wish it were otherwise, Khomeini and his associates had the backing of a strong majority
of Iranians at every major juncture in their efforts to create a postrevolutionary political order. And in the experience of most Iranians
who continue to live in their country, the Islamic Republic has made
significant progress toward the integration of Islamic governance and
participatory politics. As one defender of the system puts it:

The overwhelming majority of Iranians believe that Islamic republi-
canism and Velayat-e Faqih lead to a better society—or, at least, are
preferable to secular liberal democracy. The evidence for this is long-
term election participation rates in the Islamic Republic, election victories for candidates who affirm [its] principles, the political discourse
in which candidates appeal to voters by stressing their Islamic and
republican credentials. The advocates of secular liberal democracy
have for over 100 years been predicting the secularization of Iranians. It has only happened in parts of the elite. Many elites and the
majority of Iranians have not turned away from Islam and from seeing Islam as the basis of the organization of their personal, social,
and political life.[83]

Indeed, many of our Iranian interlocutors contend that the Guardian
Council's vetting process produces a wider range of choice for Iranian voters than the United States' two-party system offers American
voters; in particular, they argue that the Iranian system allows genuine outsiders—for example, Mohammad Khatami and Mahmoud
Ahmadinejad—to compete on an equal footing, rare in Western political systems. Empirically, the Islamic Republic has significantly higher
voter participation rates than the United States and higher or comparable rates relative to most other Western democracies.

DELIVERING A BETTER LIFE

Besides the integration of Islamic governance and participatory politics, an important part of Khomeini's revolutionary vision was the
pursuit of economic and social development. Like the proposition that
the Islamic Republic is a legitimate political system, the notion that it
is a "developmental state" flies in the face of Western stereotypes of a
society too deeply marked by financial corruption and religiously
driven social repression to offer any tangible prospect of improved
lives. Since shortly after the revolution, fictions of this sort have been
abundantly available for Western consumption. Expatriates like Jahangir Amuzegar (a former minister of commerce and finance under

the shah) and Westerners with their own animus against the Islamic Republic have made a cottage industry out of sounding the alarm that the Iranian economy is mired in crisis and may even have entered a "death spiral." Patrick Clawson—for many years the director of research at the Washington Institute for Near East Policy—has been writing about the Iranian economy's looming demise since 1981, when he published an article subtitled "Between Crisis and Collapse."[84]

But while Khomeini famously said that the Iranian Revolution was not about the price of melons, he hardly fit the caricature—still relentlessly promulgated in the West—of a leader indifferent to economic matters. In his 1970 Najaf lectures, he charged that non-Islamic government had created an "unjust economic order" that divided people "into two groups: oppressors [mostakbarin] and oppressed [mostazafin]"; the Islamic Republic's constitution takes this argument to the next level by identifying the creation of a just economic system as a requirement of Islam. In postrevolutionary Iran, positive economic development and social change have been achieved by anchoring them in religion, not by pursuing them in opposition to it. The revolution's explicitly religious aspects have enabled the Islamic Republic to achieve far more progressive outcomes in alleviating poverty, delivering health care, providing educational access, and many other areas of social policy—including the expansion of opportunities for women—than the shah's regime did. And, in political terms, the progressively better life that the Islamic Republic has delivered to its population has reinforced its legitimacy.

Here are some basic statistics. Since the end of the Iran-Iraq War, the country has posted positive GDP growth every year except two (1993 and 1994), according to the Central Intelligence Agency, the International Monetary Fund (IMF), and other international sources. While inflation has been chronically high during much of the Islamic Republic's history—as it has been for other major energy producers, both in and beyond the Persian Gulf—it has seen real, adjusted-for-inflation growth. Over the past decade, with rising oil prices, this growth has accelerated, averaging over 5 percent a year in real terms; this figure would surely have been higher but for the worldwide economic downturn that started in 2007, a corresponding drop in oil prices, and a more or less simultaneous effort by the Central Bank of Iran to restrict credit in order to lower inflation (an effort that cut the inflation rate in half, roughly from 25 to 12 percent). But even with the global financial crisis, the Iranian economy never went into recession.[85] The imposition of more stringent international sanctions against the Islamic Republic since 2008 has put additional constraints on economic growth. But a return to higher oil prices since the end of 2008 cushioned the impact of sanctions. While the most recent U.S. and EU sanctions have reduced Iran's oil exports, they have also helped keep oil prices higher than would otherwise be the case, so that the Islamic Republic continues to earn substantial revenues from oil sales.[86] (We discuss the evolution of U.S. sanctions policy in greater depth in part 3.) Starting in late 2011, sanctions-related devaluation of Iran's currency pushed inflation up again, especially on imports. But the government used this as an opening to focus its disbursement of foreign exchange on high-priority imports (like food and medicine, for which the officially administered dollar exchange rate has not dropped significantly) and to encourage greater consumption of domestically produced goods. In the long run, this should strengthen the Iranian economy and further reduce its vulnerability to U.S.-organized sanctions.

Though Iran remains dependent on oil exports as its economic mainstay, it has done a better job at cultivating the non-oil sectors of its economy than have other Persian Gulf energy producers. Its non-oil exports are rising rapidly, even in the face of tighter sanctions.[87] Iran has achieved or is approaching self-sufficiency in a growing number of basic industrial sectors, including steel, copper and copper products, paper and paper products, and cement. Using these primary industrial inputs, it has become largely self-sufficient in the manufacture of various types of industrial machinery (including many of the compressors, pipes, pumps, and related devices required by its oil, gas, and petrochemical industries), electronic components, pharmaceuticals and medical supplies, and telecommunications equipment. It has the largest stock of industrial robots in West Asia and a well-developed automobile industry that is beginning to export to neighboring markets.

It can be argued that economic growth in Iran would have been higher with a different set of economic (and foreign) policies. But to claim there has been no growth since the revolution or that the Iranian economy is collapsing is simply false. Today, the Islamic Republic has the twenty-fifth-largest economy in the world according to the CIA and the IMF.[88] With a per capita income of roughly $11,000—comparable to that of Brazil, South Africa, and several former communist states in Central and Eastern Europe—its status as a middle-income developing country is well established. To criticize it for not having a per capita income as high as that in other Persian Gulf oil-producing states is profoundly misleading, for it equates the challenge of distributing or investing oil wealth in Iran, which has 75 million citizens, with the situation in Saudi Arabia, where there are only 18 million Saudi nationals; Kuwait, which has only 1.3 million Kuwaiti nationals; the United Arab Emirates, where there are barely a million Emirati nationals; or Qatar, where less than 200,000 people hold Qatari citizenship.

Moreover, counterhistorical criticisms of the Islamic Republic's economic policy overlook its actual priorities with regard to economic development. Khomeini told Iranians that he wanted the revolution to improve their "material lives" as well as their "spiritual lives." He made clear his commitment to material progress, especially for the majority whose economic standing had improved little if at all under the shah. Among the revolution's unique features was to identify the mostazafin (the dispossessed) as one of its major intended beneficiaries, without restricting to particular classes those whose material condition was to be raised—the practice of most socialist revolutions. To fulfill this commitment, the Islamic Republic—during Khomeini's lifetime, but even more since the Iran-Iraq War—has made large and sustained investments to extend modern infrastructure (roads, electricity, piped water, and now the Internet) into rural and low-income urban areas across Iran. The result has been a sharp and well-documented reduction in poverty. Today the percentage of Iranians living in poverty—less than 2 percent by the World Bank's $1.25-per-day standard—is lower than that in virtually any other large-population middle-income country (including Brazil, China, Egypt, India, Mexico, Pakistan, South Africa, Turkey, and Venezuela).[89]

As part of its commitment to improving material conditions for the mostazafin, the Islamic Republic created and has steadily expanded a nationwide system of hospitals and primary care clinics, focusing largely on deprived areas, and has reinforced this investment with an array of other public health initiatives. Now Iranians of all classes, but especially lower-income groups, can point to substantial increases in life expectancy and substantial decreases in infant and child mortality; according to the United Nations Development Programme (UNDP), between 1980 and 2011 life expectancy in Iran increased by 21.9 years.[90] The provision of health care to rural areas has been particularly successful.[91] These results have prompted other countries to study the Islamic Republic's system as a model for improving their own services. State universities and nongovernmental organizations in Mississippi, for example, are working with the Shiraz University of Medical Sciences and the University of Tehran's School of Public Health to introduce Iranian-style health care delivery into medically underserved parts of the Mississippi Delta.[92]

The Islamic Republic has made a similarly sustained effort to expand educational opportunities. Notwithstanding the challenge of a young and rapidly growing population, its commitment to universal primary and secondary education has brought greatly expanded access for the poor along with a steadily rising average number of years of schooling completed. It has also resulted in greater female participation, with the Islamic Republic now, according to the World Bank, "well placed to achieve the [United Nations' Millennium Development Goals] target with regard to eliminating gender disparities" in educational access.[93] Since 1979, the youth literacy rate has nearly doubled; among women, it has more than tripled.[94] On top of this, the Islamic Republic has dramatically increased access to higher education.[95] These gains bolster popular perceptions that the system has delivered important economic and social benefits; as one of our interlocutors notes, at the time of the revolution "60 percent of Iranians were illiterate and 100 percent royal subjects," while "today 99 percent are literate and 100 percent get to vote for the President, their local Majles members, their local councils, and members of the Khobregan [Assembly of Experts] who appoint the Supreme Leader."[96]

Overall, the UNDP reports that Iran's Human Development Index value—"a summary measure for assessing long-term progress in three basic dimensions of human development: a long and healthy life, access to knowledge and a decent standard of living"—rose from 0.437 in 1980 to 0.707 in 2011, placing the Islamic Republic in the "high human development category."[97] One facet of this progress remains especially unappreciated in the West: the way that access to higher education is altering the status of Iranian women. While the Islamic Republic places restrictions on women (in matters of dress, for example, and access to some public events and services) that many Westerners would consider unacceptable, the majority of university students in Iran are now female, the majority of students at Iran's best universities are now female, and women's presence is increasingly being felt across an array of academic and professional disciplines—for example, the majority of Iran's medical students are now female.

The educational success of Iranian women has even prompted the initiation of what in the United States would be described as "affirmative action" programs for men at a number of Iranian universities. In 2012, the *New York Times* claimed that "thirty-six universities in Iran have banned women from seventy-seven fields of study," including accounting, chemistry, virtually all forms of engineering, and mathematics.[98] The story was factually inaccurate and misleadingly written; the University of Tehran, for example, barred women from two faculties—mining engineering and forestry—reportedly because female graduates were not going to work in these fields, where there are shortages of appropriately trained practitioners. We, of course, oppose any restrictions on educational access for women; we also recognize that there are political elements in the Islamic Republic who want to segregate Iranian universities by gender—something that Imam Khomeini rejected. But the current debate in Iran about enrolling women in particular faculties at particular universities is not a reflexively misogynistic exercise; it is at least in part a product of the enormous educational gains achieved by Iranian women since the revolution.

More broadly, a look at evolving conditions for Iranian women should put an end to facile generalizations about "progressive" Pahlavi rule versus a "backward" Islamic Republic. Under the shah, women were technically free from the veil and other formal restrictions on their behavior—an image of Iran that *Foreign Policy* magazine celebrated in a 2011 photo essay, while neglecting to inform readers that powerful social forces kept most women in prerevolutionary Iran from pursuing educational and career opportunities.[99] Today women in the Islamic Republic are legally required to cover themselves. But the biggest advances in the educational, professional, and social standing of women in Iran's history have come since the revolution, as a result of legal and policy initiatives undertaken by the Islamic Republic. Besides having ever greater educational and professional opportunities (one can even see female bus and taxi drivers in Tehran), women vote and are increasingly represented in the Iranian government. There are also far fewer restrictions on their leisure pursuits. The first two Muslim women to climb Mount Everest (in 2005) were Iranian.[100]

Official policy seeks, in multiple ways, to support women who are balancing careers with family life. By law, Iranian women are guaranteed six months of paid maternity leave, plus one hour per day paid leave for eighteen months after that—standards that exceed the International Labour Organization's guidelines for women with formal employment and that the United States and several other Western nations do not meet. On women's issues the Islamic Republic is well ahead of most of its neighbors, including two American allies, Saudi Arabia and post-Taliban Afghanistan. But broader comparisons are also revealing: a peer-reviewed study by Iranian and Scandinavian researchers found that the Islamic Republic has both better policies to promote breastfeeding and higher breastfeeding rates than many European Union countries. Another peer-reviewed study, by Australian researchers, concluded that breastfeeding rates are significantly higher in Iran than in Australia, partly because of superior maternity leave and workplace policies.[101]

Other aspects of social policy in the Islamic Republic belie Western stereotypes. While the judicial system vigorously applies the death penalty to drug dealers and traffickers, Iran's approach to dealing with drug addicts is, by international standards, highly medicalized. The Islamic Republic does not tolerate open manifestations of gay identity and culture; nor does it tolerate many manifestations of heterosexual culture (for example, singles' bars) that are commonplace in the West. Nevertheless, Iran has one of the more developed AIDS research and treatment programs in the non-Western world. Rulings from Khomeini recognizing transgendered identity as biologically grounded today provide the legal basis for free elective gender-reassignment surgery.[102]

The Islamic Republic is delivering on its promise of modernization and progress in other ways as well. Since the mid-1990s, for example, increased investment in scientific and technological research in Iranian universities and institutes has produced a remarkable burst of cutting-edge work in a wide range of fields. Measured by the number of technical papers published by Iranian researchers in internationally recognized, refereed journals—up from seven hundred in 1978 to twenty thousand in 2011—and other indices, Iran has the fastest rate of growth in scientific output of any country in the world.[103] The Islamic Republic now ranks among the top ten countries worldwide in stem cell and cloning research; it ranks among the top twenty countries in chemisty, computer sciences, mathematics, medicine, and nanotechnology. In the nuclear field, too, progress has been impressive. And investment in the sciences is translating into the development of high-tech industries, including biotechnology and nanotechnology.

———

Most Westerners are unaware of the extent of progress in post-revolutionary Iran. As a result, they cling to the myth of the Islamic Republic's illegitimacy, looking vainly for another Iranian revolution that, to say the least, is not on the horizon. In the following chapter, we explore in closer detail just how the political system crafted by Khomeini works to deliver on its promise of integrating participatory politics with religious principles.

5

A LEADER AND THREE PRESIDENTS

Islam is the main component and the spirit of religious democracy. . . . The experience we have gained over the past 33 years has shown that Islam can bring about dignity and honor for a nation. It can specify good goals and it can also prepare the way for achieving these goals. It can give rise to a scientific movement. It can give rise to a technological and industrial movement. It can give rise to a religious and ethical movement. It can make a nation feel proud in front of other nations.

        —Ayatollah Seyed Ali Khamenei, March 8, 2012

Consider two election-night scenes in Tehran, eight years apart. The first fell on May 23, 1997, when a clergyman named Seyed Mohammad Khatami burst into the world's consciousness by winning the election to succeed Ali Akbar Hashemi Rafsanjani as president of the Islamic Republic, taking almost 70 percent of the vote. Khatami's victory surprised not just Western analysts but much of Iran's political establishment, belying Western stereotypes of Iranian elections as uncompetitive exercises in authoritarian selection.

Born in 1943, Khatami was fifty-four years old at the time of his election, making him almost a full generation younger than Khamenei and Rafsanjani. Like Khomeini and Khamenei (and unlike Rafsanjani), he was a seyed, a descendant of the Prophet Muhammad. Khatami's father, Ruhollah, was a distinguished ayatollah who, decades before the revolution, had been a beloved teacher of the young Khamenei; after the revolution, Khomeini personally appointed Seyed

Ruhollah as his official representative and Friday prayer leader in Yazd, the Khatamis' hometown. Mohammad Khatami was himself a Qom-trained cleric, certified as a mujtahid. But he had also been educated in Western philosophy and spent several years before the revolution living in Germany, where he headed an Islamic study center in Hamburg.

Returning home after the revolution, Khatami was elected to the Islamic Republic's first Majles in 1980 and served two stints as minister of culture and Islamic guidance during the 1980s and early 1990s. During this period, his advocacy of intellectual and cultural pluralism antagonized conservative clerics and politicians. As long as Khomeini was alive, Khatami enjoyed the Imam's support.[1] Once Khomeini was gone, though, Khatami came under increasing political pressure. He finally resigned from the cabinet in 1992, at which point he became the head of the National Library. Five years later, Khatami's reappearance on the national stage, at the highest level of elective office and commanding what seemed to be broad public support, was widely taken to mark the arrival of the Islamic Republic's so-called reform movement as a major political force.[2] And that movement spoke a language the West was bound to find attractive, emphasizing respect for civil society, stronger rule of law, and the cultivation of what Khatami liked to call "Islamic democracy."

Now, fast forward eight years, to June 24, 2005, when Iranians witnessed another surprise election outcome. On that day, Mahmoud Ahmadinejad—a newcomer to national politics, whose highest-profile experience had been two years as mayor of Tehran—won the mandate to succeed Khatami as the Islamic Republic's president, capturing two-thirds of the vote in a second-round runoff and trouncing his opponent, former president Rafsanjani, by a two-to-one margin. Like Khatami, Ahmadinejad seemed, in many respects, an "accidental president." He also seemed as different from Khatami as night from day.

Born in 1956, Ahmadinejad was young enough to be Khomeini's grandson or the son of Rafsanjani and other members of the Islamic Republic's founding generation. Unlike them, he was neither a cleric nor a member of a clerical family; his origins, in fact, could hardly have been humbler. Born in a backwater town roughly seventy miles southeast of Tehran, he was the son of decidedly working-class parents who relocated to one of the poorer parts of the Iranian capital when he was just a boy. The family name was Sabaghian, meaning "dye masters," referring to those who dyed the woolen threads used to make carpets; before moving his wife and children to Tehran, the future president's father changed Sabaghian to a name that would not advertise the family's village background—Ahmadinejad, "of Ahmad's line."[3] (Ahmad is a traditional Muslim name derived from the Arabic *hamd*, meaning the praise that the pious accord to God.) By all accounts highly intelligent, Ahmadinejad was the first in his family to pursue higher education, doing well enough on Iran's competitive national examination for university admissions to win a place at the Iran University of Science and Technology (IUST). A supporter of the revolution, he became one of Iran's more important student leaders in the Islamic Republic's early days though, as noted earlier, he did not take part in the capture of the American embassy in November 1979, contrary to the claims of some Western journalists.

After receiving his undergraduate degree in engineering, Ahmadinejad began his political career as a provincial official in West Azerbaijan before serving in the Iran-Iraq War as part of the Basij paramilitary apparatus.[4] Following the war, he resumed political work, rising to become governor of the Azeri-majority province of Ardabil in 1993 and holding the post until the newly inaugurated President Khatami removed him four years later. Along the way, he earned master's and doctoral degrees in civil engineering and transportation from IUST, where he also taught.[5] In 2003, a coalition of conservative political groups and constituencies that Ahmadinejad had helped assemble won control of Tehran's city council. Tehran's mayor is not elected directly but appointed by the elected city council; with a conservative majority now in control, the council appointed Ahmadinejad. It was from this position that he competed for the presidency two years later. Just as Khatami's election in 1997 marked the arrival of reformists at the highest levels of Iranian political life,

Ahmadinejad's election in 2005 marked a resurgence of their ideological opposites—the conservatives, or, "principlists."[6] It also marked the advent of a new generation of top-tier players on the conservative side of Iranian politics.

Westerners' interpretations of these seemingly disparate electoral outcomes, separated by less than a decade, are distorted by their largely unquestioned assumption that Iran is inevitably headed toward liberal democracy. As a result, they tend to overestimate what Khatami's presidency said about the Islamic Republic's political trajectory and to underestimate what Ahmadinejad's rise signifies. Instead of starting from such a premise, we must look at the dynamics that actually drive the Islamic Republic's political life and consider how Iran's postrevolutionary order legitimates itself. And that means looking, first of all, at the way Ayatollah Khamenei has handled his role since succeeding Imam Khomeini as supreme leader.

KHOMEINI'S HEIRS AND FACTIONAL POLITICS

It would not have been easy for anyone to follow Khomeini, the Islamic Republic's founding father and a towering political and theological authority. It was certainly not easy for Khamenei, who came to the position of supreme leader in 1989 with considerably less standing. Politically, Khamenei had been a lieutenant of the revolution rather than one of its top leaders. Theologically, as noted, he was not widely recognized as an ayatollah at the time he succeeded Khomeini; his lack of status as a marja'-e taqlid (source of emulation) or grand ayatollah, coupled with the awareness that the constitution had to be changed to permit his accession, was a point of potential vulnerability for the first several years of his tenure.

This relative weakness meant that Khamenei had to build up his authority over time, while constantly managing his relations with senior clerics and the political order's other power centers—the popularly elected president, the Majles, the Guardian Council, Rafsanjani and the Expediency Council, the Revolutionary Guard, and the judiciary. Certainly as supreme leader he has substantial institutional resources at his disposal to solidify his position vis-à-vis the system's other major players, and over the years he has used them—to build up influence over the Qom seminaries, to establish himself as the final decision maker on major foreign policy issues, and to appoint leaders he trusts to key positions in the military and security apparatus, the state broadcasting system, and the judiciary. The Expediency Council is now dominated by his appointees (outweighing Rafsanjani's influence); so is the Guardian Council. Furthermore, he has come to exercise significant de facto influence over ministerial appointments by elected presidents that directly impact his constitutional areas of responsibility, such as foreign affairs, interior, and intelligence.

Khamenei has also built up his authority over the more than two decades he has served as supreme leader by projecting an image of moderation and modesty. One communist opponent of the Pahlavi regime who shared a cell with Khamenei in the shah's prisons before the revolution (and who became a dissident in the Islamic Republic) has recalled the future supreme leader as "a very good man"—engaging and friendly, with a strong sense of humor that helped sustain them both through their ordeal.[7] After the revolution, as Khamenei's first presidential term drew to its end, Khomeini had to ask him to stand for reelection. When, the day after the Imam died, Khamenei was formally proposed as the next supreme leader, he spoke in the Assembly of Experts against his own nomination; archival footage shows him, immediately after the final vote, looking like the weight of the world had been placed on his shoulders.[8] Khamenei has reinforced this image of moderation with a strong reputation for personal integrity. There have never been any serious allegations of corruption against him or his family, the supreme leader's house is known for the modesty of its food and carpets (two important status markers among Iranians), and he has reportedly banned his children from going into business or serving on corporate boards. Over the years these steps have bolstered his gradual accumulation of personal as well as institutional authority. He has needed it to manage the Islamic Republic's ongoing ideological conflicts.

In the years immediately following the revolution, the principal fault line in Iranian politics ran between supporters and opponents of a velayat-e faqih state. After Khomeini and his allies prevailed over their non-Islamist adversaries, politics became the purview of those displaying "practical commitment" to its constitutional order.[9] But the secularists' defeat did not end ideological differences; instead, it intensified competition among groups of Khomeini loyalists espousing different approaches to important policy questions. This was in keeping with Khomeini's political vision for Iran to be an Islamic Republic, with a constitution and institutionalized checks and balances among multiple power centers, rather than a self-described "Islamic state" like Saudi Arabia or Afghanistan under the Taliban. In the Islamic Republic of Iran, sovereignty belongs to God but accountability (at least in this world) rests with the people and with their institutions. To deal effectively with the people's problems, concerns, and aspirations, the system is set up to encourage, within its constitutional and religious parameters, genuine contestation and debate.

By the mid-1980s, two opposing currents had emerged, labeled simply the left and the right. Originally the left-right divide encompassed both domestic and international issues. While ideological disputes over foreign policy became less pronounced over time, they grew more acute on domestic matters. On economic policy, leftists argued that a statist approach was indispensable to the revolution's social goals and Islamic notions of justice. Conservatives, by contrast, opposed virtually any economic role for the state as violating the religiously recognized rights of property holders and other market actors. Through much of the 1980s, this split manifested itself inside the executive branch, with President Khamenei tending toward conservative views and Prime Minister Mousavi championing leftist ones. Outside the executive, leftists dominated the Majles elected in 1980, 1984, and 1988; using their parliamentary strength to advance their policy agenda, they passed a decadelong stream of economic laws. Conservatives took advantage of their control over the Guardian Council to declare this legislation incompatible with Islam.[10] The two sides were almost as divided over social and cultural issues.

In 1987, tensions between leftists and conservatives within the

Islamic Republican Party became so explosive that President Khamenei and Majles speaker Rafsanjani decided, with Khomeini's blessing, to dissolve the IRP before its growing dysfunction became too apparent.[11] But the following year the left-right split was publicly formalized when a group of leftist clerics, led by Mehdi Karroubi and including Khatami, received Khomeini's approval to break away from the Society of Combatant Clergy, the established pro-Khomeini clerical association, and form a competitor group, the Assembly of Combatant Clerics.[12] For English speakers, the distinction between an Assembly of Combatant Clerics and a Society of Combatant Clergy may sound comical. But the differences between the two are not superficial; they have been at least as antagonistic as the Democratic and Republican parties in the United States or left- and right-wing parties in any European country.

In the last years of his life, Khomeini was increasingly concerned about this intensifying ideological conflict, and his desire to contain it was his principal motive for creating the Expediency Council and pushing to revise the constitution in the months before his death. Since succeeding Khomeini, Khamenei has focused on keeping the Islamic Republic's deeply polarized polity in a workable equilibrium. In his own views, Khamenei is conservative, but not as conservative as the most hard-line clerics. He believes in a balance between the constitutionalist and the clerical-legalist aspects of the Islamic Republic's constitutional order; during his service as president, he was one of the few prominent conservatives prepared to tolerate the continued involvement of figures from the Liberation Movement in Iran's political life. He concentrates not on prescribing particular policy approaches, especially to domestic issues, but on upholding what he sees as the core values of the revolution, and of Islam.

As supreme leader, therefore, Khamenei has sought to occupy a strategic position, balancing the key political trends in the Islamic Republic's political life. His approach is strongly reflected in the way he conducts official business. With an extensive network of representatives throughout the government, backed by a large and independent staff covering various areas of policy, he has been careful not to let himself become dependent on incumbent administrations for information and staff support. He maintains a wide range of personal contacts and advisory relationships with important figures across the political spectrum. Before the 2005 presidential election, he explained that "the existence of two factions faithful to the constitution serves the regime. . . . [They] function like two wings of a bird, enabling it to fly."[13] Khamenei sees his primary role as ensuring that factional competition neither renders the Islamic Republic dysfunctional nor undermines its religious and revolutionary identity. This outlook has shaped his approach to dealing with both Khatami and Ahmadinejad— each, in his own way, a polarizing figure.

RAFSANJANI: THE SHARK'S LONG SHADOW

In important respects, Khatami's and Ahmadinejad's political ascendancy was conditioned by the presidency of Rafsanjani, their predecessor. Rafsanjani was elected president in 1989 virtually by acclamation, winning 96 percent of the vote against a weak candidate from what was left of Bazargan's Liberation Movement. (Bazargan's successor as head of the Liberation Movement, Ebrahim Yazdi, who had served briefly as foreign minister in Bazargan's cabinet, had wanted to run but was disqualified by the Guardian Council because he would not accept velayat-e faqih.) Acceding to the presidency in the wake of the Iran-Iraq War and of Khomeini's passing, Rafsanjani focused his administration, the Revolutionary Guard, and as much of the state apparatus as he could on the practical challenges of reconstruction. It was urgently needed, for as the 1980s drew to a close the Islamic Republic was economically devastated. The revolution and the shah's departure had prompted massive capital flight; shortly thereafter the Iran-Iraq War dealt an enormous blow to its economy, cutting per capita gross domestic product almost in half in just a few years. As the decade wore on, the heavily statist policies of the leftist Prime Minister Mousavi resulted at times in shortages of food and other critical commodities.

Rafsanjani seemed to be a man well suited to the challenge.

Although Khamenei has issued public statements discouraging it, Rafsanjani is often called *kooseh*, or "shark." The nickname's origin is a medical condition (androgenic alopecia) that prevents Rafsanjani from growing much facial hair; in contrast to other Shi'a clerics, with their full beards, he has smooth cheeks—like a shark's. But it also reflects the perception that Rafsanjani knows how to navigate in areas where clerics typically have little experience.[14] The son of a farming family and the heir to one of Iran's largest pistachio farms, Rafsanjani built up his considerable personal wealth through investments in land and in the construction industry. With his well-developed business sense, he believed that he understood what was necessary to get the Iranian economy moving again. He offered a vision for the future, an Islamic Republic that, while staying true to its core religious and revolutionary principles, would also become part of the post–Cold War globalized economic order that was already taking shape. Though he stood as the candidate of the conservative Society of Combatant Clergy, over the course of his tenure he sought to spearhead a new factional current that would champion his vision; it came to be called the "modern" right, to distinguish it from the established, or "traditional," right, as well as from the left.[15]

Rafsanjani worked through the Expediency Council to bypass legislative logjams, establishing new executive powers and using them to craft policies marking the beginning of meaningful postrevolutionary reform. Trade was partially liberalized and the Tehran Stock Exchange reopened. Large budgetary allocations were directed toward rebuilding the country's shattered infrastructure. (The pro-Rafsanjani bloc in the Majles called themselves the Executives of Construction.) And initial steps were taken toward privatizing parts of the enormous share of Iran's economy that had belonged to the shah, an effort indispensable to long-term economic rationalization. These measures helped restore growth to a badly damaged economy.

In the run-up to the 1992 Majles elections, Rafsanjani openly encouraged the Guardian Council to exclude a large number of candidates associated with the leftist Assembly of Combatant Clerics, in the hope of reducing resistance to his economic initiatives. At the same time, he sought to co-opt moderate leftists into his political orbit, in part by bringing selected leftist deputies into his parliamentary coalition and recruiting left-leaning intellectuals (some of whom would go on to help launch the reform movement) into the Center for Strategic Research, his personal think tank. He easily won reelection against very weak opposition in 1993.

But as Rafsanjani entered his second term it was evident that he was encountering formidable difficulties in delivering on the big-ticket items in his vision. During his first term, Iran had borrowed heavily from abroad to fund his reconstruction and development initiatives. While the economy started growing again, it did not grow fast enough to sustain the rising debt burden; by 1993, Iran faced a debt crisis. Rafsanjani's administration negotiated a rescheduling of payments to the country's major creditors, but the resulting reduction in new credit constrained domestic consumption, causing the economy to contract during 1993 and 1994. On the foreign policy front, as noted, both the first Bush and the Clinton administrations effectively stiffed him; the Europeans were not prepared to deal seriously with him on their own. This friction put real constraints on Tehran's integration with the various institutional mechanisms of globalized development, such as the World Trade Organization, and on attracting Western investment for Iran's oil and gas sectors.

Facing increasing resistance to his economic agenda, Rafsanjani shied away from more politically challenging reforms, including wider privatization, which promised bigger developmental payoffs but would temporarily lower living standards for significant segments of the population. In the end, his administration made at most a down payment toward serious structural adjustment. In a still strained economic climate, his policies met with greater skepticism from the left, the right, and the public at large. A widespread sense took hold that his economic liberalization initiatives, especially privatization, had disproportionately benefited a crony capitalist group of his allies—including, at least in the popular perception, members of his own family. According to independent economic assessments, both the poverty rate and various indices of income inequality declined during Rafsanjani's presidency.[16] Nevertheless, by the end of his second term, perceptions of rising corruption and of a narrow elite's enrichment had done significant damage to his image. After he left the presidency, the accusations continued to accumulate. In one complaint of bribery, the United States accused the Norwegian oil company Statoil of paying a son of Rafsanjani's, starting in 2002, to help it secure business opportunities in the Islamic Republic. (Statoil's CEO resigned over the episode in 2003, and the company settled the complaint against it in the United States in 2006.)[17] This ambiguous legacy did much to shape the political space in which both Khatami and Ahmadinejad operated.

Rafsanjani also sought to strengthen the powers of the president vis-à-vis the supreme leader—for example, by trying to fold the Revolutionary Guard into the regular military. But Khamenei rebuffed these initiatives, solidifying his status as de facto guardian of the system's overall functioning and welfare. This, too, proved critical in shaping the trajectory of both the Khatami and the Ahmadinejad presidencies.

(MIS)UNDERSTANDING THE KHATAMI PHENOMENON

When he was first elected to the presidency, it seemed to many Western and expatriate observers that Mohammad Khatami would play an important role in putting Iran's political evolution back on its naturally ordained path toward secular liberalism. There were two possible scenarios. He might remake the system from within, gradually expanding the democratic dimensions of the postrevolutionary political order and slowly but surely reducing the scope of velayat-e faqih. Alternatively, he might fail to transform the system—thereby exposing the Islamic Republic's inherent contradictions and, in the process, radicalizing the public to demand more fundamental change. But neither scenario came to pass. As subsequent events made clear, Khatami's electoral successes were not steps toward an impending metamorphosis into liberal democracy; they did not even signify the public's embrace of the reformist agenda. Nor did his repeated failures to deliver on key elements of his platform drive Iranians into revolutionary activism against the Islamic Republic.

Putting aside Western romanticization of the reform movement—a portent of the West's later glorification of the Green movement—Khatami's election was not in any fundamental sense an ideological watershed in the Islamic Republic's political life. His political career is best understood as an example of what can happen, at least for a time, when a talented politician has an opportunity to take advantage of a specific set of political conditions to which he is uniquely suited.

Khatami's rise played out against the backdrop of ongoing efforts by Iran's postrevolutionary left to reinvent and reinvigorate itself. Over the course of Rafsanjani's presidency, the left had suffered a number of serious setbacks, including its loss of parliamentary control in 1992; in the 1993 presidential election, it failed to put up a candidate owing to its own internal divisions and resistance from the Guardian Council.[18] During Rafsanjani's second term, a cadre of left-leaning intellectuals began to develop a new political program, which came to be described as "reformism." This program was the creation of two groups. One was the religious nationalists, historically rooted in the Liberation Movement, who had never believed in the velayat-e faqih state. The second was what might be described as revolutionaries turned reformers: the leftist supporters of Khomeini's revolution—including some of those involved in seizing the U.S. embassy in 1979—who judged that improving their faction's political fortunes required the articulation of a seemingly less radical agenda.[19]

On foreign policy, reformists began to moderate the left's traditional advocacy of exporting the revolution, laying the ground for the Khatami administration to embrace the core elements of the grand strategy that had been defined during Rafsanjani's presidency. To the extent that they addressed economics, reformists began to modulate the left's traditional statism, setting the stage for more open-minded consideration of at least some market-rational reforms. What they really emphasized, though, was cultural and social pluralism. They argued that intellectual freedom and a strong civil society were necessary to break what they saw as the traditional right's monopoly over the politically oriented dimensions of ijtihad (independent legal interpretation); once that monopoly was broken, the Islamic Republic could become what the reformists wanted it to be: a wholly democratic state.[20] As a movement, reformism was never clear about what this would mean for velayat-e faqih. Some reformist thinkers, however—including Akbar Ganji, Saeed Hajjarian, Mohsen Kadivar, Abdolkarim Soroush, and Ebrahim Yazdi—acknowledged explicitly that democratization would ultimately mean its demise.[21]

To be politically effective, reformism needed a champion. That is where Khatami came in, as the perfect political figure to pick up the left's new agenda and, by making the most out of political conditions at the end of Rafsanjani's presidency, to run with it. Khatami entered the 1997 presidential campaign relatively late, and only after Iran's most senior leftist politician, former prime minister Mousavi, had finally decided not to run. Once in, Khatami found himself pitted against a seemingly well-positioned conservative opponent, Ali Akbar Nateq-Nouri, then speaker of the Majles and universally regarded as the favorite. But in the course of the campaign, a number of critical factors ended up breaking in Khatami's favor.

First, perceptions of increased corruption during Rafsanjani's presidency created an opening for an untainted candidate. Polling data indicate that Khatami was widely viewed by voters as clean while Nateq-Nouri was seen as running, in effect, as Rafsanjani's successor.[22] Whatever the merits of such perceptions in reality, they badly damaged the Majles speaker's prospects. Similarly, Khatami's status as a *rouhani* (clerical) seyed, affirmed daily by his black turban, proved to be a valuable asset. (Clergy who are not descendants of the Prophet, like Rafsanjani, wear white turbans.) While the traditional right strongly backed Nateq-Nouri, through the Society of Combatant Clergy and other channels, Khatami's image as a man of religion made it hard for them to question his commitment to Islam and neutralized whatever advantage Nateq-Nouri might have derived from his own clerical status. Khatami's identity as a clerical seyed and son of a distinguished ayatollah also made him acceptable as a candidate to more traditional segments of society and helped him expand his base beyond core leftist voters.

Khatami was not as well known as Mousavi, but his service as minister of culture and Islamic guidance in Rafsanjani's cabinet had given him significant national visibility. Moreover, his advocacy of greater cultural and media freedom had proven very popular. (Reducing restrictions on what Iranians read and watch and how they conduct their private lives has always been the aspect of the reformist agenda with the broadest appeal.) In the 1997 campaign, Khatami's ministerial record was widely taken as a sign of both his commitment to the Islamic Republic and his willingness to challenge established interests in order to change things for the better, a perception that enabled him to present the reformist agenda not as radical but rather as essential to the Islamic Republic's welfare and vitality, even its very survival.

As in most other countries, being perceived as someone who cares about the problems of ordinary people helps politicians in the Islamic Republic. Compared to his religious credentials and his image as honest and well-intentioned, this was an area of relative weakness for Khatami, an educated and cosmopolitan man regularly described in media coverage as an intellectual. But neither Nateq-Nouri nor the two minor candidates had much credibility as populists, either. Furthermore, Khatami proved to be by far the most adept politician in the race: good on the stump, with crowds, and on television, with a warm and ready smile that voters found winning. On election day, these factors came together to give him a landslide victory.

In the conventional Western and expatriate Iranian narrative, the supreme leader worked to undermine Khatami's administration virtually from the day of his election. But the record does not support this story. Khatami's campaign had sparked fury from parts of the right; just as conservatives in the 1980s had decried the leftism of Mousavi and Karroubi as the prelude to the displacement of Islamic governance by warmed-over Marxism, so younger rightists in the 1990s (sometimes referred to as *hezbollahis*, from the Persianized form of the Arabic *hizballah*, "party of God") feared that reformism would put the Islamic Republic on a slippery slope to secular liberalism. When Khatami's victory was announced, riots broke out in Tehran and Esfahan. Khamenei promptly released the congratulatory message he had sent to Khatami—as a somewhat aging hezbollahi said almost a decade and a half later, a clear signal "to us hotheads" that the election outcome was to be respected. (Those who now criticize Khamenei for telling Iranians that they needed to accept Ahmadinejad's reelection in 2009 seem not to recall the leader's nearly identical position following Khatami's election in 1997.)

After Khatami's inauguration, Khamenei allowed the new president considerable latitude in assembling his cabinet and quietly supported the confirmation of his ministerial appointees by a Majles still controlled by conservatives. Though the Majles subsequently impeached Khatami's first interior minister, the leader defended several other reformist ministers against calls for their removal. During its first term, Khatami's administration made notable progress in expanding individual, cultural, and media freedom. It also took concrete steps to strengthen the rule of law, including in cases involving abuses by government security agencies (most notably the alleged complicity of officials in the so-called chain murders of Iranian dissidents).[23] None of these actions would have been possible without Khamenei's acquiescence. Khatami supporters inside Iran and Western critics of the Islamic Republic argue that it was the judiciary, ultimately under Khamenei's command, that shut down reformist newspapers and arrested prominent reformists during Khatami's presidency. While a number of reformist newspapers were indeed shut down (with many of them reopening days later under different names), newspapers that did not cross what Khamenei described as "red lines" (for example, challenging key aspects of the Islamic Republic's constitutional order, such as velayat-e faqih) were not closed. Thus, there was never a point at which multiple reformist newspapers were not widely available, on a daily basis, for Iranians to read.

The real problem for reformists lay not with Khamenei but with Khatami himself. For all his strengths as a candidate, Iran's first reformist president proved to be a poor political strategist in office.

In the early years of his first term, the same factors that had propelled Khatami to the presidency helped him build popular support for other reformists. In preparation for the 2000 Majles elections, he and Karroubi brought candidates linked to them together in a new reformist coalition, the Islamic Iran Participation Front (commonly shortened to Mosharekat, "participation"). Reformist newspapers supported their campaign with relentless criticism of former president Rafsanjani's administration and of the right, and Mosharekat candidates ended up winning a sizable majority of parliamentary seats, not only knocking out a large number of conservatives but also inflicting heavy losses on the pro-Rafsanjani Executives of Construction. (Rafsanjani's daughter could not win a seat, and the former president himself barely passed the threshold for one, which he gave up before being sworn in.)

The election appeared to be a reformist triumph. But it also reflected the inability of Khatami and his allies to form a strategic plan to advance their program. The Guardian Council remained under conservative control; the only other channel through which the reformists might promote their agenda was the Expediency Council. Yet by trashing Rafsanjani in the parliamentary election campaign, they had hardly given the former president any reason to cooperate with them in his continuing role as head of the Expediency Council—which meant that they had no way to implement the most politically challenging parts of their platform. This reality was driven home when, shortly after winning control of the Majles, they introduced a law that would have made it more difficult for judicial authorities to close media outlets. In a rare move, the leader publicly declared his opposition to the measure; with no consensus on how to proceed, the reformist bloc beat a hasty retreat.

Following the reformists' capture of the Majles in 2000, Khatami coasted to reelection the next year, against relatively weak opposition. But, even as Iranians prepared to reelect him, they were starting to see him as a politician who was not a fighter. When the mayor of Tehran, Gholam Karabaschi, who had been a key supporter of his first presidential bid, was convicted in 1998 on corruption charges that many reformists saw as politically motivated, the president had stood by silently; likewise, when student demonstrations protesting the closing of a pro-Khatami newspaper in 1999 were forcibly suppressed, he had publicly disowned the demonstrators who had risked themselves on his behalf. After his reelection, with a reformist majority in the Majles, Khatami renewed his efforts to enact his policies into law, but the reformists continued to encounter strong opposition from the Guardian Council. In a few cases, Khamenei himself intervened to persuade the council to let bills pass into law (for example, a measure enacted by parliament in 2002 authorizing equal compensation in "blood money" for Muslim and non-Muslim crime victims). But he was not about to facilitate the passage of measures that he believed threatened the integrity of the Islamic Republic's constitutional order. And this stalemate underscored Khatami's biggest failing as president: his inability to articulate a coherent argument squaring the kinds of constitutional changes it would take to realize the reformist agenda with the preservation of Khomeini's vision of Islamic government.

His failure was most graphically displayed in 2002, when Khatami presented what he described as his signature "twin bills" to the Majles. One of them sought to "clarify" (in practical effect, to expand) the president's authority relative to other institutions; the other would have eliminated the Guardian Council's power to vet and veto candidates for office. Together they would have begun changing the workings of the Islamic Republic's constitutional order in significant ways; they were certainly too radical for either Khamenei or conservative power centers to countenance. Yet even though they were, in Khatami's own words, essential to realizing the agenda on which he had twice campaigned for the presidency, he did not fight for them. When the Guardian Council declared them invalid, he withdrew both bills from the Majles—raising angry calls from reformists for his resignation.

By the end of his second term, Khatami was widely seen, even by his supporters, as a colossal disappointment. But his repeated failures to deliver on his agenda did not drive Iranians into revolutionary activism against the system. When Khatami declined to stand with the student protestors in 1999, the rest of Iranian society did not stand with them, either. In the early 2000s, as it became increasingly clear that the twice-elected Khatami was now a truly lame duck, it also became evident that people were not about to take to the streets to demand "real" reform. During his second term, some Western and expatriate analysts hypothesized that Iranians, especially younger ones, were becoming politically apathetic, tuning out politics to focus on their private lives. In reality, Iranians were not losing their enthusiasm for politics or for the Islamic Republic. As the 2005 presidential election would show, they were losing their enthusiasm for the reform movement. This shift in sentiment would result in the election of the Islamic Republic's most conservative president since Khamenei.

A NEW GENERATION OF CONSERVATIVES

Just as Khatami's election marked the arrival of reformists on the national political scene, Ahmadinejad's election eight years later marked the arrival of a new breed of conservatives. Some Iranian commentators call them the radical right; some English-language commentators describe them as neoconservatives, notwithstanding the term's rather specific connotations in American politics.[24] We prefer to call them new-generation conservatives, because their rise is the product of generational succession in the upper echelons of the Islamic Republic's conservative political circles—a process that, strikingly, has no parallel on the reformist side of the spectrum. As a result of this transition, the leading conservative political figures in Iran are no longer older clerics concentrated in the Society of Combatant Clergy but younger laymen.

This recasting of Iranian conservatism was deliberately engineered by Khamenei and some of his closest clerical allies in the early 2000s. Advisers to both Khatami and several leading conservative politicians say that the 2000 parliamentary elections left the leader worried that the political system was becoming unbalanced, in ways that could threaten the long-term survival of the Islamic Republic as a velayat-e faqih state. Sources close to Khatami say that Khamenei never doubted Khatami's fundamental commitment to the established constitutional order, even if he opposed the reformist president on a number of specific issues. The supreme leader was concerned, however, that the reformist camp included elements whose ultimate aim was to dispose of velayat-e faqih.[25] Maintaining the system's equilibrium required that those elements be balanced within the electoral arena and thereby constrained. But the reformists' rise had effectively driven the traditional right into a de facto alliance with Rafsanjani and the modern right; that alliance was proving toxic at the polls, as a consequence of Rafsanjani's own diminished popularity.

Conservatives retained statesmen-like figures—for example, former foreign minister Ali Akbar Velayati—who could potentially compete in national elections. But to make principlist political forces more electorally competitive with the reformists, Khamenei quietly but decisively worked to effect a generational transition among Iranian conservatives. The formative experience of the younger laymen who came to prominence as a result was not the revolution but the Iran-Iraq War. Many of them had discharged their wartime service in the Revolutionary Guards, known as the Pasdaran, or in the Basij paramilitary, both of which have been and continue to be important organizational channels for new conservative mobilization. More broadly, the institutional base for new-generation conservatism encompasses a network of organizations formed in the late 1980s and 1990s by war veterans, many of whom came back from the front to find the Islamic Republic, in their estimation, threatened from within, with corrupt officials (including some clerics) raking in money and revolutionary spirit in decline.

Many of those who had risked their lives and seen countless comrades killed were angry at what they found; to a significant degree, new-generation conservatism grows out of their anger. It is a movement aimed at restoring the Islamic Republic to its divinely ordained path. Younger conservatives have no use for reformism, which, to them, seems like thinly veiled liberalism. Instead of reform, their platform espouses a revived commitment to Islamic values and to Khomeini's revolutionary vision; programmatically, they favor a tactically tougher approach to foreign policy than that of either Rafsanjani or the reformists and a more populist approach to economics than that of either the traditional or the modern right.

Over the past decade and a half, three men have emerged as the most prominent figures in new-generation conservatism: Ahmadinejad; the current Majles speaker, Ali Larijani; and Tehran's current mayor, Mohammad Baqer Qalibaf. While all three are considered religious, they all also have technocratic backgrounds, with careers projecting an image of dedication to building a better, less corrupt Islamic Republic. All three ran to succeed Khatami as president in 2005; both Larijani and Qalibaf retain their ambition to succeed Ahmadinejad in 2013. While each has his own distinctive profile, their careers, taken together, constitute a history of new-generation conservatism.

If the phrase "revolutionary aristocracy" has any validity, it may surely be applied to Ali Larijani.[26] As noted earlier, Larijani's father, Grand Ayatollah Haj Mirza Hashem Amoli, was a distinguished Shi'a cleric, of equal rank to Khomeini and Iraq's Sistani. Born in 1958, Ali Larijani studied mathematics and computer science at Sharif University of Technology, before earning a Ph.D. in Western philosophy from the University of Tehran, and served in the Revolutionary Guards during the Iran-Iraq War. In 1988 he joined with a number of other war veterans to found the Islamic Society of Engineers, for the purpose of "elevating the Islamic, political, scientific, and technical knowledge of the Muslim people of Iran, defending major freedoms such as freedom of expression and gatherings, as well as continued campaigning against foreign cultural agents, whether of Eastern or Western materialism."[27] The society became one of the more important organizational channels for the new conservatives; Ahmadinejad was another early member. Larijani has close ties to the supreme leader, dating back to the time when he was a wartime commander in the Revolutionary Guards and Khamenei was president. After becoming supreme leader, Khamenei appointed Larijani to his first national-level post, director of state broadcasting, in 1994; Larijani held this position for ten years before stepping down to become one of the leader's national security advisers. Following his unsuccessful first bid for the presidency in 2005, he became secretary-general of the Supreme National Security Council and chief nuclear negotiator (an appointment formally made by Ahmadinejad but effectively arranged by Khamenei). Larijani resigned over policy disagreements with Ahmadinejad in

2007, won a Majles seat from Qom in 2008, and was chosen speaker shortly afterward.

Larijani is a politician who combines intelligence, broad erudition, and familiarity with the wider world with deep personal roots in Shi'a culture and belief. His wife is the daughter of a distinguished ayatollah who was assassinated during the MEK's terror campaign in the early 1980s. His four brothers are all prominent figures in Iranian public life; American journalists have described them as the Kennedys of Iran.[28] His older brother, Mohammad Javad, trained at both the hawza (seminary) in Qom and in electrical engineering at the Sharif University of Technology before undertaking doctoral studies in mathematics at the University of California at Berkeley. He served in the Majles and then as a deputy foreign minister during the Rafsanjani administration, generating some political controversy by advocating a strategic opening with the United States. Currently he directs the Institute for Studies in Theoretical Physics and Mathematics in Tehran, heads Iran's human rights council, and advises the supreme leader. One of Larijani's younger brothers, Sadeq, is a Shi'a cleric and scholar who was appointed by Khamenei to take over as head of the judiciary in 2009, in response to concerns about the way the arrests and trials of protestors following that year's presidential election were handled.

Ali Larijani's family connections have helped him solidify both his support across the political establishment and his public image of piety and probity; on the downside, they buttress perceptions of him as elitist. Among younger conservatives he probably has the best relationship with the traditional right and even with the modern right.[29] His record of wartime service in the Revolutionary Guards also puts him in their good stead, another potentially important asset.

Born in 1960, Mohammad Baqer Qalibaf rose to national prominence as a war hero, one of the youngest and most successful Pasdaran commanders during the Iran-Iraq War. He continued to serve in the Pasdaran after the war, eventually becoming head of its air force; thus he has many politically advantageous links to the Revolutionary Guards. Like Larijani, Qalibaf has a close relationship with

Khamenei, dating back to his service in the Pasdaran, and it has proven critical to his political career. Appointed by the supreme leader as chief of Iran's national police forces in 1999, he resigned to make his first presidential run in 2005. Later that year he was chosen by Tehran's municipal council to succeed Ahmadinejad as the city's mayor.

Since his first presidential campaign, Qalibaf has worked to expand his political base beyond his principlist constituency by appealing to younger Iranians with more modern and technocratic aspirations. As a young conservative political activist put it, Qalibaf wants to be "the candidate of the middle class." What does "middle class" mean in the Islamic Republic? Our interlocutor explained:

> Go to a coffee shop in Tehran. Look around. There may be someone husbanding his money, getting only a tea bag for which he pays 40 *toman* [less than $1]. There may be someone more prosperous, buying himself a more expensive coffee drink. And there may be someone with lots of money, buying multiple drinks for a party of people. The income differences don't matter. All of those people are middle class. They all watch or listen to the BBC Persian Service, or else would like to, if they could get access to it. Qalibaf wants to attract those people.[30]

While this strategy may prove a winning one for Qalibaf, there is the risk that it may alienate parts of his conservative base.

In no small part, Mahmoud Ahmadinejad rose faster and higher than either Larijani or Qalibaf because of his extraordinary skills as a populist politician, which enabled him to assemble a broad base of support encompassing Iran-Iraq War veterans and their families, the religious, and lower-income groups. Ahmadinejad played a vital role in the development of virtually all the main organizational channels for new-generation conservative mobilization. Although he helped found the Islamic Society of Engineers, his political ascendancy was more tightly bound up with the rise of two other organizations, Isargaran and Abadgaran. The name of the first says much about the roots of new-generation conservatism: *isar* is the Arabic word for altruism; in

Farsi, *isargaran* refers to those who give selflessly to support a sacred cause. Since the 1980s, Iranians have used the term to describe those who have worked to defend and further the revolution, particularly those who sacrificed in the Iran-Iraq War. In the mid-1990s, a group of war veterans, including Ahmadinejad, who were dissatisfied with the direction of political life founded a movement to press for the restoration of revolutionary principles. They called it (roughly translated) the Society of Devotees of the Islamic Revolution, or Isargaran for short.[31]

From its inception, Isargaran has joined an emphasis on returning to the purity of revolutionary ideals with populist economic themes—a combination that has marked Ahmadinejad's rhetoric throughout his political career. Early on, the group focused on combating the reform movement, backing Khatami's conservative opponent, Nateq-Nouri, in the May 1997 presidential election. During Khatami's first term, Isargaran issued a highly critical analysis of his presidency that stressed declining economic conditions; it helped to drive the mounting criticism of the reformists as being overly concerned with elite issues like personal liberty and the state of civil society while neglecting ordinary Iranians' bread-and-butter economic concerns. By the 2000 parliamentary elections, Isargaran had established itself as a force to be reckoned with. Although reformists won control of the Majles that year, candidates backed by Isargaran won almost 20 percent of the seats, making it the largest conservative parliamentary bloc; shortly afterward, Ahmadinejad became the group's official spokesman. Inside and outside the Majles, Isargaran articulated a simultaneously ideological and populist critique of Khatami's reform agenda; thus, the group responded to Khatami's complaints about inadequate presidential powers by defending the checks and balances spelled out in the constitution and criticizing his "twin bills" as a distraction from the challenges of raising ordinary people's living standards.[32]

In 2002, Nateq-Nouri—who after being ousted as Majles speaker became Khamenei's chief of staff—worked with Isargaran leaders, including Ahmadinejad, and with other new-conservative organizations to create an electoral coalition capable of going head to head with the reformists. Its full Farsi name is normally translated either as the Coalition of Developers of Islamic Iran or as the Alliance of Builders of Islamic Iran; in the Islamic Republic, it is usually referred to simply as Abadgaran.[33] It made its debut in the 2003 municipal council elections, capturing control of the Tehran city council, which then appointed Ahmadinejad mayor. When parliamentary elections the following year produced substantial gains in principlist representation in the Majles, the conservative victory was generally interpreted outside Iran (and among reformists inside the country) as a function of the Guardian Council's having disqualified a large number of reformist candidates. (Khamenei publicly urged the Guardian Council to reconsider its veto of so many reformists, and it reinstated some.) More important, the results showed the growing popularity of new-generation conservatism and its message, as Abadgaran provided a significant portion of the sizable majority of parliamentary seats that principlists took in the 2004 Majles elections.[34]

These developments enabled a new-generation conservative to succeed Khatami in 2005, though few predicted this outcome before the fact. Many critics of the Islamic Republic's legitimacy focus intently on Iran's 2009 presidential election to bolster their case. But in fact the 2009 election cannot really be understood without a sober analysis of the 2005 cycle and what it revealed about the nation's political trajectory.

A WATERSHED ELECTION

As various factions geared up for the 2005 presidential election, former president Rafsanjani was determined to mount a political comeback. This factor skewed almost all the electoral forecasts. Political analysts inside and outside Iran predicted, almost uniformly, that the 2005 contest would produce the Islamic Republic's first two-round presidential election and that Rafsanjani would come in first in the first round; most of them also assumed he would emerge the ultimate winner. The same Westerners who had largely spurned him when he was president in the 1990s welcomed his candidacy in 2005, hoping that once elected he would come courting them again. Very few had even an inkling that the relatively unknown mayor of Tehran, Mahmoud Ahmadinejad, would win the battle in a landslide.

When the campaign officially opened, just over a month before election day, more than a thousand Iranians registered to run as presidential candidates. Within a week, the Guardian Council had approved eight of them for the first-round ballot.

To Westerners, Iranians seem remarkably tolerant of the Guardian Council's role in their elections. Through a liberal lens, the council appears to be an unelected body engaged in the arbitrary exclusion of potential candidates from electoral contests. But that is not necessarily how Iranians see it. Every political system, a number of our Iranian interlocutors point out, has some way to vet aspirants for high office. The United States has its primary system, in which the principal criterion for moving forward has become the ability to raise money. In the United States and some European countries, parties also filter candidates, placing informal but real ideological restrictions on them. In Turkey, candidates must demonstrate their loyalty to the strictly secular constitutional order; even today, the Justice and Development Party, or AKP, cannot display its Islamist inclinations too overtly without risking disqualification from political activity by Turkish courts, backed by the military. In postrevolutionary Iran, the winnowing is done through the Guardian Council's evaluation of aspirants according to criteria laid out in the constitution, including support for "the Islamic character of the political system," endorsement of "all the rules and regulations according to Islamic criteria," recognition of Shi'a Islam as "the official religion of Iran," and acceptance of several accompanying principles—the "democratic character of the government," the doctrine of "the imamate of the umma"—as "unalterable." Political competition is limited to those who accept these parameters. But Iranians say such adherence is required in any genuinely constitutional order—including the United States, where every president, senator, and congressional representative must swear to defend the U.S. Constitution before taking office.

As Western journalists covering candidate registration at the

Ministry of the Interior in Tehran in 2005 made clear, most of the disqualified candidates were, to be generous, marginal figures in Iranian public life.[35] Other disqualifications seemed more suspect—for example, no female applicant was approved. But the eight candidates who were selected were all plausible, well-recognized figures who together represented a reasonable cross-section of the Islamic Republic's political class, covering the main points of view along its ideological spectrum.

Rafsanjani, of course, made the cut; in between the two ends of the left-right divide, the former president sought to position himself as a pragmatic centrist. There were three candidates from the reformist camp. Mehdi Karroubi, who had served as Majles speaker from 2000 to 2004, ran as the candidate of the Combatant Clerics Association, which he had helped found. The Khatami camp was skeptical that Karroubi would be able to win against Rafsanjani; their preferred candidate was Mostafa Moin, a former minister of science, research, and technology in Khatami's cabinet who ran with the backing of the Islamic Iran Participation Front. The third reformist was Mohsen Mehralizadeh, who had been head of Iran's National Sports Organization under Khatami as well as one of Khatami's junior vice presidents. (The Guardian Council originally rejected both Moin and Mehralizadeh but approved them after Khamenei publicly asked the council to reconsider.)

On the principlist side, there were four candidates. Mohsen Rezae was a founding commander of the Revolutionary Guards who, since his retirement from that post in 1998 as a result of disagreements with President Khatami, had served as secretary-general of the (Rafsanjani-chaired) Expediency Council. He quickly realized, however, that he did not have much of a popular base and withdrew before the first round. Ali Larijani had the support of the Council for Coordinating the Forces of Islamic Revolution, a body set up under Nateq-Nouri's leadership to bring new-generation conservatives and the traditional right together; for months it had sought to promote Larijani as the single conservative standard bearer in the 2005 election. But there was concern in principlist circles that Larijani was insufficiently charismatic to win a runoff against Rafsanjani; as a result, Qalibaf and Ahmadinejad, the two other emerging new-generation leaders, threw their hats into the ring. Remarkably, none of the new-conservative organizations with which Ahmadinejad had been closely associated from their beginnings endorsed him in the first round. Larijani had the backing of the Islamic Society of Engineers and the Coordination Council; Isargaran and Abadgaran both went with Qalibaf. No one, it seemed, thought Ahmadinejad would be the most effective conservative against Rafsanjani in a runoff.

The candidates emphasized a wide array of themes and messages. Rafsanjani relied heavily on his significant advantage in name recognition. Substantively, his campaign was of a piece with his presidential record. He emphasized economic growth through increased foreign investment and, to that end, claimed he could bring the negotiations with Europe over Iran's nuclear program to a successful conclusion and repair relations with the United States. On the reformist side, Karroubi ran a populist campaign, promising to pay every Iranian adult roughly $65 a month as a way of redistributing the nation's oil wealth. Moin promised to continue the policies of outgoing president Khatami. Mehralizadeh presented himself, with unintended comedy, as the candidate of the younger generation; at forty-nine, he was the same age as Ahmadinejad, two years older than Larijani, and four years older than Qalibaf.

On the conservative side, Larijani ran a lackluster campaign. Qalibaf was appreciably more energetic in presenting himself as a forward-looking leader well suited to take the Islamic Republic into a technocratic and globalized future. On the campaign trail, he favored European designer suits (without neckties, of course, since avoiding them has symbolized defiance of the West ever since the revolution). Though he had not learned to fly until after becoming commander of the Revolutionary Guards' air force in 1998, many of Qalibaf's campaign photos and posters showed him in a pilot's uniform or in the cockpit of an airplane. He touted himself as a strong manager who would get things done, but without offering much programmatic content.

Ahmadinejad, for his part, was by far the hardest-working and most populist candidate in the race, with a campaign emphasizing his humble origins and his deep religious devotion. After becoming mayor of Tehran, he had declined to live in the official mayoral residence, opting to stay in his own relatively modest apartment in a not particularly fashionable part of the city; this choice became a symbolically potent trope in his presidential campaign. In contrast to Qalibaf, Ahmadinejad eschewed suits for clothes more like those of an Iranian Everyman—a jacket paired with (often not especially well-matched) slacks, or sometimes an even more plebeian windbreaker. (To supporters of opposing candidates and journalists covering the contest his dress became a running joke: Was Ahmadinejad wearing "the brown jacket" or "the gray jacket" that day?) Substantively, his campaign tore into the elites he claimed were monopolizing wealth and power, and it promised to expand economic and social opportunities for ordinary Iranians. As Tehran's mayor, Ahmadinejad had won acclaim among the city's lower classes with a program of low-interest loans that gave young men the funds to start a household (effectively a requirement for marriage in Iranian society that many working-class city dwellers found difficult to meet). He pointed to this program as a model for the kind of initiatives he wanted to pursue as president. Moreover, he campaigned nationwide to a much greater extent than the other candidates, leaving Tehran to cover as much of the country as he could.

On June 17, 2005, 63 percent of Iran's 47 million eligible voters turned out to cast their ballots in the first round. Rafsanjani and Ahmadinejad emerged very close together as the two top vote getters, Rafsanjani with roughly 21 percent and Ahmadinejad with roughly 20 percent, and thus headed into a runoff. Karroubi came in third with 17 percent, Qalibaf fourth with 14 percent, Moin fifth with 13 percent, Larijani sixth with just 6 percent, and Mehralizadeh last with 5 percent. Another 4 percent of the ballots were judged blank or otherwise invalid. At one level, these results speak to Ahmadinejad's political skills; at another, they reveal a good deal about the relative strength of reformism and conservatism at the end of Khatami's presidency.

Ahmadinejad prevailed over Larijani, Qalibaf, and the three

reformists in the first round because in every meaningful respect he ran a better campaign, addressing voters' concerns more effectively than his rivals did. Even though the main conservative political groups had thrown their support to other candidates, Ahmadinejad's campaign organization put together a superior operation for getting out the vote on election day. The key was Ahmadinejad's ties to the Revolutionary Guards and the Basij. While Larijani and Qalibaf had their own links to these organizations, it was Ahmadinejad who most effectively used his connections to ensure that his voters got to the polls, especially in the more remote parts of Iran. In the first round's immediate aftermath, Karroubi and Moin both charged that security forces had illegally increased the vote for Ahmadinejad by bribing voters and intimidating supporters of opposing candidates; Rafsanjani professed to share the concerns of his erstwhile rivals and backed their call for an official investigation. But no evidence was presented to support the reformists' accusations (the Guardian Council recounted a small number of ballot boxes anyway), and they did not gain traction with the public at large.

The results challenge criticisms in the West that Iranians had "no choice" in the election because of the Guardian Council's role in vetting candidates. A majority of the Iranian public certainly acted as if it believed it had a choice. Turnout—which had been on a downward trend from the 2001 presidential election through the 2003 municipal elections and the 2004 parliamentary elections—was unexpectedly high in first-round balloting in 2005. There were three credible reformist candidates, two of whom (Karroubi and Moin) were prominent figures in Iranian political life; most analysts who criticize the tactical folly of splitting the reformist vote fail to acknowledge that the same dynamic was in play on the right, where three serious candidates were running.

The bottom line is that the three conservatives on the ballot (Ahmadinejad, Qalibaf, and Larijani) collectively won 40 percent of the votes cast in the first round, while the three reformist candidates (Karroubi, Moin, and Mehralizadeh) collectively took just 35 percent. More refined analyses, including comparisons with previous elections, show more clearly both a decline in popular support for reformism and a concomitant upswing in support for the right, particularly as represented by new-generation conservatives. Measured in terms of eligible voters (rather than portion of votes actually cast), Khatami had been supported by 57 percent of eligible voters in 1997, when the turnout rate was 77 percent, and 49 percent in 2001, when the turnout rate was 63 percent. In 2005, when the turnout rate was also 63 percent, only 22 percent of eligible voters cast ballots for a reformist candidate in the first round. In comparison, 25 percent of the eligible electorate in 2005 voted for a candidate on the right, while 13 percent cast ballots for Rafsanjani. Among other things, these figures show that a fair number of voters who had previously supported Khatami cast their ballots in the first round in 2005 for Rafsanjani or for one of the conservative candidates rather than for any of the three reformists.[36] The upturn in conservative support would come dramatically to light in the second-round runoff.

In the week between the first and second rounds, Rafsanjani ran a lackadaisical campaign, continuing to employ vague rhetoric of moderate reform and courting reformist voters by distributing photographs of himself with outgoing president Khatami. Like most of the pundits, Rafsanjani assumed he would win; though he was one of Iran's richest men, he claimed—with a disingenuousness that was not lost on the public—that he did not have the time or the resources to campaign outside Tehran. Even in Tehran he made few public appearances, instead spending considerable time with the foreign press. Diplomats from a major European country serving in Tehran during the campaign say that one of Rafsanjani's sons even met covertly with their embassy, asking it to relay a message to Washington conveying his father's desire for dialogue with the United States once he regained the presidency.[37]

Ahmadinejad's campaign, by contrast, gained more and more momentum in the week after the first round. His posters appeared everywhere. In response to Rafsanjani's distribution of American-style bumper stickers, Ahmadinejad supporters began displaying cheaply reproduced photos of their candidate in their cars. In a manner unprecedented for an Iranian election, the underdog campaigned intensively, across almost all of the country, emphasizing his poor background and pledging to focus as president on alleviating poverty, fighting the corruption of what he called the "oil mafia" in Tehran, and standing up for the Islamic Republic's rights against American and Western pressure—all of which underscored, in voters' perceptions, the differences between him and Rafsanjani.

On June 24, 2005, 60 percent of eligible voters went to the polls to cast their second-round ballots. Ahmadinejad routed Rafsanjani, 62 percent to 36 percent; roughly 2 percent of the votes were judged blank or otherwise invalid. It was one of the most clearly decisive outcomes in any at least minimally competitive electoral system in the last half century. Ahmadinejad attracted support not just from traditionally conservative constituencies but also from "swing" constituencies focused on the qualities of individual candidates rather than on their ideological orientation and even from reformists alienated from Rafsanjani and/or disaffected with reformism itself (think of them as Iran's "Reagan Democrats"). Even Iranian analysts sympathetic to Ahmadinejad's opponents had to concede the utter implausibility of manipulation, cheating, or electoral fraud on the scale required to account for the enormous gap between the number of votes cast for Ahmadinejad (almost 17 million) and for Rafsanjani (less than 10 million). Likewise, Western analysts normally critical of Iran's electoral system had to acknowledge that the outcome represented a stunning but also quite genuine defeat for both Rafsanjani and the reformists.[38]

It is remarkable that so many observers, inside and outside Iran, were astonished by the final result. They should not have been, given the deterioration in Rafsanjani's popularity over more than a few years, which had been patently highlighted in the 2000 Majles elections. In his 2005 presidential bid, Rafsanjani did nothing to address this decline; indeed, his Westernized campaign—with bumper stickers, headbands, and other logo items and with his partisans in elite north Tehran neighborhoods honking their car horns to show their support and holding outdoor gatherings with a street carnival atmosphere—was hardly designed to appeal to lower-than-elite strata of the electorate. (In both its Westernized quality and its ineffectiveness, Rafsanjani's campaign proved to be a precursor for Mir-Hossein Mousavi's ill-fated presidential campaign in 2009.)

The 2005 election results also offered important insights into the Islamic Republic's legitimacy just over a quarter of a century after the revolution that gave birth to it. On the one hand, they suggested that a significant portion of Iranian society—perhaps a quarter of the eligible electorate, including some reformist voters who cast ballots for Rafsanjani in the second round and those who boycotted the election altogether—were disaffected. This is not a trivial problem, as would become manifest during and after the Islamic Republic's 2009 presidential election. But the 2005 election results also indicated that a strong majority of Iranians remained committed to the political order that Khomeini's revolution had installed. For that reason, they were prepared to turn away from a reformist current they had come to view as ineffectual and possibly perilous to the Islamic Republic's long-term identity.

In line with Imam Khomeini's vision for an Islamic Republic combining religion and participatory politics, none of Iran's elected presidents have exceeded the constitution's two-term limit. *AFP/Atta Kenare*

Western observers fluctuate between exaggerating Iran's presidency into an office with almost dictatorial powers and belittling it into a post eclipsed by the authority of the supreme leader. The presidency is, in fact, a consequential office; its holders are capable of major achievements in domestic and foreign policy. But in a factionalized polity, any attempt to achieve something significant is bound to generate backlash by the opposition and frustration among supporters. Still, backlash and frustration build up slowly. Since the revolution, every president—except the impeached Bani-Sadr and the assassinated Rajai—has been elected to a second term. And every president except Khamenei has left his second term in office a reduced figure who galvanized his opposition and disappointed his supporters; this will almost certainly be the case for Mahmoud Ahmadinejad when he turns over the presidency to a successor in the summer of 2013. That presidents are limited to two consecutive terms—as in the United States—has been a safety valve by which the system vents anger and frustration and moves on. And above the presidents, the supreme leader—first Khomeini, now Khamenei—works to preserve the system's basic coherence and equilibrium.

In their devotion to the myth of the Islamic Republic's illegitimacy, Western Iran experts and political commentators have routinely failed to take account of this political history. As a result, they completely misapprehended the runup to, the results of, and the real meaning of Iran's 2009 presidential election. In the next chapter, we take a critical look at this election and the controversy it generated, the (brief) rise and (rather steep) fall of the Green movement that developed in its aftermath, and what these events tell us about the future course of Iranian politics.

6

A CONTROVERSIAL ELECTION

Elections are an important pillar of the system, and religious democracy is founded on elections.
—*Ayatollah Seyed Ali Khamenei, March 8, 2012*

On June 12, 2009, the Islamic Republic held its tenth presidential election. The incumbent, Mahmoud Ahmadinejad, who was seeking a second term, was opposed by three candidates: a former prime minister, Mir-Hossein Mousavi; a former speaker of the Majles, Mehdi Karroubi; and a former commander of the Revolutionary Guards, Mohsen Rezae. As the polls in Iran were getting ready to close, we hosted a group of Middle East specialists and foreign policy hands in Washington to talk about the election and American-Iranian relations in general. We invited a visiting Iranian academic to lead off the discussion. After telling us that he was not an Ahmadinejad supporter, he pointed out a number of factors that he felt could tip the result in the incumbent's favor. Back in Tehran, Mousavi was already declaring victory—while the polls were still open and no votes had yet been counted—saying he had received "information" that he was "the winner of this election by a substantial margin." One of his advisers was claiming he had won 65 percent of the vote.[1] At our discussion in Washington, Trita Parsi, head of the National Iranian American Council, regularly checked his

BlackBerry; eventually, he intervened to announce, elatedly, "MSNBC has called the election for Mousavi!"

Our visitor from Tehran responded that he found it strange for foreign media to be calling an Iranian election, especially when the polls might not even be closed. By the time our gathering ended, the polls in Iran had just closed and the votes were being counted; he asked if he could use a computer to check the early returns. As he pulled up reports from various Iranian news services and compared them, we quickly concluded that, whatever the basis had been for Mousavi's claim of victory and MSNBC's projection, it wasn't actual vote tallies. For as we perused the Iranian Web sites, it became clear that in the official returns Ahmadinejad was winning, and was winning big.

Though we did not fully realize it then, our experience that afternoon—with Trita Parsi, a proreformist expatriate activist excitedly citing MSNBC's proclamation of a Mousavi victory while the actual returns showed something else—was a harbinger of the controversy soon to come. Although Ahmadinejad was indeed declared the winner, with 62.5 percent of the vote, Mousavi and his supporters protested vehemently that the election had been rigged and been stolen and that the reformists and their allies, the true victors, had been disenfranchised. The continued perception that Ahmadinejad's reelection could only have been the result of fraud has had devastating consequences. It solidified the same three concerns about the Islamic Republic—WMD, terrorism, and dictatorship—that ultimately justified the invasion of Iraq, reinforcing the conviction among many that the Islamic Republic could not (or should not) be dealt with diplomatically. Even previously self-identified advocates of engaging Tehran—on the left side of the Western political spectrum as well as on the right—began advocating regime change. These misperceptions still severely constrain American policy. If the prospect of rapprochement is discredited, then war remains the only long-term option for dealing with the Iranian challenge. And if Washington judges that it cannot afford another Middle Eastern war in the near term, it will do everything short of military confrontation to isolate, pressure, and coerce Tehran—perhaps even try to negotiate a limited nuclear deal with the Islamic Republic—until war becomes affordable again. Such has been the political logic driving America's Iran policy since June 2009.

A TYRANNY OF EXPECTATIONS

In the eyes of many Western liberals and progressives, Iran's 2009 presidential election was supposed to turn out very differently. Blinded by their faith that the Islamic Republic would inevitably metamorphose into a secular democracy, they had interpreted reformist electoral successes in the late 1990s and early 2000s as clear signs that Iranians wanted to move their system in a more liberal direction. This conviction offered no explanation for Ahmadinejad's lopsided victory in 2005, but by the end of his first term a remedy seemed at hand. When Mousavi decided to challenge Ahmadinejad in 2009, Western journalists and pundits applauded his campaign as a vehicle for reviving the reform movement and restoring Iran to its correct liberal trajectory. They flocked to Tehran to report on the expected triumph of liberalism over dictatorial fundamentalism.[2] This liberal victory would also affirm the judgment of media, intellectual, and policy elites (still smarting in the wake of the strategically disastrous Iraq invasion that too few of them had opposed before the fact) that the recently retired president George W. Bush's post-9/11 strategy had been wrong. Iranians would not need to be bombed or bullied into secular democracy; they would embrace it on their own, in the process ratifying the more enlightened approach of the new American president, Barack Hussein Obama. Western coverage of the campaign focused overwhelmingly on Mousavi and his prospects, with Western experts confidently predicting Ahmadinejad's defeat.

On June 7, less than a week before the Iranian election, a majority of voters in Lebanon's parliamentary elections cast ballots for Hizballah and its allies. However, because seats are distributed along religious lines and the number allotted to the Shi'a is less than their share of the population merits, Hizballah's opponents received the mandate to form the next government. The Obama administration attributed this "victory" to the president's Cairo address to the Muslim world on June 4, three days earlier; such outlets as the *Christian Science Monitor* and the *New York Times* prattled—not just in their editorials but in their reporting—about an "Obama effect" and its potential to transform the Middle East, where the next test would be Iran.[3] On June 12, as Iranian voters were going to the polls, Obama himself all but called on them to change their government, noting from a podium in the Rose Garden that what was "true in Lebanon can be true in Iran as well," that "you're seeing people looking at new possibilities."[4]

The West was unprepared—politically, intellectually, and no doubt psychologically—for a Mousavi defeat. Ahmadinejad had grated so infuriatingly on Western sensibilities, by questioning the Holocaust, claiming there are no gays in Iran, and invoking the Mahdi's return, that for many there was simply no way he could win; the explanation had to be nefarious. Within hours of the polls' closing, the Brookings Institution's Suzanne Maloney publicly asserted that Mousavi had in fact won and that the election had been stolen. She was joined in short order by other prominent Iran experts, including Reza Aslan, Farideh Farhi, Michael Ledeen, Trita Parsi, Karim Sadjadpour, Gary Sick, Ray Takeyh, and journalists turned Iran analysts Barbara Slavin and Robin Wright.[5] On June 21, 2009, just nine days after the election, Chatham House (the Royal Institute of International Affairs, a leading British think tank) issued a "preliminary analysis" of the results by Ali Ansari, a British academic specializing in Iranian politics, providing apparently scholarly proof that the results had been falsified.[6]

A variety of pop culture platforms also promoted this proposition. One of the earliest and most potent was *The Daily Show with Jon Stewart*. Before June 12, *The Daily Show* had dispatched a correspondent, Jason Jones, to Iran to tape segments that would be aired after the election. Titled "Behind the Veil," they captured charming encounters with English-speaking Iranians who could name all of the United States' modern presidents, regularly watched *The Daily Show* (one young man reprised Stewart's trademark "Heh, heh, heh, I'm the decider" impression of former president Bush), and were blithely unresponsive to Jones's efforts to bait them into making anti-Semitic or anti-American remarks. The pieces were clearly intended to show that Iranians are, deep down, "just like us."

To be really effective, though, the premise required a Mousavi victory. After the results were in, Stewart opened his postelection coverage ("Irandecision 2009") by noting that Tehran wanted the world to believe Ahmadinejad had won "even though he's bat-shit insane!"[7] As days and then weeks went by, neither Mousavi nor Karroubi nor anyone else presented evidence of any fraud at all, much less fraud on the scale that would have been needed to hand a Mousavi victory to Ahmadinejad. Still, the story of a stolen election lived on, and it was not just *The Daily Show* that fed it. Lacking actual proof, Roger Cohen of the *New York Times* fell back on "sometimes you have to smell the truth."[8] Editors at mainstream media outlets seemed all too happy to present such fatuousness as genuine reporting and analysis.

In reality, if anyone was out to steal the election, it was Mousavi. But Western opinion leaders and decision makers, enthralled as they were by the myth of the Islamic Republic's illegitimacy, were loath to weigh Ahmadinejad's strengths as a candidate against Mousavi's weaknesses. They were blind to the polls that had been carried out by both Western and Iranian groups showing that Ahmadinejad's reelection with just over 60 percent of the vote (officially he received 62 percent) was eminently plausible. They were also disinclined to look objectively at the way the election had been conducted and at what that conduct implied about the claims of fraud or at the opposition Green movement's social base and what it represented—which was not a majority of Iranians. And because they got these things wrong, today Western elites are not able to think clearly about the future of Iranian politics.

THE INCUMBENT'S STRENGTHS

Perhaps because Americans have a hard time grasping how someone they deem "bat-shit insane" can be politically popular, they and other Westerners overlooked the strengths that Ahmadinejad brought to the 2009 election. The populist style that had helped him win in 2005 strongly shaped his approach to the presidency. He was the Islamic Republic's first truly national president, convening his first cabinet meeting in Mashhad (Iran's second-largest city, in its northeastern corner). In his first term, he visited all thirty-one provinces, something no president had ever done; he visited most of them more than once. On his trips outside Tehran, he stopped not just in provincial capitals but in remote towns and villages across a country five times the size of France. He attracted crowds of ordinary people; after addressing them, he listened to their complaints, often for hours. Following his Mashhad example, he held cabinet meetings in other provincial cities.[9]

Populism carried over into policy, too. As he had as Tehran's mayor, Ahmadinejad made his first presidential initiative an "Imam Reza love fund" (named for the Eighth Imam, entombed in Mashhad) to provide young couples with the money to marry and start households. He required banks to lower interest rates on loans to ordinary Iranians. He raised the minimum wage, the salaries of nurses and health care workers, and the pensions of civil servants.[10] To combat inflation's tightening squeeze, his administration opened the domestic market to imported goods in multiple sectors and imposed price controls in others. On a grander scale, it used revenues generated by rising oil prices to boost government spending on physical infrastructure and social welfare, including signature programs like a national school renovation campaign, and on measures targeting more remote areas of the country. In Tehran, many economists (including some at the Central Bank of Iran and the government's Management and Planning Organization) and politicians complained that Ahmadinejad was putting too much money into the economy, depleting the Oil Stabilization Fund, and wreaking havoc with budget processes.[11] But whatever the economic deficits of these programs, Ahmadinejad knew what he was doing politically. His initiatives were popular with the constituencies that supported him; if, in some cases, they did not achieve their stated objectives, these constituents tended to blame the corrupt interests against whom the president continued to rail. On foreign policy, Ahmadinejad's tougher stance on the nuclear issue and on relations with

Washington also proved popular, solidifying his image as a leader who would stand up for the Islamic Republic.

More than his predecessors, Ahmadinejad conducted his presidency in campaign mode; by the time he stood for reelection, he had, in effect, already been running for four years. In a system limiting formal campaigns to a month before an election, this resolve put almost any would-be challenger at a disadvantage. But as Ahmadinejad continued on his populist course, he also became the most polarizing president in the Islamic Republic's history. The part of the body politic that dislikes Ahmadinejad dislikes him with a vengeance. Even on the right he stirred controversy. Principlist factions that had supported his second-round campaign in 2005 were dismayed to see cabinet posts and senior positions in local government distributed overwhelmingly to Ahmadinejad loyalists, many of them either unknown or considered hostile to the political establishment. When Khatami's presidency had begun, a conservative Majles had approved all his ministerial appointees. By contrast, several of Ahmadinejad's nominees were rejected by a Majles controlled by his ostensible allies.[12]

Conservative resistance to Ahmadinejad was a major factor shaping the 2006 Assembly of Experts elections. Reformists essentially boycotted them. Ahmadinejad backed a slate headed by Ayatollah Taqi Mesbah Yazdi (frequently described as his spiritual adviser); other conservative clerics and their allies formed competitor lists. After his 2005 humiliation, Rafsanjani wanted to reassert his influence. Though he already held an assembly seat, he negotiated with anti-Ahmadinejad conservative groups to put his name atop their lists in Tehran, where he retained greater popularity than elsewhere. Rafsanjani handily won a seat; when the assembly's chairman died the next year, he became its new chairman. Similarly, in the 2006 municipal elections, a pro-Ahmadinejad slate sought control of Tehran's city council with the aim of ousting Mohammad Baqer Qalibaf as mayor; instead, an alternative principlist coalition won and reappointed Qalibaf. During his first two years as president, Ahmadinejad also clashed with the Supreme National Security Council's secretary-general, Ali

Larijani, a leading principlist rival; Larijani finally resigned in 2007. In parliamentary elections the next year, Larijani won a seat from Qom; when the new Majles convened, he became speaker. In the runup to these elections, conservative forces in the Majles divided into two coalitions, one (the United Principlists Front) functioning as the pro-Ahmadinejad bloc and the other (the Broad Principlists Coalition) attracting anti-Ahmadinejad conservatives.[13]

These developments prompted some Western commentators to assert the unraveling of Ahmadinejad's political base. But conservative animus against the president was largely a reaction to his political style and what many saw as a disproportionate distribution of patronage to his loyalists rather than to principlists more generally. Both Larijani and Qalibaf considered challenging his reelection. Larijani used his position as Majles speaker to make himself a rallying point for conservatives dissatisfied with Ahmadinejad. Qalibaf burnished his technocratic credentials as a hands-on manager who held Tehran city bureaucrats and contractors accountable for their performance; he also cultivated an international profile, traveling to the World Economic Forum in Davos in 2006.[14] In the end, though, both men chose not to run—according to advisers to one of them, because Khamenei "did not encourage" them to.[15] Only Mohsen Rezae, the Expediency Council's secretary-general and a former Pasdaran commander, ran against Ahmadinejad from the right. But, his résumé notwithstanding, Rezae was never more than a marginal candidate. As the 2009 campaign approached, the United Front and the Broad Coalition both disbanded; while there was still conservative disgruntlement, Ahmadinejad would seek reelection with more or less unified principlist support.[16]

If the president was going to be turned out, it would have to be by a candidate on the left—someone with extraordinary crossover appeal, capable of winning votes outside the established anti-Ahmadinejad and proreformist constituencies. And just as Westerners tended to ignore Ahmadinejad's strength, they glossed over Mousavi's weak points.

THE CHALLENGER'S WEAKNESSES

The way Mousavi became the president's main opponent says a lot about the difficulties that have weighed on the reform movement since Khatami's second term—difficulties reflected above all in the lack of a credible successor to Khatami. None of the first-round reformist candidates in 2005 made the runoff, and reformist votes were irrelevant in Ahmadinejad's second-round landslide. Afterward, Mehdi Karroubi resigned from the Participation Front to form his own party to contest Ahmadinejad's reelection.[17] But many reformists doubted that the septuagenarian Karroubi could succeed. Some supported him on principle, as the only real reformist running; most searched for a stronger candidate, including some who called for another presidential bid by Khatami. Khatami's advisers believed that most Iranians continued to regard him positively as a man of integrity and piety, but their esteem did not erase the disappointment over what is still widely seen as his presidency's unfulfilled promise. Even many of his admirers view him as a weak politician unwilling to fight for his agenda. And, as one prominent reformist who served in his administration notes, he is almost as polarizing a figure for conservatives as Ahmadinejad is for reformists. Thus, most reformists calculated that it would be smarter to run someone who, while acceptable to their base, might also attract conservatives disenchanted with Ahmadinejad.[18]

But there had not yet been (and has yet to be) a generational shift in the reform camp's upper echelons comparable to the emergence of the new generation of conservative leaders. As in 2005, reformists speculated about candidacies by younger figures, including Sadeq Kharrazi, the former foreign minister's nephew, who had had his own distinguished diplomatic career, and Mohammad Reza Khatami, the former president's younger brother, who was a hero of the Iran-Iraq War and an accomplished physician and who had served a term in the Majles in 2000–04, when a reformist majority had made him deputy speaker. But Kharrazi was one of those who, having had important roles in nuclear and other negotiations with the United States under Khatami, were still harshly criticized for having been soft—that is, for helping America in Afghanistan and suspending Iran's enrichment activities for nearly two years of nuclear talks with Europe without getting anything in return. So as reformists surveyed the political landscape going into 2009, most of them concluded they would have to find a compromise candidate.

Rafsanjani's 2005 defeat motivated him to work against Ahmadinejad's reelection, putting him—finally—in a de facto alliance with Khatami and the reformists. But as 2009 approached, it was clear that Rafsanjani was no longer a viable candidate. The 2006 Assembly of Experts elections had showed that he retained a measure of political skill, but there had been no significant improvement in his public image. Nor could any of his protégés fit the bill. As in 2005, those protégés who had figured prominently in Khatami's administration—for example, Hassan Rohani, the Supreme National Security Council's former secretary-general—were implicated in the same perceived foreign policy failures as some younger reformists.

These factors were behind the reformists' choice of Mousavi as Ahmadinejad's principal challenger—and while their decision may have appeared reasonable at the time, in retrospect it looks utterly misguided.

Mousavi was a year older than Khatami; he turned sixty-seven in 2009. As a former prime minister and Expediency Council member, he had enough standing to avoid disqualification by the Guardian Council. But he had not been involved in high-level electoral politics for more than twenty years and most young Iranians had no memory of him. Moreover, his record did not easily fit the profile of a reformist. His political roots lay in the most radical parts of the Islamic left. Trained as an architect, he had been a protégé of Ali Shariati, a leftist intellectual linked to the Liberation Movement. After joining the revolution, he helped found the Islamic Republican Party and briefly served as foreign minister under President Mohammad Ali Rajai. When Khamenei became president in 1981, his choice for prime minister was Ali Akbar Velayati, but the Majles's leftist majority refused to approve the conservative Velayati (who became foreign minister), handing the post to Mousavi instead. As prime minister, Mousavi was hardly a champion of expanded freedoms. He pushed statist policies that proved deeply damaging to the economy; while the pressure of the Iran-Iraq War would have tested any government, Mousavi's stewardship was widely judged to have exacerbated wartime shortages of food and other essential commodities. Furthermore, he was ill-adapted to modern campaigning. He had a Bob Dole–like persona, unexciting on the stump and, it turned out, lousy on television. For him to unseat Ahmadinejad—one of the most talented politicians in the Islamic Republic's history, with a demonstrated ability to exploit his adversaries' vulnerabilities—was, from the outset, an extremely tall order.

Mousavi was arguably the most substantial candidate ever to challenge a sitting president. But to win he would have had to mobilize all the negative reaction to Ahmadinejad and then some, at a point in the presidential cycle when, history suggests, incumbents retain much of the support that put them into office. Comparing strengths and weaknesses, there was never much chance Mousavi would beat Ahmadinejad. But he would stress the system in trying to.

THE POLLS AND THE DEBATES

In studying elections and outcomes in even minimally competitive political systems, Western analysts have come to depend on polling. Polls are never perfect, and they can sometimes be utterly misleading. But when they are reliable, they are the best tool available for exploring mass political attitudes, and they have a strong track record in predicting outcomes. In a collective display of professional malfeasance, most Western Iran experts have ignored the information provided by methodologically sound polls taken during the 2009 election and after. The key words here are "methodologically sound"—that is, drawing on samples that are both sufficiently large and random to minimize sampling error and using clear and neutrally worded questions. Polls have been conducted in Iran for more than two decades. In the weeks preceding the 2009 election, dozens were carried out—by the candidates, by news organizations, by universities, and by government agencies. The forecasts were all over the map, with some predicting a win for Ahmadinejad and others for Mousavi, and with big variations in the anticipated margins of victory. Most of these surveys, though, would never pass muster with professional pollsters.[19] Many made no pretense at scientific sampling. Some were "push polls," with questions presenting one candidate more favorably than the others. One of Mousavi's surveys sent pollsters to metro stations in north Tehran—Mousavi territory, an enclave of well-off liberals comparable to Manhattan's Upper West Side—to ask passersby whom they planned to vote for; not surprisingly, Mousavi did very well.

With methodological soundness as a standard, thirteen polls conducted in connection with the 2009 election warrant particular consideration. They were conducted by four organizations, at periods ranging from just before the campaign season officially began, on May 15, to three months after the vote. Three were well-known Western groups: the U.S.-based Terror Free Tomorrow (TFT), which has experience in surveying Muslim populations; the Canadian-based Globe-Scan, which also has international experience; and World Public Opinion (WPO), run by the University of Maryland's Program on International Policy Attitudes (PIPA). The fourth was a survey unit at the University of Tehran. Each of the Western groups ran a single poll—TFT a month before the election, GlobeScan seven to eleven days afterward, and WPO/PIPA two and a half to three months afterward. The University of Tehran unit ran ten surveys: eight before the election, starting in mid-May and ending on election eve, one some ten days later, and another roughly a month afterward. Their results were consistent with those of the Western groups, validating their reliability and their use in assessing the election.[20] Moreover, the findings from these thirteen polls were affirmed a year later by another methodologically sound poll done by Charney Research, run by a former pollster for Bill Clinton and Nelson Mandela.[21]

The data show that in the electorate's estimation Ahmadinejad started the campaign ahead of Mousavi—by a margin of more than two to one, according to TFT, and more than three to one, according to the University of Tehran. Mousavi's advisers also assessed that Ahmadinejad began the campaign well ahead, attributing his advantage to their candidate's lower name recognition, particularly among younger voters, after his long absence from politics.[22]

Backed by two former presidents, Mousavi had the resources to mount a serious campaign, with well-choreographed rallies and professionally produced media spots. He also had his own newspaper and Web site, both called *Kaleme* ("word"). Mousavi did not repeat the egregious mistakes of Rafsanjani's 2005 campaign; he made a point of campaigning outside Tehran, notably in Iran's Azeri-majority areas, where he hoped his own Azeri ethnicity would attract voters. While drawing core support from committed reformists and more upscale parts of society, he also sought to appeal to "pragmatic" conservatives (Rafsanjani voters) and principlists alienated from Ahmadinejad. Many Western journalists reported that he was reassembling the coalition that had propelled Khatami's victories, including highly visible contingents of youth and women.[23]

Ahmadinejad ran an updated version of his 2005 campaign, with a bigger budget and more sophisticated advertisements. He appealed to ideological conservatives but also to the less advantaged, the more religious, and the denizens of smaller cities and rural areas. This strategy was apparent even in Tehran. In the affluent north of the city most candidate photos in cars and shops were of Mousavi; south Tehran, which is more working class and religious, was Ahmadinejad country, with myriad displays of popular support for the incumbent. Ahmadinejad's initial advantage over Mousavi was not just a function of higher name recognition but a reflection of the breadth of his political base.[24] Mousavi had his work cut out for him.

Mousavi appeared to be moving public opinion his way during the last two weeks of May. Crowds at his campaign events grew. More concretely, the University of Tehran surveys show that he reduced the gap with Ahmadinejad, from 63–19 at the beginning of the campaign season to 57–26 a week later, 48–30 a few days after that, and 39–30 on June 1. The University of Tehran polls also indicate that at the beginning of the campaign voters evaluated Ahmadinejad's campaign as "more effective" than Mousavi's; by June 1, they judged the two campaigns equally effective. According to the TFT and University of Tehran polls, both Karroubi and Rezae started off in the low single digits; the University of Tehran data show no appreciable rise in their support in the campaign's first two weeks.

But while Mousavi's numbers improved, no methodologically sound poll ever showed him in the lead. His 30 percent score in the University of Tehran's June 1 survey, still nine points behind Ahmadinejad, was his best performance. After that, the numbers broke increasingly for the incumbent. The key factor driving this reversal was something Americans recognize as critically important in their own elections: television. Between June 2 and June 8, Iran held its first-ever televised debates among presidential candidates, injecting much the same kind of drama into the campaign that the Kennedy-Nixon debates brought to the 1960 U.S. election. The live broadcasts attracted large numbers of viewers and were quickly uploaded online, where even more people could see them. They roused the electorate, almost certainly contributing to the high turnout on June 12.

The debates did not bring all four candidates together at the same time; rather, in each of six matches, two different candidates were pitted directly against each other. The June 3 debate, between Ahmadinejad and Mousavi, seemed to give the advantage to Ahmadinejad—even Mousavi's aides say the incumbent came across as confident while their man appeared wooden and unsure of himself.[25] Ahmadinejad was particularly effective in linking Mousavi to Rafsanjani, and, by extension, to Rafsanjani's son, who had been publicly accused of corruption. Contrasting Rafsanjani's administration with his own—in which, he said, no ministers had "become millionaires"—Ahmadinejad emphasized his image as the champion of ordinary Iranians. Though expatriate supporters of Mousavi (like Trita Parsi) continue to tell Western audiences, with no supporting data at all—not even unscientific polling—that their candidate won the debate, reliable polls confirm that Ahmadinejad prevailed and thus boosted his candidacy going into the final stretch.[26] The University of Tehran surveys show Ahmadinejad's lead over Mousavi opening up again after their televised encounter: to 48–29 on June 4, 52–28 on June 6–8, 54–23 on June 9–10, and 57–27 on June 11 (election eve). While neither Mousavi nor Ahmadinejad lost many committed voters as a result of the debate, Ahmadinejad picked up the bulk of those who made up their minds after watching it. (These polls also showed Karroubi and Rezae continuing to scrape along in the low single digits.)

On election day, turnout was high, around 85 percent. Pro-Mousavi analysts assumed this factor would favor the challenger—but their optimism misconstrued the degree to which the debates had energized pro-Ahmadinejad voters. According to the official results, the incumbent won with 62.5 percent of the vote. Mousavi came in a distant second, with 33.5 percent. Rezae received less than 2 percent, Karroubi less than 1 percent, and just over 1 percent of ballots were blank or otherwise invalid. Mousavi took one of Iran's three Azeri-majority provinces and Sistan-Balochistan, its only Sunni-majority province. He carried the city of Tehran, doing well enough in north Tehran to offset his weaker performance in other parts of the city, but he narrowly lost Tehran province, which extends beyond the city to encompass less prosperous and more conservative areas.[27]

These results are in line with what the methodologically sound polls run before the election would lead any analyst not blinded by personal preferences to expect. The polls also explain why Ahmadinejad won. In the TFT and University of Tehran surveys, he outscored Mousavi by double digits (sometimes by 40–50 points) on questions asking which candidate "has a better understanding of people's problems," which is "more honest," "more unpretentious and down to earth," "more unwavering," and "will be better able to make Iran outstanding in the world." The University of Tehran polls showed that Iranians judged Ahmadinejad "better able to deal with the country's economic problems"; while many complained about inflation, TFT found that most did not hold the president responsible. Most respondents in the University of Tehran polls also saw Ahmadinejad's campaign as more positive. Asked whether a candidate's campaign was "mostly geared toward introducing his own programs or attacking the other candidates," Ahmadinejad never received less than 51 percent saying he focused on his own programs; on June 11, he led Mousavi on this measure by 13 points.[28]

These results are affirmed by the four methodologically sound polls, two from the University of Tehran and one each from GlobeScan and WPO/PIPA, conducted after the election. The percentage of respondents saying they voted is in line with the official turnout rate of 85 percent: 86 percent in the GlobeScan poll, 87 percent in the WPO/PIPA survey. The percentage saying they voted for Ahmadinejad is also consistent with official results: 61 percent in the first University of Tehran poll, 56 percent in the GlobeScan survey, 66 percent in the second University of Tehran poll, and 55 percent in the WPO/PIPA survey.[29]

Those who dislike the official election results have resisted the polls demonstrating their plausibility. Of the surveys discussed here, only the TFT poll was released prior to the election; many Western analysts dismissed it for having been conducted nearly a month before the vote and thus before the formal beginning of the campaign.[30] But the University of Tehran's pre- and postelection polls and the Globe-Scan, WPO/PIPA, and Charney Research postelection polls all gave similar results. Moreover, there is internal evidence across these polls that respondents were expressing their views honestly, without feeling compelled to deceive a pollster over a (potentially monitored) phone line: there was, for example, no "bandwagoning," with more people saying after the election that they had been with the winner all along.[31] Determined to deny the findings, some Western analysts have resorted to arguing that Iranians cannot be accurately polled because they are culturally programmed to lie to strangers.[32] Leaving aside the claim's rank essentialism, no population lies to pollsters in the same percentages across fourteen different polls based on scientifically selected samples—which is what would have had to happen to explain away the results as products of deliberate dishonesty.

MOUSAVI'S GAME PLAN

Given the polling data, it's fair to ask whether Mousavi ever had a reasonable basis to think he could win. The University of Tehran polls were not publicized before the election, but his campaign was aware of them. Based on improving poll numbers and on the growing crowds at his events, his advisers believed before the debates that he had a chance—not of winning outright on June 12 but of keeping Ahmadinejad under 50 percent, thereby necessitating a two-man runoff. And if he continued his upswing from the campaign's first two weeks, he could go into the runoff with an energized base and a sense of momentum (a key to getting late deciders to vote). After the debates, however, polls and other indicators showed such an outcome to be less and less likely.[33]

In reviewing Mousavi's campaign, he may well have understood by election day that he was not going to win at the ballot box. If so, he may also have calculated that he might still secure the presidency, if the vote were close enough and he could mount enough pressure on Ayatollah Khamenei to force the Guardian Council to annul the results and rerun the election, discrediting Ahmadinejad in the process. With this hypothesis in mind, consider the actions of the candidate and some of his supporters in the campaign's last days. On June 9, Rafsanjani sent an open letter to Khamenei asking that he make Ahmadinejad withdraw allegations of corruption against Rafsanjani and his family; it also urged Khamenei to put a stop to unspecified plots to rig the election.[34] After the election in 2005, Rafsanjani and Karroubi had accused Ahmadinejad's camp of fraud, without substantiating the charge; this time, Rafsanjani was priming the pump in advance. WikiLeaks documents show that in the days before the election a former official close to Rafsanjani, who was also advising Mousavi's campaign, regaled staffers of Voice of America (the U.S. government's external propaganda arm) with lurid tales of a plan by Khamenei's son, aided by Revolutionary Guard and Basij commanders, to manipulate the outcome—tales for which, one VOA broadcaster pointed out, he provided no proof.[35]

Two days after Rafsanjani's letter, on election eve, Mousavi sent Khamenei another open letter, deploring "measures" having "no outcome other than causing frustration and disappointment for people who are actively participating in strengthening the pillars of the Islamic Republic's system." He claimed that the Revolutionary Guards and the Basij were "interfering with the elections" in Ahmadinejad's favor, a charge reminiscent of Rafsanjani, Moin, and Karroubi's complaints in 2005. He also declared that "members of the Guardian Council . . . and some supervisors in the provinces are not observing the rule of impartiality" and were "openly supporting" Ahmadinejad and that the "Interior Ministry and provincial governors are hesitating in accepting the list of my representatives [at] places where votes are counted and at polling stations."[36] He did not document any of these allegations.

Western analysts have overlooked the real significance of the open letters, both of which—Mousavi's in particular—appear to have been crafted to lay the groundwork for discrediting the vote after the fact.

ASSESSING THE CHARGES OF FRAUD

Polls alone cannot, of course, validate the results of an election. Validation requires a careful assessment of the procedures and processes that generated the results and of whether they were subverted. Mousavi, Karroubi, and others advanced an array of complaints about the 2009 election to support their charge that the official results were fraudulent. Foreign critics and journalists picked up on their allegations and elaborated them, with enormous impact both inside and outside Iran. But not one of their contentions has ever been substantiated. Most of them do not stand up to even minimal scrutiny.

Procedures for casting and counting votes and registering vote totals in Iranian elections take place under the constant and redundant observation of Interior Ministry and Guardian Council officials, judiciary officials, and public volunteers. In addition, each candidate is entitled to have observers at polling stations and everywhere that votes are aggregated into higher-level totals; candidates register their observers in advance on an Interior Ministry Web site so that they can receive IDs allowing them access to the relevant facilities.[37] In 2009, there were 45,692 polling stations—31,398 at fixed locations and another 14,298 mobile ones, traveling (as in previous elections) to rural areas, hospitals, and other places where it would be difficult for voters to get to fixed-location stations. According to Interior Ministry data, 40,676 observers registered for Mousavi, 33,058 for Ahmadinejad, 13,506 for Karroubi, and 5,421 for Rezae.

Every Iranian aged eighteen or over, including those living abroad, may vote; in 2009, the Iranian government operated polling stations for expatriates in almost a hundred countries, including the United States. To vote, an Iranian must show an official ID with the bearer's photograph, thumbprint, and a unique number. At the polling station, the voter's name and ID number are recorded three times: by hand in a register, on a computer, and again by hand on the voter's ballot stub. Before casting the ballot, the voter must press a purple-ink thumbprint onto the stub, which is then separated from the ballot and dropped into a "stub box." (Separation of the stub prior to the casting of the ballot ensures the secrecy of the vote.) The voter marks the ballot and drops it into the ballot box; the voter's ID card is then stamped, to prevent him or her from voting again.[38]

The votes are counted at the polling stations. Before the polls open, observers at each station watch as the ballot boxes are verified to be empty. No votes are counted until after polls close. At that point observers at each station watch as the stubs and ballots are counted and their numbers compared. They then watch as each candidate's count is recorded on government-issued Form 22; at every station, multiple copies of Form 22 are signed by both officials and observers. Signed forms are placed inside the ballot box, which is sealed and turned over to local officials to hold; signed forms are also sent to the Interior Ministry and copies are given to each observer. In addition, information on these Form 22s is electronically transmitted to district-level offices, where, as candidate observers watch, vote totals from polling stations are aggregated into district-level results and recorded on government-issued Form 28s; these are sent both electronically and physically to the Interior Ministry, which aggregates them into provincial- and national-level results.[39] In 2009, for the first time, data from polling stations were also transmitted directly to the ministry.

On June 13, with results showing that Ahmadinejad had won, Mousavi began charging fraud. On June 14, he met with Ayatollah Khamenei, who the next day directed the Guardian Council to investigate the losing candidates' complaints. Formally, Mousavi made his case in three open letters to the guardians, in which he demanded "nullification of the results."[40] Published on his Web site and in his newspaper on June 14, 20, and 28, his claims boiled down to ten main points.

The first three were complaints about Ahmadinejad's conduct. Reprising Rafsanjani's objection to the incumbent's "outrageous" statements, Mousavi asserted that Ahmadinejad had falsely accused him of criminal acts. He reiterated his preelection claims that Ahmadinejad had illegally "used all the public resources provided by the state for [his] election campaign in different cities and provinces" and that laws barring the "armed forces, including the Basij," from participating in political activities "were grossly violated." And he charged that Ahmadinejad had "revealed state secrets" in the debates, thus damaging "national security."

His next three points recycled common complaints by Iranian candidates running against incumbents. He alleged that Ahmadinejad had timed development projects and increases in government salaries, pensions, and benefits for the poor and for rural residents to the election. He claimed that state media had provided "illegal extra time" to the incumbent. (In one passage, whose irony became glaring as events unfolded, he took umbrage that Ahmadinejad had "warned against violent unrest after the election" and had accused Mousavi of "conspiracy to start unrest" while "implying that his win is certain.") He also asserted that the polling stations had closed early to suppress his vote—even though they had stayed open at least three hours past the announced closing time.

Even if true, none of these six points would have constituted fraud. But Mousavi advanced four more claims that, he said, were "clear indicators for widespread and organized fraudulent activity." The first of these focused on the handling and integrity of the ballots, even before voters cast them at polling stations. He charged that "hundreds of polling stations all around the country, especially in larger cities, ran out of voting ballots many hours before the closing time of the polls" and that this was especially prevalent in areas where support for him was strong. Moreover, he wrote, "millions of additional ballot papers were printed without serial numbers," which expanded the possibilities for fraud.

Second, Mousavi averred that there had been "more than 170 voting districts" (out of 368) where "the percentage of the votes cast was between 95 percent and 140 percent of the total number of eligible voters." These figures implied that there were large numbers of votes in these districts that had been fraudulently cast or recorded.

Third, Mousavi complained about the treatment of his observers. As in his preelection letter to Khamenei, he charged that he had been denied his legal right to deploy observers at all polling stations. As noted, 40,676 Mousavi observers registered with the Interior Ministry, more than for any other candidate; Mousavi alleged that a further 5,016 had been denied credentials. He also charged that "many" of his observers had been "turned away" from stations (both fixed and mobile) and, at "most" stations, had not been allowed to witness the placing of the ballot boxes.

Finally, Mousavi complained about vote counting, claiming that the ministry had "started to announce vote counts . . . before the counting was completed in many of the polling stations." This was an especially audacious charge, given that his election-day victory proclamation and his aide's claim that he had won 65 percent of the vote had both been made while polls were still open, no votes had been counted, and no genuine "information" on returns was available. It was in response to his declaration that the Interior Ministry began releasing vote totals as they came in from the field after the polls closed, without waiting to aggregate them into a single batch. (These were the returns we were following with our Iranian colleague.)

Before and after the guardians reported on their investigation of his complaints on July 16, 2009, Mousavi amplified his formal presentations through additional open letters, statements in his newspaper and on his Web site, and declarations at protest rallies.[41] Taken together, his allegations implied two distinct theories of how the fraud had been perpetrated. Either ballot boxes had been stuffed with large numbers of bogus ballots (before the boxes' placement in polling stations and/or when they were prevented from being properly observed) or real votes had never been counted but had been replaced with precooked results. Conversations with Mousavi aides suggest that the candidate and his advisers were not able to agree among themselves on a single story—a curious situation because facts should have led them to embrace one theory or the other. If Mousavi had had real evidence of fraud, that evidence would have led him to settle on one theory or the other, but in fact he never produced evidence for either. Indeed, he never substantiated any of his myriad accusations of electoral misconduct, though virtually all of them, if true, should have been readily documentable. Instead, the point seemed to be to marshal enough pressure on Khamenei to force an annulment. The only other possible explanation for his conduct, that he was strikingly ill-informed about the electoral process and how to contest the results effectively, seems highly unlikely given that he was a former prime minister, backed by two former presidents, and counseled by experienced advisers.

Still, Western commentators and Iran experts accepted his assertions uncritically. While Ansari and his colleagues did not take up Mousavi's allegations about the treatment of his observers, they wholeheartedly embraced his claim of "excess voting" as proof of fraud.[42] The notion that more votes had been cast than there were registered voters circulated widely, endorsed not just by Iran experts but also by specialists on U.S. elections (for example, Nate Silver of FiveThirtyEight.com) and echoed by journalists for major outlets (for example, Scott Peterson of the *Christian Science Monitor* and Nazila Fathi of the *New York Times*).[43]

But the claim is nonsense. There are no "registered voters" in the Islamic Republic; every Iranian aged eighteen or over is effectively a registered voter. In presidential elections, Iranians are not required to vote in set locations—they can vote in any of tens of thousands of polling places across the country or abroad.[44] Elections are typically held on a Friday (a weekend day in the Islamic Republic) in the spring or summer; under the same conditions, the number of votes cast had exceeded the presumed number of eligible voters resident in many districts in several previous national elections, including those that Khatami won in 1997 and 2001. On June 12, 2009, many Iranians were away from home—on weekend holidays, visiting relatives, and so forth—and many expatriates had come home to vote. The Guardian Council considered all these factors, along with the mobility of military and student populations and of people moving from urban centers to suburbs while still "statistically belonging" to the cities from which they originally came, in its investigation into Mousavi's complaints.[45]

The official results indicated (and the Interior Ministry and Guardian Council affirmed) that in 2009 these factors produced three million "excess" votes spread across forty-eight cities and towns. Ansari called this discrepancy an admission that "up to three million votes had gone missing," whether through "tombstone voting," prestuffed ballot boxes, or other forms of fraud.[46] But the only way vote totals would establish fraud would be for the number of votes reported to exceed the number of eligible voters nationwide, not just in a particular district; in 2009, turnout was around 85 percent. While Mousavi claimed in his newspaper that ten million people had voted without proper identification, his submissions to the guardians specified only thirty-one such cases; he never came close to showing that a significant portion of the "excess" votes were fraudulently cast. Furthermore, the districts with comparatively high proportions of votes cast to estimated eligible voters included some that favored Mousavi.[47]

Likewise, the guardians found that the number of polling stations that had experienced temporary ballot shortages accounted for "an insignificant percentage of the entire ballot boxes across the country." In the few stations that ran out, "voters either had to wait a bit for ballot papers to be dispatched . . . [or had to] go to a nearby polling station" to cast their votes; interrupted ballot supplies could not have tipped the numbers so strongly in Ahmadinejad's favor. The guardians also explained that in previous elections every ballot had had two serial numbers, one a national number and the other a number enabling its tracking in the province where it was distributed. The vast majority of ballots in 2009 were so printed. But in anticipation of a high turnout, a final tranche of two million ballots was printed on election eve, and these received national but not provincial numbers. The guardians reported that no ballots had been illegally distributed, explaining in detail how all were accounted for; Mousavi never disputed their evidence. And, even if all two million ballots had somehow been fraudulently cast, they would still not have been enough to produce Ahmadinejad's decisive win.

As to Mousavi's allegations about unfair treatment of his observers (essential to the theory that large numbers of fraudulent ballots were cast), the guardians found that, while 40,676 Mousavi observers were registered by the Interior Ministry, 5,016 were not registered because his campaign had "failed to provide the required documents," even though the registration deadline was extended to just three days before the election.[48] Mousavi never denied this finding. His campaign identified seventy-three individuals whom it had sent to polling stations but who were turned away; the guardians found that not one had been a registered observer and that there had been "no report of any problem for those representatives who had ID cards."[49] Again, Mousavi did not dispute these findings; his campaign never identified either a single registered observer who had been excluded from a station or a single station where observers had been excluded.[50] The council also reported that Mousavi failed to identify any station where his observers "could not observe the placing of ballot boxes," noting archly that "mentioning general issues and relying on what one has heard or speculated seems to be the only evidence on the basis of which such complaints have been made."[51]

As for Mousavi's complaints about the generation of vote totals (essential to the theory that real votes were replaced with precooked results), his campaign identified seven polling stations where, it alleged, ballot boxes had been moved or otherwise handled in ways putting the vote count into question. The guardians reported that "these claims were unsubstantiated," and Mousavi did not challenge their finding.[52] He never produced a single one of his 40,676 observers to claim that the count at his or her station had been incorrect, and none came forward independently.[53] In 2009, for the first time, the Interior Ministry published vote totals from every station. Mousavi could have destroyed their credibility by identifying stations where data on his observers' Form 22s differed from the published results, but he never produced any evidence of such a discrepancy. As to his claim that his observers had not been allowed to monitor the ministry's aggregation of vote totals, the guardians concluded that the challenger was, to put it bluntly, making it up: "Representatives of the candidates were present and have observed all aspects of adding up and announcing the outcome of the election. Many of them left their desks at 6 a.m. on Saturday, June 13. . . . Creating doubt and uncertainty about the presence of the candidates' representatives at the time of adding up the votes, based on the existing evidence, is unbelievable. It is an unreal claim."[54] No observer has contradicted this finding, either.

Some Western and expatriate critics argue that, in a postelection climate of "intimidation" and "repression," it is too much to ask observers to come forward; from their perspective, instead of requiring Mousavi to document his charges, it is the Iranian government's responsibility to "establish its legitimacy"—for example, by publishing all hard-copy Form 22s.[55] But aside from its presumption, this line of reasoning ignores both Mousavi's obvious eagerness to contest the outcome and the fact that, during the first week after the election, hundreds of thousands of Iranians either did not perceive or did not care about possible government retaliation—they poured into the streets, at least partly in response to Mousavi's exhortations, to protest. Surely in this climate, and with the whole world watching, Mousavi could have dared to produce a single observer—an Iranian by definition committed to his cause—to substantiate his accusations. But he did not. He could have discredited the government's claims about the validity of the official results by presenting even one Form 22 showing a count for a polling station different from that published by the Interior Ministry. But he never did. Indeed, he never publicly displayed interest in examining any of the documents that could have validated a genuine claim of fraud. Eight days after the election, the guardians ordered that 10 percent of the ballot boxes, in six provinces, be recounted and the results checked against district-level Form 28s; Mousavi refused to send observers.[56] (The guardians reported that "no significant discrepancy was found between the announced results and the results of the recount.") A week later, Mousavi's campaign proposed recounting ballots in four provinces. When the guardians asked that Mousavi first make the request in writing—most likely so that, if the recount showed no irregularities, he would feel obliged to drop his challenge—he declined.[57]

ALTERNATE REALITIES

In the months preceding the 2003 invasion of Iraq, the American policy, intelligence, and media communities failed to exercise critical scrutiny over intellectually shoddy if not downright bogus claims about Saddam Husayn's weapons of mass destruction programs, Baghdad's ties to Al-Qa'ida and other terrorist groups, and internal Iraqi politics. Through their failure, they helped sell a manufactured case for war, enabling one of the United States' biggest strategic blunders since the end of the Cold War. In 2009, the same communities— and in some cases the same individuals—once again disgraced themselves with regard to the Iranian election. Mousavi's dissent was not a fact-based challenge to abuses that generated a fraudulent outcome. But his inability to back up his allegations did not stop Western pundits and media outlets from endorsing them as facts. In a manner distressingly reminiscent of the runup to the Iraq War, political, policy, and media elites, including the West's "best" and "most respected" Iran analysts, failed to assess the election rigorously. Rushing to judgment on the basis of exaggerated rumors and, on some points, outright inventions, they created an alternate reality, dismissing facts that got in their way. As mounting poll data undermined their unsubstantiated claims, only a few were even prepared to retreat to "we will probably never know."[58]

Some Western experts on Iran went beyond merely accepting unsubstantiated claims about electoral fraud. If Mousavi could not prove it, they tried to do so themselves by arguing that the results were too inconsistent with past voting patterns to be credible. Three flaws in this approach merit specific attention. First, many analysts compared the 2009 election to the first round of the 2005 election, when Rafsanjani and Ahmadinejad outpolled other candidates to move into a runoff; seen this way, Ahmadinejad's 2009 tally seems suspiciously large.[59] But the comparison is false—it is tantamount to holding that, because Barack Obama took just 38 percent of the vote in a multican-didate caucus in Iowa in January 2008, he could not possibly have won 54 percent of the state's vote in the general election against John McCain ten months later. As noted, high-quality polls make it clear that the 2009 election was, from the outset, a two-man race; Ahmadinejad's share of the vote in the 2005 runoff (61.7 percent) is very close to what he won in 2009 (62.5 percent).

Second, analysts argued that the 2009 results departed implausibly from some ethnic groups' previous voting behavior, finding it incred-ible, for example, that Karroubi, an ethnic Lori, did not carry his native Lorestan, as he had in 2005, and that Ahmadinejad, who had won just 7 percent of the province's vote in the first round in 2005, took 70 percent in 2009.[60] But, as also noted, high-quality polls showed Karroubi's support in the low single digits throughout the 2009 cam-paign. Nationally, many voters declined to waste their vote on a candi-date they did not think could win, and many Lors appear to have made the same choice. The results show that Karroubi did in fact benefit from an ethnic "bump," doing five times better in Lorestan than he did nationally (and twenty-five times better in his native district). But this bump did not offset reduced support from voters who concluded he could not win.[61] There is also no basis for assuming that Lori voters defecting from Karroubi would favor Mousavi. Lorestan is one of Iran's more conservative provinces; a majority of its voters supported Nateq-Nouri over Khatami in 1997.

Similarly, analysts harped on Mousavi's underperformance among ethnic Azeris. As noted, Mousavi took a majority of votes in West Azerbaijan, but not in Ardabil or East Azerbaijan (his home province). One of Karim Sadjadpour's more ill-informed (and widely repeated) assertions was that this outcome was "as plausible as John McCain winning the African-American vote against Obama" in 2008. The State Department's Iran watchers in Dubai argued likewise that, "historically, even minor presidential candidates with an Azerbaijani background win these provinces."[62] But in fact there is no such history of Azeris voting along ethnic lines; presidential candidates of Azeri origin have not always fared well with their ethnic kinsmen. (Mohsen Mehralizadeh, for example, carried just 29 percent of the Azeri vote in 2005.) Khamenei is half Azeri; in contrast to voters in Sistan-Balochistan (which Mousavi carried), Azeris were not looking to vote against the system. Like Karroubi in Lorestan, Mousavi did better in Azeri areas than he did nationally, but not well enough to offset his weak performance elsewhere. Sadjadpour's wisecrack also ignores Ahmadinejad's strengths in Azeri areas. Before entering electoral politics, Ahmadinejad was a district governor in East Azerbaijan and governor-general in Ardabil. He had learned enough Azeri to quote Azeri poetry to predominantly Azeri audiences on the campaign trail. In 2005, he won substantial majorities in all three Azeri-majority provinces.[63]

Third and finally, some analysts noted that, among the 200,000-plus Iranians voting abroad, where it was presumably more difficult for Iranian authorities to arrange whatever type of fraud they are supposed to have perpetrated, Mousavi did better than he did at home; indeed, in the official results, he won a majority of the expatriate vote. But these figures should be examined more closely. Tallies from North America, Europe, and other regions where most voters were genuine expatriates show Mousavi winning substantial majorities. But figures from Iraq, Saudi Arabia, and Syria—where Iranians routinely go for religious, business, and family reasons and voter pools were dominated by Iranians normally resident in the Islamic Republic—mirror those inside Iran: 63.5 percent for Ahmadinejad, 32.7 percent for Mousavi.[64]

Obviously, we cannot vouch for the handling and counting of the nearly 40 million ballots cast. But neither Mousavi nor anyone else in Iran nor any Western analyst has ever provided an empirically grounded or even logically sound basis for denying the legitimacy of Ahmadinejad's reelection. Tellingly, a year after the election, Ansari failed to carry through on his promised follow-up to his "preliminary analysis" of the results. Instead, he published a narrative reflection on the election, arguing that the controversy surrounding it had never been primarily about electoral fraud but rather had been about the Islamic Republic's "structure and ideology." After having released an amateurish statistical assessment of the official results, he criticized those whose "preoccupation with the detail—often statistical" had obfuscated "the broader context of developments."[65] Undoubtedly it is hard to retreat from a professional blunder. But Ansari and other pro-Green Iran specialists did real and potentially very serious damage: the canard of the stolen election discredited the Islamic Republic as a potential negotiating partner among liberals as well as among nonneoconservatives and elevated the risk of eventual war with the United States.

THE MIRAGE OF MILITARIZATION

To this day, it is easy enough to find Iranian reformists or members of elites linked to Mousavi and/or Rafsanjani who claim that highly placed (but always anonymous) sources in the Interior Ministry or the Revolutionary Guards told them, before the election, about plans to alter the results in Ahmadinejad's favor. In some of their stories, the plot is masterminded by Khamenei's son, in others by Nateq-Nouri (whom Ahmadinejad criticized along with Rafsanjani in his televised debate with Mousavi). In some accounts, the decision to fabricate results was made months before the election; in others, it was taken a week before, after it became apparent that Mousavi had won his debate with Ahmadinejad (though, as noted, there was no evidence to suggest that he had).[66] In virtually all versions, the fraud was perpetrated in close collaboration with senior leaders of the Pasdaran and the Basij.

None of these yarns even begins to explain how the (never documented) fabrication of results was actually carried out. But they do suggest an additional reason why Westerners continue to buy into them: they fit snugly with another contrived narrative, this one about the Islamic Republic's creeping militarization during Ahmadinejad's watch, with a focus on the Revolutionary Guards. Some observers compare the Pasdaran to the Praetorian Guard of imperial Rome; others turn to the aftermath of the French Revolution and depict it as the vanguard of a new Bonaparatist trend bringing Iran ever closer to military rule.[67] Along these lines, many Western pundits described the 2009 election as a de facto military coup; predictably, Secretary of State Clinton kicked this assessment up a notch with her assertion that the Islamic Republic was becoming "a military dictatorship."[68]

But analogies with classical Rome or postrevolutionary France do not match the realities in present-day Iran. To be sure, the Revolutionary Guards have a special connection to the highest levels of the Islamic Republic's political and religious leadership, and they play nonmilitary roles that the country's regular armed services do not. But it was Rafsanjani, not Ahmadinejad, who first gave the Guards a notable economic role, in the early 1990s, when he sought to marshal pools of organized manpower for postwar reconstruction by turning parts of the Pasdaran into something like the U.S. Army Corps of Engineers.[69] It is true that under Ahmadinejad an engineering and construction firm affiliated with the Revolutionary Guards received several contracts for major projects, among them developing portions of the South Pars gas field, building a section of the Tehran metro, and laying a pipeline that would enable the Islamic Republic to export gas to Pakistan.[70] But there is nothing new or subversive about the expansion of the Guards' economic activities; it hardly amounts to a Pasdaran takeover of Iran's economy. Increased resort to Pasdaran affiliates for major projects says more about Tehran's response to international sanctions than about the political and financial ambitions of Iranian factions.

Likewise, it is easy enough to document an increase in the numbers of guardsmen playing significant roles in Iranian political life, as elected members of municipal councils and the Majles and in various appointed positions. But that increase is a function of actuarial advance and political culture, not of a conspiracy among the Pasdaran and their supporters to take over the political system. Men who in their teens, twenties, and early thirties fought in the Holy Defense against Iraq are now in their forties and fifties—precisely the stage at which the politically inclined aspire to positions in public life, in a society that continues to hold military service in high esteem. When Iraq invaded the fledgling Islamic Republic just a year and a half into its existence, Iranian leaders were distrustful of the regular military establishment they had inherited from the shah. Consequently, most young Iranian men who wanted to defend their country and its new government volunteered for either the Pasdaran or the Basij, a separate apparatus that did not become formally affiliated with the Guards until 2007. Under these circumstances, it is hardly surprising that growing numbers of war veterans with backgrounds in the Pasdaran or the Basij are today winning elective office or being appointed to positions of consequence.

Today, twenty-five years after the Iran-Iraq War ended, roughly one-third of the seats in the Majles are held by former Pasdaran members.[71] By comparison, America's 91st Congress, which took office in 1969, twenty-four years after the surrender of Germany and Japan, drew 75 percent of its members (398 seats in total) from World War II veterans. In 2005, seventeen years after the Iran-Iraq War ended, the Islamic Republic elected, for the first time, a veteran of that conflict (Mahmoud Ahmadinejad, who had served in the Basij, not the Pasdaran) as its president. By 1962, seventeen years after the end of World War II, American voters had already sent two veterans of that war (Dwight D. Eisenhower and John F. Kennedy) to the White House; five more World War II veterans (Lyndon Johnson, Richard Nixon, Gerald Ford, Ronald Reagan, and George H. W. Bush) would become president. It is possible, perhaps even likely, that Ahmadinejad will be succeeded by another Iran-Iraq War veteran. In the post–World War II period, the United States did not elect a president who had never served in the military until 1992—and even then, Bill Clinton's lack of mili-

tary experience was an issue of some significance in his campaign to
unseat the incumbent George H. W. Bush, a decorated World War II
naval aviator. During Ahmadinejad's presidency, the number of Pasdaran and Basij veterans appointed as cabinet ministers and provincial governors has risen.[72] But, given Ahmadinejad's background
and his path to political prominence, it is unsurprising that veterans
from the Pasdaran and Basij would figure in his closest circles of
supporters. Most of them were apparently selected for positions
because of their standing as his longtime allies, not as representatives
of the Guards.

That a growing but still far from overwhelming number of Majles
members, the current president, and some appointed officials are
Pasdaran and Basij veterans does not constitute a seizure of the Iranian government by these organizations. The Guards' senior commanders are, of course, involved in high-level deliberations on foreign
policy matters, through the Supreme National Security Council and
other channels. But there is nothing irregular about this situation.
Making a case that the Islamic Republic is becoming a military dictatorship requires identifying policy choices—not just the distribution
of revenues from economic projects—that, save for the Pasdaran's
influence or intervention, would have been different. We are not aware
of any Western or Iranian analyses that have made such a case.

CANONIZING THE GREEN MOVEMENT

The same kind of analysis by wishful thinking fueled a heady romanticization of the Green movement, as the protest campaign sparked
by the election's outcome came to be internationally known. In the
reigning account, the Greens reflected Iranians' intense desire to
end the Islamic Republic, and the movement failed only because it
was brutally crushed. Like the notion that the election was stolen,
this narrative has further weakened support among Western elites
and publics for diplomatic engagement with Tehran. It has also bolstered the intensifying campaign to press Western governments to
de-list the MEK as a terrorist organization. Proponents of de-listing

now routinely cite the Green movement as clear evidence that Iranians reject the Islamic Republic, and promote the MEK as the ideal
platform for better organized and more effective opposition to the
current political order.

Yet the Green movement never represented anything close to a
majority of Iranian society. At most it represented a sizable chunk of
the roughly one quarter of the electorate that the 2005 election results
suggested is disaffected from the Islamic Republic's political order.
Certainly, some large demonstrations took place in the first week after
the election. There were protests in Isfahan, Tabriz, and a few other cities, but they were heavily concentrated in Tehran, where Mousavi
had won the vote. Even there, crowds came largely from the city's more
prosperous north, the most pro-Mousavi area of the country. North
Tehran is also where most Western journalists working in Iran were
based and where they could readily find English-speaking Iranians to
interview. Thus the Greens were ideally placed to attract international
attention, and indeed, notwithstanding their relatively narrow social
base, the initial demonstrations received worldwide media coverage.

These dynamics allowed the West to romanticize the Green movement on multiple fronts. But, contrary to most Western reporting, the
first week after the election was the movement's apogee; after that,
its (already minoritarian) social base contracted sharply. The turning
point was a Friday prayer sermon delivered by Ayatollah Khamenei at
the University of Tehran on June 19 (a week after election day). In this
sermon, which was heard by virtually every Iranian, the supreme
leader told Mousavi, in effect, to put up or shut up.[73]

Khamenei opened by praising all four of the candidates. Then,
condemning Ahmadinejad's "unfair" remarks "against previous governments of the past thirty years," he defended Rafsanjani as the revolution's incorruptible stalwart; "as for the next of kin, anyone who is
making an accusation, he has to prove it through legal channels." But
Khamenei also charged that Mousavi's campaign had "trampled on
ethics, law, and fairness" with its unfounded criticisms of Ahmadinejad, some of them outright "lies."

Just as all the candidates were "part of the system," Khamenei continued, "the path of revolution has 40 million votes, not just 24.5 million who voted for the president-elect." That so many Iranians had voted was a powerful rebuke to Iran's enemies, who had kept "repeating and drumming it in that the election was going to be rigged." Now, the same characters were trying "to create doubt" about the outcome: "The enemies of the Iranian nation know that when trust is gone, participation will weaken. When participation and presence on the scene is weakened, the legitimacy of the system will be questioned. This is what they want."

Declaring that "some supporters of some candidates should rest assured that the Islamic Republic does not betray votes of the people," he explained that it would not have been possible to manipulate the number of votes in Ahmadinejad's landslide: "Sometimes the difference is 100,000, 500,000 or even 1 million. In that case, one could say that there might have been vote rigging, but how can they rig 11 million votes?" Nevertheless, he said, "if there are some people who have doubts and have documents, those doubts should be investigated" by the Guardian Council. For "it should be at the ballot boxes that it is determined what the people want and what they do not want—not on the streets. If, after every election, those who do not win start street rallies and mobilize their supporters in the streets, then those who have won start street rallies in response, what is the purpose of holding elections?"

Turning to "politicians, candidates, and party leaders," Khamenei noted their duty to be "careful of their conduct" and of "what they say." Stopping just short of naming Mousavi, he urged "old friends and brothers to be patient and keep control of yourselves" and admonished them to mind "their responsibilities before God. . . . If legal frameworks are ignored today, there will be no guarantees for the health of elections in the future. In every election there will be some who win and some who lose. No elections will be safe or trusted any longer, if the law is ignored." Then Khamenei drew his line in the sand:

Street challenges are not the right thing to do. This is, in fact, challenging the principle of elections and democracy. I want everyone to end this sort of action. If they do not end it then the consequences of this lie with them. It is a wrong perception, please note, a wrong impression that through their street presence they will be creating a lever of pressure against the system. . . . Giving in to demands under pressure is itself tantamount to the start of dictatorship. . . . I am asking my friends and brothers to respect brotherhood, law, and togetherness. The legal channels are open. The channels of love and friendship are open. You should use legal and friendly methods. I hope God helps them.

Khamenei's referral of Mousavi's fraud allegations to the Guardian Council was wholly appropriate within the Islamic Republic's constitutional order; tactically, it put the onus on Mousavi to document his charges. Mousavi's failure to do so and to exhaust remedies within the system damaged his credibility among his core supporters as well as among the general public; in Tehran, it is not hard to find Mousavi voters who took part in protests the week after June 12, never imagining that their candidate would allege fraud without proof, and who then grew disillusioned when he did not back up his allegations. Strategically, too, Khamenei had redefined the situation: further protests would no longer be about the election but would be a challenge to the Islamic Republic itself. This reframing dramatically reduced the ranks of those prepared to keep protesting. The crowds after June 19 were a fraction of the size of those in the first week after the election. Polls from WPO/PIPA in late August and in September 2009 and Charney Research in September 2010 show that most Iranians (including most Mousavi backers) were repelled by radical calls for the abolition of the Islamic Republic.[74]

But precisely as popular support for the Green movement began to decline sharply in Iran, Westerners built it up as the Iranian people's salvation from an irredeemably brutal government. Their narratives were fed by stories coming out of Iran that were adroitly manipulated by the Islamic Republic's opponents. One such story was that of Neda

Soltan, a twenty-six-year-old woman who was reportedly on her way to participate in protests on June 20, the day after Khamenei's Friday prayer sermon, when she was fatally shot in the chest. While Neda Soltan's story had relatively little impact inside Iran, it gained enormous traction in the West. Her tragic death was captured on videos that, within twenty-four hours, had gone viral on the Internet, making her the Green movement's most powerfully symbolic martyr for international audiences. On June 23, barely seventy-two hours after her fatal shooting, the White House organized a press conference to give President Obama a platform to talk about her fate and, more broadly, to pivot toward a tougher rhetorical line regarding Iran.

Neda Soltan's story had such impact because it fits neatly with the Western myth of the Islamic Republic's illegitimacy. And because it fits so well with that myth, the conventional narrative about her shooting was never subjected to rigorous scrutiny, even though there are serious unanswered questions about who killed her and why. The story advanced by the opposition and its supporters outside Iran is that she was shot by a Basij sniper for exercising the basic human right of peaceful protest. But, in fact, Soltan was not protesting when she was shot; she was at least a kilometer away from the nearest demonstration. Her shooting raised alarm within the Iranian government—which denies that any of its security force personnel shot her—that the MEK, with Israeli and/or Western support, had infiltrated the protests and had killed Soltan to galvanize popular support for overthrowing the Islamic Republic. These concerns were heightened just a few months later when Soltan's fiancé traveled to Israel to be received by President Shimon Peres; even prominent figures in the Green movement say that her fiancé's high-level contacts with Israel, once they became public, were "suspicious to every Iranian."[75]

But the suspicious aspects of Neda Soltan's case did not inhibit the Greens and their supporters from moving quickly and aggressively to capitalize on her image as a martyr. To augment the impact of the videos of her death, oppositionists organized a Facebook page dedicated to the "Angel of Iran." Wanting still photos of the murdered woman, they appropriated the photo of a different young Iranian

A protestor in New York holds up a photo supposedly showing Neda Soltan, the young woman mysteriously slain after Iran's June 2009 election. In fact, the photograph depicts a different, unrelated Iranian woman. *Getty/Mario Tama*

woman, named Neda *Soltani*—a graduate student at Tehran's Islamic Azad University who was very much alive and well—from another Facebook page. The "Angel of Iran" page became an overnight sensation. Photos of Neda Soltani, falsely labeled Neda Soltan, went viral; media outlets around the world, including Voice of America, circulated them as images of the murdered Neda Soltan. The misappropriation of Soltani's image was not an innocent mistake. When Soltani reached out to VOA and several Internet sites to correct what she originally believed to be a simple case of mistaken identity and to request that her photos be taken down, VOA used the additional photos she sent to back up her request as new, "exclusive" images of the slain protestor. Internet forums supporting the Iranian opposition refused to take down her pictures and accused her of being a stooge for the Iranian government; one such forum posted, "You won't take our angel away from us, you bastard."[76]

Similarly, preconceived notions of Iranians wanting to be just like us conditioned Western receptivity to the idea that the Islamic Republic was being liberated by a "Twitter revolution." Three days after the election, the U.S. State Department asked Twitter to postpone scheduled maintenance of its worldwide network that would have cut daytime service in Iran for several hours.[77] The idea that the Greens were an unprecedented social media–driven movement—as the *Atlantic*'s Andrew Sullivan headlined, "The Revolution Will Be Twittered"—became a staple of Western journalists' postelection coverage. Sullivan, Robert Mackey of the *New York Times*, and Nico Pitney of the *Huffington Post* all developed vast and influential online readerships—including President Obama—by republishing tweets, ostensibly from inside Iran, that graphically described purported exercises in security force brutality and appeared to be helping protestors organize their next moves. The *New York Times* columnist Tom Friedman went so far as to crow that social media like Facebook and Twitter had "replaced the mosque" as networking sites for change in Iran.[78] But while the story of Iran's Twitter revolution was gratifying for Western elites convinced that Iran was ready to embrace secular liberalism, it was not true. Within days of the election, the manager of a popular Farsi-language Web site told the *Washington Post* that most of the tweets about protests were not originating inside Iran; they were, instead, being generated by "Americans tweeting among themselves."[79] Even an Iranian expatriate correspondent for Radio Free Europe/Radio Liberty—which, along with VOA, provided a steady stream of U.S. taxpayer–funded pro-Green propaganda—concluded that "there was no Twitter Revolution inside Iran. . . . Western journalists who couldn't reach—or didn't bother reaching?—people on the ground in Iran simply scrolled through the English-language tweets posted with tag *#iranelection*. Through it all, no one seemed to wonder why people trying to coordinate protests in Iran would be writing in any language other than Farsi."[80]

Not only did Western journalists exaggerate the extent and significance of Iran's purported Twitter revolution; they also, in a dismaying number of instances, made uncorroborated tweets an important source for their reporting. The weekend after Ayatollah Khamenei's June 19

Friday prayer sermon, for example, Western media outlets circulated a story—based on demonstrably false tweets—of Western embassies in Tehran accepting gunshot victims for medical treatment because the Basij was monitoring hospitals for injured protestors. In the months that followed, similarly unsubstantiated stories were regularly featured in Western media coverage on Iranian developments—for example, police throwing protestors off bridges and pouring acid and boiling water on demonstrators.[81]

Relying on this kind of propaganda, Western analysts, journalists, and officials looked to the Green movement to bring about what they believed was desperately needed fundamental change in the Islamic Republic—if not to topple it entirely. But the movement's social base was shrinking even before the end of June 2009. Its decline accelerated over the next several months. As Mousavi's fraud claims dwindled, the Greens became less focused on championing his candidacy and split into factions, with liberals following an essentially reformist agenda and radicals devoted to transforming the Islamic Republic into a secular state. Western attention to the radicals reinforced Khamenei's portrayal of continuing protests as a challenge to the Islamic Republic. It did not help Mousavi that public figures linked to his campaign, like the filmmaker Mohsen Makhmalbaf, presented themselves in Western capitals as his representatives, fostering a perception inside Iran that Mousavi was willing to collaborate with foreign powers. As a result, Mousavi had to issue statements emphasizing "the Islamic and national identity of the Green movement, its opposition to foreign rule, and its loyalty to our constitution," as well as his own commitment "to the independence of this country."[82]

These problems were only too evident by the end of 2009. On December 27, crowds turned out across Iran to commemorate Ashura, which coincided with mourning observances for Grand Ayatollah Montazeri, who had died a week before. Mousavi and Karroubi tried to use these events to mobilize their followers. A relatively small number of protestors gathered in Tehran; some attacked police stations, sparking clashes with security forces. Opposition Web sites numbered them in the tens of thousands; others in Iran estimated two to four thousand. Even the higher figures were embarrassingly low, considering that huge crowds pour out in Tehran and other cities every year for Ashura. Moreover, many Iranians were upset by the use of a holy day to make a political statement (especially one most of them did not endorse). Three days later, many more took part in government-organized demonstrations in support of the Islamic Republic; a Web site that had opposed Ahmadinejad's reelection estimated the turnout in Tehran at over a million, making it perhaps the largest crowd in the city since Khomeini's funeral.[83] In its wake, Mousavi had to reject the Ashura protestors' "unacceptable radicalism."

The episode also underscored the Greens' lack of a coherent agenda. On January 1, 2010, Mousavi issued a five-point "solution to the current problems and present crisis," which Western journalists and pundits hailed as a Green manifesto. Rather vaguely it exhorted the government to make itself "directly accountable to the nation," to provide "transparent and credible regulation of the election process," to "free and exonerate political prisoners," to expand "freedom of the press and media," and to respect the right to "establish political groups and parties." Days later, concerned that Mousavi was "backing off" his challenge to the government, five of the Islamic Republic's most visible critics-in-exile—Abdolali Bazargan, Akbar Ganji, Mohsen Kadivar, Ataollah Mohajerani, and Abdolkarim Soroush—put out a ten-point manifesto, which was also widely acclaimed in the West.[84] It laid out "optimal demands" beyond anything Mousavi, Karroubi, or Khatami could have proposed, including Ahmadinejad's resignation, new presidential elections, an end to Guardian Council vetting of candidates, a new election commission with "representatives of the opposition and protestors," the barring of government statements and "orders" at Friday prayers, and making all offices elective and subject to term limits. Soroush described these demands as a first stage; in the next stage, he said, the movement "may demand a redrafting of the constitution."[85] The Greens were torn along the same dividing line that had afflicted the reformists during the preceding decade: on one side, those who saw the movement as a campaign to move the Islamic Republic in a more liberal direction; on the other, those who wanted to do away with it altogether.

Western observers like Barbara Slavin and Robin Wright who had already exaggerated the Green movement's import now insisted on reading the Ashura protests as a show of its vitality and the intellectual disarray of early January as a sign of "emerging consensus" on goals.[86] But as we pointed out in the *New York Times* on January 6, 2010, none of these observers could answer three basic questions: "First, what does this opposition want? Second, who leads it? Third, through what process will this opposition displace the government in Tehran?"[87] Even though they had no answers to these questions, Western and Iranian expatriate pundits almost universally predicted that February 11, Islamic Revolution Victory Day, would see overwhelming protests marking (as some put it) the beginning of the end of the Islamic Republic. Mousavi, Karroubi, and Khatami fed the frenzy by exhorting their followers to turn out on February 11.

No indicator of a social movement's decline can be more clear than a waning ability to mobilize. By this measure, February 11 was a disaster for the Greens, as even their partisans could not deny (though some, like Reza Aslan, tried to).[88] Few protestors came out; when observances ended, the movement's "strength" was hardly noticeable. Borzou Daragahi, a pro-Green *Los Angeles Times* reporter who had sent us an e-mail warning us that our Iranian contacts were "government mouthpieces" and should be ignored, ruefully concluded that the movement's leaders needed to reevaluate their strategy and tactics.[89] Galvanized by attacks on our analysis of the Green movement and its shortcomings by editorialists at the *Atlantic*, the *New Republic*, and various neoconservative outlets, the *New Republic* assigned a reporter to interview us, our employers and colleagues, and many of our critics and to scour our work and our backgrounds for points of professional or personal vulnerability. But when the story was published at the end of February 2010, even Michael Crowley, the reporter, had to acknowledge, "It's not obvious that [the Leveretts'] analysis is wrong—especially in the wake of disappointing Green turnout last week on the anniversary of the 1979 Iranian revolution."[90]

Western and expatriate Iranian analysts hoping for the demise of the Islamic Republic also claimed that Khamenei's inept handling of the election and of the Greens' rise had so undermined his standing that disaffected political elites were about to bring him down along with Ahmadinejad.[91] (Khamenei, it was said, was so worried that he had a plane standing by to fly him to Russia or some other foreign destination if necessary.) Some held that Rafsanjani would use his influence over the Assembly of Experts to press the leader. Mousavi and Rafsanjani advisers told Western diplomats that Rafsanjani was working to rally a majority of the Experts for Khamenei's removal, hoping to use such pressure to force a new election.[92] But the strategy was doubtful at best. Rafsanjani's personal and political ties to Khamenei went back too far for such a challenge to be plausible.[93] Moreover, as early as June 20, 2009—barely a week after the election and just a day after Khamenei's sermon at the University of Tehran—the Assembly of Experts endorsed his handling of the situation.[94] Whether Rafsanjani was unwilling to move or unable to, it became evident after February 11 that there was going to be no significant challenge to Khamenei. In late February 2010, Rafsanjani publicly realigned with Khamenei, declaring at an Assembly of Experts meeting that "those who care for the revolution must clarify their position vis-à-vis supporters of regime change and opponents of the Supreme Leader, and must regard him as the center of unity."[95]

Indeed, after February 11, Mousavi and Karroubi lost virtually all their high-level political support. Khatami pulled away; since February 2010, he has not joined calls for more protests. Others decried the Green movement's "hijacking" by radicals who had undercut its popularity; reformist legislators with an eye to their own political futures followed Khatami's example and distanced themselves. By March 2010, Mousavi was reduced to declaring, "We have to call the next year the year of patience and endurance until the aims of the Green movement are achieved."[96] He still could not say what those aims were or explain how "patience and endurance" were going to achieve them.

Faced with the undeniable reality of the Greens' decline, Western observers fell back to arguing that the opposition had not really faded but rather had been cruelly suppressed by an illegitimate regime using every tool available to keep itself in power. Emblematically, Gary Sick alleged in January 2010—with no evidence—that "agents of the Iranian government must be considered the prime suspects" in the assassinations of Iranian nuclear scientists; in Sick's assessment, the Iranian government was out to "amplify their campaign of intimidation against the Green opposition."[97] (Of course, it is increasingly clear that the assassinations are the work of Israel's intelligence service.) More generally, the image of a dark night of repression falling over heroic, freedom-seeking Iranians took deep root in Western perceptions and writing. In a typical example, the street protests were described as having been met with

> paroxysms of brutality as the Islamic Republic's repressive security apparatus went into overdrive, its forces attacking peaceful demonstrators, killing dozens and injuring hundreds. Hoping to crush the growing movement and deter further expressions of dissent, the state arrested virtually every leader, journalist, or activist associated with or even sympathetic to the Green movement, filling its prisons—in which, we soon learned, crimes of a truly horrifying nature were systematically committed. Stalinist-style show trials were conducted. Iran witnessed a full-blown reign of terror.[98]

Claims like this should be treated with some skepticism. Clearly, criminal acts were committed in the course of the government's response to the demonstrations; the government itself acknowledges them. Even as early as his June 19, 2009, sermon, Ayatollah Khamenei said that "one's heart is torn apart" to see progovernment forces "raid university dormitories and harm young students, not rioting students but pious students, and then chant slogans in support of the Leader." Where security actions exceeded public tolerance, Khamenei imposed accountability—for example, Kahrizak Detention Center, where some detainees were physically abused and others murdered, was closed and twelve of its personnel indicted; two were sentenced to death.[99]

The political significance of the security forces' behavior after the June 2009 presidential election should be considered in the context of Iran's history. In the fifteen months preceding the shah's departure in

1979, troops gunned down thousands of protestors, but the crowds demanding the shah's removal kept growing. In comparison, the government's response to the unrest in 2009–10 was relatively restrained (Mousavi's Web site was never taken down, for example), yet even so the Greens retreated and their base contracted. Opposition sources say that just over seventy people died in clashes with security forces after June 12, 2009 (the government puts the toll at thirty-six).[100]

This is not the stuff of which revolutions are made. Moreover, while most demonstrators were nonviolent, especially during the first week, the Western media either overlooked or rationalized episodes where antigovernment mobs attacked police and Basij personnel, tried to storm security force installations where weapons were stored, attacked other facilities with fire bombs and Molotov cocktails, and damaged storefronts and other property. Western human rights groups estimate that four to six thousand were arrested in connection with the postelection disturbances—protests that some of the same groups estimated to have involved millions of people, meaning that the authorities detained a very small percentage of demonstrators.[101] More than 90 percent of those detained were released without charge; the International Campaign for Human Rights in Iran found that about 250 people were convicted of crimes stemming from the unrest. All but a handful were pardoned by Khamenei; most who were not are free on bail pending appeals.[102]

The behavior of Iranian security forces after the June 2009 presidential election should also be considered in comparison with other cases. Reaction in the West to the Iranian government's handling of the 2009–10 protests stands in stark and telling contrast to Western attitudes about analogous cases. In 1992, during the Rodney King riots in Los Angeles, a significant segment of the population—by no means a majority—protested, often violently, against a perceived failure of justice (the acquittal of four Los Angeles police officers who had been videotaped beating a black suspect). Troops from the National Guard and, ultimately, the U.S. Army and Marine Corps were deployed; fifty-three people were killed—and Americans called it a riot, not a protest. Americans also praised the Egyptian military for its restrained and even statesmanlike response to the protests in early 2011 that drove Hosni Mubarak from power. In fact, 986 people were killed by Egyptian military and security forces in the course of those protests. In August 2011, the police shooting of a black man in London sparked large protests in British cities that prompted large-scale police deployments across several London boroughs and the arrest of at least thirty-one hundred people. More than a thousand were criminally charged—at least four simply for using Facebook to organize some of the protests. The *Guardian* (one of the Greens' most ardent champions in the West) called on the public to back the police: "Britain's 2011 riots have become a defining contest between disorder and order ... there is only one right side to be on."[103] The *Daily Telegraph* (another vocal supporter of the Greens) held that "there can be only one response if the law-abiding majority is to be protected: the thugs must be taught to respect the law of the land the hard way."[104] Prime Minister David Cameron—who considered shutting down all social media in Britain during the episode—condemned the "sickening scenes" of unrest and violence, telling protestors, "You will feel the full force of the law. And if you are old enough to commit these crimes, you are old enough to face the punishment."[105]

In this context, one can understand why, by objective measures of public opinion, a majority of Iranians saw their government's response to the 2009–10 protests as legitimate, contrary to Western caricatures of it as a bloody crackdown. In the 2010 Charney Research poll, 59 percent of respondents said the government's reaction had been "correct"; only 19 percent thought it "went too far."[106]

BEYOND THE GREEN MOVEMENT

Romanticizing the Green movement remains a powerful urge in Western discourse about Iran. As recently as October 2011, as the Obama administration was alleging Iranian government involvement in a plot to assassinate the Saudi ambassador in Washington, Republican senator John McCain argued that if President Obama had supported the Greens in 2009, "they could have overthrown the government then."[107] But the future of Iranian politics will not be charted by the Greens. Some of the movement's expatriate partisans, such as Hamid Dabashi and Hooman Majd, later argued that the Greens were never out to bring down the Islamic Republic but should instead be understood as a "civil rights" campaign.[108] At this point, though, the movement cannot even serve as a platform for a reformist revival. A year after the 2009 election, Mousavi tried again to lay out an agenda, in an article that included sections on "roots and goals," "fundamental strategies," "Green identity," the "Green movement's values," and "abiding by the law and negotiating."[109] Western journalists, apparently oblivious to the events of the preceding year, hailed it as a "political charter [that] attempts, for the first time, to unite the opposition movement behind a clear set of goals."[110] But fewer and fewer Iranians were paying attention. As Mousavi and Karroubi became marginalized, conservatives in and out of parliament began agitating for their arrest and trial on sedition charges.

When the Arab Spring broke out, as 2010 passed into 2011, Western pundits and Iran experts expected developments in Tunisia, Egypt, and other Arab countries to reenergize the opposition in Iran. Once again, they underestimated the Islamic Republic as a system and Khamenei as a leader. While Secretary of State Hillary Clinton was still asserting that Mubarak's government was stable, Khamenei had moved to claim the Arab awakening as an extension of Iran's Islamic Revolution. When, three days after Mubarak's resignation, Mousavi and Karroubi called on their supporters to assert the Green movement's primacy in sparking the Arab Spring, both men and their wives were placed under house arrest—where, apparently, they remain, with no appreciable public outcry.

However much many Westerners and expatriate Iranians may wish it were otherwise, the future of Iranian politics will be charted within the current constitutional order. Too many Western analysts persist in trying to depict Iranian politics as a binary, all but Manichaean conflict between reformists and principlists. In this view, if conservatives gain the upper hand over reformists, repression must be the cause. And if there are political disagreements among conservatives, they must surely be a sign that the political order is falling apart. Thus, Western pundits, journalists, and policy makers reflexively treat virtually any sign of policy conflict in the Islamic Republic (something considered normal politics everywhere else in the world) as "unprecedented" and a sign of "crisis."

Contrary to much speculation in the West, Ahmadinejad will in all probability finish out his current term. Indeed, his administration is likely to be regarded as consequential, even transformative, on a number of fronts. His closest advisers believe that he has changed the nature of campaigning and communicating with the public in ways that will survive his presidency. Substantively, his government is overseeing a meaningful restructuring of the Iranian economy, starting with the most significant reform of domestic subsidies in the Islamic Republic's history—an issue that both Rafsanjani and Khatami said they wanted to take on but that Ahmadinejad has actually tackled.[111] The devaluation of Iran's currency for all but the most essential imports is another important initiative. (In his second term, he has also tried to do something no Iranian president has done before: to lay the ground for exercising substantial influence after leaving office—via efforts to elect a parliamentary bloc that would be loyal to him after his presidency ends and to position his chief of staff to run for president in 2013. Neither plan has played out successfully.)

Parliamentary elections in 2012 suggested that the Islamic Republic has weathered the controversy surrounding the 2009 presidential contest. Turnout was around 65 percent, slightly higher than average for parliamentary elections, which are held separately from presidential elections. In fact, turnout was much higher than in analogous off-year congressional elections in the United States (just under 38 percent in 2010), and higher even than in American presidential elections (just under 57 percent in 2008). Although Mousavi and Karroubi urged a boycott of the 2012 elections, the most prominent reformist figures—including Khatami and Khomeini's grandson Hassan Khomeini—and Rafsanjani all made a public display of voting, to show their support for the system. While the campaign was dominated by competing principlist slates, there were reformists on the ballot, as well as a significant number of independents. In the end, principlists took roughly two-thirds of the seats; reformists and independents won about a third.

Conservatives are much better positioned than reformists to compete in the next presidential election, in 2013; there is little reason to expect reformists to resolve their problems with leadership and message before then. Some reformists are arguing for another tactical choice in 2013, such as supporting a new-generation conservative sympathetic to at least some parts of the reform agenda; Qalibaf seems to be the figure most frequently mentioned. (Alternatively, some look to former foreign minister Velayati, Supreme National Security Council Saeed Jalili, and Gholam-Ali Haddad-Adel as other conservatives who might run, though it is not clear how much appeal they would have for nonprinciplists.) Reformists thinking along these lines hope that electing a less polarizing conservative might help create a "vital center" in Iranian politics that could serve as a platform for reinvigorating the reform movement. This prospect, however, is at best a long-term recovery strategy for the reformists—all of which means that the center of the action in Iranian politics will remain on the conservative side of the spectrum for at least the next several years.

It is critical for Americans and other Westerners to recognize that the Islamic Republic is not going away. Such an understanding is essential if the United States is to deal with the Islamic Republic rather than try to overthrow it or wait in vain for it to turn into what some Westerners wish it were but most Iranians manifestly do not. In part 3, we explore the reasons Washington finds it so difficult to come to terms with Iranian realities and pursue policies toward the Islamic Republic that would actually serve American interests.

PART THREE

THE ISLAMIC REPUBLIC AS AMERICAN TARGET

PROLOGUE

Myths about the Islamic Republic's strategic irrationality and domestic illegitimacy have fostered the image of a severe threat to international security and vital American interests. A threat so dire requires a strong response, and that response has been shaped by Washington's attachment to what we have called the "isolation myth"—the notion that through diplomatic action, economic pressure, military moves, and other coercive measures, the United States will succeed in marginalizing the Islamic Republic and slowly strangling it.

Since the 1979 revolution, America's Iran policy has emphasized three main elements, all grounded in hostility. The first is diplomatic ostracism. The United States does not have diplomatic relations with the Islamic Republic and leans on other states to minimize their ties to Tehran. Beyond the matter of formal relations, it has worked to limit the Islamic Republic's diplomatic involvement in regional and international affairs. Over time, this posture has undermined Washington's ability to understand, much less influence, Iranian political developments and policy deliberations.

The second hostile element is economic pressure. Virtually from the founding of the Islamic Republic, the United States has subjected it to sanctions and, for nearly the whole of the past two decades, to what is effectively a comprehensive economic embargo. Washington continues to squeeze the Iranian economy more and more tightly by regularly adding to an already daunting array of prohibitions. It also seeks to keep foreign companies and financial institutions based in third countries from doing business in Iran, threatening them with secondary sanctions (almost certainly illegal under the World Trade Organization, though no one has litigated the question yet) and various types of political pressure.[1] Besides these unilateral steps, the United States encourages other states to levy their own sanctions on Iran and periodically pushes the U.N. Security Council to expand multilateral sanctions against it.

The third core element is a barely veiled support for regime change. Washington has yet to formally declare this goal, as it did with Saddam Husayn's Iraq, Muammar Qadhafi's Libya, and Bashar al-Assad's Syria. Nevertheless, American politicians have openly called for a secular, liberal, and presumably pro-Western regime to replace the Islamic Republic. More directly, Washington supported Iraq's war of aggression against Iran's fledgling postrevolutionary political order during the 1980s. Subsequently, it has pursued both public diplomacy campaigns and a variety of initiatives under the rubric of "democracy promotion" to weaken domestic support for the Islamic Republic. It has maintained ties to a variety of groups dedicated to the Islamic Republic's overthrow and/or dismemberment. It has steadily intensified covert operations against Iran and has repeatedly raised the threat of direct military action. In 2011, the Obama administration opened a "virtual embassy" to Iran, set up to bypass the government and engage the Iranian public directly, for the express purpose of stimulating popular discontent with the existing order.[2] In 2012, as noted, the same administration removed the MEK's terrorist designation, positioning it to become the vanguard of an explicit regime change strategy.

This approach has manifestly not worked, even on its own terms. The Islamic Republic is not isolated in any strategically meaningful sense. Iran's election to the chairmanship of the Nonaligned Movement—with 120 members representing a majority of the world— in 2012 is clear evidence of this. According to the United Nations Conference on Trade and Development's 2012 *World Investment Report*, foreign direct investment to Iran rose from $1.9 billion in 2008 to $3.6 billion in 2010 and $4.2 billion in 2011, even with intensifying sanctions.[3] A wide array of political and policy elites in the West claim sanctions are "biting"; some even say they are "working." But while sanctions unquestionably affect economic conditions inside Iran—creating hardships for people in their day-to-day lives, raising transactional costs and obstacles for Iranian businesses, suppressing the value of Iranian currency, and so forth—the country's economy is not collapsing. Sanctions have reduced Iranian oil exports, but they are also forcing international oil prices well above the levels that market supply and demand would normally impose. As a result, Iran has a substantial current account surplus—today, the world's twelfth largest, at roughly $42 billion, according to the C.I.A.[4] Even with intensifying sanctions, the I.M.F. projects that the Iranian economy will continue to grow while the World Bank projects only a modest contraction.[5]

Indeed, sanctions can encourage greater self-sufficiency. In 2010, when President Obama authorized a new round of Iran-related second-ary sanctions that, among other things, threatens to penalize third-country entities selling gasoline to Iran, sanctions proponents claimed the measure would bring the Islamic Republic—then still reliant on foreign refiners to meet its gasoline demand—to its knees. Instead, Iran accelerated efforts to expand its refineries. In 2011, Iran became a net exporter of gasoline; one of its biggest customers is Afghanistan. Sanctions are also encouraging Iran to build its indigenous scientific and technological base, to rein in imports and its consumer culture, and expand its domestic production and non-oil exports.

The notion that sanctions and other economic pressures will gener-ate strategic leverage over Tehran's decision making is counterhistorical (Iran went through eight years of a de facto international embargo during its war with Iraq) and, ultimately, illusory. A substantial majority of Iranians remain invested in the present political system: as noted, turnout in the 2012 parliamentary elections, the most recent national political contest, was 65 percent, slightly higher than the historical average for legislative elections since the revolution.

Washington's established Iran policy has proven grossly counterproductive to American interests, not just in the Middle East but also globally. The persistent enmity of the United States has prompted Iranian policy makers to devote more attention to what they call the "Eastern option"—to cultivating strategic relationships with non-Western powers, epitomized by the BRICS countries: Brazil, Russia, India, China, and South Africa. In this regard, Tehran's strategy for responding to sanctions goes well beyond the forms of subterfuge (smuggling, the use of front companies for overseas procurement) and sanctions-busting trade that Saddam's Iraq pursued, including with American allies like Jordan and Turkey. The Islamic Republic is also working with rising powers in the global south to create alternative financial and trade mechanisms. For example, in 2012, China—today both Iran's biggest customer and its largest source of imports—paid for some of the oil it bought from the Islamic Republic in renminbi, obviating the need for Western financial institutions to mediate transactions and accelerating the erosion of the dollar's supremacy as a reserve and transactional currency.[6] Washington's expanding reliance on secondary sanctions—which, since 2012, cover simple purchases of crude oil and most non–energy-related commercial exchanges with the Islamic Republic—to press Tehran rests on an assumption that even countries resistant to American hegemony will go along, in the belief that participation in the global economy requires access to the U.S. financial system. But American policy is now incentivizing emerging powers to develop alternatives to established, U.S.-dominated mechanisms for conducting, financing, and settling international transactions.[7] As Washington continues on this course, it will hasten the shift of economic power from West to East.

Yet even with the mounting drain on its strategic position, the United States' Iran mythology remains unshakable, hindering a more rational and constructive approach at every turn. To be sure, every

American administration since the Iranian Revolution has at some point had to recognize Iran's importance in the regional balance and request its assistance on matters of concern to the United States. The Reagan and George H. W. Bush administrations sought Tehran's help in freeing American hostages in Lebanon; the Clinton administration coordinated with Iran to supply weapons to the beleaguered Bosnian Muslims when American law prevented Washington from doing so; and the George W. Bush administration benefited from Iranian cooperation against Al-Qa'ida and the Taliban following 9/11. In all of these episodes, Tehran did much of what was asked of it, calculating that cooperation would prompt Washington to reconsider its hostile posture. And in each case Washington pocketed Tehran's help without reciprocation and then cut off dialogue, either out of anxiety over domestic political blowback or because of some perceived and unrelated Iranian provocation. The Obama administration, for its part, has hardly done better. On Obama's watch, the total time spent by American diplomats in substantive bilateral discussions with their Iranian counterparts has amounted to forty-five minutes so far.

Now the risk that the United States will initiate a war against the Islamic Republic is rising. Americans should have no illusions about the consequences of such a course or of a U.S.-facilitated attack by Israel. As senior Obama administration officials acknowledge, the inevitable rise in oil prices would have severe consequences for Western nations, at a time when their economies are already seriously challenged.[8] Politically, a new show of force by the United States in any way reminiscent of its 2003 invasion of Iraq would elevate the already high levels of anti-American sentiment in the Middle East, threatening its remaining allies there and, for most, rendering their continued cooperation with Washington practically impossible. The damage to America's global standing would also be severe. U.S. military action against the Islamic Republic would have no international legitimacy: no authorization by a Security Council resolution, no legal justification that most governments and publics would accept, no allies but Israel, Britain, and some minor European nations. The larger part of the international community would inevitably consider an attack illegal, ratifying the United States' image in much of the world as an outlaw superpower.

Instead of thinking about starting another war in the Middle East, American decision makers need to acknowledge that the United States has to come to terms with the Islamic Republic if it wants to maintain standing and influence in the Middle East and broader leadership in world affairs. The only truly meaningful questions are: when will Washington finally wake up and how much higher will the price be for dithering?

In the next three chapters, we examine the reasons the United States keeps getting it wrong on Iran—that is, why American political and policy elites cling to dangerous myths about the Islamic Republic and to a failed Iran policy. We explore the factors that drive the United States' actions in the Middle East—for its dysfunctional Iran policy is, in many respects, a manifestation of broader problems in its grand strategy since the end of the Cold War. We then take up the matter of what has to happen for the United States to avert strategic disaster in the Middle East and finally set its relationship with the Islamic Republic on a more positive and productive course.

7

MYTHS AND MYTHMAKERS

It is part of American folklore that, while other nations have interests, we have responsibilities; while other nations are concerned with equilibrium, we are concerned with the legal requirements of peace.

—*Henry Kissinger, 1968*

On January 29, 2002, ten weeks after the United States avenged the 9/11 terrorist attacks by overthrowing the Taliban government in Afghanistan, President George W. Bush delivered his annual State of the Union address, outlining the next phase in America's "global war on terror." Beyond the ongoing imperative to "shut down terrorist camps, disrupt terrorist plans, and bring terrorists to justice"—which was ostensibly what the Afghan phase of the war had been about—Bush declared that he was determined to "prevent regimes that sponsor terror from threatening America or our friends and allies with weapons of mass destruction." Three such regimes stood out. While they had been "pretty quiet since September 11," Bush was confident that

we know their true nature. North Korea is a regime arming with missiles and weapons of mass destruction, while starving its citizens. Iran aggressively pursues these weapons and exports terror, while an unelected few repress the Iranian people's hope for freedom. Iraq continues to flaunt its hostility toward America and to support terror. . . . States like these, and their terrorist allies, constitute an axis of evil, arming to threaten the peace of the world. . . . In any of these cases, the price of indifference would be catastrophic. . . . The United States of America will not permit the world's most dangerous regimes to threaten us with the world's most destructive weapons.

To counter this dire threat, Bush invoked basic features of American political culture to mobilize his compatriots behind a campaign to remake the Middle East in line with American preferences. Updating a century-old view that the United States' security requires transforming states (especially unfriendly ones) into democracies, he tapped into the old mix of liberalism and exceptionalism that American presidents and other elites have long drawn on. The rhetorical formulas are well known: "manifest destiny" (devised by proponents of westward expansion to justify the Mexican War), the "imperialism of righteousness" (deployed by proponents of American colonial power to legitimize the Spanish-American War), and the call to make the world "safe for democracy" (issued by President Woodrow Wilson in his 1917 war message). The constant references to the United States during the Cold War as the "leader of the free world" and in the post–Cold War period as "the indispensable nation" extended the pattern.[1]

After 9/11, Bush relied on formulas like "the forward strategy of freedom" to persuade Americans that the United States had a moral as well as strategic mandate to remake the Middle East. The criteria he listed for inclusion in the axis of evil—pursuit of WMD, support for terrorism, and political repression—became the constituent elements of his case for invading Iraq. But these arguments did not spring from the ether—they were manufactured by interested elites both inside and outside the administration. For Iraq, four groups were especially important: neoconservatives on the right, liberal internationalists on the left (joined by less overtly hawkish progressives interested in promoting human rights and Western-style democracy in the Islamic world), the pro-Israel lobby, and Iraqi expatriates and their U.S.-based representatives. In the decade preceding the invasion, these four clusters of political entrepreneurs converged to push Washington toward war with Iraq—and to manipulate the public into supporting their project.[2]

Now the same or similar groups are converging to push the United States toward war with the Islamic Republic. These are the myth-makers who have created America's view of Iran. And they have created it for a reason: to facilitate American dominance in the Middle East by demonizing the state posing the biggest indigenous challenge to it. Resting on the same presumption that drove the Iraq War—that the United States must pursue the quintessentially imperial mission of subduing and remaking the Middle East—this mythology combines self-justifying narratives about the American role with deeply negative readings of Iranian Shi'a culture. It claims that the strain of Shi'ism embodied in the Islamic Republic has given rise to an aggressively millenarian mentality that is strongly resistant to rational calculations of cause and effect, risk and benefit, means and ends. It further justifies Washington's imperial agenda by insisting on the illegitimacy of an Islamic Republic dedicated to resisting Washington's hegemonic ambitions. And in doing so, it traps policy makers in positions that, while favored by all four groups we are about to consider, are counterproductive to American interests and ruinous for the region.

THE ROOTS OF THE MYTHS

America's Iran mythology continues long-established patterns of thinking, not just about foreign policy but also, more broadly, about the Muslim world. For as long as the Middle East has been a focus of Western attention, ill-informed and stereotype-ridden ideas have distorted Western discourse about it. With the Europeans' arrival, en masse and in force, at the end of the eighteenth century, came the broader dilemma of "liberal imperialism." Liberal states pondered what their stance should be vis-à-vis the nonliberal societies they encountered: respecting self-rule and noncoercion or encouraging "progress" and universalizing "the rule of law"? The British, the French, and, in time, the Americans debated; in each case, the faction holding that liberalism justified imperialism ultimately won.[3]

These debates shaped the way that liberal states crafted their impe-rial narratives. John Stuart Mill, one of nineteenth-century Britain's most influential liberals, argued that "despotism is a legitimate mode of government in dealing with barbarians, provided the end be their improvement, and the means justified by actually effecting that end."[4] By this logic, the legitimation of a liberal empire depended on a view of indigenous societies as backward—or, in more "scientific" parlance, traditional, rooted in what Max Weber called "the eternal yesterday."[5]

For Iran and other parts of the Muslim world, these assessments were conditioned by "orientalism," an enterprise that, as the late Edward Said argued in his influential 1978 book, unites the scholarly study of Islam and the Middle East with the promulgation of essentialist nar-ratives. Orientalism, according to Said, gave rise to a "style of thought" about the Muslim world that reflected Western liberal powers' impe-rial ambitions. Through the first half of the twentieth century, Western orientalists focused mainly on mastering Middle Eastern languages in their "highest," or most literary, forms and studying religious and his-torical texts. On this basis, they constructed summaries of Islamic culture and societies, ascribing qualities to them that were the dia-metric opposites of "modern" Western values like rationality, equality, and individuality. For the British and French, such summaries helped legitimize their regional interventions.[6]

Though American engagement in the Middle East during the early twentieth century was limited, American images of the region were much the same as their British and French counterparts.[7] Orientalist attitudes strongly influenced Woodrow Wilson's approach to the Mid-dle East following World War I. Believing that few non-Western nations were ready for real independence, the United States' self-appointed champion of self-determination supported Britain and France as they divided up the Ottoman Empire into colonial mandates to share between themselves. This outlook shaped the American approach to Iran as well. At the 1919 Paris Peace Conference, Britain, determined to protect its position in Iran from outside scrutiny, worked to keep Iranian delegates who had the opposite end in view from being seated. London feared that the American delegation might meet with them separately, but it need not have worried—the Wilson administration did not consider the Iranians any more prepared for sovereignty than the Arabs.[8]

The "backwardness" of specific populations takes on more weight the more they affect the great powers' ambitions. Starting with World War II, the Persian Gulf and the Middle East became increasingly important to the United States. The region's hydrocarbons were, in the words of one American diplomat, "the greatest prize in history"; coming out of the war, Washington was determined to maintain a decisive influence over their production and marketing. This resolve was not so much a matter of American needs. The United States was self-sufficient in oil; indeed, it had supplied most of the oil its allies had used and would not become a net oil importer until the 1970s.[9] Rather, American policy makers judged that a reliable flow of Persian Gulf oil was critical to the postwar recovery of Europe and Japan, which they considered essential to the United States' own long-term economic prospects. U.S.-provided energy security would also help bind these allies to Washington.[10]

As the United States became more deeply enmeshed in the Middle East after World War II, narratives about its role there became more and more inflected with negative appraisals of the region's culture, society, and politics. Said argued in one of *Orientalism*'s sharper passages that

> so far as the United States seems to be concerned, it is only a slight overstatement to say that Muslims and Arabs are essentially seen as either oil suppliers or potential terrorists. Very little of the detail, the human density, the passion of Arab-Moslem life has entered the awareness of even those people whose profession it is to report on the Arab world. What we have is a series of crude, essentialized caricatures of the Islamic world presented in such a way as to make that world vulnerable to military aggression.[11]

Since then, notions of an unreformed Islam "at war" with the West, if not with modernity itself, have been widely embraced in the United States.

American discourse about the region has updated the old orientalist dichotomy between the traditional (or backward) and the modernized (or Westernized) into a strategic distinction between "moderates" and "radicals." Washington's post–World War II strategy in the Middle East had little interest in democratization. Western Europe and Japan were different; there, Washington calculated, democracy was a path into the American-led political and security order. But, in the Middle East, American policy makers recognized (at least until they were blinded by neoconservative ideology) that democratization would empower Islamists and other groups resistant to the American imperial project. That is why, for Washington, a Middle Eastern political order's status as moderate or radical has been largely divorced from its domestic governance. The standard of moderation is, first and foremost, receptivity to an American-led regional order and, second, an openness to peace with Israel, at least theoretically. Conversely, radicals have been those who challenged American ambitions in the region and rejected peace with Israel, at least on American-specified terms. Thus, in Iran, Mohammad Mossadeq's government may have been democratically elected, but with a platform that urged the nationalization of Western oil interests and an independent (even if not anti-American) foreign policy, Mossadeq was unacceptably radical. In comparison, Mohammad Reza Pahlavi—an autocrat so unpopular that he was ultimately deposed by one of the most broadly based revolutions in modern history—was a moderate.

After the CIA-instigated 1953 coup that brought down Mossadeq, the willingness of the shah to embrace Western templates for economic and social (if not political) development led a bevy of American officials, academics, and media commentators to certify him as a legitimate leader with substantial popular support. Liberalism and Westphalian concepts underlay the West's commitment to the consolidation of secular states; after World War II, new theories of development enshrined secularization as a key to modernization. On this front, too, the shah seemed to be taking Iran in the right direction; owing to his authoritarian White Revolution development program, American social scientists and journalists routinely assessed him as a modernizer—a verdict ratified for mass audiences by his frequent appearances on American television, with high-profile interviewers like Barbara Walters and in popular venues like *60 Minutes.*

Hence the failure of so many American foreign policy experts and pundits to grasp what was happening even when the revolution was far advanced. Emblematically, in a late November 1978 *People* magazine interview conducted as mass protests burgeoned in Tehran and other cities, Marvin Zonis of the University of Chicago, one of the United States' most renowned students of Iranian politics, declared that the shah had improved his country's standard of living "immeasurably," was not torturing people "at this moment," and would continue in power because "a vast number of Iranians still support him as a symbol of unity and stability, whose experience and wisdom—which are considerable—can be called upon."[12] Less than seven weeks later, Mohammad Reza Pahlavi left Iran, never to return.

The same culturally conditioned outlook gave rise to the Western view of the revolution as a liberally oriented uprising that was "captured" by unrepresentative Islamists. In 1981 Said extended his criticism of Western commentary on the Muslim world with *Covering Islam,* arguing that the media's response to the revolution and the Islamic Republic's early days, including the hostage crisis, grew out of a "longstanding attitude to Islam, the Arab and the Orient." He found lamentably "little inclination to accept the revolution itself as much more than a defeat for the United States (which in a very specific sense, of course, it was), or a victory of dark over light."[13]

One does not have to agree with every word of Said's work to recognize that American discourse on Iranian politics and foreign policy has rarely taken the full range of relevant facts and nonexpatriate Iranian perspectives into account. It is hard for most Americans to accept the legitimacy of a political order that seeks to combine religious authority with democratic institutions and practices—especially when it also has the audacity to question the goodness of American ambitions in the Middle East. The seizure of the hostages in the Islamic Republic's early days put the seal on its radical nature; it is now all too easy to imagine the Islamic Republic as a backward, repressive, and brutally misogynistic place where, as Jay Leno jokes, the Flintstones are known as the Jetsons. In American popular culture and opinion, Iran remains the embodiment of an extremist Islam that is no more rational than, and functionally indistinguishable from, the Salafi extremism of Al-Qa'ida and the Taliban.

NEOCONSERVATIVES: PHILOSOPHER ACTIVISTS OF AMERICAN EMPIRE

Neoconservatives have been at the forefront of efforts to make the United States' Iran policy more bellicose, and their animus toward the Islamic Republic is of a piece with their larger vision. Since the 1970s, neoconservative thinkers have developed an internally coherent narrative about America's role in the world, a narrative whose influence derives partly from its incorporation of ideas from older traditions. Like foreign policy realists, they believe that military power is the trump card in international affairs; unlike the realists, they scorn what they see as the squandering of hard-power advantages in balancing, containment, and other status quo strategies. Like foreign policy liberals, they consider the character of a state's regime the most important driver of its international conduct—they enshrine liberal democracies as the world's good guys doing battle with the hostile ideologies of fascism, communism, or, now, Islamism; but, unlike liberals, they doubt that diplomacy, economic openness, and soft power (divorced from hard power) can do much to defeat those rivals. Bringing these threads together, they hold that the United States can assure its security only by shaping the international environment, including other states' domestic orders, through a combination of military force and liberal principle. John Mearsheimer calls this "Wilsonianism with teeth."[14]

During the Cold War, neocons argued that, beyond curtailing communist expansion while waiting for the Soviet Union's internal contradictions to bring it down, the United States should actively undermine it. While the nuclear balance of terror precluded direct military action, Washington could nonetheless win the Cold War by driving the Soviet Union to the point of economic collapse with an arms race, pursuing covert action and other forms of pressure, and relentlessly delegitimizing alternative strategies of engagement, such as Kissingerian détente and European *Ostpolitik*.[15]

The Islamic Republic's first decade overlapped with the Cold War's last. Recognizing the struggle with Moscow as the highest priority, neocons were prepared to apply balance-of-power logic to Iran, particularly as it became apparent that Saddam was not going to win his war against it. As long as the Soviet Union was on the scene, even the most hawkish foreign policy hands could stomach "talking to the ayatollahs." That is how, during Reagan's presidency, neoconservatives became embroiled in the secret outreach to Tehran that imploded in the Iran-contra scandal. The scheme had several goals, among them obtaining Iranian assistance in securing the release of American hostages in Lebanon. The most strategically consequential was identifying and engaging figures in the Iranian leadership (like Rafsanjani) who saw the benefits of improving relations with the West. White House officials hoped to develop ties to Iranian moderates who might be induced, over time, to help balance American interests against Soviet designs in the region (such as the expansion of Iraqi military power). This aim was short-circuited—rather spectacularly—by a display of lawlessness and incompetence that foreshadowed the neocons' manufactured case for invading Iraq and their utter failure to plan for the country's post-Saddam occupation.

Once the Iran-contra scandal broke, in 1986, the Reagan administration judged it politically impossible to try engagement again. It is noteworthy, though, how balance-of-power logic moved even some of those neocons who would later emerge as vocal advocates of regime change to continue arguing for engagement. In a July 1988 *New York Times* op-ed, Michael Ledeen—a former consultant to the National Security Council on Iranian issues—argued that the imminent succession to Ayatollah Khomeini offered the United States a chance to bolster Iranian elites who favored improving relations with the West. (He mentioned Rafsanjani.) "Past mistakes," he wrote, "should not prevent the Administration from pursuing the clear chance for a potential breakthrough in one of the more strategically sensitive areas of the world."[16]

Once the Cold War was over, neocons argued the case for an unembarrassed American pursuit of empirelike hegemony, largely through military action. The proponents—many of them linked by ties of family, education, and mentorship—included Elliott Abrams, John Bolton, Max Boot, David Brooks, Eliot Cohen, Jackson Diehl, Douglas Feith, David Frum, Francis Fukuyama, Reuel Marc Gerecht, Jeffrey Goldberg, Robert Kagan, Frederick Kagan, Zalmay Khalilzad, Charles Krauthammer, William Kristol, Joshua Muravchik, Richard Perle, Danielle Pletka, Gary Schmitt, Paul Wolfowitz, former director of central intelligence R. James Woolsey, and David Wurmser. Many of them cut their teeth in the Reagan and first Bush administrations before gaining prominence in the foreign policy intelligentsia. Their efforts to shape public debate have been reinforced by opinion makers like Niall Ferguson and Robert Kaplan, who, while not necessarily identified as neoconservatives, nonetheless advocate the creation of a new "liberal empire."

The Middle East is a special focus for neocons, who believe their Cold War terms of reference still hold there, with Western civilization, embodied by Israel, under threat from illiberal zealots committed to hostile ideologies, especially Islamism—or, as Norman Podhoretz labeled it, "Islamofascism." With no other superpower to constrain the United States since the Soviet Union's demise, they have urged that, in the Middle East, Washington follow a more robust version of the strategy they championed during the Cold War: assertive application of hard power to root out bad regimes and replace them with ones prepared to accept American hegemony and Israeli regional dominance. After 9/11, Podhoretz and others exalted this vision as "World War IV."[17]

The starting point for their strategizing was their disappointment with the dénouement of the first Gulf War, which had left Saddam Husayn in power. Throughout the 1990s, they focused on Saddam's removal through unilateral American action as an essential first step in their larger project to remake the Middle East—a project that would ultimately require the transformation of other problematic orders, including Syria's Assad regime as well as the Islamic Republic.[18] For neocons and other GOP hawks, the end of the Cold War and the weakening of Saddam through his defeat in the first Gulf War devalued any gains to be had from engaging Tehran. A few years after his 1988 *Times* op-ed, Ledeen was staunchly advocating regime change in Iran, and he still is.[19] Over the past two decades, most neocons of any stature have agreed that the Islamic Republic has to go. As Eliot Cohen wrote in the wake of 9/11, "The overthrow of the first theocratic revolutionary Muslim state and its replacement by a moderate or secular government . . . would be no less important a victory in this war than the annihilation of bin Laden."[20] One argument for regime change in Baghdad was that it would also weaken the Islamic Republic—by empowering reformists and others disaffected with it to press for internal transformation and by positioning Najaf as an alternative to Qom that would challenge the Islamic Republic's religious authority and draw Shi'a away from its influence.

Virtually all of the neoconservative figures mentioned above (joined, in recent years, by younger propagandists like Jennifer Rubin and Bret Stephens and former George W. Bush administration officials like Michael Singh) have done their part in crafting America's Iran mythology. In doing so, they frequently display a cavalier regard for facts; Ledeen, for example, has published multiple articles over the past several years citing "reliable" sources that Ayatollah Khamenei has died or is near death.[21] They almost uniformly describe the Islamic Republic as illegitimate (Krauthammer: Iranians want "to bring down the tyrannical, misogynist, corrupt theocracy that has imposed itself" on them) and irrational (Brooks: "Iranian leaders do not think in a linear fashion" but "live in a world of shadows and fantastical notions, beyond fact," and "we are wrong to think that the people inside the regime are cool customers carefully manipulating symbols and events"). They claim the regime is beyond engagement (Robert Kagan: "The problem is not the United States; it's the leaders in Tehran who don't want to make a deal"). They all accept as fact (without offering evidence) that the 2009 election was a fraud and that the Greens reflected a majority wish for a secular system. Many of them chastised Obama for too weakly backing the Greens.[22]

To support their case for regime change, they have developed the arguments about the Islamic Republic's vulnerability to pressure and coercion that lie at the heart of the isolation myth. Some, like Ledeen, question the use of force, preferring to see Washington support Iranian oppositionists (including, for some, the MEK) and levy debilitating sanctions to undermine the system.[23] Others hold that U.S. and/ or Israeli military action against Iran's nuclear infrastructure (which many hawks think is warranted anyway) would mobilize Iranians against the system.[24] But, tactical disagreements aside, encouraging the Islamic Republic's implosion is a high priority for them all. It has also become the dominant position in Republican Party circles, as underscored, for example, by the evolution of Richard Haass's views. Currently president of the Council on Foreign Relations, Haass is a self-styled realist who previously supported limited American-Iranian engagement but now favors regime change in Tehran.[25]

Starting in the 1990s, neoconservatives took over the foreign policy shops at several right-leaning think tanks in Washington (including the American Enterprise Institute and the Hudson Institute) and at the Stanford University–based Hoover Institution. They also established new ones—the Project for a New American Century in 1997; after 9/11, the Foundation for Defense of Democracies; and, after Obama's election, the Foreign Policy Initiative. And they forged ties to traditional hard-liners like Dick Cheney and Donald Rumsfeld, who, while not concerned about spreading democracy, shared their enthusiasm for using force to topple resistance to American hegemony. After the Bush administration came to office in 2001, these ties gave neocons inside and outside the government great influence over foreign policy and a virtual lock on Republican foreign policy debates, which they have maintained despite the Bush administration's strategic debacles.[26]

Neoconservatives have not been bashful about judging the foreign policies and the politics of countries they have never visited, whose languages they have never seriously studied, and whose cultures and histories they do not know. None of the individuals cited above has real expertise on the Middle East; Ledeen, for example, is a scholar of Machiavelli and Italian fascism. Indeed, neocons frequently seem contemptuous of country- or region-specific knowledge and analysis, though they are always happy to recruit congenial academic specialists to bolster their credibility.[27] In the Cold War, sympathetic Sovietologists like the Harvard historian Richard Pipes helped make their case for harder-line policies toward Moscow. In the post–Cold War era, Bernard Lewis and Fouad Ajami have played the same role for the Middle East.

At the age of ninety-six, Lewis is routinely hailed by neocons as "the greatest living historian of the Middle East." In 2005, in a symbolically potent gesture, the neoconservative *Weekly Standard* profiled him as "the last orientalist" (a term he had defended vigorously against Said's critique).[28] A British-born scholar of Islam and the Middle East, Lewis came to the United States in 1974 to fill a chair at Princeton University and the Institute for Advanced Study. He entered neocon circles soon afterward, becoming part of the late Senator Henry Jackson's foreign policy "brain trust" (along with Richard Pipes) and writing for *Commentary* as well as more mainstream publications like the *New York Review of Books* and the *Atlantic*.[29]

Over his career, Lewis has forged an unflattering portrait of Islam, emphasizing "the authoritarianism, perhaps we may even say the totalitarianism, of the Islamic political tradition."[30] In the 1950s, he held that Pakistan's experiment with an Islamic republic was "a contradiction in terms" and argued that Muslim societies were at special risk of communist subversion because communities

> brought up on such doctrines will not be shocked by disregard of political liberty or human rights. [They] may even be attracted by a regime which offers ruthless strength and efficiency in the service of a cause—anyway in appearance—in place of the ineptitude, corruption, and cynicism which in their mind, one may even say in their experience, are inseparable from parliamentary government.[31]

In his popular books and magazine articles, Lewis gave his imprimatur to the neoconservatives' Middle East agenda. Before Samuel Huntington foresaw the clash of civilizations, Lewis was writing that the West should see Islamism's rise as "the perhaps irrational but surely historic reaction of an ancient rival against our Judeo-Christian heritage, our secular present, and the worldwide expansion of both." (Huntington quotes this passage in the 1993 *Foreign Affairs* article that formed the basis for his 1996 book.) After 9/11, Lewis became an informal consultant to Vice President Cheney and other Bush administration officials and a cheerleader for the Iraq War.[32]

One might think that Iran's revolution would have caused him to reevaluate his notion of Islam as a religion counseling slavish obedience to authority; instead, he has denigrated the outcome of the revolution, drawing parallels "between what happened in the Islamic world in our day and what happened in Europe and beyond following the Russian and French Revolutions—the same upsurge of emotion, the same uplifting of hearts, the same boundless hopes, the same willingness to excuse and condone all kinds of horrors, and the same questions."[33] One might also think that Iranian politics after 1979 would have prompted him to reconsider his claim that the concept of an "Islamic republic" is an oxymoron. But, while conceding that "Iran holds contested elections and allows more freedom of debate and criticism in the press and in its parliament than is usual in most Muslim countries," he has focused mainly on how it fails by liberal standards it was never designed to meet. On elections, he complains that "there are exacting and strictly enforced limitations on who may be a candidate, what groups may be formed, and what ideas may be expressed. It goes without saying that no questioning of the basic principles of the Islamic revolution or the republic is permitted."[34] (Of course, questioning the basic principles of the U.S. Constitution—which, as noted, every president, senator, and representative must swear to defend before taking office—is not so well tolerated in American elections, either.)

Lewis also propounds the myth of Iranian irrationality, maintaining that there is a radical difference between the Islamic Republic of Iran and other governments with nuclear weapons, [which] can only be described as the apocalyptic worldview of Iran's present rulers. This worldview and expectation, vividly expressed in speeches, articles and even schoolbooks, clearly shape the perception and therefore the policies of Ahmadinejad and his disciples. . . . School textbooks tell young Iranians to be ready for a final global struggle against an evil enemy, named as the U.S., and to prepare themselves for the privileges of martyrdom. . . . In Islam, as in Judaism and Christianity, there are certain beliefs concerning the cosmic struggle at the end of time—Gog and Magog, anti-Christ, Armageddon, and for Shiite Muslims, the long-awaited return of the Hidden Imam, ending in the final victory of the forces of good over evil, however these may be defined. Mr. Ahmadinejad and his followers clearly believe that this time is now, and that the terminal struggle has already begun.[35]

Fouad Ajami was born to a Lebanese Shi'a family in 1945 and came to the United States as a teenager, eventually taking a Ph.D. at the University of Washington. After beginning his career at Princeton, in 1980 he moved to the Johns Hopkins University School of Advanced International Studies (SAIS), where he held a chair in Middle East studies for three decades; he is now a Hoover Institution fellow. He entered neoconservative circles when he arrived at SAIS, which was also when he began writing for the *New Republic*, the *Wall Street Journal*, and *Foreign Affairs*. Like Lewis, he was a Bush administration consultant and a staunch champion of the Iraq War.[36]

Without ever specializing in Iran, Ajami has advanced a reading of its revolution that combines the "inherently regressive" interpretation with the "captured revolution" narrative. In his view, the "liberal secularists" in Khomeini's coalition

were doomed all along—because theirs was a fragile, tentative liberalism that could not survive on Iranian soil. When the hurricane swept Iran and a confused, atomized society grafted onto a cleric who had returned from a long exile its yearning for order and for purity, there wasn't much a fragile liberalism, or a foreign power, could do. In reality the Iranian liberals' politics were not part of Iran's political culture. Men and women in Iran broke old chains only to forge new ones. They demolished the rule of one man and then submitted to the tyranny of another. They mimicked the ways of the outside world and then came to rail against those ways.[37]

Ajami is subtler with the irrationality myth, seeing Iranian leaders as cunning but not self-destructive. He nonetheless rejects engaging them. In 1988, as Ledeen was still arguing for outreach to pro-Western elites, Ajami countered that "there is no need for guesswork about 'radicals' and 'moderates' in the ranks of the Iranian political class and the clerical estate. The country's protean leadership makes a mockery of these categories."[38] Since 2000, he has denounced what he (inaccurately) calls Madeleine Albright's "outright apology" for the 1953 coup.[39] He blamed problems in post-Saddam Iraq on the "Persian menace" in a 2008 *Wall Street Journal* op-ed, accusing the Iranians of playing "arsonists and firemen at the same time. They could fly under the radar, secure in the belief that the U.S., so deeply engaged there and in Afghanistan, would be reluctant to embark on another military engagement in the lands of Islam." He refused to believe that Iranian politics would ever produce better interlocutors—"the clerics have had no interest in any bargain with the U.S." Washington might "tell the Iranians that the military option is 'on the table,'" he wrote, "but decades of playing cat and mouse with American power have emboldened Iran's rulers," who "will have to be shown that there is a price for their transgressions."[40] Not surprisingly, he endorses regime change as the goal of American policy.

In 2007, Lewis and Ajami started their own professional society, the Association for the Study of the Middle East and Africa. Over the years, they have become lodestars to younger neoconservative academics like Patrick Clawson of the Washington Institute for Near East Policy; Daniel Pipes, founder of the Middle East Forum, which publishes the neoconservatively oriented *Middle East Quarterly* and runs Campus Watch to "review and critique Middle East studies in North

America"; and Michael Rubin of the American Enterprise Institute—all of whom have provided additional scholarly veneer to what is really a propaganda campaign for regime change in Tehran.[41]

Among neoconservative initiatives to isolate, stress, and undermine the Islamic Republic, the Foundation for Defense of Democracies (FDD) stands out. It sponsors an Iran Energy Project, which promotes energy sanctions "as part of a comprehensive strategy to pressure the Iranian regime to abandon its pursuit of nuclear weapons, support for terrorism, and brutal oppression of its own people."[42] It has been so successful in developing sanctions legislation that in 2012 the Senate sponsors of a recently enacted measure cited its analysis to exhort the Obama administration to impose tough conditions on countries seeking sanctions waivers.[43] The FDD has also received money from the U.S. government–funded National Endowment for Democracy to train Iranian oppositionists.

LIBERAL INTERNATIONALISTS: IMPERIALISTS WITH THE BEST OF INTENTIONS

Not only have few notable neoconservatives ever acknowledged that any of their judgments might seem, in retrospect, dubious, few of their ostensible political opponents have held them to account. One important reason is the substantial overlap between their hard-line approach and that of the liberal internationalists—or, as John Mearsheimer calls them, "liberal imperialists"—who dominate Democratic foreign policy circles.[44]

Like neoconservatives, these liberals regard a state's domestic order as the main determinant of its foreign policy. They have a similar commitment to the spread of democracy as a strategic priority for the United States and a similar receptiveness to force as a means for reshaping key parts of the world. Indeed, both groups' common grounding in America's liberal tradition has contributed to what Harvard's Stephen Walt describes as a "neocon-liberal alliance" in contemporary foreign policy debates.[45] They are especially close together on Middle East policy, and both subscribe to the prevailing Iran mythology. As a result, the Iran debate has become increasingly narrow, hostile to the Islamic Republic, and closed to engagement.

From World War II until the 1960s, liberal internationalism was the Democratic Party's reigning foreign policy approach. Introduced by Woodrow Wilson, it was embraced by the Roosevelt, Truman, Kennedy, and Johnson administrations. But in the 1960s the Vietnam War deeply divided Democrats. Those who supported it feared that antiwar elements were making the party look soft on foreign policy in voters' eyes. In the 1970s, some of these hawkish Democrats—including former staffers for Senator Jackson (Elliott Abrams, Richard Perle) and foreign policy academics (Jeane Kirkpatrick)—left the party altogether, fattening the GOP's neoconservative cadre. Those hawks who remained—including senior officials in the Carter administration (Madeleine Albright, Richard Holbrooke) and prominent legislators (Al Gore, Joseph Lieberman, Sam Nunn, Charles Robb)—argued that their party had to restore public confidence in its ability to steward the country's security and international standing. During Reagan's presidency, these "new Democrats" organized the Democratic Leadership Council and the Progressive Policy Institute (where Josh Block, former spokesman for the American Israel Public Affairs Committee, now runs an Iran task force), which unapologetically defended the principles and practices of Cold War liberalism and, as the Cold War ended, promoted them as the basis for future foreign policy.[46]

By that time, these hawkish internationalists—Holbrooke called them "national security Democrats"—had largely reasserted control over the party's foreign policy deliberations. They staffed much of Bill Clinton's national security apparatus, giving it an imperial cast that supported military interventions in Haiti, Bosnia, and Kosovo and a militarized, economically draconian standoff with Saddam Husayn. In theory, liberals diverge from neoconservatives over international organizations—neocons deride them as a useless constraint on the United States, while liberals promote them as useful tools for legitimating American initiatives. In practice, the Clinton liberals were as unilateral as the neocons: it was Clinton who added the phrase "coalition of the willing" to the diplomatic lexicon (in discussing military options against North Korea), and the Kosovo war and the no-fly zones over Iraq were prosecuted by just such a coalition, without Security Council authorization.

Liberal internationalists cast an imperial eye on the Middle East as well. Following Jimmy Carter's success in brokering the Camp David Accords, they saw Arab-Israeli diplomacy as a valuable tool for reshaping the Middle East's balance of power in favor of the United States and Israel. (By taking Egypt out of the military equation, Camp David had effectively blocked another generalized Arab-Israeli war and made Egypt a well-subordinated American ally.) It was certainly a major dimension of the Clinton administration's approach to the region. While neoconservatives have criticized this emphasis on Middle East peacemaking as a distraction, if not outright appeasement, their disagreement is only tactical—liberal interest in the peace process is motivated by the same hegemonic ambitions. Likewise, it was Bill Clinton—not George W. Bush—who formally committed the United States to coercive regime change in Iraq, by signing the Iraq Liberation Act in 1998.[47] This pursuit of dominance in the Middle East extended to Iran. The Islamic Republic posed a challenge to liberal internationalists' assumption that modernization necessarily leads to secularization, liberal democratization, and acceptance of American aspirations to regional and global hegemony. Liberals have pushed back: in 1995, as noted, Clinton issued two executive orders imposing a comprehensive American economic embargo on the Islamic Republic in response to Tehran's offer of a contract to Conoco.

Liberal hawks continued to dominate Democratic debate after Clinton left office. Besides Albright and Holbrooke (who died in 2010), leading figures in this camp include the New York Times columnist Thomas Friedman, former Council on Foreign Relations president Leslie Gelb, SAIS professor Michael Mandelbaum, and Strobe Talbott, president of the Brookings Institution and Clinton's deputy secretary of state. After 2000, their ideas were embraced by foreign-policy-focused Democratic senators, including Joseph Biden, John Kerry, Carl Levin, and Hillary Clinton. This influence was bolstered by the rise of younger foreign policy hands, many of whom served in the

Clinton administration (and, in some instances, joined the Obama administration)—Kurt Campbell, Derek Chollet, Michèle Flournoy, G. John Ikenberry, and Suzanne Nossel (who, after a second stint in the State Department during the Obama administration, became executive director of Amnesty International USA), along with Michael O'Hanlon, Kenneth Pollack, and Susan Rice of Brookings.[48] As this roster suggests, liberal internationalists have been well represented at mainstream think tanks; like the neocons, they also established new ones for themselves, most notably the Center for a New American Security, founded by Campbell and Flournoy in 2007.

After 9/11, liberal internationalists were crucial to mustering Democratic support for the invasion of Iraq. Less than a year before the invasion, Kenneth Pollack, a former CIA analyst and Clinton National Security Council staffer at the Council on Foreign Relations, published *The Threatening Storm: The Case for Invading Iraq*. Beyond its best-selling status, the book elicited wide Democratic backing for war, even though every major reason Pollack came up with was wrong.[49]

This liberal enthusiasm for the war had little to do with any role Iraq might have played in 9/11. (None.) Rather, many liberals bought the neocon idea that replacing Saddam with a "democratic Iraq" would transform the region. Their posture had an explicitly hegemonic cast, reflecting a view that Washington had to reassert its dominance in the Middle East. As Thomas Friedman intoned in 2003, what the region "needed to see was American boys and girls going house to house, from Basra to Baghdad, and basically saying, 'Which part of this sentence don't you understand? You don't think . . . we care about our open society? . . . Well, Suck. On. This."[50] The Iraq War also had the backing of less overtly hawkish progressives focused on human rights and on bringing Western-style democracy to the Islamic world, a stance that the late scholar Tony Judt criticized as "a commitment to the abstract universalism of 'rights'—and uncompromising ethical stands taken against malign regimes in their name"—that leads "all too readily to the habit of casting every political choice in binary moral terms."[51]

Following the Iraq debacle, these groups made even more explicit common cause with neoconservatives in urging a tougher approach to the Islamic Republic. In 2007, Princeton's Anne-Marie Slaughter— who endorsed the Iraq invasion and would go on to serve in the Obama administration as Secretary of State Hillary Clinton's first director of policy planning—offered an assessment of the Iranian "threat" that could have come from almost any neocon:

> An Iran with a popular, accountable, and rights-regarding govern-ment would not be a threat, even if it developed a nuclear weapon. But an Iran with a president who denies the Holocaust, who will not deny that he called for the eradication of Israel, and who won popu-lar election through a rhetoric and a radicalism that worry even the mullahs is a grave potential threat.[52]

While liberals are more inclined than neocons to value diplomacy, they too are skeptical that negotiations will ever secure Tehran's sur-render to American diktats.[53] But they do see diplomacy as a way of legitimizing more coercive measures to domestic and international constituencies. Thus, Susan Rice, one of Obama's earliest foreign pol-icy advisers, wrote in 2004 that "we cannot get Europe to apply sanc-tions against an Iran destined to go nuclear until we've done our best to negotiate a solution"; similarly, Samantha Power, the human rights professor at Harvard's Kennedy School who became a close adviser to Senator and, eventually, President Obama, argued in 2008 that a big part of "what negotiations can do is diminish perceptions of U.S. arro-gance."[54]

Liberal internationalists tend to take a graver view of military action than neocons do. But they are no less bent on coercing Tehran's capitulation on both the nuclear issue and its support for groups the United States designates as terrorist organizations. Six years after the Iraq invasion, Leslie Gelb made the remarkable admission that "my initial support for the war was symptomatic of unfortunate ten-dencies within the foreign policy community, namely the disposition and incentives to support wars to retain political and professional credibility."[55] Yet Gelb and other liberal internationalists—seemingly oblivious to the lessons of the Iraq debacle—have been key players in several bipartisan initiatives to marshal political backing for intensified economic pressure on Iran and to prepare the public for eventual military action against it. In 2007, hawkish Democrats and neoconservative Republicans founded the Bipartisan Policy Center (BPC), which has been effective in recruiting Democrats to a quintessentially neoconservative Iran agenda. A 2012 report from the BPC's Iran Initiative—by a task force including former Democratic Virginia senator Charles Robb, longtime Democratic Party donor Mortimer Zuckerman, and John Hannah, former national security adviser to Vice President Cheney—called on the Obama administration to commit the United States to military action to keep Iran from acquiring nuclear weapons, intensify covert operations against its nuclear program, build up military forces in the Persian Gulf in preparation for blockading and/or attacking Iran, and provide Israel with more powerful "bunker-busting" bombs and better aerial refueling capabilities to strike Iranian targets.[56]

Similarly, in 2008, Gelb and Richard Holbrooke joined with Fouad Ajami, former George W. Bush speechwriter Michael Gerson, former Bush adviser Karen Hughes, former Bush administration counterterrorism chief Frances Townsend, former director of Central Intelligence R. James Woolsey, and others to found United against a Nuclear Iran (UANI), an advocacy group that "seeks to prevent Iran from fulfilling its ambition to obtain nuclear weapons" via "sanctions campaigns and state and Federal legislative initiatives" that "focus on ending the economic and financial support of the Iranian regime by corporations, firms, entities and individuals." UANI is also the hub for the Coalition against a Nuclear Iran, which encompasses the neoconservative Foundation for Defense of Democracies, a number of groups affiliated with the Israel lobby, and several Iranian American organizations committed to the Islamic Republic's overthrow.[57]

Like neoconservatives, liberal internationalists have found the prevailing Iran mythology extremely useful in selling their strategic agenda. One of UANI's objectives is to "inform the public about the nature of the Iranian regime, including its desire and intent to possess

nuclear weapons, as well as Iran's role as a state sponsor of global terrorism, and a major violator of human rights at home and abroad."[58]
In Thomas Friedman's more colorful words, the Islamic Republic is a
"brutal, cynical, corrupt, anti-Semitic regime that exploits the Palestinian cause and deliberately maintains a hostile posture to the West
to justify its grip on power."[59] Not surprisingly, he and other liberal
hawks see regime change as inevitable. Virtually all of them inflated
the significance of the Greens in the 2009 election into a force that was
going to transform Iranian politics along secular, liberal lines.

THE ISRAEL LOBBY: (MIS)APPROPRIATORS
OF AMERICAN INTERESTS

While the Israeli government has myriad channels of communication
with executive branch agencies in the United States and with Congress, its efforts to influence decision making in Washington are substantially bolstered by the "Israel lobby"—shorthand for a loose coalition
of groups and individuals that works to promote the U.S.-Israel "special relationship" and to push American foreign policy in a pro-Israel
direction.[60] The lobby comprises a complex of U.S.-based organizations that number by various estimates between seventy-five and
ninety; among the most prominent are the American Israel Public
Affairs Committee (AIPAC), the Conference of Presidents of Major
American Jewish Organizations, and the Anti-Defamation League.[61]
They operate in three main ways: by directly lobbying the executive
and legislative branches in Washington, by influencing public opinion
and discourse, and, in AIPAC's case, by evaluating candidates' positions for pro-Israel political action committees and donors. The lobby
also encompasses networks of influential individuals focused on
encouraging close U.S.-Israeli relations.[62]

The lobby seeks to link hegemonic narratives about America's role
in the Middle East to assertions about its special relationship with
Israel being rooted not just in "shared democratic values" but also
in Israel's importance as a "strategic asset" to the United States. Besides
working to maximize American economic, military, and political

support for Israel and to make it as unconditional as possible, the lobby has long focused on ensuring that the United States conducts its Middle East policy in line with Israeli preferences—a particularly high priority where Iran is concerned.

The end of the Cold War, the removal of the Iraqi military as a factor in the regional balance of power as a result of the first Gulf War, and the collapse of the Soviet Union allowed Israel to consolidate an unprecedented level of regional dominance—to which only Iran has presented an obstacle. Iranian policies that Israel disliked but tolerated in the 1980s—for example, Tehran's support for anti-Israeli Lebanese and Palestinian groups—were redefined by Israeli policy makers in the 1990s as major threats to Israel's security, if not its very existence. They are not. In reality, Hizballah and HAMAS now constitute an increasingly effective rebuke to the Israeli strategy of open-ended occupation and unilateral military initiative. In Lebanon, Hizballah's accumulation of military hardware is problematic because it constrains, to some degree, Israel's military decision making. Israeli planners must now worry that air strikes against targets in Lebanon, Syria, or Iran could elicit rocket barrages that would paralyze northern Israel. Likewise, Hizballah's demonstrated ability to fight Israeli forces to a standstill with what has been called high-intensity insurgency has raised the threshold for another ground invasion of Lebanon.[63]

Similarly, the Islamic Republic's nuclear development became a major concern for Israel only from the early 1990s. Israel did not object to Iran's purchase of nuclear fuel for the Tehran Research Reactor in the 1980s. Today—putting aside the heated rhetoric produced for public consumption—Israeli leaders are not focused on Iran's fuel cycle capabilities out of fear of a nuclear holocaust.[64] Some have even admitted publicly what more say privately: they do not believe that Iran would use nuclear weapons against Israel. As Defense Minister Ehud Barak concedes, "I don't think the Iranians, even if they got the bomb, [would] drop it in the neighborhood. They fully understand what might follow. They are radical but not totally crazy. They have a quite sophisticated decision-making process, and they understand reality."[65] Rather, Israeli leaders want to preserve a regional balance of power strongly tilted in Israel's favor; in Prime Minister Netanyahu's words, a nuclear Iran would "create a sea change in the balance of power in our area."[66] In the view of senior Israeli military and intelligence officials and politicians, the perception that the Islamic Republic had achieved even just a "breakout" capability would start to erode Israel's nuclear weapons monopoly in the region, chipping away at both the image and the reality of its regional hegemony. And a nuclear-capable Iran could begin constraining, at least on the margins, what Israeli generals call their country's "freedom of military action"—in other words, it might, in some circumstances, make Israeli decision makers think twice about initiating conflict. As Barak puts it,

> Imagine if we enter another military confrontation with Hezbollah, which has over 50,000 rockets that threaten the whole area of Israel, including several thousand that can reach Tel Aviv. A nuclear Iran announces that an attack on Hezbollah is tantamount to an attack on Iran. We would not necessarily give up on it, but it would definitely restrict our range of operations.[67]

This view is widely shared among Israeli national security professionals.[68]

Thus, since the 1990s, there has been an emphatic consensus among Israeli elites that the Islamic Republic must be marginalized and kept weak. Israel seeks to accomplish this aim on its own through intelligence operations, assassinations, covert support for separatist and other antiregime groups inside Iran, military preparation, and the threat of military attack. But Israeli administrations have also worked to influence Washington's posture toward Iran—both through their own channels to the executive and legislative branches and through the Israel lobby. Together, they seek to persuade the American government to adopt policies that will keep Iran strategically subordinated.

To this end, they work to preclude serious diplomacy between Washington and Tehran; currently, AIPAC and other members of the lobby back legislation that would bar any diplomatic contact between American and Iranian officials unless Congress is notified at least fifteen days in advance.[69] If completely forestalling diplomacy proves impossible, the lobby hopes at least to put severe limits on it. On the nuclear issue, for example, it insists that Washington require a complete termination of Iranian enrichment—an outcome that would prevent the Islamic Republic from constraining Israel's military autonomy by achieving a "nuclear weapons capability" (AIPAC's alarmist formulation for mastering the nuclear fuel cycle).[70] Such a posture guarantees the failure of nuclear diplomacy in advance.

With AIPAC at the forefront, the lobby has also spearheaded efforts to impose ever tougher sanctions on the Islamic Republic, with the ultimate objective of cutting off Iranian oil exports. As noted, during the 1980s AIPAC argued against imposing sanctions on Iran; since then, however, AIPAC and others in the lobby have made expanding and intensifying anti-Iranian sanctions a top priority.[71] In 1995, this pressure was a major driver of the Clinton administration's decision not to accept Rafsanjani's invitation for American energy companies to return to Iran and, instead, to impose a comprehensive U.S. economic embargo against the Islamic Republic. According to a former AIPAC senior staffer, AIPAC then drafted what became the 1996 Iran-Libya Sanctions Act (ILSA), which authorized the imposition of secondary sanctions against third-country entities investing in developing Iranian hydrocarbons; ILSA's provisions were renewed with minor modifications in 2001 and, under the title of the Iran Sanctions Act (ISA), in 2006.[72]

For diplomatic, legal, and political reasons, American administrations have shown reluctance actually to impose the sanctions authorized under ILSA and ISA—a source of mounting frustration for the Israel lobby. Consequently, AIPAC joined with the Iran Energy Project, run by the neoconservative Foundation for Defense of Democracies to campaign for the Comprehensive Iran Sanctions, Accountability, and Divestment Act (CISADA). Signed by President Obama in 2010, CISADA expands the range of third-country commercial activities in Iran that are subject to sanction by the United States; more important, it sharpens the punishment for doing business with Iran to include an effective cutoff from the American financial system and makes it harder for the executive branch to avoid sanctioning foreign entities. In 2011, AIPAC and FDD were key players behind an amendment to the defense authorization bill mandating the application of CISADA-like sanctions against foreign entities purchasing Iranian oil or transacting business with the Central Bank of Iran—the strongest effort yet to embargo Iranian oil. In 2012, Obama signed the Iran Threat Reduction and Syria Human Rights Act, which is designed to make it even harder for the executive branch to avoid imposing secondary sanctions. As the number of sanctions has increased, AIPAC, the Anti-Defamation League, and the rest of the lobby have focused intently on ensuring that these are strictly enforced.[73] Israeli pressure is also a major factor behind American efforts both to marshal the U.N. Security Council to authorize sanctions and to persuade other countries to enact their own.

Contrary to conventional wisdom, a unilateral Israeli attack against the Islamic Republic's nuclear infrastructure would work against the logic of Israel's national security strategy. The upside would be paltry. The relatively small number of Israeli aircraft able to reach targets in Iran and (assuming that Israel would not use nuclear weapons against Iranian nuclear facilities) the IDF's lack of ordnance suitable for destroying hardened underground sites like the enrichment centers at Natanz and Fordo mean that the damage Israel could do on its own would be very limited. The prospective downsides could be enormous: the level of international consensus that has been achieved to support economic sanctions and political pressure against the Islamic Republic would be badly undermined, and Israel would face potentially severe backlash, not just from Iran but from other regional neighbors (for example, sustained rocket barrages from Hizballah in Lebanon). That is why Israel's professional security establishment—including most of the current and retired leadership of the IDF and the country's intelligence services—opposes overt unilateral Israeli military action against Iran. If Prime Minister Netanyahu orders such action, it will be for reasons outside the framework of Israeli strategy. Israel's security establishment has determined that, if the Islamic Republic is to be struck militarily, it is better for the United States to do the deed.

Thus, beyond sanctions, the lobby is working to turn American public opinion in favor of eventual military action against Iran. At the beginning of 2002, as the world was trying to discern which part of the axis of evil was going to be the war on terror's next target, Israeli officials made it clear that they considered Iran a bigger threat than Iraq. (Flynt Leverett learned this firsthand as a U.S. government representative at Israel's Herzliya security conference that January.) When Bush decided on Iraq, administration hawks assured Israel and the lobby that Saddam was not their last target—Iran and Syria were both on their post-Iraq hit list.[74] But the Bush administration never moved on to large-scale military operations against the Islamic Republic, and so Israel shifted to urging "surgical" American military strikes against Iranian nuclear targets.[75] Prime Minister Ehud Olmert pushed for them in 2007–08, with Vice President Cheney's support; Bush rebuffed them after the U.S. Intelligence Community's December 2007 National Intelligence Estimate disputed that Iran was working on a nuclear weapons program.[76] Olmert's successor, Binyamin Netanyahu, has continued the drumbeat during Obama's presidency, while also becoming more vocal in asserting Israel's right to strike on its own if international steps to squeeze Iran prove inadequate.[77]

To raise the alarm, Israeli leaders often deploy the irrationality myth, comparing the Islamic Republic to Nazi Germany, and the Israel lobby echoes this trope.[78] Both groups also present a deeply distorted view of Shi'a Islam in order to back up their claim that the Islamic Republic is so collectively bent on destroying "the Zionist entity" that it is willing to become a "suicide nation."[79] Thus, senior Israelis insist that Tehran's "irrational regime" cannot be allowed indigenous fuel cycle capabilities (because "you can't rely on the fact that they'll obey the calculations of cost and benefit that have governed all nuclear powers since the rise of the nuclear age after Hiroshima and Nagasaki").[80] The Israel lobby concurs. The American Jewish Committee's executive director, David Harris, has questioned whether a country "driven by Shiite theology" could be "a rational actor" and resist using nuclear weapons against Israel, "whose destruction it has called for." For that matter, "Could it be trusted not to share its weapons with allies like Venezuela or terrorist groups [such] as HAMAS or Hezbollah?"[81] The Anti-Defamation League's Abraham Foxman simply defames Iran as "a country that is not rational."[82]

In tandem with Israeli political and security officials, the lobby also regularly hauls out the illegitimacy myth, since it helps mobilize public support for harder-line measures, increases obstacles to diplomacy, and shores up the idea that the Islamic Republic is vulnerable to outside pressure. So when Obama released his March 2009 Nowruz video to "the people and leaders of the Islamic Republic of Iran," Israeli president Shimon Peres responded with his own video, exhorting Iranians to rise up and overthrow their government.[83] In 2010, the executive director of the Conference of Presidents of Major Jewish Organizations, Malcolm Hoenlein, released a video, too, assuring the Iranian people that "we" do not have any grievance against them and want to help them create a government that would not divert resources away from "health care and other domestic needs" and toward nuclear weapons—even though the Islamic Republic, as noted, has made internationally recognized advances in delivering health care and education to its people and ameliorating poverty.[84] Today, the Anti-Defamation League tells visitors to its Web site that "the Iranian regime denies basic freedoms to Iran's citizens, including freedom of speech, freedom of assembly, freedom of religion, and freedom of the press. The rights of women, workers, homosexuals, juveniles, religious and ethnic minorities, and political opposition are brutally suppressed."[85]

The lobby has also taken steps to influence the American political establishment by setting up policy research institutes. The oldest is the Jewish Institute for National Security Affairs, founded in 1976 by conservative Zionists disturbed by what they saw as Washington's slowness in resupplying Israel during the October 1973 War; it seeks to "improve awareness in the general public as well as in the Jewish community about the importance of an effective US defense capability" and to "engage the American defense and foreign affairs community about the important role Israel can and does play in bolstering democratic interests in the Mediterranean and the Middle East."[86] The most prominent is the Washington Institute for Near East Policy (WINEP), founded in 1985 by a network of AIPAC donors; its first director, Martin Indyk, left an AIPAC staff position for his new post. While WINEP has, on occasion, published genuine scholarship on Iran, most of its work is strongly agenda-driven, depicting Tehran as an aspiring regional hegemon with a nihilistic determination to destroy Israel.[87] In 2002, the Saban Center for Middle East Policy opened at the Brookings Institution, endowed by Haim Saban, an Israeli American media magnate who forthrightly tells reporters that he is "a one-issue guy, and [that] issue is Israel."[88] Its first director was the same Martin Indyk. Its first major hire was Kenneth Pollack, fresh from his commercial success cum looming embarrassment with *The Threatening Storm*; from his platform at Brookings, Pollack has devoted a lot of attention to Iran, with much the same faulty analysis he brought to Iraq. He has dismissed Iranian security concerns as the self-generated fantasies of a regime "obsessed with the United States," embraced the myth of the Islamic Republic's illegitimacy, and consistently backed the failed dual-track strategy—to the point of encouraging the Obama administration to "double down" on it. He has even recommended exploring ways to "goad" Iran into a "provocation" ostensibly justifying American airstrikes against Iranian targets—which might otherwise prove "unpopular in the region and throughout the world."[89]

One of the chief functions of lobby-affiliated think tanks is to position pro-Israel policy specialists for high-level government posts. Indyk is a good example. A former analyst with Australia's intelligence service, he came to the United States to work for AIPAC in 1982 and three years later helped found WINEP with AIPAC donors. In 1992, he advised presidential candidate Bill Clinton on Middle East issues; following Clinton's election, he joined the National Security Council staff as senior director for Near East and South Asian affairs. (Because he was an Australian national, his application for American citizenship had to be expedited with unusual speed to get him the requisite security clearances.) He went on to serve two tours as ambassador to Israel, with a stint as assistant secretary of state for Near Eastern affairs in between. When Clinton left office, Indyk established the Saban Center.

Another example is Dennis Ross, who has maintained ties to the Israel lobby, liberal internationalists, and neocons alike. Trained as a Sovietologist, Ross began his career in the Carter administration's Defense Department, where, under Deputy Assistant Secretary Paul Wolfowitz (later the Bush administration's leading Iraq War proponent), he contributed to the analysis and planning that culminated in the Carter Doctrine. He continued working on Persian Gulf security at the Pentagon and the National Security Council in the Reagan administration. In 1985, Ross became WINEP's first senior fellow and wrote its first monograph, in which he called for the appointment of a "non-Arabist Special Middle East envoy" who would "not feel guilty about our relationship with Israel" and would take an approach to Arab-Israeli peacemaking referred to around WINEP as "motion without movement."[90] The aphorism would later summarize his view on Iran policy. During the George H. W. Bush administration, he served as Secretary of State James Baker's director of policy planning; he was then retained by the Clinton administration as its (non-Arabist) special Middle East coordinator. After Clinton left office, Ross returned to WINEP until the Obama administration appointed him to run its Iran policy, first at the State Department and later at the National Security Council. In 2012, he returned to WINEP, where he continues advising the administration but also played an overtly political role supporting Obama's reelection campaign. Though neocons have criticized Ross's commitment to a (highly Israel-friendly and never productive) peace process—and though he can boast few concrete policy successes—his extensive connections to the lobby make him a perennially attractive candidate for senior government positions.

During the primary season in every presidential election cycle, WINEP combs the ranks of candidates' foreign policy advisers to create a bipartisan "presidential study group." WINEP selects candidate advisers who it believes are already sympathetic to its point of view, do not yet have strongly developed views on the Middle East, or see the benefit of having the lobby's backing. The study group convenes to hear pro-Israel presentations on Middle East issues, travels to Israel to hear Israeli policy perspectives firsthand, and produces a high-profile set of policy recommendations for the next American president. Signatories to the report receive a boost to their attractiveness as potential officials in the next administration—a dynamic that helps the lobby, through WINEP, to influence candidates' advisers and to position suitably pro-Israel policy hands for posts in the incoming administration.[91]

EXPATRIATES: NATIVE AUTHENTICATORS (AND ENABLERS?)

Disaffected Iranian expatriates—both dissidents in exile and politically influential Iranian Americans—have just as eagerly promulgated the Iran mythology, which is hardly surprising: almost by definition, they have an axe to grind with the government from which they or their families fled. It is more difficult to understand why they have been so widely accepted as unimpeachable purveyors of truth—or prospective agents of change—when many of them have not been in Iran for years, even decades.

Following the Cold War and 9/11, the American project of reshaping the Middle East created a demand for regional expertise. But Washington's strategic goals and tactical preferences defined the limits of the knowledge that would be acceptable—euphemistically termed "policy-relevant analysis"—inside the Beltway. Thus the sought-after "expertise" validates Washington's received opinion about regional politics, especially in target countries. If it comes from sources that seem natively authentic, all the better—and better still if those sources claim to be in a position to help the United States realize its policy goals.

Such an environment is tailor-made for a man like Ahmad Chalabi. An expatriate opponent of Saddam Husayn's, Chalabi was a highly intelligent and entrepreneurial con artist with both a Ph.D. in mathematics from MIT and a conviction for bank fraud in Jordan. In the 1990s, with support from Kanan Makiya, an émigré Iraqi architect who wrote best-selling books about the horrors of life under Saddam and now teaches Middle Eastern politics at Brandeis University, and from a few other Iraqi exiles, Chalabi forged alliances with prominent neocons and with the Israel lobby. As a result, he played a uniquely significant role in steering American Iraq policy toward regime change over the course of the decade. After 9/11, he and his Iraqi National Congress (INC) were instrumental in facilitating the decision to invade Iraq, providing manufactured intelligence about Saddam's WMD programs and serving as the face of the neocons' fantasy, a post-Saddam government. Of course, since returning to Iraq, neither Chalabi, the INC, nor the secular nationalism they claimed to represent has ever attracted much support.

Today, an array of high-profile disaffected Iranian expatriates is playing much the same role, with much the same sort of distorting impact on policy deliberations. While, according to polls, most Iranian Americans oppose military action against Iran, substantial majorities also believe that Iran should be a secular democracy (only 6 percent support some form of "Islamic republic") and that "promoting human rights and democracy" should be the top priority of American policy toward the Iranian government.[92] One of the more broadly based political initiatives within the diaspora calls for a referendum on changing the constitution to make the Islamic Republic a secular state. Among the more established Iranian American groups, only the American Iranian Council, founded in 1997, has consistently opposed sanctions and backed engagement with the Islamic Republic.

For some, the desire for regime change translates into support for the MEK—"the best-funded and best-organized" opposition group.[93] Indeed, Iranian Americans have been key to the MEK's ongoing effort to sell itself as the vanguard of real opposition to the Islamic Republic. During the 1970s, the MEK assassinated a number of American military and civilian personnel in Iran; as noted; in 1994 the group reportedly worked with Ramzi Yousef (just a year after he helped bomb the World Trade Center in New York) to blow up a widely revered mosque in Iran. In 1997 the MEK become a charter member of the U.S. government's list of foreign terrorist organizations (FTOs). Nevertheless, it was allowed to continue operating in the United States, through affiliates like the National Council of Resistance of Iran, until 2002.

After that, its expatriate supporters campaigned to rehabilitate it and, in particular, to remove it from the list of FTOs—through lobbying, public relations initiatives, and litigation in the federal courts. Many of them hope that it can serve, much as the INC did, as the cutting edge of an American-sponsored regime change strategy.

Through this campaign expatriate supporters established ties to both neoconservatives and the Israel lobby. To be sure, some neocons—notably Michael Ledeen, Danielle Pletka, and Michael Rubin—have warned against involvement with the MEK; in a rare display of analytic sobriety, Ledeen has pointed out that "most Iranians hate the MEK, because it is based in Iraq and operated on behalf of Saddam Hussein, killing many Iranians."[94] Many more, though—including John Bolton, Max Boot, WINEP's Patrick Clawson, and Daniel Pipes of the Middle East Forum—have called on the U.S. government to de-list the MEK; some of them want to see it trained and equipped as a paramilitary force.[95] Fox News acknowledges that one of its longtime paid commentators on Iran and the Middle East, Alireza Jafarzadeh, worked "for a dozen years as the chief congressional liaison and media spokesman for the U.S. representative office of Iran's parliament in exile, the National Council of Resistance of Iran," an MEK affiliate; he held the position until the U.S. government shut down the NCRI's Washington office in 2002.[96] The MEK has expanded its support among neocons and in the pro-Israel community through the Iran Policy Committee, organized by Raymond Tanter, an NSC staffer in the Reagan administration, professor emeritus at the University of Michigan, and a longtime WINEP associate.[97]

Over the past few years, the campaign to "de-list" the MEK was taken to a new level with infusions of funding from Iranian Americans and perhaps others. A number of prominent Republicans were recruited to agitate publicly on the MEK's behalf: Newt Gingrich, Rudolph Giuliani, former attorney general Michael Mukasey, former State Department policy planning director Mitchell Reiss (the chief foreign policy adviser to GOP presidential candidate Mitt Romney), former homeland security secretary and Pennsylvania governor Tom Ridge, former White House homeland security and counterterrorism

The MEK takes its well-financed campaign to overthrow the Iranian government into the halls of power in Washington. *EPA/JIM LO SCALZO*

coordinator Frances Townsend, and House Foreign Affairs Committee chair Ileana Ros-Lehtinen.

In 2010 a federal district court in California ordered the State Department to review its designation of the MEK as an FTO—and with this development, the public campaign for de-listing went bipartisan and big time. The roster of prominent figures recruited to flack for the MEK expanded to include former Democratic representative Lee Hamilton, former Democratic presidential candidate and party chair Howard Dean, former New Mexico governor and Clinton administration cabinet member Bill Richardson, and former New Jersey Democratic senator Robert Torricelli, as well as former FBI director Louis Freeh, retired U.S. Marine Corps general Anthony Zinni, and (after he stepped down as President Obama's first national security adviser in November 2010) retired Marine Corps general James Jones. A Washington consulting firm—Executive Action, LLC, which describes itself as "a McKinsey & Company with muscle, a private CIA and Defense Department available to address your most intractable problems and difficult challenges"—was engaged to organize a series of high-visibility events and initiatives on the MEK's behalf. Many of the above individuals were paid five- or even six-figure sums to speak out for the MEK's de-listing.[98] U.S. officials believe that the MEK continues to conduct attacks inside Iran—including, as noted earlier, some carried out in cooperation with Al-Qa'ida—and that it is currently collaborating with Israel to assassinate Iranian scientists. Nevertheless, in the fall of 2012, the Obama administration decided to remove the MEK's FTO designation.

Other segments of the Iranian American community, in contrast, prefer what might be called "soft" regime change, accomplished not through military confrontation but by nonviolently undermining the Islamic Republic and somehow setting Iran on what they see as its natural—that is, secular and liberal—trajectory. While eschewing the MEK's militant tactics, the goal of these activists is regime change all the same, to be achieved through stepped-up criticism of the Islamic Republic's human rights record and support for reformists and secular liberals inside Iran. At its core, this is neoconservatism without guns, effectively indistinguishable from the position of Michael Ledeen and other neocons who believe that military action would be counterproductive. Nevertheless, over the last decade, organizations like George Soros's Open Society Institute and the Rockefeller Brothers Fund have worked, often through expatriate activists and groups, to promote the soft regime change agenda under the guise of building "civil society" in Iran.[99] And Iranian-American endorsement of this agenda has been critical to the adoption of the illegitimacy myth as the reigning narrative about the Islamic Republic's domestic politics in America's distorted Iran debate.

In particular, dissident expatriates have functioned as native authenticators of that myth. Certainly it has not been hard for Westerners to find high-profile dissidents like Akbar Ganji, Mohsen Kadivar, Mehdi Khalaji, and Mohsen Sazegara to affirm for them that the Islamic Republic has failed to live up to the revolution's promises and is thus an illegitimate state. Others, like 2003 Nobel Peace laureate Shirin Ebadi, hold that its legitimacy has been undermined by systematic human rights abuses. (Many Iranians living inside the Islamic Republic view the West's adulation of Ebadi with suspicion because, as a judge in prerevolutionary Iran, she failed to criticize the shah's judicial apparatus that systematically abused Iranians' human rights.) Nor has it been difficult to find expatriate intellectuals such as Hamid Dabashi, Abbas Milani, and Azar Nafisi to declare (again, without serious supporting evidence) that most Iranians do not want to live in an Islamic republic at all, regardless of whether it achieves the goals it has set for itself.

American elites ratify such messages without much scrutiny: Ganji received the Cato Institute's 2010 Milton Friedman Prize for Advancing Liberty; Kadivar is a visiting professor at Duke University; Khalaji is a senior fellow at WINEP; Milani is codirector of the Hoover Institution's Iran Democracy Project and director of Iranian studies at Stanford University; Nafisi is writer in residence at SAIS; and Sazegara is a fellow at the George W. Bush Institute at Southern Methodist University. For Columbia University's Hamid Dabashi, that is as it should be. Dabashi lashed out at our questioning of the rush of Iran "experts" to declare Iran's 2009 election as stolen with a classically fallacious argument from authority: "Among the 'experts' who had corroborated these charges, and whom the Leveretts placed in quotation marks by way of denigrating and dismissing them, were the leading Iranian scholars within and outside their homeland—from Iran to Europe to the US to Japan to Australia—and the Leveretts would do well to exercise a degree of humility in the face of their superior competence and knowledge of their homeland."[100] But we all know what came from deferring to the "superior competence and knowledge" of agenda-driven expatriates regarding the attitude of Iraqis toward being invaded and occupied by the United States and about the state of Saddam's WMD.

The messages of these dissident expatriates are reinforced by a cadre of highly visible Iranian American commentators who may have spent some part of their childhood in Iran but have made their lives and careers in the West—for example, Reza Aslan, Nader Hashemi, Azadeh Mouaveni, Karim Sadjadpour, and Ray Takeyh. Though they may not all be as outlandishly off base as Amir Taheri, they have, as we have noted throughout, been wrong about multiple major turning points in Iranian politics over the past several years. Most exaggerated popular support for Mousavi before the 2009 presidential election; all subsequently pushed unsubstantiated claims of electoral fraud. They were also severely off the mark regarding the alleged implosion of Aya-tollah Khamenei's authority and the Islamic Republic's legitimacy among most Iranians.[101] Sadjadpour's and Takeyh's analytic misper-ceptions extend to foreign policy: both have championed the false proposition that the Islamic Republic is too dependent on legitimiz-ing itself via anti-Americanism to have a rational diplomatic strategy, and Takeyh has, under various rubrics, stubbornly defended the United States' failed dual-track approach.[102] Despite their poor track record, this group continues to enjoy easy access to mainstream media outlets and is regularly called on to advise administrations—including the Obama administration—about Iran-related issues.[103]

Abbas Milani's ascendancy is instructive as regards both the influ-ence of expatriate Iranian commentators and the allure of soft regime change for American policy makers. Born in Iran in 1949, Milani came to California as a teenager. He completed high school and col-lege in the Bay Area, became a devotee of Maoist Marxism, and took a Ph.D. in political science at the University of Hawaii in 1974. He then taught at Iran's National University before being imprisoned by the shah's government for his Marxist views. After the revolution, he joined the faculty at the University of Tehran, then returned to Cali-fornia in 1986. He taught at a small Catholic college in the Bay Area and published intermittently in obscure nonacademic outlets with little impact on the field of Iranian studies. In 2001, a group of Iranian Americans (several of whom had made fortunes in Silicon Valley start-ups) endowed a fellowship for Milani and his Iran Democracy Project at the Hoover Institution. He began teaching as a visiting professor in Stanford's political science department; in 2005, pros-perous Iranian Americans endowed the directorship of the universi-ty's (one-man) Iranian studies program for him.[104] From this platform and a contributing editorship at the *New Republic*, Milani works assiduously to depict Iran as a nation destined to become a secular democracy.

Milani and his colleagues at the Iran Democracy Project elaborated on their ideas for soft regime change in a 2005 monograph. They proposed a "new strategy for dealing with Iran," according to which Washington would pursue diplomacy with Tehran over the nuclear issue and other hot-button security challenges, eschew military confrontation while championing human rights and democratization, and replace the existing sanctions, which afflicted all Iranians, with "smart sanctions" targeting the Iranian government. At the same time, Washington should encourage greater contact between the United States and Iran, which, Milani and his colleagues argued, would undermine popular support for the existing political order.[105]

Although the George W. Bush administration mostly ignored the recommendations dealing with diplomacy and expanded U.S.-Iranian contacts, Milani's ideas about soft regime change had an appreciable impact. During Bush's second term, U.S. government funding for "democracy promotion" in Iran rose sharply, from $1.5 million in 2005 to $75 million in 2008. The Obama administration repackaged these appropriations under new labels that somewhat disguised their Iran-specific purposes, but it has maintained a comparable level of support for Iranian democratization. A number of prominent dissidents, including Ebadi and Ganji, have warned that "no truly nationalist and democratic groups will accept such funds" since to do so would compromise them, in Iranian eyes, as tools of a foreign power.[106] However, several Iranian Americans have put themselves forward as prospective engines of political transformation and have welcomed funds from the State Department's democracy promotion accounts, as well as from the government-funded National Endowment for Democracy.

Expatriates have created several organizations, such as the International Campaign for Human Rights in Iran, that aim to delegitimize the Islamic Republic by focusing attention on its human rights record; at least one of them, the Iran Human Rights Documentation Center (IHRDC), has received U.S. government support. That their activism is hardly apolitical is clear from a closer look at their leaders. Ramin Ahmadi, a physician and founder of the IHRDC, received several years' worth of U.S. government financing for his Iranian Center for Applied Nonviolence. Government and other funds were also funneled to his group through the neoconservatively oriented Freedom House. The center ran workshops in Dubai to train Iranian oppositionists in nonviolent civil disobedience, inviting members of the youth movement that had brought down Serbian president Slobodan Milošević, with the idea of fostering an Eastern European–style color revolution in Iran. Participants came to Dubai thinking that they were going to attend U.N.-sponsored workshops on "human rights reporting"; instead, they say they were instructed in how to use encrypted e-mail and secure software to organize antigovernment protests. They did not learn until after the fact that their training had been funded by the American government.[107]

The National Iranian American Council (NIAC) also seeks to link human rights activism to soft regime change. Its founder and president, Trita Parsi, emigrated from Iran to Sweden as a child; his family, he has said, wanted "to escape political repression." After serving as a Swedish diplomat at the United Nations, he remained in the United States to attend graduate school and, in 2002, to launch NIAC in order "to enable Iranian-Americans to condemn the September 11, 2001 terror attacks." While promoting American-Iranian engagement as a way to "enhance our national security by helping to stabilize the Middle East and bolster the moderates in Iran," he has been especially focused on supporting "the Iranian-American community's aspirations for democracy in Iran" and "ensuring that human rights are upheld in Iran." Parsi and NIAC back the "pro-democracy movement" as "a peaceful path for changing Iran's political system from within," a goal to which their advocacy of engagement is ultimately subordinate. After the 2009 election, which they insisted was fraudulent without producing any evidence, they called for a "strategic pause" in U.S. engagement with Tehran, to avoid "legitimating" the established order. While they now once again favor diplomacy, they stipulate that any diplomacy must include "human rights as a core issue," with the goal of "a world in which the United States and a democratic Iran"—no mention of the Islamic Republic—"enjoy peaceful, cooperative relations."[108]

Parsi and NIAC do not want the United States to attack the Islamic Republic or to back terrorist campaigns against it by the MEK, because, in their view, these tactics are unlikely to turn Iran into the secular, liberal, and pro-Western country they dream of. Their periodic support for diplomatic engagement attracts angry criticism from groups that back the MEK or otherwise call for a more hard-line approach to regime change, but their policy positions enable the pursuit of neoconservative ends. NIAC's unsubstantiated portrayal of the 2009 election as stolen helped make real rapprochement between the United States and Iran less likely and war more likely. Its advocacy of "targeted sanctions" against the Iranian government serves only to facilitate the passage of broad-based sanctions, which also increase the long-term risk of war. Moreover, its ultimate vision for Iran is not fundamentally different from that of neoconservatives. NIAC notes on its Web site that, "with the support of grants from the National Endowment for Democracy," it has "conducted nonpolitical trainings for non-governmental organizations (NGOs) in Iran to help foster a stronger Iranian civil society"—which it regards as key to realizing its goal of a secular Iranian state.[109] It has received funding as well from the Rockefeller Brothers Fund, which supported similar efforts to encourage political change in the former Yugoslavia and former Soviet-block states. (The Rockefeller Brothers Fund also underwrote Ali Ansari's substantively flawed work to delegitimate the Islamic Republic's 2009 election.)[110]

Some expatriates and their Western supporters are even more flagrant in their pursuit of soft regime change. A case in point is Scott Lucas, a U.K.-based academic activist and supporter of soft regime change whose Enduring America Web site purports to draw on expatriate networks and anonymous sources in Iran to report alleged Iranian internal problems, from economic malaise to police brutality. While we cannot document that Lucas was inciting Iranians to protest in 2009, we know that he was doing so in 2012. He used multiple e-mail and IP addresses to try to break into our Web site, which is read in Iran, so as to post places Iranians should gather to protest on the 2012 anniversary of 22 Bahman. He desisted only after we alerted the dean at his university that he was using university e-mail and IP addresses to hack into our site.

Western liberals who do not favor another U.S.-instigated war in the Middle East have sometimes asked us what we find wrong with the notion of soft regime change, or at least of advocating for a more secular and liberal order in Iran in the name of human rights. As we have noted, criminal abuses are committed by authorities in the Islamic Republic, as they are elsewhere. (This is one reason we are personally opposed to capital punishment, for when it is abused there is no possibility of correction.) But the only way human rights conditions in the Islamic Republic, as defined by Western liberals, are likely to improve is in a context of U.S.-Iranian rapprochement, whereby the United States had credibly given up regime change as a policy goal.

Even with the establishment of normal diplomatic relations, the real motives for American interest in human rights remain suspect in many non-Western political orders resistant to domination by the United States (China is a good example). Would it have helped the cause of civil rights in the United States if the Soviet Union had provided financial and political support—and perhaps even military training and weapons—to groups seeking to challenge a racist American order? By the same token, we are deeply skeptical that the U.S. government can be an objective advocate for human rights in countries and regions of the world that it has long sought to dominate.[111] All four groups discussed in this chapter—neoconservatives, liberal internationalists, the Israel lobby, and Iranian expatriates—use human rights issues as a tool to support American dominance over the Islamic Republic. (Former GOP senator and presidential candidate Rick Santorum, for example, opposes equal rights for homosexuals in his own country but made allegations about the treatment of gays in the Islamic Republic part of his case for adopting regime change as the goal of America's Iran policy.) That is precisely what the U.S. government tries to do itself, but on a broader scale and with vastly more resources. Washington has never demonstrated that it cares about human rights in the

Middle East for their own sake. It cares about them when and where caring appears to serve other policy goals. In situations where this is not useful—for example, Bahrain—Washington is, in concrete terms, indifferent to human rights.

———

The United States' Iran mythology is the basis for its Iran policies. In the next chapter, we examine how that mythology and those who champion it have constrained and distorted Washington's approach to the Islamic Republic, spurring actions that inflict ever greater damage on America's strategic position, in the Middle East and globally.

8

IRAN AND AMERICA'S IMPERIAL TURN

The war in Vietnam is but a symptom of a far deeper malady within the American spirit, and if we ignore this sobering reality we will find ourselves organizing clergy-and-laymen-concerned committees for the next generation. . . . We will be marching [and] attending rallies without end unless there is a significant and profound change in American life and policy.

—*Martin Luther King Jr., 1967*

On December 16, 2011—nearly a decade after President George W. Bush's "axis of evil" speech—PBS *NewsHour* presented its regular Friday review of the past week's events, featuring liberal commentator Mark Shields and conservative *New York Times* columnist David Brooks. The American military presence in Iraq was nearing its end; it was an occasion to reflect on the invasion and eight-year occupation of Iraq. The discussion, moderated by *NewsHour*'s chief anchor at the time, Jim Lehrer, included the following exchange:

SHIELDS: Let's be very blunt about it. Al-Qa'ida was responsible for 9/11. Iraq had nothing to do with it. Iraq had no weapons of mass destruction and no ability or capacity to deliver those weapons that were nonexistent.

LEHRER: And you don't dispute that, David?

BROOKS: No. Well, we obviously thought what we thought back then. But I always thought that the need to disrupt the Middle East was one of the reasons why it was necessary.[1]

Brooks's response captures much of what is wrong with the United States' post–Cold War grand strategy in the Middle East—and, specifically, with its Iran policy. The 2003 invasion of Iraq was an all too blatant manifestation of the American ambition to consolidate hegemony over the Middle East. The public case for war relied on arguments about Saddam Husayn's WMD and his ties to Al-Qa'ida, but when those arguments were shown to be false and manufactured, true believers in the enterprise did not abandon their support. To them, the most resounding reason for the invasion had nothing to do with (flawed) technical assessments of Saddam's nuclear infrastructure or (bogus) intelligence reporting about Iraqi contacts with the 9/11 hijackers. In Brooks's phrase, the war was fundamentally about the "need to disrupt the Middle East"—to shake the region to its political and cultural foundations and then remake it in accordance with American preferences. It was thus a prime example of what we have described as the imperial turn in the United States' post–Cold War Middle East strategy. It was also a contemporary manifestation of what Martin Luther King Jr., in his 1967 sermon about the Vietnam War and American foreign policy, called the "deeper malady within the American spirit" and the "deadly Western arrogance that has poisoned the international atmosphere for so long."

The Iraq War provides a powerful case study in the damage that the quest for hegemony can do to American interests and stature. To begin with, this bloody experiment in projecting the neoconservative worldview caught up millions of Iraqis who had no opportunity to give their "informed consent," and their suffering—the massive death, injury, and displacement—is a permanent stain on the record of American foreign policy. It is never good to lose a war, and make no mistake: the United States lost the war in Iraq. It was compelled to withdraw its military forces without having achieved its core political objectives there. And the war's results were hardly what the policy makers who pushed it advertised. Americans were promised that overthrowing Saddam would lead to a secular, democratic order in Iraq that would be, almost by definition, pro-American and that the country's transformation would pave the way for similarly pro-American secular democracies around the region. Instead, the war ended up creating a state that, in keeping with its Shi'a-majority demographics, is naturally aligned with the Islamic Republic. Not only did the campaign fail on its own terms; it turned the regional balance of power against the United States. In the process, it did massive harm to the nation's broader strategic position and accelerated the erosion of its international leadership role.

But the war was not merely an aberration in American foreign policy attributable to the idiosyncrasies of George W. Bush and his neoconservative advisers or their fear of the uniquely menacing Saddam Husayn. The United States' imperial turn in the region was focused not only on Iraq but rather on all potential challenges to its primacy there. The imperial thrust began in George H. W. Bush's presidency, at the opening of the post–Cold War era (with strategic and political roots going much further back), and accelerated during Bill Clinton's. Nor did it end with George W. Bush's departure from Washington. Barack Obama pledged to move away from the hegemonic thinking that had produced the Iraq War and restore the legitimacy of American leadership in the Middle East and globally. Instead, with a few tactical modifications, he has continued down the same self-destructive path—and with predictably similar results. His attempt to salvage Washington's failed drive for regional hegemony could wind up doing more damage to American strategic prospects than George W. Bush's debacles did.

The competitive dynamics of international politics, like those of a market, tend to punish states (even superpowers) that act in nonstrategic ways—for example, by pursuing policies that bend to domestic ideologies and pressures at the expense of political and economic reality. Unquestionably, the international political market has begun to punish the United States for the policy failures it has accumulated in its quixotic quest for dominance in the Middle East. Today, this quest is most visible in the escalating struggle between Washington and Tehran. Once again, establishment voices are saying the Middle East could benefit from armed attack. The historian Niall Ferguson, for example, recently extolled the idea of an Israeli strike on Iran, with American

Regardless of political party, America's post–Cold War presidents have followed strikingly similar policies, pushing the United States further and further toward confrontation with the Islamic Republic. *Official White House photo/Pete Souza*

forces providing "all necessary support" to ensure the destruction of Iran's nuclear and military infrastructure, as an example of "creative destruction."[2] In fact, an American military confrontation with the Islamic Republic would almost certainly prove even more damaging to the United States than its Iraq misadventure has been. But, captive to the prevailing Iran mythology, Washington's approach to Iran and the rest of the region remains stubbornly single-minded, despite the mounting risks and clear harm to American interests.

THE AMERICAN WAY OF STRATEGY

As already noted, when confronted by a more formidable state, most countries—including medium-sized powers like Iran—have to either balance against it or bandwagon with it. A great power like the United States, however, has a different set of options; it chooses between balancing and hegemony. Balancing strategies are fundamentally defensive: a state seeks security by marshaling the resources it takes to prevent other great powers from challenging its core interests, either militarily or economically. Hegemonic strategies, by contrast, are inherently expansionist: a state uses military, political, and economic power not just to defend its interests but to bend others into accommodating them.

Americans generally like to think that their country has exercised its power only reluctantly—to defend itself and advance the welfare of others. But the United States has been, virtually from its inception, expansionist. Through the first half of the nineteenth century, it spread relentlessly westward across North America, maneuvering Britain, France, and Spain out of their holdings, displacing Native Americans, and, in the Mexican-American War of 1848, annexing roughly a third of Mexico's territory. Starting in the second half of the nineteenth century, it extended its military power and political and economic influence into Latin America and the Pacific basin, through the forcible annexation of Hawaii and other Pacific island territories, the Spanish-American War (with the attendant colonization of the Philippines, the de facto colonization of Cuba, and the annexation of Guam and Puerto Rico), and President Theodore Roosevelt's enunciation of a regime-change policy against any Latin American government that Washington deemed problematic.[3]

By the end of the nineteenth century, the United States was the Western Hemisphere's hegemonic power. From the beginning of the twentieth century, its foreign policy was increasingly shaped by a more ambitious idea: that, to be truly secure, it had to deploy the full panoply of its military, economic, and ideological power across the world to ensure access both to markets (for American goods and capital) and to critical raw materials. To this end, it had to be capable of leveraging political outcomes—of fostering regimes that would cooperate with its objectives without trying to become independent strategic actors themselves. President Wilson captured this quintessentially hegemonic program in his exhortation, during his 1917 war message to Congress, that "the world must be made safe for democracy." By the time the United States entered World War II, a critical mass of American elites had internalized the idea, and its logic guided the Roosevelt administration's deliberations over the kind of postwar world that Washington would shape. As a result, the United States emerged from the war seeking strategic dominance in Europe, East Asia, and the Persian Gulf—the three areas outside the Western Hemisphere that American policy makers deemed essential to global primacy.[4]

Washington's determination to dominate these regions was not, as most Americans preferred to think, a function of the Cold War. Investments in military capabilities and a worldwide network of bases from the late 1940s on obviously helped the United States implement the Cold War strategy of containment first put forward by George Kennan in 1947.[5] But these investments were not driven primarily by the requirements of the new strategy; they reflected, rather, Washington's determination to reshape the global order so as to ensure its own prosperity and dominance. Tellingly, NSC-68 (the document that, in 1950, first designated containment as the American plan for dealing with the Soviet Union) held that the United States had to pursue "the development of its military and economic strength" in order to "foster a world environment in which the American system can survive and flourish"—a policy, the authors noted, that "we would probably pursue even if there were no Soviet threat."[6]

As originally conceived by Kennan, containment was a balancing strategy, designed to let the United States protect its vital interests without courting a disastrously destructive general war. By the time NSC-68 was prepared, he feared that his idea was being used to justify a drive for global dominance. In short order, he was replaced as chief policy planner to Secretary of State Dean Acheson by Paul Nitze, who oversaw the drafting of NSC-68. (A quarter of a century later, Nitze allied himself with neoconservative critics of Henry Kissinger's détente strategy.) As the Cold War unfolded, Kennan and other realist critics took issue with the overmilitarization of the United States' posture toward the Soviet Union and its repeated misidentification of marginal theaters like Vietnam as indispensable bulwarks of democracy—all policy aspects that grew out of the tension between the balancing logic of containment and the aspiration to hegemony.[7]

For the past seventy years, "defending the American way of life" has meant not so much defending the United States' territorial and political integrity as cultivating and defending international conditions favorable to its continuing economic growth. In the post–World War II period, the United States conducted its Cold War struggle against the Soviet Union as part of a massive exercise in empire building.[8] Military power has been a pillar of American supremacy, but the United States has built up its unique form of empire far less through the application of force and direct political control over other societies than through alliances and security relationships with at least nominally sovereign states. Its primacy has been buttressed by the dollar's role as an international currency and by a multifaceted process of economic liberalization and reinforced, to different degrees in different parts of the world, by the diffusion of American ideas and values.[9]

In important ways, the Cold War actually constrained Washington's quest for hegemony in the Middle East, where it would have brought the United States and the Soviet Union into direct confrontation. The imperial nature of the modern American strategy became more obvious after the Cold War ended. Survey data show a high degree of continuity from the last decade of the Cold War into the early years of the post–Cold War period in the attitudes of American elites toward their country's international role and objectives, notwithstanding profound changes in the structure of international politics.[10] This consensus translated into a bipartisan endorsement of dominance over the Middle East as a high priority for the country's post–Cold War foreign policy.

BETWEEN BALANCING AND HEGEMONY

From World War II on, the United States has seen itself as having vital interests in the Middle East. Even as the war raged, American policy makers were angling for the United States to displace Britain as the dominant power in the Persian Gulf. In particular, the Roosevelt administration wanted American energy companies, which already had an exclusive concession in Saudi Arabia, to secure another one in Iran, where the Anglo-Iranian Oil Company (whose majority shareholder was the British government) held a monopoly position. Since then, Iran has been a focus for Washington—as a critical strategic partner and, after the Islamic Republic's creation, as the most persistent obstacle to America's hegemonic aspirations in the Persian Gulf.

In many respects, the Cold War started in the Middle East—and specifically in Iran. American leaders wanted to prevent the Soviet Union from gaining control over Persian Gulf oil reserves, and to that end it became involved in the bargaining over the Soviet withdrawal from northern Iran after the end of World War II. While the United States had large military forces in both Europe and Asia, it had no such presence in the Middle East. But Washington was determined to keep Iran out of the Soviet sphere of influence, and so it threatened to add its own troops to the British forces already there if the Soviets did not pull theirs out.[11] Once the Soviets did pull out, though, sending in U.S. troops was no longer feasible; it would only prompt Moscow to do the same. So, as the Cold War heated up, Washington had to rely on the British as its first line of defense in securing Persian Gulf oil flows.[12]

The CIA-instigated coup that brought down Mohammad Mossadeq in 1953 was a low-profile way for the United States to advance its agenda. The coup allowed the United States to displace Britain as the dominant power in Iran and set the stage for Washington, during the Suez crisis three years later, to assume London's mantle of strategic leadership for the Middle East as a whole. It also boosted American influence over Persian Gulf hydrocarbons: following the shah's reinstatement, American oil companies finally broke the British monopoly in Iran. And Washington began cultivating the shah as an important strategic partner.[13]

The British withdrawal from the Persian Gulf in 1971 marked another critical juncture in the regional balance, coinciding with American efforts to recalibrate the nation's military commitments under the Nixon Doctrine. In the view of Nixon and Kissinger, Vietnam and the relative decline of the United States' international economic position made military retrenchment imperative, and they were reluctant for the United States to take on day-to-day responsibility for Gulf security. Nixon was keen on the shah, whom he saw as the capable pro-American leader of a strong and stable state. Under its "twin pillars" policy, the United States provided infusions of military hardware so that Saudi Arabia and, especially, the shah's Iran could police the Gulf on its behalf.[14]

Despite the mounting disconnect between the shah's agenda and Iranian sensibilities, most clearly marked in the growing receptivity to Khomeini's message, the Nixon, Ford, and Carter administrations embraced the shah: he projected power and influence and kept the Soviets at bay. All three worried that his top-of-the-line U.S. weaponry and the lavish revenues flowing into his coffers from the higher oil prices engineered by OPEC might allow Iran to become an independent strategic actor. But real danger came from a different direction. Even before the close of the Ford administration, some policy makers suspected that the United States had helped the shah construct a politically unsustainable edifice. By Carter's tenure, they were tracking the rise of Khomeini's revolutionary movement with mounting alarm.[15] But the persistent drive for hegemony in the Middle East made it impossible for high-level decision makers to take seriously, and plan around, the possibility that a regime so strong, both militarily and financially, and pro-American could fall.

Its collapse and the founding of the Islamic Republic in 1979 gutted the twin-pillars approach; later that year, the Red Army's invasion of Afghanistan raised the specter of the Soviets' penetrating Iran and gaining access to the Persian Gulf. These developments compelled Washington to assume direct responsibility for the security of Gulf oil flows. But even as the United States built up its naval presence and arms capabilities in the Gulf, becoming the region's dominant military power, the Cold War continued to necessitate restraint. The United States refrained from deploying substantial forces on the ground, operating as an "offshore balancer" from an over-the-horizon position.

Washington pressed Tehran, for the most part indirectly, especially by supporting Saddam's war against Iran from 1980 to 1988.

As it became apparent that Saddam would not succeed in bringing the Islamic Republic down, the United States was forced to rely even more on strategic balancing in its approach to the Persian Gulf and to reconsider its diplomatic options vis-à-vis Tehran. A declassified National Security Decision Directive on "U.S. Policy toward Iran," circulated to National Security Council principals in June 1985, spells out the problem:

> Instability caused by the pressures of the Iraq-Iran war, economic deterioration and regime infighting creates the potential for major changes in Iran. The Soviet Union is better positioned than the U.S. to exploit and benefit from any power struggle that results in changes in the Iranian regime, as well as increasing socio-political pressures. . . . Soviet success in taking advantage of the emerging power struggle to insinuate itself in Iran would change the strategic balance in the area. . . . The U.S. position in Tehran is unlikely to improve without a major change in U.S. policy.[16]

It was this analysis that motivated Reagan's National Security Council staff to turn to Tehran with the plan that imploded in the Iran-contra scandal. But within just a few years such initiatives were off the table. For under Reagan's successor, George H. W. Bush, American strategy in the Middle East would shift decisively away from balancing and toward the unequivocal pursuit of hegemony—a development that deeply affected American-Iranian relations in the post–Cold War era.

THE EROSION OF REALISM

The first Bush administration boasted what seemed, at least on the surface, close to a foreign policy realist's dream team. Bush himself was an experienced foreign policy hand. His national security adviser, Brent Scowcroft, had served as Henry Kissinger's deputy in the early

1970s before becoming President Gerald Ford's national security adviser; he was steeped in balance-of-power politics. Initially Bush and Scowcroft were willing to explore a diplomatic opening to Tehran.[17] But the overlap of the Iraqi invasion of Kuwait and the ensuing Gulf War with the collapse of the Soviet Union moved them in a different direction, suggesting that Washington could now safely disregard balance-of-power considerations. In turn, the belief that the United States could finally consolidate its hegemony in the Middle East killed any serious interest in engaging the Islamic Republic.

When the Bush administration came to office, policy planners were still smarting from the loss of the shah a decade earlier. To make matters worse, the Reagan administration's regional initiatives had ended in disaster: American forces deployed to Lebanon to oppose Iranian-supported resistance to the Israeli invasion had been routed by Shi'a suicide bombers; following that failure, Washington had exhibited an appalling lack of strategic preparation and tactical competence in its efforts to cultivate Iranian moderates as part of its Iran-contra project. Bush saw the persistent problem of American hostages in Lebanon as a constant reminder to the world of these recent setbacks. As Scowcroft later recounted, the hostage issue "overshadowed everything we did in the Middle East. When we wanted to make a diplomatic move, what effect would that have on the hostages? Would some of them be killed in retribution for some action that we take. It infused every act we took on the Middle East."[18] Bush used his inaugural address to tell Tehran, "Good will begets good will." Subsequently, Scowcroft communicated indirectly but repeatedly with Tehran through U.N. envoy Giandomenico Picco, promising positive American steps in return for efficacious Iranian engagement with the hostage takers. Yet, as we have seen, after Iran helped to effect the release of the last American hostages and quietly aided the United States in the first Gulf War, the Bush administration reneged on its pledges of reciprocity.

According to some former officials, the administration's reneging was a function of election-year politics.[19] Scowcroft was more attuned than Bush's other advisers to the strategic benefits of engagement, but

Secretary of State James Baker, who had masterminded Bush's first presidential campaign, had always been more leery—a position that his director of policy planning, Dennis Ross, reinforced. In this account, as Bush's reelection campaign faltered, Baker came to regard engagement as politically radioactive, and the president, with his advisers, opted to defer major policy changes toward Iran to a second term.[20] Other former officials hold that the administration would never have engaged Tehran as long as the Islamic Republic continued supporting what they describe as "acts of terrorism" in the Arab-Israeli arena and against expatriate Iranian dissidents. Those advocating this view within the administration included neoconservatives and other hawks who, two decades later, would help formulate the George W. Bush administration's hard-line Middle East policies; they also included Richard Haass (the National Security Council's senior director for the Near East and South Asia under Bush 41, a position he won largely as a result of his role in WINEP's 1988 presidential study group).[21]

Scowcroft later admitted that he "lost the argument" over the direction of the Bush administration's Iran policy.[22] But neither the political explanation for why he lost nor the Iran-as-unacceptably-bad-actor explanation makes sense. The Islamic Republic was not more politically radioactive in early 1992 than it had been in January 1989, when Bush reached out to Tehran in his inaugural address; by then, moreover, Tehran had helped free the American hostages in Lebanon and had quietly supported the United States in the first Gulf War. Likewise, there was nothing new about Iranian ties to organizations and individuals that the United States considered malefactors—those ties were the reason both the Reagan and Bush administrations had sought Tehran's assistance with the hostage holders in Lebanon. In early 1992, the Islamic Republic was not yet supporting HAMAS. From an American perspective, Iran had not changed its strategic orientation to any significant degree for better or worse.

What had changed was the context in which Washington was now assessing the importance of Iran in the regional balance of power. Thus a more compelling explanation for its reneging on engagement is offered by other top advisers to Baker, who say that the administration had considered including Tehran in its plans for the post–Gulf War Middle East but decided that it didn't need to.[23] The demise of the Soviet Union, it judged, had liberated the United States from balance-of-power constraints. And the defeat of Iraq left no Arab army in the region with viable offensive capabilities. The United States was looking at an unprecedented opportunity to erect a political and security order that would allow it to dominate the Middle East well into the future. Washington no longer had to come to terms with an Islamic Republic that insisted on maintaining its strategic independence. American policy makers thought that, in this new world order, they could dictate their terms in the Persian Gulf—and that, for the first time, they could back up those terms with the ongoing deployment of tens of thousands of American troops on the ground.

Scowcroft has written that, going into the Gulf War, the administration wanted to "reduce Saddam's military might so that he would no longer pose a threat to the region, yet to do so in such a way that Iraq was secure from external threats and the balance with Iran was preserved."[24] But that is not what happened. According to Chas Freeman, the American ambassador to Saudi Arabia during the war, the U.N. sanctions and U.S. pressure on Iraq that followed the war had pernicious consequences: "the failure to craft a sustainable postwar order for the Gulf and to assign Iraq an appropriate role in it meant that there was no postwar regional balance."[25] Iraq's removal from the balance should have bolstered American incentives for an opening to Tehran, but the Bush team threw away its opportunity to establish better relations and, in the triumphalist postwar atmosphere, decided that the United States could fill the power vacuum it had created. Not only did the Bush administration snub Tehran after its help with American hostages and the Gulf War, it also chose to launch a Middle East "peace" process designed to win Arab buy-in to a highly militarized and U.S.-led regional order that excluded the influence of both Iran and Iraq.

By the time Bush left office, his administration's goals for the Middle East—including a militarily predominant Israel, Arab dependence on Washington for security, and a steady supply of reasonably priced hydrocarbons to fuel both American and global economic growth—had achieved strong bipartisan support. And so the Bush administration's pursuit of hegemony continued under Bill Clinton's presidency, with corrosive effects on his handling of Iran.

GLOBALIZATION AS EMPIRE BUILDING

Bill Clinton's approach to the Middle East was shaped by his eagerness to broaden and deepen those processes of economic liberalization that, after the Cold War, came collectively to be called globalization. In part, his emphasis on growth and prosperity grew out of his domestic agenda. But there was a strategic component, too: from the beginning, his administration calculated that expanding participation in the liberal economic order that the United States had promoted in Europe and Asia could induce more nations around the world to align with it and ensure American global dominance.[26] Primacy in the Middle East was indispensable to this agenda, enabling the United States to position itself as the provider of energy security to its allies and competitors alike—making them all dependent on Washington for their economic lifeblood.

Clinton's strategy relied on regional order building to persuade more players to support the United States. An important influence on his thinking was Martin Indyk, who wanted Washington to leverage the extraordinary preeminence it enjoyed to create a Middle East that not only embraced the United States as the ultimate guarantor of regional security but also accepted Israel as its dominant military power. This favoritism reflected the unquestionable influence of the pro-Israel lobby in Washington. But it also stemmed from the conviction that a strong Israel was central to America's own ambitions. This belief had started with Israel's victory in the 1967 war, when it seized large tracts of territory from its Arab neighbors, including, especially, Soviet-allied Egypt; the proposition took root among neocons in the Reagan administration during Israel's 1982 invasion of Lebanon. By the time Clinton entered the White House, many Democratic policy makers also believed that Israeli military superiority helped keep the rest of the region subordinated. Thus, in the so-called peace process, the United States has regularly sought Arab acquiescence to a dominant Israel and a highly circumscribed role for the Arab states.

From this perspective, Iran was a problem, both because it insisted that providing its own security was essential to its strategic independence and because it refused to accept a quasi-hegemonic Israel. During the 1992 presidential campaign, Indyk had won Clinton the candidate over to the Yitzhak Rabin–Shimon Peres strategy, then just taking hold in Israel, of marginalizing Iran so that Israel could reach "peace" (or, more accurately, end-of-conflict) agreements with weaker Arab neighbors. And those agreements would further marginalize Iran. But though Indyk's role in Clinton's campaign and administration is a testament to the Israel lobby's influence, Clinton already had his own hegemonic inclinations. Indyk later recounted that

> Tony Lake, Sandy Berger, and I had flown to New Orleans to brief Clinton at one of his campaign stops on policy toward Iran and Iraq. I had argued that both nations were hostile to our interests and that we should therefore work to contain them while we pressed ahead with Arab-Israeli peacemaking. Clinton had responded that containing them was not a tough enough policy. We had to find a way to change their behavior or change the regimes, he said.[27]

Once he became senior director for Near East and South Asian affairs on Clinton's National Security Council staff, Indyk crafted a strategy that melded a strongly pro-Israel agenda with liberal internationalist precepts to generate, as he later explained, "a dramatic shift in the regional balance of power" through "a comprehensive Arab-Israeli peace." Curbing the "destabilizing activities" of Iran as well as Iraq was a critical element: the more Arab-Israeli diplomacy advanced, "the more isolated Iran and Iraq would become." Indyk called it "a neat and logical design."[28]

In this design, the Islamic Republic could not be viewed as anything but a grave threat to American interests—or, more precisely, ambitions. So, in a policy-setting address delivered to WINEP in May

1993, Indyk declared that the United States would no longer play the game of balancing Iraq against Iran; instead, it would pursue "dual containment." With the help of its regional allies—Egypt, Israel, Saudi Arabia and the other states in the Gulf Cooperation Council, and Turkey—it was now sufficiently strong to "counter both the Iraqi and Iranian regimes. We will not need to depend on one to counter the other."[29]

Although Scowcroft derided dual containment as "a nutty idea," the Clinton administration was, in many respects, merely naming the strategic error that the Bush administration had already committed. Containment was, in fact, something of a misnomer, since the imperative to change behavior or change regimes was very much in play. In his WINEP address, Indyk had delivered the administration's verdict that Saddam was "irredeemable"; American officials later said that, even if Iraq complied with all the requirements the U.N. imposed after the invasion of Kuwait, sanctions would stay in place until Saddam was removed.[30] The task of containing Iran, Indyk argued, was more challenging than that of containing Saddam's Iraq, since the Security Council had adopted no sanctions against the Islamic Republic. Indyk pledged that Washington would work energetically to dissuade other nations from engaging in military transactions or even "normal commercial relations" with Iran.[31] By seeking to apply the same tools against Iran that were already in place against Iraq, the administration was serving notice that Tehran could either surrender to America's regional ambitions or, eventually, face the same treatment as Saddam.

The message was underscored in a 1994 *Foreign Affairs* article by Anthony Lake, Clinton's first national security adviser. Lake cited the Islamic Republic, Iraq, Libya, and North Korea as a small group of "recalcitrant and outlaw states that not only choose to remain outside the family [of nations] but also assault its basic values." These "backlash states" under regressive dictatorships—a precursor to George W. Bush's "axis of evil"—had shunned the community of nations that were "committed to the pursuit of democratic institutions, the expansion of free markets, the peaceful settlement of conflict and the promotion of collective security." In the administration's view, "as the sole superpower, the United States has a special responsibility for developing a strategy to neutralize, contain, and, through selective pressure, perhaps eventually transform these backlash states into constructive members of the international community."[32]

The strategy's defects quickly became apparent. By affirming its intent to contain (and sooner or later remove) Saddam—rather than simply to maintain commitments to protect Persian Gulf oil supplies and the territorial and political integrity of its regional allies—the Clinton administration bound itself to an open-ended and resource-draining standoff with the Iraqi dictator. The number of U.S. forces deployed in the region rose significantly, with no positive payoff and considerable damage to the perceived legitimacy of American aims.

In the case of Iran, a similarly hegemonic ambition prompted Washington to systematically reject Rafsanjani's repeated offers to work together on the basis of mutual interest. In 1995, Clinton issued the executive orders imposing an American economic embargo against the Islamic Republic. Indyk later wrote that, while Rafsanjani's decision to offer Conoco a contract "may have been designed to signal his desire to engage more constructively with the United States," the Clinton team "read it as an attempt to thwart our pressure on European oil companies by highlighting our hypocrisy."[33] Likewise, his team insisted that Iran be excluded from pipeline projects to bring oil and gas from post-Soviet Central Asia to international markets. It was also Clinton—who had committed the United States to the World Trade Organization, under which secondary sanctions and other extraterritorial applications of national trade law are illegal—who signed the initial authorization for secondary sanctions against foreign companies investing in Iranian energy projects. Even more significantly, it was Clinton who, in 1995, signed the first-ever appropriation for U.S. government initiatives aimed at destabilizing the Islamic Republic—a significant step toward making regime change, the goal of his Iraq policy, the goal of his Iran policy as well. In 1997, his administration considered retaliatory strikes against Iran for the 1996 Khobar Towers attack in Saudi Arabia in which nineteen American servicemen were killed, even though the case for Iranian complicity was—and still is—weak.

These moves were all of a piece with the administration's support for Israeli regional supremacy. Clinton came to office when Israel's focus was shifting to the Islamic Republic as the main bar to its regional ambitions. While Israel had refused Reagan's request to impose sanctions on Iran after the 1983 bombing of the Marine Corps barracks in Lebanon, by the early 1990s, it had turned as truculent as the United States toward the Islamic Republic and was depicting it as an "existential threat," the most serious challenge to post–Cold War peace, and the world's leading sponsor of terrorism. In Washington, the Israel lobby's priorities had also shifted toward exerting pressure on Congress and the executive branch to make American policy even more implacably anti-Iranian. The administration's close ties to AIPAC reinforced its growing emphasis on sanctions.

The Clinton team defended its Iran policy by arguing that, if Israel was going to "take risks for peace," it needed assurance that the Iranian threat would be kept in check. With Dennis Ross held over from the Bush administration to run Arab-Israeli diplomacy, Israeli preferences were prioritized over other considerations. Ross's deputy, Aaron Miller, has described the Clinton administration—perfectly— as "Israel's lawyer."[34] Yet the administration's behavior was not solely the product of domestic political cravenness. Clinton and his advisers saw Israeli agreements with weakened Palestinian, Jordanian, and Syrian counterparts, on terms ensuring its military dominance and containing Arab power, as integral components of a pro-American order in the Middle East.

From the administration's vantage, the Islamic Republic and its allies HAMAS and Islamic Jihad were the most effective and thus the most dangerous opponents of this project. During Clinton's first term, his team consistently rebuffed overtures from the Rafsanjani government and engaged in what can only be described as shameless duplicity after having secured the provision of Iranian weapons to Bosnian Muslims (see chapter 3). It justified this conduct with a willful misreading of the historical record, as a typical statement by Indyk confirms: "Tehran's unremitting hostility toward America as the 'Great Satan' rendered engagement an unrealistic option at the beginning of the Clinton administration."[35] Indyk advanced that assessment after Rafsanjani's government had helped free the last American hostages in Lebanon and had quietly supported the United States during the Gulf War and as it was making overtures—despite the Bush administration's having reneged on its pledges of reciprocity—to the new American administration of which Indyk was a part.

By the beginning of Clinton's second term, though, his Middle East strategy was in trouble. His administration's approach to Arab-Israeli diplomacy had ensured that Israel never felt any meaningful American pressure; as a result, Israel took no real risks and peace never materialized.[36] And even with its escalating pressure on Tehran, the Clinton team was ineffective in containing Iran or curbing its opposition to an American-sponsored "peace" process. After the killing of Israeli prime minister Yitzhak Rabin in 1995 by an Israeli assassin and a series of bomb attacks by HAMAS and Islamic Jihad that sealed Binyamin Netanyahu's election as Israel's new prime minister in 1996, the process was in shambles and the United States' regional position in free fall.

Under these circumstances, Mohammad Khatami's election as president of Iran shortly after the beginning of Clinton's second term prompted a number of Clinton's advisers to reexamine his administration's posture toward the Islamic Republic. Clinton had appointed Madeleine Albright to replace Warren Christopher as secretary of state; one of Albright's top aides, State Department spokesman Jamie Rubin, was engaged and then married to the half-Iranian television journalist Christiane Amanpour, who conducted CNN's widely watched January 1998 interview with the newly installed President Khatami. Both Rubin and Deputy Secretary of State Strobe Talbott urged Albright to reach out to Khatami; up to then, the Clinton team had not even offered Tehran the option of acquiescing to its vision of a U.S.-dominated regional order—which was what senior diplomats now wanted to give it the chance of doing. They thought that, in return for better relations with the United States (though without specifying exactly what that meant), Khatami might be willing to take steps to reduce Iranian pressure on the Palestinian and Syrian leadership to hold fast in their negotiations with Israel. As Talbott said, "If Khatami is able to moderate Iran's behavior, it will change everything."[37] Rather than tailor a deal that Tehran might actually accept, the Clinton team tried to go around Khamenei and other so-called hard-liners to make an arrangement with Khatami, an effort to game Iranian politics that exemplifies Washington's unwillingness to take the Islamic Republic seriously as a system.

Put bluntly, the Clinton administration thought of engagement as a way of getting the Islamic Republic to submit to a U.S.-led order for the Middle East—not as a channel for rapprochement based on mutual accommodation. Since leaving office, Clinton and several of his colleagues have tried to spin the story of their diplomacy during Khatami's first term (which largely overlapped with Clinton's second term) as one of repeatedly reaching out to Tehran and being rebuffed.[38] But in reality this outreach was far too geared to American priorities to hold any interest for the Iranians.

IMPERIAL OVERREACH

George W. Bush entered the White House in January 2001 without, it seems, a clear sense of what he wanted to do in the Middle East. He rejected Clinton's vision of reshaping the regional balance of power through an Arab-Israeli agreement, but he had no alternative vision of his own—until 9/11. The attacks on the twin towers and the Pentagon opened the way for him to take the United States' drive for hegemony in the Middle East to a new level, with the war on terror, the "axis of evil" construct in his 2002 State of the Union address, the 2003 invasion of Iraq, and a clearly enunciated ambition to remake the region along liberal Western lines. That is why his administration disregarded what was probably the best opportunity for a diplomatic opening with the Islamic Republic that the United States has ever had.

A hegemonic strategy strongly influenced by neoconservative ideas was hardly consistent with the positions Bush had taken as a candidate, when he had seemed to pull back from the more imperial ambitions of American foreign policy during the 1990s. In a debate with his Democratic opponent, Vice President Al Gore, Bush observed: "If we're an arrogant nation, they'll resent us; if we're a humble nation, but strong, they'll welcome us. And our nation stands alone right now in the world in terms of power, and that's why we've got to be humble." More pointedly: "The Vice President and I have a disagreement about the use of troops. He believes in nation building. I would be very careful about using troops as nation builders. . . . I just don't think it's the role of the United States to walk into a country and say, we do it this way, so should you." Yet the "Vulcans"—the Bush campaign's foreign policy advisers—included not only figures who seemed to endorse a more modest foreign policy, like Condoleezza Rice, but also high-profile neocons like Richard Perle and Paul Wolfowitz.[39]

This diversity of views continued after Bush's election. During the first eight months of his presidency, Iran policy was one of many issues on which his national security team was split, at both the cabinet and subcabinet levels. On one side of the divide were Secretary of State Colin Powell, Deputy Secretary of State Richard Armitage, and some of their advisers, who were all open to the possibility of engaging Tehran over issues of mutual interest. In the spring of 2001, as noted earlier, Hillary Mann Leverett, then working in the State Department as a political adviser to the U.S. Mission to the United Nations, started meeting regularly with Iranian counterparts to discuss Afghanistan-related issues under the U.N.'s 6 + 2 framework (the six nations bordering Afghanistan plus the United States and Russia). At the State Department, the policy planning staff began to sketch out ways to improve American-Iranian relations.

On the other side of the divide, neocons and hard-liners at the National Security Council (NSC), the office of the vice president, and the office of the secretary of defense all strongly opposed any engagement with Tehran. These officials—including Elliott Abrams at the NSC; the vice president's chief of staff and national security adviser, Lewis ("Scooter") Libby; his deputy national security advisers Eric Edelman and John Hannah; Deputy Secretary of Defense Paul Wolfowitz; Undersecretary of Defense for Policy Douglas Feith; and Undersecretary of State for Arms Control and International Security John Bolton, the hard-liners' Trojan horse in Powell's State Department—argued that the United States should adopt regime change as the explicit goal of its Iran policy, just as it had for Iraq.

In the wake of 9/11, the debate over Iran intensified as it got tangled in issues of broader strategy. Starting on September 11, the administration's ideological camps struggled over how to wage what came to be called the global war on terror. Should the United States focus on destroying Al-Qa'ida, its Taliban supporters, and its worldwide support network, using the campaign as an occasion to strengthen and expand America's international partnerships? This model was solidly grounded in the logic of balancing. Or should the United States conceive of the war not as a fight against terrorists per se but as a campaign against those illiberal and revisionist states that (in the neoconservative view) spawn terrorist networks, illicit WMD programs, and other challenges to the international order as defined by the United States? This alternative model was just as clearly grounded in the logic of hegemony.[40]

The debate on these questions had enormous implications for the administration's Iran policy. For some of those who favored a balancing-oriented approach—including us—the reaction of the Islamic Republic to 9/11 afforded an opportunity to effect a realignment with it. Tehran's own antipathy toward Al-Qa'ida and the Taliban and its offer of unconditional cooperation in responding to the 9/11 attacks provided the United States an opening to work with it—as well as the potential to leverage Iran's cooperation (not to mention its anxiety over becoming a target itself) into a broader dialogue, based on a contingent American offer of strategic rapprochement.

But for the neocons and their allies, the Islamic Republic and its Hizballah surrogates represented the Shi'a complement to Al-Qa'ida's militant Sunni extremism. Their view was not a matter of simple ignorance about Islamic history and theology. From a neoconservative perspective, all of these actors posed the same basic threat: they challenged American primacy under the cloak of Islam—and thus, in a post–Cold War, post-9/11 context, Washington could not cooperate with the Islamic Republic without ceding its ambitions to hegemony in the Middle East. The United States might have to content itself, for a time, with containing Iran, they reasoned, but ultimately the logic of hegemony would require the diminution if not overthrow of the Islamic Republic.

The clash of these perspectives produced an ambivalent, even incoherent posture toward Iran following 9/11. The United States intensified its dialogue with Iran on Afghan issues in the 6 + 2 framework, developing an essentially independent bilateral channel. There remained within the administration, however, significant opposition to this collaboration, and certainly to genuine strategic dialogue. Important parts of the foreign policy team, including the offices of the vice president and the secretary of defense, opposed any engagement with Iran, which they saw as the prime target once the Taliban and Saddam had been dealt with. Some of the officials who favored diplomacy—Powell, Armitage, Deputy Assistant Secretary of State for Near Eastern Affairs Ryan Crocker, and Hillary Mann Leverett—backed an ongoing dialogue with Tehran about Afghanistan and Al-Qa'ida, but, with the exception of Hillary, they were not inclined to go beyond incremental engagement on specific issues.

National security adviser Condoleezza Rice, our boss at the White House, recognized there could be tactical benefits to engaging Iran. However, she regarded Khatami, then in his second term, as a "Gorbachev-like" figure who was inadvertently paving the way for the demise of the Islamic Republic. (The Yeltsin who would follow him and galvanize radical change she never identified.) She also bought Bush's argument that Saddam's overthrow would be a catalyst for change in Iran. Consequently, she was reluctant to "legitimate" a political order that, through the lens of her background as a Sovietologist, appeared to her to be on its last legs. And so the administration continued its dialogue with Tehran over Afghanistan and Al-Qa'ida while simultaneously both rebuffing the Iranian invitation to build on that dialogue and resisting pressure from its own neoconservatives to publicly and explicitly embrace regime change.

The deciding factor was Iraq. The invasion resolved the impasse in favor of hegemony, which had profound ramifications for the administration's approach to Iran. As it drew near, there was less and less space within the administration to argue for continuing, let alone expanding, the dialogue with Tehran. Once the invasion was launched, the dialogue was terminated at the earliest opportunity.

Hence the Bush administration's perverse reaction to the Iranian non-paper that came to the State Department in May 2003, outlining a "roadmap" for negotiations (see chapter 3). Within days of the Roadmap's arrival in Washington, Flynt Leverett—who had just resigned from the CIA after leaving the White House two months before that— met with Mohsen Rezae, the former Revolutionary Guards commander and incumbent secretary-general of the Expediency Council. In their conversation, Rezae confirmed that Tehran was interested in strategic realignment with Washington. He noted, though, that it needed clarity as to the United States' intentions; Iran, he said, "could not realign to nothing."

We both thought that Rezae's remarks underscored the diplomatic opportunity embodied in the Roadmap. Though Flynt had left the White House in disagreement over the administration's Middle East policies, he provided a report on his meeting with Rezae to Rice, CIA Director George Tenet, and Assistant Secretary of State for Near Eastern Affairs William Burns. Soon afterward, Hillary Mann Leverett— who had left the White House with Flynt but had returned to the State Department to serve on the policy planning staff—prepared a memorandum for Powell laying out the case for strategic engagement with Tehran, drawing on her experience negotiating with Iranian counterparts over Afghanistan and Al-Qa'ida; she included both the Roadmap and Flynt's report on his meeting with Rezae.

A few weeks later, we were able to speak with Powell directly, on the margins of a State Department ceremony. He complimented Hillary on her "great memo" but lamented that he "couldn't sell it at the White House." His longtime chief of staff, Lawrence Wilkerson, later suggested to us that Powell had, in effect, made a trade whereby he would refrain from pushing for engagement with Iran—to which both the White House and the vice president were, by this point, irrevocably opposed—in exchange for greater maneuvering room in the United States' ongoing nuclear diplomacy with North Korea.

The fact was that by May 2003, when the Roadmap arrived in Washington, enough Bush administration heavyweights had decided they did not want rapprochement with the Islamic Republic, even if it was possible. In a sense, these players—Cheney, Rumsfeld, Wolfowitz, Libby, their subordinates in government and their supporters outside it, and the president himself—understood that the United States could not simultaneously realign relations with Iran and pursue hegemony in the Middle East. But whereas we viewed the pursuit of hegemony as inevitably counterproductive and the strategic payoff from rapprochement with Tehran as enormous, they thought that true hegemony in the region was at last within their grasp. And Powell, the one person in the administration who might have been able to articulate an alternative framework for post-9/11 policy making—and get the president's attention—lacked the political wherewithal to pull it off.

The same agendas that had scuttled opportunities for progress during Bush's first term continued to block any meaningful improvement during his second term. To its final day in office, the administration remained unwilling to accept the Islamic Republic as an enduring political entity with legitimate interests. Granted, Bush and his team always stopped short of formally endorsing regime change. After becoming secretary of state, Rice publicly denied on several occasions that regime change was American policy. But the president consistently declined to back up her denials, even when interviewers asked him directly.[41] More concretely, he signed intelligence findings supporting covert actions aimed at destabilizing the Islamic Republic; Congress authorized at least $400 million for this purpose, along with funding for overt "democracy promotion."[42] Other aspects of the administration's Iran policy, like its refusal to recognize the continuing validity of the 1981 Algiers Accord (under which the United States had pledged not to intervene in Iranian affairs) or to agree to the prin-

ciple of uranium enrichment on Iranian soil, also leaned in the direction of regime change. Even after the Iraq Study Group (a bipartisan
panel appointed by Congress to assess the situation in Iraq and chaired
by former secretary of state James Baker and former representative
Lee Hamilton) recommended in 2006 that the administration engage
Iran on all relevant issues "without preconditions," the president
declared publicly that he would not authorize U.S. participation in
nuclear discussions with Tehran until it suspended enrichment.[43]

In practical terms, Bush's unwillingness to accept the legitimacy
of the Islamic Republic, let alone its right to enrich, meant that his
team was never prepared to offer it a positive security assurance—
which inevitably doomed diplomacy on the nuclear issue. Rice's point
man on Iran, Undersecretary of State for Political Affairs R. Nicholas
Burns, insisted that the United States should never offer Iran a security guarantee as long as it remained, as the State Department's
Patterns of Global Terrorism report perennially puts it, "the world's
leading state sponsor of terrorism." This justification for diplomatic
stasis could just as well have been viewed as an argument for comprehensive American engagement, but that was something the administration would not countenance.

During Bush's last two years in office, as it became ever more clear
that the Islamic Republic would not accede to Washington's nuclear
demands, Vice President Cheney pushed the president to launch military strikes against Iranian nuclear targets—or at least help Israel to
do so—and Israel's Olmert government joined in the lobbying effort.[44]
Two factors kept Bush from ordering the attack. First, in December
2007 the U.S. Intelligence Community produced a National Intelligence Estimate—including a publicly released set of unclassified "Key
Judgments"—concluding that the Islamic Republic had stopped purely
weapons-related aspects of its nuclear activities in 2003.[45] Bush himself has affirmed that he did not believe he could order strikes when
Iran was not pursuing a nuclear weapons program.[46] Second, after the
massive Republican losses in the 2006 congressional elections, former
deputy national security adviser and Director of Central Intelligence
Robert Gates replaced Donald Rumsfeld as secretary of defense—and

unlike Rumsfeld, Gates thought that a third Middle Eastern war would be profoundly damaging to the United States' strategic position. For the rest of Bush's presidency, he steadfastly opposed an attack. (Gates continued his opposition to airstrikes into the Obama administration and, in a speech at West Point in 2011, went so far as to say, "In my opinion, any future Defense Secretary who advises the President to again send a big American land army into Asia or into the Middle East or Africa should have his head examined.")[47]

In its last year, the administration considered opening a U.S. interest section at the Swiss embassy in Tehran, comparable to the one Iran maintains at the Pakistani embassy in Washington. But in the end it declined to take even that small step.[48]

FAILING TO CORRECT COURSE

Like Richard Nixon, Barack Obama came to the White House at a time of mounting foreign policy overreach and deepening economic crisis. Like Nixon, he held out the promise that he would restore the country's strategic position by extricating the United States from foreign quagmires and coming to terms with key foreign powers. Obama was awarded the Nobel Peace Prize before completing his first year in office, simply for articulating this idea. But he was, in fact, no less committed than his predecessors to American hegemony in the Middle East. He arrived with no understanding of what strategic engagement with the Islamic Republic would take. And once in the White House, he flinched from the task. His efforts at engagement have been almost completely rhetorical, with no new policy substance to entice Iranian leaders. Indeed, a sober examination of his administration's interactions with Iran reveals a dismaying mix of dishonesty and incompetence that has done profound damage to American interests and credibility. Even before Tehran declined to play by his rules, Obama was resorting to the same coercive tools as his predecessors, but even more recklessly, with little regard for the declining relative power of the United States and the new realities in the Middle East.

Obama took office amid what appeared to be an unprecedented

American openness to diplomatic engagement with the Islamic Republic. The Bush administration's wars in Afghanistan and Iraq had imposed severe "capacity constraints" on the new president; he could no longer maintain the same logistically and financially draining course in the Middle East. American foreign policy circles showed a growing awareness of Iran's rising regional influence and thus an enhanced appreciation of the potential benefits of talking.[49] Obama himself seemed well attuned to this new climate. He had made his opposition to the Iraq War a cornerstone of his campaign, declaring himself out to end not just the United States' military involvement in Iraq but also "the mindset that got us into [the] war in the first place." In keeping with this approach, he took a relatively forward-leaning position on engaging the Islamic Republic. When, as a candidate in the Democratic primaries, he had come under fire from Senator Hillary Clinton over the issue, he had rejected his political consultants' advice to pull back, arguing that his position on Iran helped differentiate his foreign policy from hers.

Once Obama entered the White House, his initial outreach to Tehran in various statements seemed to flow naturally from his campaign stance. At the same time, though, several of his high-level personnel choices raised doubts about his dedication to changing Washington's hegemonic stance on the Middle East. He appointed Hillary Clinton (who, during the primaries, had threatened to "totally obliterate" Iran if it attacked Israel) secretary of state, named Rahm Emanuel (who had volunteered with the Israeli army in a civilian capacity and was one of the most pro-Israel Democrats in Congress) White House chief of staff, retained Stuart Levey (a neoconservative lawyer who had spearheaded the Bush administration's Iran sanctions policy) as undersecretary of the treasury for terrorism and financial intelligence, and placed Dennis Ross in positions of influence over Iran policy, first at the State Department and then at the NSC. All of these appointments showed pronounced deference to the liberal hawks who had provided high-level Democratic support for the Iraq invasion, to the Israel lobby, and even to neoconservative views on Iran.

Obama formulated his Iran policy through a broad-based

interagency process—thereby guaranteeing all these groups ample opportunity to forestall any serious effort at strategic engagement. He also opened the process to consultations with allies who, for reasons of their own, oppose diplomacy with Tehran. Israel favors the Islamic Republic's continued strategic subordination and, as noted, insists on zero enrichment as the ultimate outcome of any nuclear deal. Britain and France are just as hard-line on the enrichment issue; they consider the (already declining) strategic value of their own small nuclear arsenals threatened by the rise of nuclear-threshold states in the global south (for example, Brazil) and want to hold on to the one continuing justification for their status as "great powers" with permanent seats on the Security Council. Saudi Arabia, while uneasy about the risks of another U.S.-instigated war in its neighborhood, fears that an American-Iranian rapprochement would diminish the kingdom's value to Washington as a regional partner.[50] None of these concerns have anything to do with American interests, yet Obama allowed them all a part in distorting his Iran policy.

More important, the Obama administration failed to follow up on the president's early rhetorical gestures with substantive proposals and concrete action. It did nothing to rein in the anti-Iranian covert programs it inherited from its predecessor; indeed, leaked documents show that such programs (including ties to groups whose actions in Iran, had they been taken in Israel or many other countries, would be condemned in Washington as terrorism) intensified after Obama came in.[51] The administration designated the Kurdish separatist movement PJAK a terrorist organization in February 2009, but as a gesture to Turkey, not Iran.[52] At the same time, it declined to so designate Jundallah, the deadlier Balochi separatist group that was a more serious security concern for Tehran—according to American intelligence officials we have spoken to, because U.S. intelligence and the military wanted to maintain contact with it. Washington did eventually put Jundallah on its list of terrorist organizations in November 2010, nearly two years into Obama's presidency and months after Iran had captured and executed the group's leader.[53]

The administration's diplomatic efforts focused almost exclusively on the nuclear issue. Yet Obama advisers say that in his first months in office the president decided against modifying the P5+1 nuclear incentives package (see chapter 3) to address Iranian concerns about security. Likewise, he refused to back away from the Bush administration's insistence that Iran suspend all activities related to uranium enrichment. These positions indicated to Tehran that there had been no real change in the American attitude and they undermined the efforts at nuclear diplomacy.

In fact, the Obama administration used nuclear talks with Iran primarily as a way to set the stage for more coercive measures—tougher sanctions and, at some point, military strikes—and to bring international partners and the American public on board. In an op-ed published in the *New York Times* in May 2009, we warned that the administration's approach had already betrayed the early promise of Obama's initial rhetoric. We recounted what Dennis Ross had told us before joining the Obama administration, that he believed a strategy of "engagement with pressure" toward Iran would not stimulate productive diplomacy but would be necessary to lay the groundwork for further sanctions and, eventually, military strikes against Iranian nuclear targets.[54] Many commentators who supported the idea of engaging Iran criticized our assessment as at best premature. After we published the article, Ross let us know indirectly how unhappy he was about our exposing his views; subsequently, he had his assistant at the State Department, Ray Takeyh, offer an on-the-record comment about him to Roger Cohen for a July 2009 *New York Times Magazine* story: "The idea that he's just looking for engagement with Iran to tick some box before moving to harsh measures is just wrong and fraudulent."[55]

But the next three years all too grimly vindicated our judgment. In his celebrated March 2009 Nowruz message, Obama had said that American-Iranian rapprochement "will not be advanced by threats." He was absolutely correct: strategic engagement is not the same as carrots-and-sticks diplomacy. In fact, it requires a deliberate decision to put sticks aside in order to assure Iran of American seriousness about realigning relations. Despite Obama's words, that is something his administration has never been willing to do. Thanks to WikiLeaks, we now know that, even as Obama was taping his Nowruz message, officials in his administration were telling their European counterparts that the White House remained committed to the pressure track of the dual-track approach.[56] Likewise, State Department talking points from the time confirm that "the two elements of the P5+1 strategy—engagement/incentives and pressure—were always intended to run in parallel."[57] Even more tellingly, former State Department officials who worked on Iran policy in the early months of Obama's presidency now say that senior decision makers "never believed that diplomacy could succeed" and were "never serious" about engagement.[58]

From the outset, then, there was something fundamentally contradictory in the Obama administration's approach. The problem was compounded by a decision taken before Obama took office to set up a structure of "listening posts" at U.S. diplomatic missions in countries neighboring Iran—Azerbaijan, Iraq, Turkey, Turkmenistan, and the United Arab Emirates—where American embassy or consulate officials could meet Iranians. Most Iranians whom these Iran watchers meet are expatriates; a significant portion come into American embassies or consulates to procure visas or establish relationships with American officials for other self-interested reasons—for example, to be paid for information. The quality of their information is extremely dubious. The Bush administration's reliance on such conduits for intelligence on Iraq—such as the spurious reporting from "Curveball" and other Iraqi National Congress sources, whom Ahmad Chalabi later praised as "heroes in error"—is now regarded as a scandal. Yet the State Department's Iran watcher program effectively institutionalized the practice. And the Obama administration has relied heavily on reports from would-be Iranian defectors, disaffected expats, and others who simply want to come to the United States.[59] Several dozen WikiLeaks cables released in 2011 show that information about the Islamic Republic's 2009 presidential election and other developments provided by these sources was almost uniformly critical of the Islamic Republic and, almost as uniformly, out-and-out wrong.[60] The administration has also regularly consulted with individuals it regards as Iran experts on the best way for Washington to communicate with

Iranian officials and the public, on the design and implementation of sanctions and on other policy issues; they include Afshin Molavi, Trita Parsi, Karim Sadjadpour, and Ray Takeyh, and his wife, Suzanne Maloney, along with the pseudonymous defector Reza Kahlili.[61] But these experts, too, a disproportionate number of them Iranian expatriates, have almost all provided public analyses of Iranian politics and foreign policy that we have shown to be deeply flawed.

That the Obama administration was not interested in real rapprochement with the Islamic Republic came to the fore during the complicated machinations over the refueling of the Tehran Research Reactor (TRR). In early June 2009, just before the Iranian presidential election, Iran's ambassador to the IAEA sent a letter to its director general, Mohamed ElBaradei, requesting IAEA help in finding a supplier of new fuel for the TRR. Tehran had intended the letter as a straightforward confidence-building measure: if it could buy the fuel, then it would not need to produce it. And, by any reasonable standard, it should not have been a problem to refuel a reactor that, under the Islamic Republic, had never been implicated in proliferation activities, especially one as well safeguarded by the IAEA as the TRR.

But the Obama administration refused to treat Tehran's request as a technical matter (as the Reagan administration did in 1987, when Iran had last gone on the market to purchase fuel for the TRR, which Argentina then supplied). Instead, it came back with a convoluted plan that put Tehran in a bind. The plan involved Iran's stockpile of low-enriched uranium (LEU), or uranium enriched to the less than 20 percent level; the LEU in question was enriched to the 3-4 percent level needed to fuel power reactors but not to the nearly 20 percent level that the TRR requires. The administration proposed taking most of Iran's LEU in exchange for a promise that France and Russia would supply new fuel for the TRR, perhaps two years later. Such a swap, Washington held, would put off for at least eighteen months any possibility of Iran's accumulating sufficient LEU so that, if put through centrifuges again, it might yield enough weapons-grade fissile material for a bomb. A deal along these lines would also set a precedent for the removal of uranium enriched in Iran, which would slow down its nuclear development without requiring the United States to give up anything in return. If Tehran balked, Washington could cite its reluctance as further evidence of its unwillingness to accept a "cooperative" solution. This scenario was, in all probability, exactly what the administration wanted, since, as we know from classified cables made public by WikiLeaks, Obama had agreed with Netanyahu to set the end of 2009 as a deadline for progress in nuclear talks with Iran; after that, the administration would be committed to launch a campaign for new sanctions.[62] (This plan was, of course, fully consistent with the Iran strategy Dennis Ross had described to us.)

When the Obama administration put forward its swap proposal, in October 2009, Tehran accepted "in principle"—for several reasons. First, it needed to refuel the TRR, which it uses to make medical isotopes for hundreds of thousands of cancer patients, and acquiring new fuel from international suppliers was the easiest way to do so. (For several years, these isotopes have been subject to intermittent worldwide shortages, which have also affected the United States. The situation has motivated Iran to produce them indigenously, under IAEA scrutiny, rather than rely on an unreliable world market.) Second, from a strategic perspective, Iran still wanted to use a TRR deal as a confidence-building measure, with ElBaradei, a winner of the Nobel Peace Prize who had shown he could stand up to American pressure during the run-up to the Iraq War, directly involved to help the parties reach agreement. Third, it hoped that concluding a swap would pave the way for Washington to recognize Iran's right to enrich.

At the same, time, though, Tehran wanted to negotiate details of timing and implementation to guarantee that it actually received the new fuel. The Obama administration and its supporters portrayed this response as evidence of division and paralysis among Iran's leaders after the June election.[63] But this was a Western projection. From the start of the swap discussions, Tehran had repeatedly cited the bitter experience it had already had with multilateral nuclear fuel arrangements. (In the 1970s, the shah had invested $1 billion in a 10 percent stake in the Eurodif uranium enrichment consortium to ensure Iran a reliable supply of nuclear fuel. After the revolution, the French government suspended Iranian participation but refused to return Iran's $1 billion. It took the Islamic Republic more than a decade to recover the bulk of its money.)[64] Tehran was also consistent about its terms for a deal on refueling the TRR: It required either a simultaneous exchange of LEU for new fuel or the deposit of Iranian LEU in a third country, which would return it if the new fuel was not provided by an agreed-upon time.

Washington spun this stance as a rejection. In truth, the administration did not want to negotiate, since an agreement would not advance its real goal of getting the Security Council to adopt new sanctions. (British officials told us in late 2009 that their government also wanted the TRR proposal to fail, and for the same reason.) So the administration made its proposal a take-it-or-leave-it proposition: if Iran would not agree to its plan by December 31, 2009, it would focus its strategy exclusively on sanctions. In November 2009, at the IAEA's behest, Turkey put itself forward as a depository for Iran's LEU, pending receipt of new fuel for the TRR, but Tehran kept seeking specific guarantees about the size and timing of its LEU shipment, which were unacceptable to Washington.[65]

In February 2010, with talks broken down, Iran began enriching uranium to the near–20 percent level needed to make TRR fuel (which is also closer to the 90 percent–plus level required for weapons-grade material than was its previous LEU production), announcing that it would convert indigenously produced near–20 percent LEU into fuel for the TRR on its own, under IAEA monitoring. The Obama administration condemned the move as "wholly unjustified."[66] Some Western specialists, including David Albright, said there was no benign explanation for it, as Iran was not capable of making fuel plates for the TRR. (In February 2012, when Iran inserted its first indigenously produced fuel plate into the TRR, giving the lie to such assessments, Albright brazenly told the Washington Post that the plates are not hard to produce.")[67]

At the same time, Turkey and Brazil—both nonpermanent members of the Security Council—jointly stepped forward as potential mediators of a multilateral arrangement to refuel the TRR. Though the administration had agreed with Israel to an end-of-2009 deadline for diplomatic progress and was already discussing the terms of a new sanctions resolution with other permanent members, the White House thought it politically unwise to publicly reject any possibility of a deal. American, Turkish, and Brazilian diplomats who were directly involved in the process later said that a group of administration officials headed by Dennis Ross came up with a way to manipulate Turkish prime minister Recep Tayyip Erdoğan and Brazilian president Luiz Inácio Lula da Silva, with a big diplomatic payoff in mind. While encouraging the two leaders to travel to Tehran to try to reach a solution, Washington would set terms so strict that the Iranians would surely balk; once the effort had failed, Washington would be in a position to insist that both governments support intensified sanctions, giving it a unanimous vote in the Security Council.[68]

So in April 2010 Obama sent virtually identical letters to his Turkish and Brazilian counterparts laying out his conditions for a deal.[69] Recalling that he had been "prepared to support and facilitate action on a proposal that would provide Iran nuclear fuel using uranium enriched by Iran," he affirmed that the door was still "open to engagement." He agreed to having Iranian LEU held in escrow in Turkey but stipulated that the full amount under discussion—1,200 kilograms, the larger part of Iran's stockpile—had to come out in a single batch at the start of the process. He also assured Lula that the letter presented "a detailed explanation of my perspective" and that he would be prepared to work with an arrangement that met his terms.

Ross and company thought the terms laid out in Obama's letters would be a deal breaker when Erdoğan and Lula went to Iran the next month. Our Iranian contacts, however, told us more than a week before the two leaders arrived in Tehran that they were "friends" who would not go home empty-handed. And, indeed, on May 17 Erdoğan and Lula persuaded their Iranian interlocutors—partly by showing them Obama's letters—to agree to the Tehran Declaration, which met all of the American president's conditions.[70] Washington promptly rejected it. The Washington Post reported that administration officials were "thoroughly irritated" by Erdoğan and Lula's success.[71] The next day, Secretary Clinton tabled a U.S.-drafted Security Council resolution imposing further sanctions on Iran, calling it "as convincing an answer to the efforts undertaken in Tehran over the last few days as any we could provide."

The Turkish and Brazilian governments were deeply disappointed, to say the least. On May 24, Turkish foreign minister Ahmet Davutoğlu and his Brazilian counterpart, Celso Amorim—following several unsatisfying exchanges with Secretary Clinton—conveyed their frustration in an op-ed for the *International Herald Tribune*:

> The joint declaration that was signed by Turkey, Brazil and Iran in Tehran on May 17 reflected a major breakthrough. . . . Iran agreed to remove from its territory 1,200 kilograms of low-enriched uranium—the exact amount specified by the IAEA proposal—within one month once the appropriate arrangements are concluded. The low-enriched uranium would be deposited in Turkey in one batch. The deposit will be made at the beginning of the process before any amount of nuclear fuel is delivered to Iran. . . . The Tehran declaration needs to be given the opportunity to work. . . . There is now sufficient substance to give negotiations a chance. Missing it may well be regretted for generations for come.[72]

As the Obama administration persisted in its rejection of the Tehran Declaration, Turkish and Brazilian officials concluded that Obama had not been honest in his letters to Erdoğan and Lula. The Turkish prime minister and Brazilian president came to believe that, in reality, they had been set up to fail; their main offense, from an American perspective, was that they had gone to Tehran and succeeded in brokering a deal. Three days after the Davutoğlu-Amorim op-ed, the Brazilian Foreign Ministry leaked Obama's letter to Lula to a Brazilian Web site, to show the extent of the White House's duplicity.[73]

The Obama administration, in its official response to the IAEA, noted several deficiencies in the Tehran Declaration: it did not freeze

Iran's enrichment at the near–20 percent level; it set an unrealistically short deadline of one year for delivery of finished fuel; and, most problematically, it recognized Iran's right to continue enriching uranium. But the one-year deadline had in fact been suggested in Obama's letters to Erdoğan and Lula, which also made no mention of freezing enrichment at the near–20 percent level as a condition. As to the right to enrich, ElBaradei noted that despite U.N. resolutions calling on Iran to "stop enrichment completely as a confidence-building measure,"

> we all know that these issues can only be resolved through negotiations. . . . We know in negotiations that you will not get everything before the start of the negotiations. In fact, that insistence to get everything before you start negotiating, the result of that was six years of wasted time on resolving the Iranian issue. We wasted six years in the past because the Western approach was that Iran should give everything before the start of the negotiation.[74]

The Obama administration went stubbornly on with its sanctions resolution, which the Security Council adopted in June—with Turkey and Brazil voting against it. Before the vote, the representatives from those two nations asked for an open debate, but the United States would agree only to a closed-door meeting. When the council finally voted, the Brazilian ambassador expressed her regret that the Tehran Declaration "has neither received the political recognition it deserves nor been given the time it needs to bear fruit." She also conveyed her government's "grave concern" about "the way in which the permanent members, together with a country that is not a member of the Security Council" (a reference to Germany's inclusion in the P5+1), "negotiated among themselves for months behind closed doors," warning that, "by adopting sanctions, this Council is actually opting for one of the two tracks that were supposed to run in parallel—in our opinion, the wrong one."[75] After the vote, Amorim published an op-ed in the New York Times decrying what he saw as the hegemonic impulse underlying the administration's Iran policy. Reiterating that Erdoğan and Lula's negotiations had "followed precisely the script that had been on the table for some months and whose validity had been recently reaffirmed at the highest level," he wrote:

> The insistence on sanctions against Iran—effectively ignoring the [Tehran Declaration]—confirmed the opinions of many analysts who claimed that the traditional centers of power will not share gladly their privileged status. . . . The fact that Brazil and Turkey ventured into a subject that would be typically handled by the [P5+1]—and, more importantly, were successful in doing so—disturbed the status quo.[76]

It is indeed hard to avoid the conclusion that Obama simply lied in his letters to Erdoğan and Lula, setting them up to fail so that he could get their votes for the sanctions resolution. Their success thwarted his plan—but he got the resolution all the same. Senior Obama administration officials acknowledge privately that they "mishandled communications" with Turkey and Brazil. While they are pleased to have gotten the sanctions resolution, one lamented that "it was not our finest hour."

Since the rejection of the Tehran Declaration, the Obama administration's Iran policy has grown ever more coercive. As noted, the administration has sought to raise the pressure on Tehran by intensifying economic sanctions—a drive that has already boosted international oil prices above the normal dictates of supply and demand. Since the start of the Arab awakening in late 2010, it has also tried hard to manage indigenous forces for political change (when it could not stymie them) so as to protect the United States' hegemonic ambitions in the Middle East—and, of course, to marginalize the Islamic Republic. Between January 25 and February 11, 2011, the administration tried unsuccessfully to engineer a transition in Egypt from the beleaguered Hosni Mubarak to his longtime intelligence chief, which would have let Washington preserve Mubarakism without Mubarak. It then partnered with Saudi Arabia and other conservative regimes to remove the Saudis' nemesis, Muammar Qadhafi, from Libya while quietly endorsing the Saudis' "invasion by invitation" of Bahrain (where the U.S. Fifth Fleet is based) to help the Sunni Khalifa monarchy suppress demands by the Shi'a-majority population for political change. None of these actions did any more to produce stable, pro-American political orders or boost the United States' popular standing in the region than the Bush administration's interventions in Afghanistan and Iraq did. Yet now the Obama administration is taking the same tack in Syria, seeking through diplomatic and economic pressure and support for antigovernment forces to topple the Assad government— in no small measure, as a way of isolating Iran. This approach has already backfired, solidifying Russian and Chinese resistance to the American position and driving post-Saddam Iraq even closer to Iran.

In early 2012, Obama and his advisers made it clear that they did not want to consider a military confrontation with the Islamic Republic before the American presidential election and did not want Israel to, either. In April 2012, the Obama administration, along with its P5+1 partners, resumed nuclear talks with Iran. But the administration was no more willing than previously to deal constructively with the main barriers to diplomatic progress—American refusal to acknowledge Iran's right to pursue safeguarded enrichment and, more broadly, to accept the Islamic Republic as a legitimate political entity with legitimate national interests. At the April 2012 round of discussions, the P5+1—at Washington's insistence—tabled a proposal whereby Iran would halt 20 percent enrichment, send all its near-20 percent LEU to a third country, and shut down its enrichment site at Fordo. Two months later, in Moscow, Iranian negotiators outlined (in 48 PowerPoint slides) a comprehensive proposal for resolving the controversy over the Islamic Republic's nuclear activities, including steps by Tehran to increase the transparency of its nuclear program along with reciprocal confidence-building measures culminating in the "normalization" of Iran's nuclear file in the Security Council and the IAEA and the "total termination of the UNSC, unilateral, and multilateral sanctions." Washington, though, continues to withhold recognition of Iran's right to enrich or to incorporate meaningful sanctions relief as part of a negotiated settlement. Iran's proposal also calls for nonnuclear cooperation, including on regional issues like Syria and

Bahrain; senior Iranian diplomats have told us that this item was intended as a litmus test of U.S. and Western intentions. The Obama administration has declined the offer.[77] The administration's 2012 decision to lift the MEK's terrorist designation strongly suggested that, even if Obama were reelected, there is little interest in Washington in a fundamentally different relationship with the Islamic Republic—which would require the United States to accept the Islamic Republic as a legitimate political entity representing legitimate national interests.

––––––

Through 2012, Washington's Iran policy remained locked in a trajectory that, unless fundamentally altered, will ultimately lead to war. The Iran myths have become ever more deeply entrenched as conventional wisdom. In mainstream discourse, the problems in American-Iranian relations are blamed almost entirely on the intransigence of an ideologically driven and illegitimate leadership in Tehran; hardly any attention is paid to the last four U.S. administrations' strategically damaging approaches to Iran. Western commentary on Iranian affairs comes disproportionately from expatriates with agendas, from neoconservative and liberal internationalist policy entrepreneurs with no expertise on the Islamic Republic, and from the Israel lobby. The media are regularly guilty of serious professional lapses in their coverage of Iran-related issues.

The Iran debate in the United States is coming more and more to resemble the public discussion that accompanied the run-up to the Iraq War. Then, too, conventional wisdom—pushed by a mix of Iraqi expatriates, neocons, self-promoters, and journalists—took hold in political and policy circles. That conventional wisdom was wrong in virtually all of its particulars, but very few legislators, journalists, or even public intellectuals were willing to question it; instead of being held to account, many were rewarded with influential and/or lucrative positions. As Washington has shifted its focus from Iraq to the next major challenge to its hegemonic ambitions in the Middle East, American elites have once again bought into a false and intellectually lazy but politically convenient set of assumptions. This is the reason we have pointed out in detail the role of specific individuals and groups in promoting such assumptions about the Islamic Republic.

There is a way out: strategically grounded engagement with the Islamic Republic. It is politically demanding and dauntingly counter-intuitive for many Americans. But it is the only way to set U.S.-Iranian relations on a more constructive trajectory and to halt the erosion of America's regional and global strategic position. Taking this more constructive path will require, in particular, two things. First (and with a rhetorical nod to President Kennedy's admonition about the dangers of myth), Americans must "disenthrall" themselves from the prevailing Iran mythology and those who promote it. Since the end of the Cold War, the American political system—and American society more generally—have utterly failed to impose accountability on those who contributed to the United States' most significant strategic failures. As Glenn Greenwald, Michael Massing, and other astute commentators have pointed out, Americans have hardly disenthralled themselves from those—the Hillary Clintons, Tom Friedmans, Leslie Gelbs, Ken Pollacks, Anne-Marie Slaughters, Andrew Sullivans, and countless neocons who dominate their country's foreign policy establishment—that displayed such contemptibly bad strategic and moral judgment regarding the 2003 Iraq invasion.[78] Now many of these same analysts, policy makers, and pundits—aided by a cadre of Iran "experts" who have been consistently wrong about their subject over many years—are laying the ground for yet another war of aggression by the United States in the Middle East.

Second, Americans' capacity to take a more constructive approach toward the Islamic Republic necessarily rests on a proactive and nuanced understanding of what strategic engagement means and what a genuine realignment of U.S.-Iranian relations would require of the United States. In the final chapter, we examine the critically important precedent of America's opening to China in the early 1970s to map out the path for U.S.-Iranian rapprochement.

9

THE ROAD TO TEHRAN

This will shake the world.
—*Zhou Enlai to Henry Kissinger in 1972, upon completing
negotiations over the Shanghai Communiqué*

The story of American policy toward the Islamic Republic is an unrelieved account of bad ideas, of high-level officials unable to learn from past failures and unwilling to break with unworkable approaches, of a great power that cannot free itself from the allure of hegemony over the Middle East. In these respects, it is tellingly similar to the story of American policy toward another rising revolutionary power—the People's Republic of China, during the first quarter century of the Cold War.

Just as Iran has been critical to the United States' strategic calculations about the Middle East, China has been critical to its calculations regarding Asia. The success of the Chinese Revolution followed by the establishment of the People's Republic of China in 1949, like the success of the Iranian Revolution followed by the establishment of the Islamic Republic of Iran in 1979, was viewed as an unacceptable challenge to American ambitions to dominate a strategically vital region. As products of revolution, both the People's Republic and the Islamic Republic have strongly ideological identities. But as much as both revolutions were defined by their ideologies, they were also marked by a commitment to restoring their nations' independence after long periods of Western domination—which, by the time each one took place, the United States had come largely to embody. And the American reaction in both cases was what a Chinese historian has described as "typically the mentality of a dominant Western power in the face of a rising revolutionary country"—a blending of "hostility with contempt."[1]

Given these parallels, the record of American policy toward the People's Republic can show us much about what is wrong with the United States' current approach to the Islamic Republic. Likewise, the reorientation of U.S. policy toward the People's Republic in the early 1970s—the outstanding example in American diplomacy of real rapprochement with a rising revolutionary state—can help us see what it would take for the United States to get its Iran policy right.

THE CHINA PROBLEM

George Kennan argued, in his famous "Long Telegram" from Moscow in 1946 and his "Mr. X" article in *Foreign Affairs* the following year, that tensions between the Soviet Union and national communist movements around the world would inevitably escalate and that the United States could derive significant strategic advantage from this development.[2] But the Truman administration transmuted Kennan's notion of containment into a crusade against international communism, leaving little space for nuanced, fact-based assessments of communist politics or the internal political struggles of pivotal states. This was especially the case regarding China, where the U.S.-backed Kuomintang under Chiang Kai-shek was locked in a civil war with the Chinese Communist Party (CCP) under Mao Zedong.

Washington's commitment to the Kuomintang originated not in the Cold War but rather in their alliance against imperial Japan during World War II. Looking beyond the war, Washington viewed a pro-American China as a critical element in a U.S.-led order in Asia, and it regarded the Kuomintang as a more suitable partner than the CCP, which was resolutely focused on restoring Chinese independence and sovereignty after a century and a half of Western domination. In fact, the CCP's own assessment was that the United States' primary strategic objective was not to confront the Soviet Union but to expand its own influence into the "intermediate zone" of nonaligned nations. Thus, a communist government would need not only to defend China's sovereignty but also to contest American dominance in Asia—a posture broadly similar to the one that, following the Iranian Revolution, the Islamic Republic took toward the United States and its strategic goals in the Middle East.[3]

As the Chinese Civil War escalated and American relations with the Soviet Union deteriorated, the CCP's challenge to U.S. ambitions in Asia grew ever more acute. In this climate, American political and policy elites came up with an essentialist narrative about Chinese communism in which the CCP was not a nationalist party committed to returning China to great-power status but rather the Chinese wing of a worldwide communist movement controlled from Moscow.[4] Yet American propaganda could not change reality: the CCP's victory over the Kuomintang and the resulting creation of the People's Republic were a huge blow to Washington's Asia strategy.

Citing the State Department's own postmortem on the Chinese Civil War, a few foreign policy realists like Walter Lippmann argued that the idea of using a Kuomintang-ruled China as an anchor for a U.S.-led Asian order had been doomed from the outset.[5] The implication of these analyses was clear: Washington needed, in its own interest, to come to terms with geopolitical reality in Asia, including China's new communist order. The People's Republic was not, in fact, implacably anti-American; it was prepared to normalize relations with the United States—so long as Washington accepted the Chinese Revolution and respected China's independence. As Mao himself put it, the new China was "willing to discuss with any foreign government the establishment of diplomatic relations on the basis of the principles of equality, mutual respect for territorial integrity and sovereignty." To demonstrate its seriousness, however, the United States would have to "sever relations with the [Kuomintang], stop conspiring with them

or helping them and adopt an attitude of genuine, and not hypo-
critical, friendship toward People's China."[6] The Islamic Republic's
leaders have assumed much the same position.

Dealing with China on its stated terms would have meant stepping
back from Washington's more far-reaching ambitions in Asia. But
American leaders were no more prepared to take such an approach
toward the People's Republic in the first two decades after 1949 than
they have been with regard to the Islamic Republic since 1979. The
detention of American consular officials in late 1948 by communist
forces in Shenyang and their subsequent arrest, trial, and conviction
for injuring one of their local employees had almost as destructive
an impact on Sino-American relations as the 1979–81 Tehran
embassy hostage crisis did on Iranian-American relations. Washington demanded that Beijing accept "basic international principles"
before ties could improve—which, since 1979, has also been a constant
refrain in its rhetoric about the Islamic Republic.[7]

American decision makers knew that the United States had no
choice but to coexist with the Soviet Union in a divided Europe. They
also judged that it could do so and still attain most of its major economic and strategic objectives in the western part of the continent. In
contrast, official Washington was almost uniformly concerned that
attempting to coexist with the People's Republic would undermine
American interests in Asia. Policy makers worried in particular that
they would not be able to integrate Japan into their projected Asian
order if Tokyo restored economic links to China, with political links
sure to follow.[8] Consequently, the policy of containment was applied
to "Red China" with greater comprehensiveness and intensity than to
the Soviet Union—eschewing diplomatic relations, imposing a near-
total ban on political and commercial contacts, and recognizing the
Kuomintang's Taiwan-based Republic of China as a political alternative to the People's Republic.[9] Again, this approach was remarkably
similar to the way the U.S. has treated the Islamic Republic since 1979,
emphasizing diplomatic isolation, economic pressure, and support for
regime change.

With the outbreak of the Korean War in June 1950, Sino-American antagonism devolved into open confrontation. Believing that Japanese security—and, along with it, American dominance in Asia—required a quiescent Korean peninsula, the United States initially sent four divisions to South Korea to repel invading North Korean troops. It also, for the first time, deployed the Seventh Fleet to the Taiwan Strait, breaking the Truman administration's previous pledge not to interfere in the ongoing civil war between the CCP and the Kuomintang, now based on Taiwan. Within a few months, American troops were advancing across the 38th parallel into North Korea itself. Ignoring clearly signaled Chinese concern over the deployment of American troops so close to the Chinese–North Korean border, American units advanced to the Yalu River, triggering Chinese military intervention in October 1950 and a bloody defeat for U.S. forces. Chinese troops—nearly a million soldiers over the course of the conflict—then stayed on in Korea for three more years of fighting. In total, the United States deployed just over 300,000 troops to Korea and estimated that it killed roughly 400,000 Chinese soldiers. This was the first of its post–World War II military interventions in Asia, motivated, like the later one in Vietnam, by the perceived need to push back against the Chinese challenge to its hegemonic ambitions in the region.

More generally, Washington decided that the People's Republic had to be isolated, delegitimized, and, if possible, eliminated. From that resolve flowed a China mythology that distorted American discourse and policy deliberations for two decades—just as, today, the Iran mythology distorts debates about the Islamic Republic and how to deal with it.

One element of America's China mythology stressed the illegitimacy of the People's Republic, drawing on themes of revolutionary betrayal and rule by an unrepresentative clique that would reappear in its Iran mythology. Hence, according to Secretary of State Dean Acheson's public evaluation, a laudable revolutionary process had been "captured" by the communists, who, rather than helping their country achieve "true national independence," were reducing it to "a mere dependency in the Soviet orbit."[10] Calling on already established depictions of the

CCP as a tool of Moscow, Acheson's assistant secretary for Far Eastern affairs, Dean Rusk—later secretary of state under Presidents Kennedy and Johnson—went so far as to assert that China's communist rulers were "not Chinese."[11] Deriding the CCP for its foreign loyalties and anti-Chinese character remained a central motif in American propaganda through the 1960s.[12]

Another element of the China mythology stressed the irrationally aggressive nature of the People's Republic, particularly under Mao's leadership. As with the Islamic Republic, the idea was grounded in a willful misreading of Beijing's national security strategy. China's communist leaders have always considered their country's security inextricably connected to the regional balance of power. For at least the first two decades after the revolution, one of their more important policy tools for fending off American designs to contain and isolate the People's Republic was ties to proxy allies—typically described as "national liberation movements"—in other Asian countries. Of course, such ties have also been central to the Islamic Republic's national security strategy, and American officials have not liked them in either case. Nearly three decades before the U.S. government began keeping a list of state sponsors of terrorism, it was already expressing grave concern over Beijing's encouragement of "militant dissidence" across the non-Western world. Its formulations evoked nineteenth-century alarms over the Yellow Peril and other racist tropes, as when President Eisenhower warned, "We are always wrong when we believe that Orientals think logically as we do."[13]

Still another element—again mirrored in today's Iran mythology—stressed the imperative of isolating the People's Republic. At the 1954 Geneva Conference, convened in the aftermath of the Korean War to determine the future of the Korean peninsula and Vietnam, Secretary of State John Foster Dulles famously refused to shake hands with Chinese premier and foreign minister Zhou Enlai, setting the United States' China policy on a path of open-ended hostility toward the People's Republic. From the mid-1950s on, American intelligence agencies launched covert action programs designed to fan separatist sentiment among minority (non-Han) segments of China's population, particularly in Tibet. At the same time, President Eisenhower drew on contradictory images of the People's Republic as part of a monolithic communist threat and as a carrier of revolutionary nationalism to propound the domino theory. This construct, in turn, was used to justify American military intervention in Vietnam and then to maintain that the political costs of withdrawal would be unacceptably high—even after the Eisenhower, Kennedy, and Johnson administrations all concluded that victory there was beyond reach.[14]

The powerful "China lobby" included prominent businessmen (the *Time-Life* media mogul Henry Luce), well-known newspaper columnists (Joseph and Stewart Alsop), and military heroes (Claire Chennault, commander of the famed "Flying Tigers" squadrons). The China mythology they promoted was matched with a ferocious effort to block any consideration of strategic alternatives. A case in point is the fate of the "China hands," a cadre of American diplomats and journalists who worked in China during the 1930s and 1940s, mastering its language along with its culture, history, and politics. The China hands had forecast a CCP victory over the Kuomintang; most of them recommended that Washington engage China's new communist leaders. But the idea of replacing American ambitions for hegemony in Asia with a balancing strategy was a foreign policy heresy. The China lobby went after anyone who challenged its mythology, recruiting its own experts (like the University of Washington historian George Taylor, who could not discredit the substance of the China hands' analysis but was still happy to smear their political loyalties before congressional committees and federal investigators). On Capitol Hill, a hardline "China bloc" of pro-Kuomintang congressmen and senators offered support reflexively. As a result, over the course of the 1950s several of the most accomplished American diplomats of their generation, including John Paton Davies, John Service, and John Carter Vincent, were drummed out of the State Department. Some were put under criminal investigation and threatened with prosecution. Eminent Sinologists like Owen Lattimore, who had served the U.S. government as an expert adviser in China during World War II, were hounded by criminal probes, congressional inquisitions, and prosecution. Journalists of the caliber of Edgar Snow and Theodore White were turned away from prominent newsmagazines.[15]

Speaking personally, the two of us, like the China hands, have no political agenda—other than presenting the most objective analysis of Iranian politics, Iranian foreign policy, and American-Iranian relations that we possibly can and drawing from that analysis the correct prescriptions for American foreign policy. As we have tried to tell the truth about important but vehemently politicized issues of American policy toward the Islamic Republic, we, too, have experienced sharp backlash from elements in the American body politic opposed to a more rational and constructive Iran policy. The George W. Bush administration censored an op-ed we wrote in December 2006 that documented Iranian cooperation with the United States on Afghanistan; the *New York Times* published it with the redacted passages blacked out because we demonstrated to the newspaper that all of the material that the White House excised was publicly available elsewhere, a fact that clearly suggested that the Bush administration was out to silence us for political reasons.[16] We know what it means to have to leave careers in government service because of unpopular analytic and policy views and—in Flynt's case—to be forced out of a prominent Washington think tank because of those views. By 2010, we had become such a lightning rod in the Iran debate that, according to the *Economist,* much of it was about "what we should think of Hillary and Flynt Leverett."[17] With the experience of the China hands in mind, we take these criticisms as confirmation that we are looking at reality straight on.

By the mid-1950s, events compelled Washington to begin pursuing limited diplomatic engagement with the People's Republic. But this engagement was purely tactical, not strategic. A month after the 1954 Geneva Conference ended, Washington and Beijing had become embroiled in the first Taiwan Strait crisis, sparked by conflicts between the People's Republic and the Taiwan-based Republic of China over control of the islands of Quemoy and Matsu. Thereafter low-level consular contacts between the two sides in Geneva were upgraded to ambassadorial rank; after a second Taiwan Strait crisis in 1958, the venue for these sporadic talks shifted to Warsaw. But accepting "Red China" and abandoning the goal of Asian hegemony appeared to be a politically impossible step for any administration, of either party, to take.

When John F. Kennedy won the presidency, in November 1960, he privately complained that he found the absence of diplomatic relations between Washington and Beijing "stupid."[18] But on the eve of his inauguration, he met with Eisenhower at the White House, and, as he later recounted to his brother Robert, Eisenhower told him, "I'm going to try to support you every way I can on foreign policy. But there is one point on which I would oppose you strongly—the seating of Communist China in the U.N. and bilateral recognition." As one Kennedy biographer writes, "That took care of that." Avoiding Ike's disapproval on a high-profile international issue was "a more compelling concern" than crafting a rational Asia policy.[19]

When it became evident in the early 1960s that the People's Republic was working to build nuclear weapons, another round of frenzied argument began in American political and policy circles. Foreshadowing the contemporary polemic on the Islamic Republic's nuclear activities, columnists decried the "madness of Mao Tse-tung."[20] Just as President Obama has warned that "it will not be tolerable to a number of states" in the Middle East for Iran to have nuclear weapons while they do not, the Kennedy administration raised the alarm that China's nuclear development would trigger a cascade of proliferation in Asia.[21] The real issue, however—as Kennedy himself told his National Security Council—was that "the development of nuclear capabilities by the Chinese communists" would endanger the United States' regional position. His administration even approached the Soviet Union about a possible preventive attack against China's nuclear infrastructure. China's first nuclear weapons test, in 1964, motivated the Johnson administration to broach the idea with the Soviets again.[22]

Even when, under pressure of reality, Washington was periodically compelled to return to its diplomatic dialogue with the People's Republic, as the United States periodically does today with the Islamic Republic, the China lobby's fanatical enforcement of the China mythology forced it to hedge its engagement so thoroughly that progress was impossible. Under both the Kennedy and the Johnson administrations, the American agenda for the Warsaw talks centered on getting the People's Republic to address American grievances and surrender to American diktats (especially regarding Taiwan) rather than on real rapprochement—the same kind of unpalatable diplomacy that, at multiple junctures since 1979, has undermined prospects for any meaningful improvement in American-Iranian relations.

In 1966, the U.S. representative to the Warsaw talks referred publicly to "the People's Republic of China," marking the first time an American diplomat had formally used the nation's official name. As Henry Kissinger later noted, such gestures "were put forward as abstract hopes geared to some undefined change in Chinese attitudes," yet "no practical conclusion followed."[23] In 2009, commentators made much of Barack Obama's similarly groundbreaking reference to the Islamic Republic of Iran by its official name. But "no practical conclusion" has followed from that rhetorical gesture, either.

The prospect that President Obama might change the U.S.-Iranian relationship was front-page news in the Islamic Republic. *AFP/Behrouz Mehri*

THE NIXONIAN MOMENT

Only when Richard Nixon reoriented American strategy along more interest-based lines was the United States able to break away from its failed China policy and its disastrous military commitment in Vietnam. Nixon sliced through the twenty-year-old conceptual and rhetorical constraints that kept the country bound to counterproductive policies, tacitly acknowledging that an unreflective quest for hegemony in Asia had actually undermined the American position there. The story offers valuable insights into how the United States might finally break out of its Iran policy straitjacket.

Nixon recognized that rapprochement with Beijing was a strategic imperative for the United States, not an aid or a reward for the People's Republic. His rationale was grounded in classic balance-of-power logic. On coming to office, as Kissinger later wrote,

> Nixon found himself in the position of having to guide America through the transition from dominance to leadership . . . for the age of America's nearly total dominance of the world stage was drawing to a close. America's nuclear superiority was eroding, and its economic supremacy was being challenged by the dynamic growth of Europe and Japan. . . . Vietnam finally signaled that it was high time to reassess America's role in the developing world, and to find some sustainable ground between abdication and overextension.[24]

Nixon sought to navigate this transition, Kissinger wrote, "according to a concept of America's national interest—repugnant as that idea was to many traditional idealists." Both men understood that such an approach is ultimately incompatible with the reflexive pursuit of global hegemony:

> If the major powers, including the United States, pursued their self-interests rationally and predictably, Nixon believed—in the spirit of the eighteenth-century enlightenment—that an equilibrium would emerge from the clash of competing interests. Like Theodore

Roosevelt—but unlike any other twentieth-century American president—Nixon counted on a balance of power to produce stability, and considered a strong America essential to the global equilibrium.[25]

Through this balance-of-power prism, Nixon understood that the United States needed an opening to China in order to shore up its position in Asia and to revive its standing as a global power.[26] Some have argued that Nixon was motivated primarily by an interest in "triangulating" with China against the Soviet Union; this interpretation, however, defines his vision—and his accomplishment—too narrowly. The triangulation argument undoubtedly helped him ameliorate resistance to realigning relations with "Red China."[27] Yet Kissinger and other Nixon associates affirm that, among his motives for an opening to Beijing, getting out of Vietnam was more significant than triangulating against Moscow.[28]

More important, Nixon saw rapprochement in broad terms. The diplomat Chas Freeman—who worked on China policy intensively during the initial years of his career and served as Nixon's interpreter on his historic 1972 trip to Beijing—recounts that, "from the very outset, the United States made it clear that it sought its opening to China not as a matter of expediency but as a long-term and strategic move."[29] In Kissinger's account, Nixon treated rapprochement "as an opportunity to redefine the American approach to foreign policy and international leadership. He sought to use the opening to China to demonstrate to the American public that, even in the midst of a debilitating war, the United States was in a position to bring about a design for long-term peace."[30]

The primary impetus for rapprochement was not a common enemy but a common need to align American and Chinese interests in order to deal with an array of strategic challenges. As Kissinger wrote, "Excluding a country of the magnitude of China from America's diplomatic options meant that America was operating internationally with one hand tied behind its back."[31] That is why the relationship has grown even more consequential since the Cold War era—contrary to what the triangulation thesis would predict.

It is no less imperative today for the United States to make the transition from a self-damaging quest for dominance—especially in the Middle East—to effective international leadership, based above all on successful management of the balance of power. Its post–Cold War hegemony is eroding, its economic supremacy is being challenged by the rise of China and the rest of Asia, and its failures in Afghanistan and Iraq have demonstrated the limits of what its military power can accomplish. Against this backdrop, it clearly needs to find the ground "between abdication and overextension"; realigning relations with Iran has moved from the "nice to have" to the "need to have" category. But political and policy elites in the United States remain deeply resistant to this reality. Just as presidential leadership was essential to sway elite and, by extension, mass opinion on ties to China, it can also play a critical role in reorienting American attitudes about an opening to Iran. Unfortunately, we have not yet seen any such leadership.

Nixon did not merely grasp the need for Sino-American rapprochement; he also understood how to accomplish it. Specifically, he recognized that realigning relations with Beijing would require at least four fundamental changes in Washington's posture, and, just as important, he was prepared to carry them out.

First, Nixon knew that, for rapprochement to move forward, the prevailing American narrative about the People's Republic and its ambitions would have to be recast. Kissinger recalls that, at the outset of Nixon's presidency,

> the vast majority of informed opinion . . . considered Communist China incurably expansionist, fanatically ideological, and intransigently committed to world revolution. America had involved itself in Indochina in large part to blunt what had been perceived as a Chinese-led communist conspiracy to take over Southeast Asia. Conventional wisdom had it that, even more than was the case with the Soviet Union, the Chinese communist system would need to be transformed before negotiations could be considered.[32]

The Nixon administration rejected these myths of communist Chinese irrationality. Its first foreign policy report to Congress stated, "We will regard our Communist adversaries first and foremost as nations pursuing their own interests as *they* perceive these interests, just as we follow our own interests as we see them."[33] (This assertion was, of course, very much in keeping with Nixon's focus on American national interests as the touchstone for formulating foreign policy.)

Far from rejecting myths about the Islamic Republic's irrationality and illegitimacy, every American administration since the Iranian Revolution has publicly indulged them. And President Obama, aside from a few rhetorical gestures early on—intended more for Iranian audiences than for American ones—has done nothing to construct a counternarrative. Those American elites willing to argue that the Iranian leadership might be even minimally rational define that rationality very narrowly—as a focus on maintaining a grip on power, not as a broader strategic orientation.

Compare the Nixon administration's willingness to treat the People's Republic and other communist states as "nations pursuing their own interests as *they* perceive these interests, just as we follow our own interests as we see them" with Obama's statements about Iranian leaders in a 2012 interview:

> They have a very ingrown political system. They are founded and fueled on hostility towards the United States, Israel, and to some degree the West. And they have shown themselves willing to go outside international norms and international rules to achieve their objectives. All of this makes them dangerous. They've also been willing to crush opposition in their own country in brutal and bloody ways.

Obama acknowledged that Iranian leaders were "self-interested," but only in the limited sense of wanting to preserve their hold on power.[34] His portrait of Iran conjured up a country that might modify its behavior in response to the "negative reinforcement" of sanctions, not one that could ever be engaged in a genuine strategic dialogue, as Nixon engaged China.

Second, Nixon understood that the incremental, step-by-step diplomacy being intermittently pursued in the Warsaw channel would never achieve a real breakthrough. To be sure, he authorized a resumption of the Warsaw talks almost immediately upon taking office. At the same time, though, he knew that relying solely on the talks would, as he told Kissinger, "kill this baby before it is born." What was needed was a top-down, comprehensive approach.[35] Thus, in the summer of 1969, he made what Kissinger calls the "extraordinary" decision

> to put aside all the issues which constituted the existing Sino-American dialogue. The Warsaw talks had established an agenda that was as complex as it was time-consuming. Each side stressed its grievances: China's had to do with the future of Taiwan and Chinese assets sequestered in the United States; the United States sought the renunciation of force over Taiwan, China's participation in arms-control negotiations, and the settlement of American economic claims against China. Instead, Nixon decided to concentrate on the broader issue of China's attitude toward dialogue with the United States. . . . If relations improved on that basis, the traditional agenda would take care of itself; if relations did not improve, the traditional agenda would remain insoluble. In other words, the practical issues would be resolved as a consequence of Sino-American rapprochement, not chart the path toward it.[36]

Two and a half years later, this approach bore rich fruit with the announcement of the Shanghai Communiqué—which, as Chas Freeman notes, "served as the basic charter for the Sino-American relationship" from Nixon's trip in 1972 until relations were normalized in 1979, under the Carter administration.[37] Once Nixon focused on the basic issue of "China's attitude toward dialogue with the United States," Chinese leaders knew they had a serious partner—and responded accordingly. Kissinger recalls:

While drafting the Shanghai Communiqué with Zhou Enlai, I at one point offered to trade an offensive phrase in the Chinese draft for something in the American version to which Zhou might object. "We will never get anywhere this way," he replied. "If you can convince me why our phrase is offensive, I will give it to you." Zhou's attitude was not the product of abstract goodwill but of a sure grasp of long-term priorities.[38]

And so the two sides defined a top-down framework for bilateral rapprochement. As the Shanghai Communiqué's core paragraphs note,

> There are essential differences between China and the United States in their social systems and foreign policies. However, the two sides agreed that countries, regardless of their social systems, should conduct their relations on the principles of respect for the sovereignty and territorial integrity of all states, non-aggression against other states, non-interference in the internal affairs of other states, equality and mutual benefit, and peaceful coexistence. International disputes should be settled on this basis, without resorting to the use or threat of force. The United States and the People's Republic of China are prepared to apply these principles to their mutual relations.

The two sides then committed themselves to several concrete benchmarks, among them making "progress toward the normalization of relations" (which was "in the interests of all countries"), reducing "the danger of international military conflict," and developing their "economic relations based on equality and mutual benefit." They also stipulated formulas for resolving—or at least managing—the most serious disputes between them, especially Taiwan.

Nixon used to tell his staff, "You pay the same price for doing something halfway as for doing it completely. So you might as well do it completely."[39] As we have seen, no American president has been willing to take anything like a similarly top-down and comprehensive approach to diplomacy with the Islamic Republic—to put aside specific grievances and demands in order to "concentrate on the broader issue" of Iran's "attitude toward dialogue" with the United States. As a result, there has been no effort to engage Tehran with the aim of producing a Shanghai Communiqué–like roadmap for realigning relations.

Third, Nixon realized that it was incumbent on the United States, as the stronger party and one with a record of stubborn hostility toward the People's Republic, to demonstrate its bona fides proactively to the Chinese leaders. Chas Freeman relates how, on Nixon's orders, the Seventh Fleet quietly ended its nineteen-year patrolling of the Taiwan Strait. Likewise, Nixon ordered the CIA to pull back from its long-standing covert action program in Tibet.[40] His administration relaxed restrictions on travel to and small-scale commercial exchanges with the People's Republic.[41] When Soviet and Chinese military units clashed along the Sino-Soviet border in 1969, Washington told Moscow that it would not quietly acquiesce to a major strategic defeat of the People's Republic.[42]

Analogous actions vis-à-vis the Islamic Republic might include pulling back from anti-Iranian covert actions and from military deployments that threaten it. But so far no American president has been prepared to take these proactive steps. Clinton did designate the MEK a foreign terrorist organization, but he permitted MEK affiliates to continue operating in the United States. During his last year in office, he allowed sanctions to be modified slightly, to allow the import of such innocuous products as Iranian carpets, pistachios, and dried fruits, but he refused to let American energy companies pursue business opportunities in Iran and publicly pressured non-American companies not to do so, either. Early in his tenure, Obama refused to order a pullback from the anti-Iranian covert action programs he inherited from his predecessor; in fact, as we have seen, these programs have actually intensified on his watch. And, of course, the Obama administration took the decision to lift the MEK's terrorist designation, positioning it to become the vanguard of a new American strategy for regime change in Iran. Escalating sanctions, rigid negotiating positions, and growing support for Iranian oppositionists all display an ever-increasing hostility toward the Islamic Republic.

———

Fourth, Nixon understood that refashioning policy after twenty years of intense hostility toward the People's Republic would not be easy, politically or bureaucratically. Both he and Kissinger have recounted that, coming into office in 1969, they knew that holding a "normal" interagency process on a potential opening to Beijing would kill any chance of success.[43] Such success demanded that those opposed to rapprochement or motivated by other interests to throw up obstacles be excluded from policy planning and development. So Nixon and Kissinger remade the policy themselves, working largely in secret with probably no more than ten people. They also knew that they would have to find new channels for communicating with their Chinese counterparts. Kissinger has described the bureaucratic encumbrances surrounding the Warsaw talks: "Two dozen members of Congress had to be briefed on every step, and new approaches were bound to be lost in the conflicting pressures of briefings of some fifteen countries, which were being kept informed about the Warsaw talks and included Taiwan—still recognized by most of them, and especially the United States, as the legitimate government of China."[44] Working first through Romanian and then through Pakistani intermediaries, Nixon and Kissinger established lines of communication to the top of the Chinese leadership—which they treated as a whole, without trying to play Mao and Zhou against each other. These lines of communication made possible Kissinger's secret visit to Beijing in July 1971, which he followed with a public visit in October 1971, preparing the way for Nixon's historic trip in February 1972. Throughout, the focus was on providing the basis for a positive outcome that would then draw public support. Allies and domestic constituencies found out what Nixon and Kissinger were up to only after it was too late for them to sabotage it.

No American president, including Obama, has assumed anything close to the same kind of leadership role in charting a new course toward Iran. Obama's decision to start his administration's strategic work on Iran with a broad-based interagency policy review, including extensive consultations with allies opposed to a realignment of American-Iranian relations—among them Israel, Britain, France, and Saudi Arabia—was a telltale sign that he was not serious about rapprochement.

A WAY FORWARD

The result of Nixon and Kissinger's efforts was the greatest achievement of American diplomacy in the past half century. When Nixon made his epochal visit to the People's Republic, Mao was still presiding over the CCP; probably three million Chinese citizens had been killed in the ongoing Cultural Revolution that he had launched six years earlier. The People's Republic was still providing the North Vietnamese military and Vietcong guerrillas with weapons, ordnance, and other equipment that was being used to kill American soldiers in South Vietnam. It was an act of extraordinary statesmanship for Nixon to go anyway. Today, it would be hard to find even the most ardent neoconservative, the most stalwart liberal internationalist, or the most committed human rights advocate to argue that the world would be better off had he not gone.

The opening to the People's Republic thoroughly reoriented the United States' China policy. Less obviously but just as importantly, it reoriented the American grand strategy in Asia. In effect, the United States backed away from its counterproductive quest for absolute hegemony in the region—a posture that, among many self-inflicted wounds, had driven the open-ended and calamitously draining war in Vietnam. The Shanghai Communiqué stated that neither the United States nor China "should seek hegemony in the Asia-Pacific region and each is opposed to efforts by any other country or group of countries to establish such hegemony." The United States still had vital interests in the region, of course, and would remain deeply engaged there. But after the opening to China it would no longer seek to coerce every political outcome. Instead, it would adapt its behavior to the logic of strategic balancing. This change of course was initially disorienting for some Asian allies—but they adjusted. Just seven months after Nixon's visit, Japan's prime minister made his own trip. Today, none of these countries would maintain that it would have been better for them if Washington and Beijing had stayed estranged. Indeed, the strategic situation of Japan and other American allies in Asia would be far less secure if a hostile environment had persisted between the two great powers.

The United States' Iran policy has yet to experience its Nixonian moment. The deficiencies of that policy become all the more glaring in contrast to Nixon and Kissinger's accomplishment. At the same time, an informed appreciation of the Islamic Republic's foreign policy and its national security strategy, reinforced with insights gleaned from the opening to China, allow us to outline a potentially far more efficacious diplomatic approach—in reality, the only one that can work.

Such an approach must be predicated on American acceptance of the Islamic Republic as an enduring and legitimate political entity, with legitimate national interests. For more than two decades, the People's Republic remained willing to consider rapprochement with the United States, but only once the United States accepted the Chinese Revolution and the political order it had produced; the Islamic Republic has a similar perspective. As part of acceptance, the United States will need to demonstrate that it is genuinely prepared to abide by the portion of the Algiers Accord (the 1981 agreement that ended the hostage crisis) committing it "not to intervene, directly or indirectly, politically or militarily, in Iran's internal affairs"—first of all, by stopping its support for groups seeking the Islamic Republic's overthrow. While Americans might retain a principled interest in the human rights of individual Iranians, their government should refrain in its official rhetoric and policy from favoring the opposition Green movement over the elected government and otherwise constitutionally legitimate authorities.

At a minimum, this new and very different American diplomatic strategy would mean that diplomacy could not be used as the cutting edge of soft regime change. It is fantastical to think that the Islamic Republic of Iran—any more than the People's Republic of China—would be willing to negotiate its internal political transformation with the United States. Such a fantasy is, as we noted earlier, neoconservatism without guns. It is also a recipe for diplomatic failure. Rejecting it is essential for making productive diplomacy possible.

A comprehensive top-down approach is absolutely essential for Washington and Tehran to come to terms with each other, and the record indicates that the current Iranian leadership would be as receptive to such an approach as the Chinese leaders were in the early 1970s. To invoke one of Nixon and Kissinger's crucial points: if both sides are committed to comprehensive realignment, individual items will take care of themselves; without that commitment, the rest of the agenda will remain insoluble. Without an understanding of where the two sides intend to go in their bilateral relations, there will always be an alleged terrorist attack, an arms shipment, or a nasty statement that can be used as a justification for cutting off negotiations.

Without a clear American commitment to comprehensiveness, Tehran will be obliged to continue assuming that the ultimate objective of Washington's Iran policy is the Islamic Republic's overthrow—which will reduce Iranian negotiators' flexibility on contentious individual issues, as well as on trade-offs across issues. From an Iranian perspective, diplomatic progress requires an American willingness to extend an effective security assurance to the Islamic Republic—that is, a commitment not to use force to change the borders or form a government of postrevolutionary Iran.

The United States, however, cannot extend such an assurance solely as part of a negotiated resolution of the nuclear issue, or of any other specific dispute. As we have seen, the American agenda vis-à-vis Iran extends well beyond the nuclear issue, encompassing the management of regional conflicts (such as in Afghanistan), Iranian ties to what Washington considers terrorist organizations, and Tehran's posture toward a negotiated settlement of the Arab-Israeli conflict. Without a reciprocal Iranian commitment to resolve—or, where resolution is not possible, to manage—outstanding bilateral differences through diplomacy and negotiation, no American administration would be able to provide security guarantees to the Islamic Republic.

At this juncture, resolving any of the significant bilateral differences between the Islamic Republic and the United States necessarily means resolving all of them. That is why we have long argued that meaningful improvement in American-Iranian relations will require the negotiation of a "grand bargain" between Tehran and Washington, in which all the major disputes between the two sides are put on the table and resolved in a package.[45] In recent years, American and Western diplomacy toward the Islamic Republic has focused on its nuclear development. That issue will obviously remain a high priority on the international agenda, and the multilateral P5+1 process will continue to be an important venue for dealing with it. But real rapprochement cannot be achieved over the nuclear question alone or through progress on any other single issue. Even a long-term solution to the country's nuclear development will have to be embedded in a broader strategic understanding—primarily between the United States and Iran, reached primarily through bilateral U.S.-Iranian discussions. Ideally, two levels of diplomatic interaction will reinforce each other: representations and contingent communications in bilateral discussions should facilitate progress in multilateral nuclear negotiations, and vice versa.

The goal of these bilateral discussions would be to produce a framework for restructuring American-Iranian relations similar to the Shanghai Communiqué. The substantive portion of the communiqué opens with parallel Chinese and American statements about what was then the current international situation. One can imagine that the Islamic Republic's statement might sound something like the Chinese declaration:

> Wherever there is oppression, there is resistance. Countries want independence, nations want liberation and the people want revolution—this has become the irresistible trend of history. All nations, big or small, should be equal: big nations should not bully the small and strong nations should not bully the weak. China will never be a

superpower and it opposes hegemony and power politics of any kind. The Chinese side stated that it firmly supports the struggles of all the oppressed people and nations for freedom and liberation and that the people of all countries have the right to choose their social systems according to their own wishes and the right to safeguard the independence, sovereignty and territorial integrity of their own countries and oppose foreign aggression, interference, control and subversion. All foreign troops should be withdrawn to their own countries.

It would be an enormously positive step toward correcting the hegemonic distortions in the United States' post–Cold War foreign policy for an American administration to endorse ideas like those that Nixon and Kissinger put into the Shanghai Communiqué:

Peace in Asia and peace in the world requires efforts both to reduce immediate tensions and to eliminate the basic causes of conflict. The United States will work for a just and secure peace: just, because it fulfills the aspirations of peoples and nations for freedom and progress; secure, because it removes the danger of foreign aggression. . . . The United States believes that the effort to reduce tensions is served by improving communication between countries that have different ideologies so as to lessen the risks of confrontation through accident, miscalculation or misunderstanding. Countries should treat each other with mutual respect and be willing to compete peacefully, letting performance be the ultimate judge. No country should claim infallibility and each country should be prepared to reexamine its own attitudes for the common good.

Following the Shanghai Communiqué model, a framework document would, after opening statements of each side's view of international conditions, lay out a set of agreed-upon principles to guide the development of bilateral relations, including "respect for the sovereignty and territorial integrity of all states, non-aggression against other states, non-interference in the internal affairs of other states, equality and mutual benefit, and peaceful coexistence." The document would then specify concrete benchmarks for dealing with major bilateral disputes and common challenges (the nuclear issue, postconflict stabilization in Afghanistan, the Arab-Israeli conflict) and for developing relations in areas of mutual interest. Where American and Iranian interests are not aligned, the two sides would commit to resolving their differences in an atmosphere of mutual respect and without resort to violence or economic warfare. As bilateral relations developed, the latter commitment would motivate the executive branch in Washington to pull back on the implementation of unilateral sanctions against the Islamic Republic.

On the nuclear issue, the parameters of a deal are virtually self-evident. Iran is going to enrich uranium; the international community should want safeguards in place sufficient to assure that the proliferation risks associated with those fuel cycle activities are under control. In practical terms, this means that, in return for American (and, more generally, Western) recognition of its right to enrich, Tehran would ratify and implement the Additional Protocol to the NPT and would agree to other, more intrusive verification measures and notification requirements.[46] These steps would give the IAEA as robust a level of access to Iranian nuclear facilities as it enjoys anywhere in the world. Once the terms of the deal were finalized through discussions with the P5+1 countries, the U.N. Security Council would roll back the multilateral sanctions that have been imposed on the Islamic Republic over its nuclear activities.

Additionally, the United States and its international partners should lock in a deal on the nuclear issue through expanded nuclear cooperation with the Islamic Republic. President Ahmadinejad and Foreign Minister Salehi have both suggested that the United States and other countries concerned about aspects of Iran's nuclear activities should send scientists and technicians to work collaboratively on those activities in joint ventures with Iranian counterparts. Iranian officials have said for years that Tehran would be open to associating the Islamic Republic's nuclear program with multilateral nuclear consortia (including for producing nuclear fuel) and joint venture arrangements; Washington and its partners should take up these expressions of openness to international nuclear cooperation.

Such an outcome would, of course, aggrieve any number of U.S. allies, at least in the short run—principally Israel, along with Britain, France, and Saudi Arabia. But, as we have seen, their unhappiness has little to do with American interests or the integrity of the international nonproliferation regime. On the contrary, their continuing insistence on zero enrichment will only ensure that negotiations fail—an eventuality that is no more in their long-term interest (since in the final analysis they rely on the United States for their security) than it is in the United States'. For Washington's Middle Eastern and European allies, as for those Asian allies who were initially discomfited by the opening to China, it is far better that the U.S. reestablish itself as a great power able to shape strategic outcomes than that it continue in the downward spiral of a failing hegemon.

Beyond the nuclear issue, the United States should invite Iran into regional negotiations about postconflict Afghanistan and a prospective political settlement in Syria. In Afghanistan, a process in which various states bring their influence to bear on the range of Afghan factions will be indispensable to stabilizing Afghanistan (and, by extension, Pakistan). In particular, getting to a sustainable political settlement will require the cooperation and support of Iran's allies there—the Hazara, Tajik, and Uzbek communities that together comprise almost half of the population. The Pakistani- and Saudi-backed Taliban will have to be balanced by these non-Pashtun groups, which makes Iranian participation essential. By bringing Iran into these negotiations and inviting it to play a central role in dealings with non-Pashtun constituencies, the United States could persuade Iranian policy makers that power sharing can be done in a manner that addresses their concerns—about the Taliban's relative standing, about Afghan-based narcotics production and trafficking, and about the regional balance of power. In Syria, as in Afghanistan, Iran's contribution is crucial to any effort at attaining a political settlement based on negotiated power sharing. The Assad government and its constituencies are vital participants in forging a more representative and stable political order in Syria—and that means Iran's involvement is vital, too.

By including cooperation on Afghanistan and Syria in a broader strategic dialogue with Tehran, Washington could, at the same time, reinforce a more positive message about its stance toward the Islamic Republic. Washington should also engage Tehran on the daunting array of issues gathered under the heading "the Arab-Israeli conflict." To recover its strategic position in the Middle East, the United States urgently needs to reinvent the peace process. The reasons are not directly connected to Iran, but for any such process to be meaningful, Iran will have to be treated as a major player—and the United States will have to make clear that it recognizes the Islamic Republic's important regional role. The key will be American willingness to engage all relevant parties. The so-called Quartet conditions—whereby Washington insists on Israel's behalf that nonstate actors, even democratically elected ones, must accept Israel, renounce violence, and recognize all previous peace agreements before being allowed to participate or even to be engaged by the United States—make serious diplomacy impossible. At this point, there is no way that a two-state solution can be negotiated and implemented without HAMAS's agreement. Likewise, a peace settlement between Israel and Lebanon—or even Israel and Syria—is simply no longer feasible without Hizballah's acquiescence, if not its active support.

Thus, Iranian participation is critical for real diplomacy to move forward. While the Islamic Republic may not be prepared, for the foreseeable future, to formally accept Israel, it has said that it will respect decisions by its allies to reach negotiated settlements. Bringing Iran into the process and demonstrating that no agreement will be forged that aims to marginalize the Islamic Republic or its allies will maximize the chances that Tehran abides by this pledge.

Finally, once the various elements of a framework document for rapprochement have been negotiated, it should be sealed by a direct meeting between the American president and his Iranian counterparts. A direct meeting of this kind, especially if it took place in Tehran, would be the clearest possible demonstration, to American, Iranian, and international onlookers, that the United States has now accepted the Islamic Republic. As with Nixon's trip to China and Sadat's to Jerusalem, it is a form of recognition that cannot be taken back. While there will inevitably be bumps on the road as the two sides work to reorient their relationship, the recognition bestowed by a presidential visit cannot be reversed. It would undergird all future diplomacy and underscore confidence that a reconciliation will come.

As another presidential term gets under way, the United States faces no challenge more pressing than getting its Iran policy right. The reasons for rapprochement with the Islamic Republic are crystal clear.

It is time for an American president to go to Tehran.

AFTERWORD TO THE 2014 EDITION

On June 14, 2013, as voters began casting ballots in Iran's presidential election, the *Washington Post* intoned that former nuclear negotiator Hassan Rohani "will not be allowed to win." The statement reflected American pundits' near-consensus position. For months, Iran "experts" at Washington's most prominent foreign policy think tanks (e.g., Brookings' Suzanne Maloney, RAND's Alireza Nader, the Carnegie Endowment's Karim Sadjadpour, and the Atlantic Council's Barbara Slavin) had declared that the contest would be "a selection rather than an election," engineered to install Ayatollah Seyed Ali Khamenei's "anointed" candidate—in most versions, Saeed Jalili.

Of course, Rohani won, as trusted polls predicted he would—something that the institutional overseers of Washington orthodoxy never took into account. Their contrived analyses extended American elites' thirty-four-year failure to understand Iran's 1979 revolution, to take seriously the system this revolution created, and to accept the Islamic Republic as it is, rather than subjecting it to fantasies of hard or soft regime change. Distorted analyses of Iran's 2013 election flowed from the same agenda-driven assumption as mainstream commentators' equally warped assessments of its 2009 presidential race: that Iran's "regime" is fundamentally estranged from its public. Consequently, the theory goes, Iranian leaders must manipulate electoral processes to subjugate popular will—for if popular will were allowed unconstrained expression, it would threaten the Islamic Republic's foundations.

After Rohani's victory, America's foreign policy elite manufactured two explanations for it. One was that disaffection from Iran's current order had become so deep as to exceed the capacity of Khamenei and his minions to wangle Jalili's election through their usual machinations. This explanation, though, contradicted what Rohani represents and how he won.

Rohani is a significant figure in the Islamic Republic's establishment. As we document in *Going to Tehran*, his four predecessors in the presidency—Ali Khamenei, Ali Akbar Hashemi Rafsanjani, Mohammad Khatami, and Mahmoud Ahmadinejad—were all accomplished holders of the office, winning reelection and shaping both domestic and foreign policies. Rohani, too, is likely to have a consequential presidency—but he is unlikely to bring about the secular, liberal, pro-American political order Washington elites want.

While candidate Rohani emphasized "moderation," he is not a reformist. The only cleric on the ballot, Rohani belongs to the Society of Combatant Clergy, the conservative antipode to the Assembly of Combatant Clerics founded in 1988 by Mehdi Karroubi, Mohammad Khatami, and other notables in what would become Iran's reform movement. For more than twenty years, Rohani's most important patron has been former president Ali Akbar Hashemi Rafsanjani, the seminal figure for the Islamic Republic's "modern" (or "pragmatic") right. But his ties to Khamenei are also strong. After Rohani stepped down as Secretary of Iran's Supreme National Security Council in 2005, Khamenei made Rohani his personal representative on the Council. Supporting Rohani in 2013 was thus unlikely to be seen by most Iranians as a demand for radical change, especially given that an eminently plausible reformist candidate had been approved by the Guardian Council—Mohammad Reza Aref, a Stanford Ph.D. in electrical engineering who served as vice president to reformist President Khatami.

Rohani's background aside, his victory hardly constituted a

reformist takeover of the state—much less a radical challenge to the Islamic Republic. The parliament elected just one year before is dominated by principalists, and on the same day Rohani won the presidency, conservatives won 70 percent of the more than 200,000 local council seats across Iran. Even in the presidential contest, there was no reformist groundswell. Aref's résumé notwithstanding, methodologically sound polls showed his popular support never exceeded single digits; he ultimately left the race, just three days before Iranians voted.

Another explanation advanced by avatars of America's foreign policy establishment cited Rohani's victory as proof that U.S.-instigated sanctions were finally "working." In this account, sanctions are fueling popular discontent with policies—especially on the nuclear issue—that have prompted escalating international pressure. This discontent supposedly drove Iranians to elect a candidate inclined to cut concessionary deals with the West.

In fact, it was not sanctions but a functioning political system that worked to produce Rohani's election. Between May 21, when the Guardian Council approved eight presidential candidates, and June 14, Iran experienced a real political contest. Candidates advertised, held campaign events, and had broad and regular access to national media. They also participated in three nationally televised (and widely watched) debates. High-quality polls showed that these debates and the perceived quality of candidates' campaigns played a significant role in many Iranians' decisions for whom to vote. Rohani won because he did well in the debates, ran an effective campaign, and broadened his base through adroit politicking.

Rohani's debate performance helped to offset his biggest weakness: foreign policy. Between 2003 and 2005, when Rohani was chief nuclear negotiator, Tehran agreed to suspend uranium enrichment for nearly two years, but got nothing from the West in return. Criticism of Rohani's approach was a factor in Mahmoud Ahmadinejad's initial election in 2005, and it was bound to resurface in 2013 with Rohani on the ballot. During the campaign—especially in the debates—Rohani effectively addressed this potential vulnerability, arguing that his approach let Iran avoid sanctions while laying the ground for subsequent development of its nuclear infrastructure. While Rohani advocated a diplomatic solution to the nuclear issue, he also pledged to defend Iran's nuclear rights—including enrichment. His campaign video featured praise from armed forces chief of staff General Seyed Hassan Firuzabadi, bolstering Rohani's perceived credibility on security.

Forging coalitions was key to Rohani's success. After the Guardian Council declined Rafsanjani's bid to run for president yet again, Rafsanjani threw his support—including a public endorsement—behind Rohani, solidifying Rohani's center-right base. Rohani drew votes from more hard-core principlist constituencies, too; polls show that, largely because he is a cleric, his vote share was higher in small towns and villages, where people are more conservative, than in most larger cities. At the same time, Rohani's rejection of "extremism" made him acceptable to reformists. After Aref withdrew, many reformists did as we anticipated in the first edition of *Going to Tehran*: They threw their support behind a conservative (Rohani) sympathetic to parts of their agenda, with Khatami adding his endorsement to that of Rafsanjani's. While reformists were not the core of Rohani's base, they got him over the 50-percent threshold for victory.

In the week between the last debate and election day, polls showed Rohani was one of three candidates building momentum with voters (along with Mohammad Baqer Qalibaf and, to a lesser degree, Mohsen Rezae). By election day, polls showed Rohani pulling ahead; we were among the few Western analysts to take these surveys seriously, defying the Washington establishment to predict a possible Rohani victory.

One of *Going to Tehran*'s most controversial points—that there is no hard evidence Iran's 2009 presidential election was "stolen"—finds striking affirmation in the 2013 election. Just as we took high-quality polls seriously in 2013, we also took them seriously in 2009—when no methodologically sound survey ever showed Mir-Hossein Mousavi ahead of the incumbent Ahmadinejad. We called out journalists and think-tank pundits who fundamentally misrepresented the election and its aftermath, and they excoriated us in turn for believing Iranians could be reliably polled like other populations. But our focus on objective data was, and is, right.

Even though no evidence of fraud was put forward, in 2012 the Islamic Republic created an Election Commission to oversee the Interior Ministry's management of the 2013 election. The biggest difference from 2009, however, was candidates' behavior. In 2013, all candidates agreed not to make post-election statements until all votes had been counted and results officially announced. They stuck to this commitment as the Interior Ministry announced partial results coming in from across Iran. Though Rohani won by just 261,251 votes over the 50-percent threshold, his rivals immediately congratulated him, as did Khamenei. Compare that to 2009, when—while polls were still open and no votes had been counted—Mousavi claimed to have official "information" he had won "by a substantial margin," setting himself up to cry fraud and call for protests. The 2013 election showed that the Islamic Republic has moved beyond the Green movement, which was always stronger in the fantasies of Iranian expatriates, pro-Israel advocates, and Western liberals than among Iranians inside Iran.

Rohani's election underscores the strategic challenge facing Washington: To come to terms with the Islamic Republic as an enduring entity representing legitimate national interests. In this regard, Rohani's election is an opportunity. If America wants to resolve the nuclear issue with a deal grounded in the Nuclear Non-Proliferation Treaty (NPT), Rohani—who holds advanced degrees in Islamic and Western law—and his foreign minister, Javad Zarif, are ideal interlocutors. But engaging Tehran constructively requires Washington to accept the Islamic Republic as a sovereign NPT signatory, by acknowledging its right to enrich under international safeguards.

Washington, though, remains unwilling to do this—because it would mean accepting the Islamic Republic as the legitimate government of a fully sovereign state with legitimate interests. Such unwillingness reflects familiar deficiencies of American strategic culture: difficulty coming to terms with independent powers; hostility to non-liberal states, unless they subordinate their foreign policies to U.S. preferences (like Egypt under Sadat and Mubarak); and an unreflective belief that U.S.-backed rules and transnational decision-making processes apply to others, not to America. Because these attitudes are strong, a president will have to invest considerable political capital to realign U.S.-Iranian relations. Obama—notwithstanding a fifteen-minute phone conversation with Rohani on the margins of the United Nations General Assembly in September 2013—has shown no such inclination.

Obama's highly public failure to master political support for military strikes against the Assad government following the use of chemical weapons in Syria on August 21, 2013, has effectively undercut the credibility of U.S. threats to use force against Iran. If Washington does not engage in serious diplomacy with Tehran, it will ultimately be forced to surrender—publicly and humiliatingly—its hegemonic pretensions in the Middle East. Moreover, hostility toward the Islamic Republic exacerbates America's inability to deal with participatory Islamist governance elsewhere in the Middle East. Less than a month after Rohani's election, the United States supported a military coup that deposed Egypt's first democratically elected (and Islamist) government. The coup in Egypt hardly obviates the reality that, when given the chance, majorities in Middle Eastern Muslim societies choose to construct Islamist orders. Refusing to accept this reality will only accelerate the erosion of U.S. influence in the region.

The United States is not the first imperial power in decline whose foreign policy debate has become increasingly detached from reality—and history suggests that the consequences of such delusion are usually severe. Strategic recovery must start with a thoroughgoing revision of America's Iran policy. That requires a U.S. president to do what Richard Nixon did to enable the historic breakthrough with China—going to Tehran, metaphorically if not physically, and accepting a previously demonized order as a legitimate sovereign entity representing legitimate national interests. If America does not do this, it condemns itself to a future as an increasingly flailing—and failing—superpower.

Flynt Leverett
Hillary Mann Leverett
October 2013

INTRODUCTION: WILL THE UNITED STATES LOSE THE MIDDLE EAST . . . OR COME TO TERMS WITH THE ISLAMIC REPUBLIC OF IRAN?

1. On the imperial turn in America's post–Cold War Middle East strategy, see also John Mearsheimer, "Imperial by Design," *National Interest* 111 (Jan.–Feb. 2011).

2. The U.S. Defense Department's "Iraq War Logs," published in 2010 by WikiLeaks, show that, by the end of 2009, more than 100,000 Iraqi civilians had been killed in military action following America's 2003 invasion; see Simon Rogers, "WikiLeaks Iraq War Logs: Each Death Mapped," *Guardian*, Oct. 22, 2010, http://www.guardian.co.uk/world/datablog/interactive/2010/oct/23/wikileaks-iraq-deaths-map, and "The Iraq Archive: Strands of a War," *New York Times*, Oct. 22, 2010, http://www.nytimes.com/2010/10/23/world/middleeast/23intro.html?_r=1. This is in line with mainstream nongovernmental assessments; see, e.g., www.iraqbodycount.org and the Brookings Iraq Index, www.brookings.edu/iraqindex. Johns Hopkins researchers using established epidemiological techniques estimated in 2006 that more than 600,000 Iraqi civilians had been killed in the war; see Gilbert Burnham et al., "Mortality after the 2003 Invasion of Iraq: A Cross-Sectional Cluster Sample Survey," *Lancet*, Oct. 2006. The Defense Department does not regularly report on civilian deaths in Afghanistan. Mark Herold, a University of New Hampshire economist who studies civilian casualties in war, estimated in late 2011 that almost 9,000 Afghan civilians had been killed since the U.S. invasion of Afghanistan in October 2001; see "A Dossier on Civilian Victims of U.S. Aerial Bombing of Afghanistan: A Comprehensive Accounting" and

"A Day-to-Day Chronicle of Afghanistan's Guerilla and Civil War: June 2003 to Present," http://pubpages.unh.edu/~mwherold/dossier.htm.

3. Paul Kennedy, *The Rise and Fall of the Great Powers: Economic Change and Military Conflict, 1500–2000* (New York: Random House, 1987).

4. See Flynt Leverett and Hillary Mann Leverett, "The United States, Iran and the Middle East's New 'Cold War,'" *International Spectator* 45, no. 1 (March 2010), 75–76.

5. Vice President Biden's national security adviser, Antony Blinken, made these comments to the Israel Policy Forum on Feb. 27, 2012; see http://www .israelpolicyforum.org/blog/antony-j-blinken-speaks-ipf-video.

6. See, e.g., Secretary of Defense Leon Panetta's response when asked if the Arab Spring would spread to Iran: "Absolutely. . . . It's a matter of time before that kind of change and reform and revolution occurs in Iran as well." See "Leon Panetta, Secretary of Defense," *Charlie Rose*, Sept. 6, 2011, http://www .charlierose.com/view/interview/11878.

7. Louis Hartz, *The Liberal Tradition in America* (New York: Harcourt, Brace, 1955), 12, 285.

8. David Crist, *The Twilight War: The Secret History of America's Thirty-Year Conflict with Iran* (New York: Penguin, 2012), 5.

9. Amir Taheri, "A Colour Code for Iran's 'Infidels,'" *National Post*, May 19, 2006, http://www.canada.com/nationalpost/story.html?id=398274b5-9210 -43e4-ba59-fa24f4c66ad4&k=28534.

10. See Yossi Melman, "Canada's *National Post* Retracts Report That Iranian Jews Will Be Forced to Wear 'Yellow Patches,'" *Haaretz*, May 24, 2006, and "Our Mistake: Note to Readers," *National Post*, May 24, 2006, http://www .canada.com/nationalpost/news/story.html?id=6df3e493-f350-4b53-bc16 -53262b49a4f7.

11. Jonathan Schwarz, "The Amir Taheri Story," *Mother Jones*, Nov. 18, 2007, http://www.motherjones.com/mojo/2007/11/amir-taheri-story.

12. Larry Cohler-Esses, "Bunkum from Benador," *Nation*, June 14, 2006, http:// www.thenation.com/article/bunkum-benador.

Part One: The Islamic Republic as Rational Actor

PROLOGUE

1. See, e.g., Emmanuele Ottolenghi, "The High Price of Deterring Iran," *Wall Street Journal*, May 18, 2009, http://online.wsj.com/article/SB124259185 503527891.html, and Gerald Steinberg, *Deterrence Instability: Hizballah's Fuse to Iran's Bomb*, Jerusalem Center for Public Affairs, April 1, 2005.

2. Peter Hirshberg, "Netanyahu: It's 1938 and Iran Is Germany; Ahmadinejad Is Preparing Another Holocaust," *Haaretz*, Nov. 11, 2006; "Israel: Iran Is Like 'Nazi Germany,'" *Al Jazeera English*, April 22, 2009, http://www.she

bacss.com/mediac/news.php?id=19748; Walter Russell Mead, "Goo-Goo Genocidaires: The Blood Is Dripping from Their Hands," *American Interest*, June 8, 2010, http://blogs.the-american-interest.com/wrm/2010/06/08/goo-goo-genocidaires-the-blood-is-dripping-from-their-hands/; Bret Stephens, "Iran Cannot Be Contained," *Commentary*, July–August 2010; and Karim Sadjadpour, "The Sources of Soviet Iranian Conduct," *Foreign Policy*, Nov. 2010.

3. In Shi'a theology, the Twelfth Imam, Muhammad al-Mahdi, was placed by God into a state of "occultation," rendering him invisible so as to protect him from enemies, in AD 873, when he was four years old. His return, accompanied by Jesus, will prepare mankind for judgment day and bring justice and peace to the world.

4. Bernard Lewis, "August 22," *Wall Street Journal*, Aug. 8, 2006. Michael Ledeen, a longtime neoconservative foreign policy hand who has focused much of his energy since 1979 on Iran, has offered similar predictions; see, e.g., his "Into the Quagmire: Important Days Ahead for Iran," *National Review Online*, Oct. 13, 2003, http://old.nationalreview.com/ledeen/ledeen200310140838.asp.

5. *Diplomat's Dictionary*, 2nd ed. (Washington, D.C.: United States Institute of Peace, 2010), 115.

6. Robert Pape and James Feldman, *Cutting the Fuse: The Explosion of Global Suicide Terrorism and How to Stop It* (Chicago: University of Chicago Press, 2010), 32.

7. Neoconservative commentator Kenneth Timmerman argued that Osama bin Laden had received sanctuary in the Islamic Republic; see "Kenneth Timmerman Reports: Bin Ladin in Iran," *The Michael Savage Show*, May 13, 2009, and "Iran Is Hiding Bin Ladin," *The Michael Savage Show*, Nov. 1, 2009. The allegation was elaborated in the film *Feathered Cocaine*; see Ed Barnes, "Usama bin Laden Is Living Comfortably in Iran, Documentary Asserts," Fox News, May 3, 2010, http://www.foxnews.com/world/2010/05/03/usama-bin-laden-living-comfortably-iran-documentary-asserts/.

8. "Transcript: George Stephanopoulos Interviews Iranian President Mahmoud Ahmadinejad," ABC News, May 5, 2010, http://abcnews.go.com/GMA/transcript-george-stephanopoulos-interviews-iranian-president-mahmoud-ahmadinejad/story?id=10558442.

9. See *Letters from Abottabbad: Bin Ladin Sidelined?* (West Point: Combating Terrorism Center at West Point, 2012).

10. *Constitution of the Islamic Republic of Iran*, trans. Hamid Algar (Berkeley: Mizan Press, 1980), article 154.

11. *Kayhan Hava'i*, April 4, 1993, as cited in Henner Fürtig, *Iran's Rivalry with Saudi Arabia between the Gulf Wars* (Reading, U.K.: Ithaca Press, 2002), 33–34.

12. See "Dan Meridor: We Misquoted Ahmadinejad," *Al Jazeera English*, April 16, 2012, http://www.aljazeera.com/programmes/talktojazeera/2012/04/2012413151613293582.html.

13. Initially presented in Nazila Fathi, "Wipe Israel 'Off the Map,' Iranian Says," *New York Times*, Oct. 26, 2005.

14. We have adjusted the word order slightly in our translation. To translate strictly word for word: *een rezhim-e ishghalgar-e qods* ("this regime occupying Jerusalem") *bayad* ("must") *az safheh-ye ruzgar* ("from the pages of time") *mahv shavad* ("disappear"). See also Juan Cole, "Hitchens Hacker and Hitchens," *Informed Comment*, May 3, 2006, http://www.juancole.com/2006/05/hitchens-hacker-and-hitchens.html; Jonathan Steele, "Lost in Translation," *Guardian*, June 14, 2006, http://www.guardian.co.uk/commentisfree/2006/jun/14/post155; Arash Norouzi, "'Wiped off the Map'—the Rumor of the Century," Antiwar.com, May 26, 2007, http://original.antiwar.com/arash-norouzi/2007/05/26/wiped-off-the-map-the-rumor-of-the-century/; and Glenn Kessler, "Did Ahmadinejad Really Say Israel Should Be 'Wiped Off the Map'?," *Washington Post*, Oct. 5, 2011, http://www.washingtonpost.com/blogs/fact-checker/post/did-ahmadinejad-really-say-israel-should-be-wiped-off-the-map/2011/10/04/gIQABJIKML_blog.html. For an inhouse (and unpersuasive) defense of the original *New York Times* article, see Ethan Bronner, "Just How Far Did They Go, Those Words against Israel?," *New York Times*, June 11, 2006.

15. For a well-sourced review, see Nima Shirazi, "Some Notes on Ahmadinejad's 'Insult to Humanity' Comment," *Wide Asleep in America*, Aug. 18, 2012, http://www.wideasleepinamerica.com/2012/08/some-notes-on-ahmadinejads-insult-to.html.

16. On Israel's covert war against Iran, see, e.g., Dan Raviv and Yossi Melman, *Spies against Armageddon: Inside Israel's Secret Wars* (Sea Cliff: Levant, 2012).

17. Greg Myre, "Soft-Spoken but Not Afraid to Voice Opinions," *New York Times*, March 11, 2003.

18. Kayhan Barzegar, "Iran's Foreign Policy after Saddam," *Washington Quarterly* 33, no. 1 (Jan. 2010), 174.

1: A REVOLUTIONARY STATE IN A DANGEROUS WORLD

1. United Nations Special Commission (UNSCOM), *Report to the Security Council*, Jan. 25, 1999, annex B.

2. On Iranian estimates, see Moosa Zargar et al., "Iranian Casualties during the Eight Years of Iraq-Iran Conflict" (letter to the editor), *Revista de Saúde Pública* 41, no. 6 (Aug. 2007). Western estimates tend to be higher; see H. W. Beuttel, "Iranian Casualties in the Iran-Iraq War: A Reappraisal," *International TNDM Newsletter*, Dec. 1997.

3. Iran's government estimated that the war cost the country $440 billion in direct losses and $490 billion in indirect losses—more than the total revenue it earned from oil exports during the twentieth century. See Kamran Mofid, *The Economic Consequences of the Gulf War* (London: Routledge, 1990).

4. "Address by Hojjat-ul-Islam Seyed Ali Khamenei, President of the Islamic Republic of Iran," 42nd General Assembly, Provisional Verbatim Record of the 6th Session, Sept. 22, 1987 (New York: United Nations General Assembly, A/42/PV.6, Sept. 24, 1987); for video, see http://www.youtube.com/watch ?v=hn2djK9Fxno. We have modified the translation slightly.

5. Different writers have used different terminology. E. H. Carr focused on "the fundamental divergence of interest between nations desirous of maintaining the *status quo* and nations desirous of changing it" in *The Twenty Years' Crisis, 1919–1939: An Introduction to the Study of International Relations* (London: Macmillan, 1939). Hans Morgenthau juxtaposed "status quo" states and "imperialist" states in his *Politics among Nations: The Struggle for Power and Peace*, 5th ed. (New York: Knopf, 1978). Henry Kissinger introduced the term "revolutionary states" in his *A World Restored: Metternich, Castlereagh, and the Problems of Peace, 1812–1822* (Boston: Houghton Mifflin, 1957).

6. Randall Schweller, "Neorealism's Status-Quo Bias: What Security Dilemma?," *Security Studies* 5, no. 3 (Spring 1996).

7. Michael Hunt, *Ideology and U.S. Foreign Policy* (New Haven: Yale University Press, 1987), 92–124.

8. Stephen Walt, *Revolution and War* (Ithaca: Cornell University Press, 1996), 8–11.

9. The International Institute for Strategic Studies estimates military spending by the United States at nearly $739 billion, by Saudi Arabia at $46 billion, by Israel at over $18 billion, and by Iran at just under $12 billion; *The Military Balance 2012* (London: Routledge, 2012).

10. Walt, *Revolution and War*, 19–22, 32–37.

11. For an Iranian scholar's assessment, see Mahmood Sariolghalam, "Decision-Making Inputs: Iraq's Premises before the War," in *Iranian Perspectives on the Iran-Iraq War*, ed. Farhang Rajaee (Gainesville: University Press of Florida, 1997).

12. Seyed Mohammad Marandi, "The Islamic Republic of Iran, the United States, and the Balance of Power in the Middle East," *Race for Iran*, Jan. 14, 2011, http://www.raceforiran.com/the-islamic-republic-of-iran-the-united -states-and-the-balance-of-power-in-the-middle-east.

13. Thomas Schelling, *The Strategy of Conflict* (Cambridge: Harvard University Press, 1960).

14. Alastair Iain Johnston, "Thinking about Strategic Culture," *International Security* 19, no. 4 (Spring 1995).

15. Shireen Hunter, *Iran and the World: Continuity in a Revolutionary Decade* (Bloomington: Indiana University Press, 1990), 21–28.

16. Multiple sources estimate Iran's proven reserves of conventional crude oil at 137 billion barrels—the world's third largest, after Saudi Arabia and Venezuela; see, e.g., the *BP Statistical Review of World Energy, June 2011*, http://

www.bp.com/liveassets/bp_internet/globalbp/globalbp_uk_english/reports
_and_publications/statistical_energy_review_2011/STAGING/local_assets
/pdf/oil_section_2011.pdf. (Iraq claims that its reserves are now larger than
Iran's, but the claim has not been widely accepted. The *Oil and Gas Journal*
estimates Canada's proven oil reserves at 175 billion barrels; see "Petroleum
Insights: World's Top 23 Oil Reserves Holders—OGJ," Jan. 1, 2012, http://
petroleuminsights.blogspot.com/2012/01/worlds-top-23-proven-oil
-reserves.html. This, however, is mostly oil that can potentially be
extracted from tar sands, not conventional crude.) Multiple sources estimate Iran's proven reserves of natural gas at 1,046 trillion cubic feet—the
world's second largest, after Russia; see http://www.bp.com/liveassets/bp_
internet/globalbp/globalbp_uk_english/reports_and_publications/statistical
_energy_review_2011/STAGING/local_assets/pdf/natural_gas_section
_2011.pdf.

17. The great game is usually described as running from the Russo-Persian
Treaty of Golestan in 1813—which formally ceded Azerbaijan, Dagestan,
and eastern Georgia from Iran to Russia—to the Anglo-Russian Conven-
tion of 1907. See Nikki Keddie, *Modern Iran: Roots and Results of Revolution*
(New Haven: Yale University Press, 2003), 34–72, and Michael Axworthy,
Empire of the Mind (New York: Basic, 2008), 177–87, 192–211.

18. Keddie, *Modern Iran*, 73–105; Axworthy, *Empire of the Mind*, 211–30; and
Gholam Reza Afkhami, *The Life and Times of the Shah* (Berkeley: University
of California Press, 2009), 3–23, 61–80.

19. Stephen Kinzer, *All the Shah's Men: An American Coup and the Roots of
Middle East Terror* (Hoboken: Wiley, 2008), and James Bill, *The Eagle and
the Lion: The Tragedy of American-Iranian Relations* (New Haven: Yale University Press, 1989), 51–97.

20. *Islam and Revolution: Writings and Declarations of Imam Khomeini*, trans.
and annot. Hamid Algar (North Haledon: Mizan Press, 1981), 172.

21. "The Granting of Capitulatory Rights to the U.S.," Oct. 27, 1964, in *Islam
and Revolution*, 181–88. On U.S.-Iranian relations from the 1953 coup
through the 1960s, see Bill, *The Eagle and the Lion*, 98–182.

22. *Constitution of the Islamic Republic of Iran*, article 9.

23. Stephen Walt, *The Origins of Alliances* (Ithaca: Cornell University Press,
1987), 17–33.

24. See, e.g., Shahram Chubin, "Iran's Strategic Predicament," *Middle East
Journal* 54, no. 1 (Winter 2000), 13; Anoush Ehteshami, "Iran's International
Posture after the Fall of Baghdad," *Middle East Journal* 58, no. 2 (Spring
2004), 185; and Shireen Hunter, *Iran's Foreign Policy in the Post-Soviet Era:
Resisting the New International Order* (Santa Barbara: Praeger, 2010), 12–16,
76–77, 209–11.

25. "Iran: Assessing Geopolitical Dynamics and U.S. Policy Options," Testimony before the Committee on Armed Services, U.S. House of Represen-

tatives, June 8, 2006, and "The Iran Puzzle," *American Prospect*, May 22, 2007.

26. This goal is presented in the twenty-year *Perspective* document, prepared by the Expediency Council in the early 2000s, approved by the supreme leader in 2005 and published the following year; see *Cheshmandaz-e Jomhouri Eslami Iran dar Ofoq-e 1401* (Tehran: Jamal-al-Haq, 2006).

27. For discussion by a scholar who served as an Iranian diplomat during the 1970s, see Hunter, *Iran and the World*, 29–35. That states bandwagon not only as "appeasement" but also to maximize certain types of strategic gains is treated in Randall Schweller, "Bandwagoning for Profit: Bringing the Revisionist State Back In," *International Security* 19, no. 1 (Summer 1994).

28. See also Heinz Halm, *Shi'ism*, 2nd ed. (New York: Columbia University Press, 2004), 152, fn. 245.

29. Khomeini, *Islamic Government: Governance of the Jurist*, trans. Hamid Algar (Tehran: Institute for the Compilation and Publication of Imam Khomeini's Works, n.d.), Kindle ed., introduction.

30. The phrase was coined in Alastair Crooke, *Resistance: The Essence of the Islamist Revolution* (London: Pluto, 2009), 86–109.

31. Hamid Algar, *Roots of the Islamic Revolution in Iran* (Oneonta: Islamic Publications International, 2001), 78.

32. Khomeini delivered a series of lectures on Islam and politics in Najaf in early 1970, published the following year as *Hukumat-e Eslami* ("Islamic government"); after the revolution, they were republished as *Velayat-e Faqih* ("rule of the religious jurist"). The best English translation is *Islamic Government*; the quotations cited are from the introduction.

33. Khomeini, *Islamic Government*, introduction.

34. "Address by Hojjat-ul-Islam Seyed Ali Khamenei, President of the Islamic Republic of Iran."

35. See, e.g., Ahmadinejad's address to the UN General Assembly on Sept. 23, 2009; the quotes are from a translation provided by the Permanent Mission of the Islamic Republic of Iran to the United Nations.

36. http://www.youtube.com/watch?v=brEqnxf3OOI&feature=related. The passage cited was translated by the authors.

37. "Address by Hojjat-ul-Islam Seyed Ali Khamenei, President of the Islamic Republic of Iran."

38. Ibid.

39. On the Revolutionary Guards and the Basij, see Wilfried Buchta, *Who Rules Iran? The Structure of Power in the Islamic Republic* (Washington, D.C.: Washington Institute for Near East Policy and the Konrad Adenauer Stiftung, 2000), 65–72; Buchta, "Iran's Security Sector: An Overview," Conference Paper (Geneva Centre for the Democratic Control of Armed Forces, July 2004); and Frederic Wehrey et al., *The Rise of the Pasdaran: Assessing the Domestic Roles of Iran's Islamic Revolutionary Guards Corps* (Santa Monica: Rand, 2009).

40. Beuttel, "Iranian Casualties in the Iran-Iraq War."

41. Elaine Sciolino, *The Outlaw State: Saddam Hussein's Quest for Power and the Gulf Crisis* (New York: Wiley, 1991), 113.

42. Javed Ali, "Chemical Weapons and the Iran-Iraq War: A Case Study in Noncompliance," *Nonproliferation Review* 8, no. 1 (Spring 2001), 46.

43. For a participant's account, see Gustav Anderson's foreword in Shahriar Khateri and Ahmad Janati Moheb, eds., *Iraq's Use of Chemical Weapons against Iran: UN Documents* (Tehran: Foundation of Preservation of Works and Dissemination of the Values of Holy Defense, 2007).

44. "Address by Hojjat-ul-Islam Seyed Ali Khamenei, President of the Islamic Republic of Iran." See also Bahran Mostaghami and Masour Taromsari, "Double Standard: The Security Council and the Two Wars," in *Iranian Perspectives on the Iran-Iraq War.*

45. "Address by Hojjat-ul-Islam Seyed Ali Khamenei, President of the Islamic Republic of Iran." We have modified the translation slightly.

46. Richard Engel and Robert Windrem, "Israel Teams with Terror Group to Kill Iran's Nuclear Scientists, U.S. Officials Tell NBC News," NBC News, Feb. 9, 2012, http://rockcenter.msnbc.msn.com/_news/2012/02/09/10354553 -israel-teams-with-terror-group-to-kill-irans-nuclear-scientists-us-officials -tell-nbc-news?lite.

47. Ibid. U.S. intelligence officials say that Israel is funding and otherwise help- ing the MEK to carry out the assassinations. Dan Raviv and Yossi Melman report that Israeli operatives are perpetrating the attacks, with support from the MEK; see their *Spies against Armageddon.*

48. Seymour Hersh, "Our Men in Iran?," *New Yorker*, April 6, 2012.

49. "Address by Hojjat-ul-Islam Seyed Ali Khamenei, President of the Islamic Republic of Iran." We have modified the translation slightly.

50. Iran shares land borders with seven states (Pakistan, Afghanistan, Turkmeni- stan, Azerbaijan, Armenia, Turkey, and Iraq), maritime borders with six (Kuwait, Qatar, Bahrain, the United Arab Emirates, Saudi Arabia, and Oman), and littoral borders across the Caspian Sea with Russia and Kazakhstan.

51. Barzegar, "Iran's Foreign Policy after Saddam," 180.

52. As reflected in statements by Iranian officials, military writings, and other sources; see Steven Ward, "The Continuing Evolution of Iran's Military Doctrine," *Middle East Journal* 59, no. 4 (Autumn 2005).

53. Gary Sick, *All Fall Down: America's Tragic Encounter with Iran* (New York: Random House, 1986), 3–25, and Bill, *The Eagle and the Lion*, 183–215.

54. "The Iranian Revolution 25 Years Later: An Oral History with Henry Precht, Then State Department Desk Officer," *Middle East Journal* 58, no. 1 (Winter 2004), 17, 26.

55. Bruce Riedel, in *Iran and the West* (London: BBC, 2009), part 1, *The Man Who Changed the World*, http://www.youtube.com/watch?v=ZOaGmK8aTHQ. Riedel served as the CIA's Iran desk officer during the revolution.

56. "The Iranian Revolution 25 Years Later," 17, 26.

57. John Limbert, *Negotiating with the Islamic Republic of Iran: Raising the Chances for Success—Fifteen Points to Remember,* Special Report 199 (Washington, D.C.: United States Institute of Peace, Jan. 2008), 10.

58. Ibid., 13.

59. http://www.parstimes.com/history/algiers_accords.pdf.

60. Bruce Riedel, interview transcript for *Iran and the West,* archived at Liddel Hart Center for Military Archives, King's College, London; Riedel in *The Man Who Changed the World*; Walter Mondale, interview transcript for *Iran and the West,* archived at Liddel Hart Center for Military Archives, King's College, London.

61. See Sciolino, *The Outlaw State*; Alan Friedman, *Spider's Web: The Secret History of How the White House Illegally Armed Iraq* (New York: Bantam, 1993), 3–121; Bruce Jentleson, *With Friends Like These: Reagan, Bush and Saddam, 1982–1990* (New York: Norton, 1994); Arshin Adib-Moghaddam, *Iran in World Politics: The Question of the Islamic Republic* (New York: Columbia University Press), 83–122; and Barry Lando, *Web of Deceit: The History of Western Complicity in Iraq, from Churchill to Kennedy to George W. Bush* (New York: Other, 2007), ch. 3. For U.S. government documents showing the extent of Washington's backing for Saddam's war, see *Iraqgate: Saddam Hussein, U.S. Policy, and the Prelude to the Persian Gulf War, 1980–1994* (Washington, D.C.: National Security Archive, 1995).

62. *Iran and the West,* part 2, *Pariah State,* http://www.youtube.com/watch?v=UfuzlnB0YB8&feature=relmfu.

63. On U.S.-Iranian conflict in the Persian Gulf during the 1980s, see Crist, *The Twilight Wars,* 206–371; On Rumsfeld's meeting with Tariq Aziz, see Howard Teicher, interview transcript for *Iran and the West,* archived at Liddel Hart Center for Military Archives, King's College, London.

64. Commander David Carlson, "The *Vincennes* Incident" (letter to the editor), U.S. Naval Institute *Proceedings* 115, no. 9 (Sept. 1989).

65. See, e.g., "Public War, Secret War," *Nightline,* July 1, 1992, and John Barry, "Sea of Lies," *Newsweek,* July 13, 1992. Even Crist—who inexplicably defends Rogers as having "made the correct decision to fire"—is compelled to judge Washington's response to the shooting down of Iran Air 655 as deliberately dishonest; see *The Twilight War,* 368–69. In 1996, to settle claims that Iran had brought in the International Court of Justice, the U.S. government agreed to pay $131.8 million, but only ex gratia—meaning that Washington accepted no responsibility or liability.

66. Formally, the Islamic Republic accepted the terms of United Nations Security Council Resolution 598, which had been adopted in July 1987.

67. Crist, *The Twilight War,* 465. In 2012, Republican Congressman Dana Rohrabacher urged the Obama administration to support independence for Iranian Azeris; see "Rep. Rohrabacher Urges Secretary Clinton to Back Freedom

from Iran for Azeris" (press release), July 26, 2012, http://rohrabacher.house
.gov/news/documentsingle.aspx?DocumentID=304840. For discussion of
the 2010 Nuclear Posture Review, see Flynt Leverett and Hillary Mann Leverett, "Is Iran Now a Nuclear Target for the United States?," *Race for Iran*,
April 5, 2010, http://www.raceforiran.com/is-iran-now-a-nuclear-target-for
-the-united-states.

68. "Imam's Message in Support of Palestine," Nov. 10, 1972, *Sahifa-ye Nur*
(Tehran: Markaz-e Madarek-e Farhangi-ye Enqelab-e Eslami, 1983), vol. 1, 193.

69. "Imam's Message to the Muslim Governments," Nov. 7, 1973, *Sahifa-ye Nur*,
vol. 1, 201.

70. On Israel's dealings with Tehran during the war, see Trita Parsi, *Treacherous
Alliance: The Secret Dealings of Israel, Iran, and the United States* (New
Haven: Yale University Press, 2007), 97–126. Iranian officials take issue with
elements of Parsi's account, particularly regarding direct dealings between
the Islamic Republic and Israel.

71. "Imam's Message on the Anniversary of the 15 Khordad Uprising," June 5,
1983, *Sahifa-ye Nur*, vol. 18, 12.

72. "Imam's Message," Sept. 6, 1983, *Sahifa-ye Nur*, vol. 19, 101.

73. Efraim Inbar and Shmuel Sandler, "Israel's Deterrence Strategy Revisited,"
Security Studies 3, no. 2 (Winter 1993–94).

74. Parsi, *Treacherous Alliance*, 139–71.

75. David Sanger, "Obama Order Sped Up Wave of Cyberattacks against Iran,"
New York Times, June 1, 2012, http://www.nytimes.com/2012/06/01/world
/middleeast/obama-ordered-wave-of-cyberattacks-against-iran.html?_r=2
&pagewanted=all.

76. Engel and Windrem, "Israel Teams with Terror Group to Kill Iran's Nuclear
Scientists, U.S. Officials Tell NBC News," and Yaakov Lappin, "Book: Israeli
Agents Killed Iranian Scientists," *Jerusalem Post*, July 11, 2012, http://www
.jpost.com/IranianThreat/News/Article.aspx?id=277016.

77. Parsi, *Treacherous Alliance*, 172–89.

78. Gilles Kepel, *Jihad: The Trail of Political Islam*, trans. Anthony Roberts
(Cambridge: Harvard University Press, 2002), 137.

79. Afghan Pashtuns are overwhelmingly Sunni, with extensive cultural, familial, and tribal connections to Pakistani Pashtuns. Afghanistan's other major
ethnic and sectarian groups—Tajiks, Uzbeks, and Hazara—have ethnic, linguistic, and/or religious ties to Iran (for Uzbeks, to Turkey, too.)

80. See Steve Coll, *Ghost Wars: The Secret History of the CIA, Afghanistan, and
Bin Laden, from the Soviet Invasion to September 10, 2001* (New York: Penguin, 2004), 216.

81. The word, taken into Pashto and Farsi from Arabic, means "students," evoking the movement's origins among madrassa students.

82. See Flynt Leverett and Hillary Mann Leverett, "Obama: Stop Covert Activities against Iran and Dump Bush's Policy of Playing the Sunni-Shi'a 'Card,'"

Race for Iran, Oct. 20, 2009, http://www.raceforiran.com/obama-stop-covert
-activities-against-iran-and-dump-bushs-policy-of-playing-the-sunni-shia
-%E2%80%9Ccard%E2%80%9D, and "Is the Obama Administration Supporting Violent 'Regime Change' in Iran?," *Race for Iran*, March 4, 2010,
http://www.raceforiran.com/is-the-obama-administration-supporting
-violent-%e2%80%9cregime-change%e2%80%9d-in-iran.
83. These are the goals identified in the Islamic Republic's military regulations,
codified in 1992; see *Iran: Complete Regulations of the Islamic Republic of
Iran Armed Forces*, Near East and South Asia Supplement, FBIS-NES-94
-208-S, U.S. Foreign Broadcast Information Service, Oct. 27, 1994.

2: RATIONALITY, REALISM, AND IRANIAN GRAND STRATEGY

1. Mohsen Aminzadeh, interview transcript for *Iran and the West*, archived at
Liddel Hart Center for Military Archives, King's College, London. We have
modified the translation slightly.
2. "OSC: Khamenei's Speech Replying to Obama," *Informed Comment*, March
23, 2009, http://www.juancole.com/2009/03/osc-khameneis-speech-replying-
to-obama.html and http://video.afghanmania.com/video/t_oAHcsYqIs.
3. In Farsi, *majma'-e tashkhis-e maslahat-e nezam*.
4. Seyed Mohammad Marandi, "Ayatollah Khamenei and a Principled Foreign
Policy," paper presented at a conference entitled "Renovation and Intellectual Ijtihad in Imam Khamenei," Beirut, June 6–7, 2011.
5. See Paul Kennedy, "Grand Strategy in War and Peace: Toward a Broader
Definition," *Grand Strategy in War and Peace*, ed. Paul Kennedy (New
Haven: Yale University Press, 1991), 4–6, and Geoffrey Parker, *The Grand
Strategy of Philip II* (New Haven: Yale University Press, 2000), 1.
6. International relations scholars distinguish between "internal balancing"
(mobilizing additional defensive capabilities) and "external balancing"
(forming alliances); see John Mearsheimer, *The Tragedy of Great Power Politics* (New York: Norton), 156–57.
7. In its 2012 "Annual Report on Military Power of Iran," the Defense Department
holds that "Iran's security strategy remains focused on deterring an attack,"
with a military doctrine "designed to slow an invasion; target its adversaries'
economic, political, and military interests; and force a diplomatic solution to
hostilities while avoiding any concessions that challenge its core interests."
8. Joseph Nye, *Bound to Lead: The Future of American Power* (New York:
Basic, 1990), 31.
9. The consolidation of strategic consensus after the Iran-Iraq War has been
described to us by multiple Iranian interlocutors; also see Houchang
Hassan-Yari, "Iranian Foreign Policy in the Postwar Era," in *Iranian
Perspectives on the Iran-Iraq War*, and Abbas Maleki, "Iran's Regional For-
eign/Energy Policy," *Politika* (2007).

10. The Supreme National Security Council (*shura-ye ali-ye amniyat-e melli,* literally "high council for national security" but routinely translated as Supreme National Security Council) is formally chaired by the president. It includes the Majles speaker, the head of the judiciary, two representatives of the supreme leader, the ministers of foreign affairs, interior, and intelligence, the commanders of the Revolutionary Guards and the regular military, and the head of the Planning and Budget Organization. See Buchta, *Who Rules Iran?,* 23–24.

11. See also Barzegar, "Iran's Foreign Policy Strategy after Saddam."

12. On Shi'a populations, see Central Intelligence Agency, *World Factbook,* https://www.cia.gov/library/publications/the-world-factbook/; *Mapping the Global Muslim Population: A Report on the Size and Distribution of the World's Muslim Population* (Washington, D.C.: Pew Forum on Religion and Public Life, 2009); and Ahlul Bayt World Assembly, www.ahl-ul-bayt.com.

13. *The Pike Report* (Nottingham, U.K.: Spokesman, 1977), 215–17.

14. Ties to Shi'a Islamist and Kurdish groups were reinforced by geography; Iran's long border with Iraq connects with Kurdish areas in the north and with Shi'a-majority provinces in the south.

15. "Iran-U.S. Relations: Referendum" (interview with Ali Akbar Hashemi Rafsanjani), *Discourse: An Iranian Quarterly* 4, nos. 3–4 (Winter–Spring 2003), 292.

16. E.g., Crist, *The Twilight War,* 467.

17. Tehran's enforcement of a cease-fire among Shi'a militias from 2007 contributed at least as much to reducing violence as the U.S. "surge." Even Ray Takeyh acknowledges that "contrary to Washington's claims, the clerical state has always seen its fortunes [in Iraq] as best served by elections and plebiscites"; see *Guardians of the Revolution: Iran and the World in the Age of the Ayatollahs* (New York: Oxford University Press), 253. For discussion by an Iranian analyst, see Kayhan Barzegar, "Iran's Foreign Policy toward Iraq and Syria," *Turkish Policy Quarterly* 6, no. 2 (Summer 2007), and "Iran's Foreign Policy in Post-Invasion Iraq," *Middle East Policy* 15, no. 4 (Winter 2008).

18. Jason Burke, "Are the Shias on the Brink of Taking Over the Middle East?" *Guardian,* July 22, 2006.

19. For an Iranian perspective on Iran's use of Shi'a proxies against American military and intelligence assets in Lebanon during the 1980s, see Mohsen Rafiqdoost (one of the Revolutionary Guards' founders), interview transcript for *Iran and the West,* archived at Liddel Hart Center for Military Archives, King's College, London; for an American perspective, see Crist, *The Twilight War,* 108–57.

20. Pape and Feldman, *Cutting the Fuse,* 28.

21. Crooke, *Resistance,* 185.

22. See Flynt Leverett and Hillary Mann Leverett, "Iran's 'Soft Power' Increasingly Checks U.S. Hard Power," *Race for Iran,* Oct. 13, 2010, http://www

.raceforiran.com/irans-%E2%80%9Csoft-power%E2%80%9D-increasingly -checks-u-s-power. The quote is from Nicholas Blanford, "Iran's Ahmadine- jad Receives Rapturous Welcome in Lebanon," *Christian Science Monitor*, Oct. 13, 2010.

23. E.g., during Tajikistan's civil war in the early 1990s, Tehran recognized that helping an Islamist insurgency would put it at odds with Moscow and other regional governments; so Iran withheld support and helped mediate nego- tiations among the warring parties. Likewise, Tehran adopted a relatively "pro-Russian" posture—our Iranian contacts describe it as "neutral"— vis-à-vis the conflict in Chechnya.

24. For a discussion from an Iranian perspective, see Kayhan Barzegar, "Region- alism in Iran's Foreign Policy," *Iran Review*, Feb. 8, 2010.

25. Associated Press, "World," Jan. 1, 2000 and "Supreme Leader: Iran Will Always Support Palestinian Nation, Resistance," *Al Manar*, Feb. 12, 2012, http://www1 .almanar.com.lb/english/adetails.php?eid=45409&frid=23&seccatid=32& cid=23&fromval=1.

26. "HAMAS Official in Tehran Praises Iran's 'Limitless Support,' " *Daily Star*, March 16, 2012, http://www.dailystar.com.lb/News/Middle-East/2012/Mar -16/166822-hamas-official-in-tehran-praises-irans-limitless-support.ashx #axzz1veM6iRR8; Franklin Lamb, "Will Islamic Republic Support the 'Sacred Palestinian Resistance' in Lebanon?," *Al Manar*, Feb. 18, 2012, http:// www1.almanar.com.lb/english/adetails.php?fromval=1&cid=41&frid=41& eid=45969; and "Supreme Leader: Iran Will Always Support Palestinian Nation, Resistance."

27. For discussion, see Milani, "Iran's Policy toward Afghanistan," 239–46, and Barnett Rubin, *The U.S. and Iran in Afghanistan: Policy Gone Awry*, Audit of the Conventional Wisdom (Center for International Studies, MIT, Oct. 2008), 2.

28. The fact that U.S. and Iranian officials held talks and cooperated in 2001 and 2002 has been publicly displayed on the State Department's Web site since 2009; see Bureau of Near Eastern Affairs, "Background Note: Iran," Department of State, http://www.state.gov/r/pa/ei/bgn/5314.htm. Hillary Mann Leverett's participation in these meetings is also well documented in the public record. See *Showdown with Iran*, PBS *Frontline* (Oct. 2007), http://www.pbs.org/wgbh/pages/frontline/showdown/; *The Pariah State*; and Hillary Mann Leverett, "U.S. Diplomacy with Iran: The Limits of Tacti- cal Engagement," Testimony to the Subcommittee on National Security and Foreign Affairs, U.S. House Committee on Government Oversight and Reform, Nov. 7, 2007, https://www.hsdl.org/homesec/docs/testimony/nps37 -111907-03.pdf&code=85ec99835f6130c26b6dlf290bdab367.

29. This cooperation has been acknowledged by, among others, Richard Armi- tage (former U.S. deputy secretary of state) in *Pariah State* and in Crist, *The Twilight War*, 427–36.

30. For additional discussion by another former U.S. diplomat engaged with postconflict stabilization in Afghanistan, see James Dobbins, *After the Taliban: Nation-Building in Afghanistan* (Washington, D.C.: Potomac, 2008).

31. Pape and Feldman, *Cutting the Fuse*, 112–37.

32. Much of Iran's aid, investment flows, and trade ties appears to focus on the western (Herat) and northern (Mazar-e-Sharif) parts of Afghanistan— precisely the areas Tehran would want as a buffer against the Taliban and its backers under conditions of renewed civil war.

33. Barzegar, "Iran's Foreign Policy after Saddam," 183.

34. On Iran's ballistic missile program, see Mark Fitzpatrick, ed., *Iran's Ballistic Missile Capabilities: A Net Assessment* (London: International Institute for Strategic Studies, 2010).

35. For a range of views, see Caitlin Talmadge, "Closing Time: Assessing the Iranian Threat to the Strait of Hormuz," *International Security* 33, no. 1 (Summer 2008); *Iran's Naval Forces: From Guerilla Warfare to a Modern Naval Strategy* (Suitland: Office of Naval Intelligence, 2009); Joshua Shifrinson and Miranda Priebe, "A Crude Threat: The Limits of an Iranian Missile Campaign against Saudi Arabian Oil," *International Security* 36, no. 1 (Summer 2011); and Jonathan Schroden, *A Strait Comparison: Lessons Learned from the 1915 Dardanelles Campaign in the Context of a Strait of Hormuz Closure Threat* (Washington, D.C.: Center for Naval Analysis, Sept. 2011).

36. Julian Borger, "War Games Were Fixed to Assure Victory, Charges General," *Guardian*, Aug. 20, 2002, and Scott Peterson, "How Iran Could Beat Up on America's Superior Military," *Christian Science Monitor*, Jan. 26, 2012.

37. *Iran's Ballistic Missile Capabilities*, 128. During its entry into the CWC, Iran declared one CW production facility, which inspectors certify as having been disabled. On U.S. intelligence assessments on Iran's CW capabilities, see Nuclear Threat Initiative, *Iran Profile*, http://nti.org/e_research/profiles/Iran/Chemical/index.html.

38. Report of the NSSM 219 Working Group, "Nuclear Cooperation Agreement with Iran," April 1975, http//www.gwu.edu/~nsarchiv/nukevault/ebb268/doe05a.pdf.

39. Dafna Linzer, "Past Arguments Don't Square with Current Iran Policy," *Washington Post*, March 27, 2005.

40. Seyed Hossein Mousavian, "Iran's Nuclear Diplomacy: Current Options and a Road Map for the Future," public lecture, Princeton University, Feb. 24, 2011.

41. See Nuclear Threat Initiative, *Iran Nuclear Chronology*, http://www.nti.org/media/pdfs/iran_nuclear.pdf?_=1316542527. Iran's postrevolutionary government also wanted to continue developing a nuclear power plant under construction at Bushehr. However, the German firm that was building the plant withdrew under American pressure and the facility was badly dam-

aged by air strikes during the Iran-Iraq War. In 1995, Russia's state-owned nuclear industry contracted to rebuild the plant, which started operating, under full safeguards, in 2010.

42. The quote is from an Oct. 2009 cable by the U.S. mission to the IAEA, published in 2010 by WikiLeaks; see Flynt Leverett and Hillary Mann Leverett, "Pulling the IAEA into the 'Attack Iran' Debate Will Backfire," *Race for Iran*, Nov. 8, 2011, http://www.raceforiran.com/pulling-the-iaea-into-the-%e2%80%9cattack-iran%e2%80%9d-debate-will-backfire, and Julian Borger, "Nuclear Watchdog Chief Accused of Pro-Western Bias over Iran," *Guardian*, March 22, 2012.

43. For a critical assessment by an American nuclear scientist who served as an IAEA inspector, see Robert Kelley, "Nuclear Weapons Charge against Iran No Slam Dunk," Bloomberg, Jan. 10, 2012, http://www.bloomberg.com/news/2012-01-11/iran-nuclear-weapons-charge-is-no-slam-dunk-commentary-by-robert-kelley.html.

44. In fact, some Western countries that joined as nonweapons states have conducted research into aspects of weapons fabrication at least as advanced as anything Iran is said to have undertaken; these include Sweden and Switzerland. Likewise, South Korea and Taiwan have done work on producing weapons-grade fissile material well beyond anything Iran has been shown to have undertaken.

45. Kenneth Waltz, "Why Iran Should Get the Bomb: Nuclear Balancing Would Mean Stability," *Foreign Affairs* (July–Aug. 2012).

46. For critical overviews, with links or references to articles in the *New York Times* by William Broad, Steven Erlanger, James Risen, and David Sanger, in the *Washington Post* by David Ignatius and Joby Warrick, in the *Los Angeles Times*, and to stories broadcast by ABC, CBS, and NBC, see, e.g., William Beeman, "Commentary on America's Deadly Dynamic with Iran by David Sanger," *Culture and International Affairs*, Nov. 6, 2011, http://wbeeman.blogspot.com/search?q=new+york+times&max-results=20&by-date=true; Robert Naiman, "Judy Miller Alert! The *New York Times* Is Lying about Iran's Nuclear Program," *Truthout*, Jan. 8, 2012, http://truth-out.org/index.php?option=com_k2&view=item&id=5957:judy-miller-alert-the-new-york-times-is-lying-about-irans-nuclear-program; William Beeman, "Commentary on Bill Keller: 'Bomb-Bomb-Bomb, Bomb-Bomb Iran," *Culture and International Affairs*, Jan. 23, 2012, http://wbeeman.blogspot.com/search?q=new+york+times&max-results=20&by-date=true; Thomas Wark, "Do You Feel Your Strings Being Pulled—Again?," *A Bordello Pianist*, Jan. 31, 2012, http://bordellopianist.blogspot.com/2012/01/do-you-feel-your-strings-being-pulled.html; Gareth Porter, "How the Media Got the Parchin Access Story Wrong," *lobelog*, Feb. 2012, http://www.lobelog.com/how-the-media-got-the-parchin-access-story-wrong/; "Report: Broadcast News Networks Misrepresent Intelligence on Iranian

Nuclear Issues," *Media Matters*, April 18, 2012, http://mediamatters.org/blog
/2012/04/18/report-broadcast-news-networks-misrepresent-int/184478;
Thomas Wark, "Riding a Misinformation Train to War," *A Bordello Pianist*,
April 20, 2012, http://bordellopianist.blogspot.com/2012/04/riding-misin
formation-train-to-war.html. For the ombudsmen's views, see Patrick Pex-
ton, "Getting Ahead of the Facts on Iran," *Washington Post*, Dec. 9, 2011,
http://www.washingtonpost.com/opinions/getting-ahead-of-the-facts-on
-iran/2011/12/07/gIQAAvvCjO_story.html, and Arthur Brisbane, "Lessons
from Another War," *New York Times*, March 10, 2012, http://www.nytimes
.com/2012/03/11/opinion/sunday/lessons-from-another-war.html?_r=2&
ref=thepubliceditor.

47. See Brzezinski's address to the conference, "Understanding Iran: Domestic
and Foreign Policy on the Eve of the Presidential Election," sponsored by the
RAND Center for Middle East Public Policy, Arlington, Va., June 5, 2009,
http://www.c-span.org/Events/RANDs-Centers-for-Middle-East-Public
-Policy-Conference-on-Understanding-Iran/14057-2/.

48. "Iran Will Never Make the Mistake to Build Nuclear Weapons; Envoy,"
Tehran Times, Nov. 3, 2010, http://old.tehrantimes.com/index_View.asp
?code=229718.

49. "In Iran, Leader Slams US Nuke Threats," *Press TV*, April 11, 2010, http://
edition.presstv.ir/detail/123015.html. On Iranian perceptions of the Obama
administration's Nuclear Posture Review, see Leverett and Leverett, "Is Iran
Now a Nuclear Target for the United States?" and "Iran Reacts to Becoming
a US Nuclear Target," *Race for Iran*, April 11, 2010, http://www.raceforiran
.com/iran-reacts-to-becoming-a-u-s-nuclear-target.

50. For a similar assessment, see Gareth Evans, "Inside Iran's Nuclear Reasoning," *Project Syndicate*, Sept. 17, 2010, http://www.project-syndicate.org
/commentary/inside-iran-s-nuclear-reasoning.

51. "CBS Interview with Ali Akbar Salehi," CBS News, April 13, 2010, http://www
.cbsnews.com/2100-202_162-6390463.html.

52. Ayatollah Seyed Ali Khamenei, "Supreme Leader Speaks to Nuclear Scientists," Feb. 22, 2012, http://english.khamenei.ir//index.php?option=com_
content&task=view&id=1595&Itemid=4.

53. For discussion, see Ebrahim Mohseni, "Coercive Persuasion: Measuring the
Effectiveness of Sanctions as a Way of Persuading Iran to Comply with
United Nations Security Council Resolutions," unpublished paper, Univer-
sity of Maryland, 2011; see also Sara Beth Elson and Alireza Nader, *What
Do Iranians Think? A Survey of Attitudes on the United States, the Nuclear
Program, and the Economy* (Santa Monica, Calif.: Rand, 2011), 11–16, and
Jay Loschky and Anita Pugliese, "Iranians Split, 40% to 35%, on Nuclear
Military Power," *Gallup World*, Feb. 15, 2012.

54. Peter Jenkins, "Iran as a Threshold Nuclear State?," *Race for Iran*, Oct. 10,
2010, http://www.raceforiran.com/iran-as-a-threshold-nuclear-state.

55. "A New Global Security System towards a World Free from Nuclear Weapons: A Conversation with Mohamed ElBaradei," John F. Kennedy School of Government, Harvard University, April 27, 2010, http://www.iop.harvard.edu/Multimedia-Center/All-Videos/A-New-Global-Security-System-Towards-a-World-Free-From-Nuclear-Weapons-A-Conversation-With-Mohamed-ElBaradei.

56. See Alvin Richman et al., "Iranian Public Is Not Monolithic: Iranians Divide over Their Government but Unite over Forgoing Nuclear Weapons," WorldPublicOpinion.Org, May 19, 2009, http://www.worldpublicopinion.org/pipa/pdf/may09/IranianPublic_May09_rpt.pdf, and "Two-Thirds of Iranians Ready to Preclude Developing Nuclear Weapons in Exchange for Lifting Sanctions," WorldPublicOpinion.Org, Sept. 22, 2009, http://www.worldpublicopinion.org/pipa/articles/brmiddleeastnafricara/640.php.; Elson and Nader, What Do Iranians Think?, 11–12; and Loschky and Pugliese, "Iranians Split." See also Mohseni, "Coercive Persuasion."

57. Western commentators made much of an Internet poll conducted in early July 2012 by Iranian state television in which a majority of respondents reportedly favored giving up enrichment in exchange for sanctions relief; see, e.g., Ramin Mostaghim and Alexandra Sandels, "Iranians Want End to Sanctions, Short-Lived Poll Finds," Los Angeles Times, July 4, 2012. It should be noted, however, that the respondents to this poll did not constitute a scientific sample. Respondents were self-selecting individuals with online access; there were also no real safeguards against multiple submissions by a single respondent.

58. "Iran Will Not Back Down, Will Confront Threats at Right Time," Feb. 3, 2012, http://english.khamenei.ir//index.php?option=com_content&task=view&id=1581&Itemid=2.

59. This reading is confirmed by two former nuclear negotiators and a well-connected Iranian analyst; see Kayhan Barzegar, "Tit for Tat Diplomacy," Bulletin of the Atomic Scientists 66, no. 6 (2010).

60. See Kayhan Barzegar, "The Paradox of Iran's Nuclear Consensus," World Policy Journal 26, no. 3 (Fall 2009), and "Capabilities of Iran's Nuclear Program," Iran Review, Dec. 19, 2009.

61. "A New Global Security System towards a World Free from Nuclear Weapons."

62. Joseph Nye, Soft Power: The Means to Success in World Politics (New York: PublicAffairs, 2004), 11.

63. Abbas Maleki, "Soft Power and Its Implications on Iran," presentation at the Institute for North American and European Studies, University of Tehran, May 15, 2007.

64. The United States Information Agency defined public diplomacy as promoting the national interest "through understanding, informing, and influencing foreign audiences"; http://publicdiplomacy.org/pages/index.php?page=about-public-diplomacy.

65. Arshin Adib-Moghaddam and Abbas Maleki, "Iran, Netanyahu, and the Holocaust," *Veterans Today*, April 30, 2012, http://www.veteranstoday.com/2012/04/30/iran-netanyahu-and-the-holocaust/?utm_source=rss&utm_medium=rss&utm_campaign=iran-netanyahu-and-the-holocaust.

66. Robert Tait, "Iran's Jews Reject Cash Offer to Move to Israel," *Guardian*, July 12, 2007. The monetary incentives to emigrate were offered in the wake of an episode in which thirteen Iranian Jews were arrested in 1999 on allegations of spying for Israel. In 2000, ten of the thirteen were convicted and sentenced to prison; over the next three years, higher courts communted their sentences and released the ten from jail.

67. For a discussion, see Derek Sands, "Analysis: Iran's Soft Power Pays Off," UPI, Aug. 14, 2007; Ethan Chorin and Haim Malka, "Iran's Soft Power Creates Hard Realities," *CSIS Middle East Notes and Comment* (April 2008); and Flynt Leverett and Hillary Mann Leverett, "Who Says Iran Is Becoming Isolated in the Middle East?," *Race for Iran*, Aug. 8, 2010, http://www.raceforiran.com/who-says-iran-is-becoming-isolated-in-the-middle-east.

68. See, e.g., Marc Lynch, "Why Put an Attack on Iran Back on the Table?" *Foreign Policy*, July 19, 2010, http://lynch.foreignpolicy.com/posts/2010/07/19/is_an_attack_on_iran_really_back_on_the_table.

69. See Lynch, "Why Put an Attack," and Jeffrey Goldberg, "The Saudis Are Neocons, and Other First WikiLeaks Impressions," *Atlantic*, Nov. 28, 2010, http://www.theatlantic.com/national/archive/2010/11/the-saudis-are-neocons-and-other-first-wikileaks-impressions/67094/#.

70. See, e.g., the University of Maryland's 2010 Arab Public Opinion Poll, Aug. 5, 2010, http://sadat.umd.edu/new%20surveys/surveys.htm, and its 2011 Arab Public Opinion Poll, Nov. 21, 2011, http://www.brookings.edu/~/media/Files/events/2011/1121_arab_public_opinion/20111121_arab_public_opinion.pdf.

71. Ibid.

72. See Zbigniew Brzezinski, *Second Chance: Three Presidents and the Crisis of American Superpower* (New York: Basic, 2007), 202–3, and "The Global Political Awakening," *New York Times*, Dec. 16, 2008, http://www.nytimes.com/2008/12/16/opinion/16iht-YEbrzezinski.1.18730411.html?pagewanted=all.

73. Personal communications with the authors.

74. See the 2010 Arab Public Opinion Poll, the 2011 Public Opinion Poll, and Arab Center for Research and Policy Studies, *The Arab Opinion Project: The Arab Opinion Index*, March 2012.

75. Marandi, "The Islamic Republic of Iran, the United States, and the Balance of Power in the Middle East," *Race for Iran*, Jan. 14, 2011, http://www.raceforiran.com/the-islamic-republic-of-iran-the-united-states-and-the-balance-of-power-in-the-middle-east.

76. See, e.g., Dalia Dassa Kaye, "Iran Might Not Be the Big Winner of Mideast Uprisings," *Washington Post*, March 4, 2011; Karim Sadjadpour, "Arabs

Rise, Tehran Trembles," *New York Times*, March 5, 2011; Simon Tisdall, "Iran Has Been Isolated by the Arab Spring," *Guardian*, May 17, 2011; Scott Peterson, "Iran Sees Threat to Clout amid Arab Spring," *Christian Science Monitor*, May 31, 2011; Colin Kahl, "Supremely Irrelevant," *Foreign Policy*, Jan. 25, 2012; Gregory Gause and Ian Lustick, "America and the Regional Powers in a Transforming Middle East," *Middle East Policy* 19, no. 2 (Summer 2012); and F. Stephen Larrabee, "The Turkish-Iranian Alliance That Wasn't: How the Two Countries Are Competing after the Arab Spring," *Foreign Affairs*, July 11, 2012.

77. "Muslim Brotherhood Hails Iran's Role in Reinvigorating Muslim Unity," Fars News Agency, Feb. 28, 2011, http://english.farsnews.com/newstext.php?nn=8912081371, and "Conference on Islamic Awakening Held in Tehran," *Tehran Times*, Feb. 28, 2011, http://old.tehrantimes.com/Index_view.asp?code=236516.

78. Thomas Friedman, "Morsi's Wrong Turn," *New York Times*, Aug. 28, 2012.

79. See, e.g., Karim Sadjadpour, "Assad Regime Crucial to Iran," Council on Foreign Relations and *CNN Global Public Square*, Aug. 30, 2011, http://carnegieendowment.org/2011/08/30/assad-regime-in-syria-crucial-to-iran/8kgi; Clifford May, "The Battle of Syria," *National Review Online*, June 7, 2012, http://www.nationalreview.com/articles/302053/battle-syria-clifford-d-may; and Larrabee, "The Turkish-Iranian Alliance That Wasn't."

80. See Javad Mansouri, "Crisis in Syria Influenced by Foreign Meddling," *Tehran Times*, June 28, 2011, http://www.tehrantimes.com/opinion/101-crisis-in-syria-influenced-by-foreign-meddling, and Mehdi Mohammadi, "Syria's Developments and Iran's National Security Equation," *Iran Review*, July 22, 2012, http://www.iranreview.org/content/Documents/Syria-s-Developments-and-Iran-s-National-Security-Equation.htm.

3: ENGAGING AMERICA

1. "CBS Interview with Ali Akbar Salehi."

2. See, e.g., Reuel Marc Gerecht, "Diplomatic Illusions: Why Diplomacy with Iran Will Never Work," *Weekly Standard*, Dec. 13, 2010, and Michael Rubin, "Diplomacy Is Not Enough," *Prospect*, June 25, 2006.

3. See, e.g., Sadjadpour, "The Sources of Soviet Iranian Conduct" and "Engagement with Iran: An Assessment of the Options" (interview), *Middle East Progress*, Dec. 8, 2009; Takeyh, "Domestic Politics Color Iran's Susceptibility to Western Courtship," *Washington Post*, Sept. 19, 2010; and Scott Peterson, "Is Iran Prepared to Undo 30 Years of Anti-Americanism?," *Christian Science Monitor*, Feb. 6, 2009.

4. Harold Rhode, *The Sources of Iranian Negotiating Behavior*, Strategic Perspectives no. 5 (Jerusalem: Jerusalem Center for Public Affairs, 2010); see

also Michael Rubin, "Talking to Iran: They've Sold Us This Rug Before," *Weekly Standard*, Feb. 16, 2009, and "What Iran Really Thinks about Talks," *Wall Street Journal*, April 13, 2009.

5. "Flynt Leverett Debates Michael Ledeen on Iran Policy," Atlantic Council of the United States, March 3, 2010, http://www.youtube.com/watch?v=uNpVn Gkjz9I.

6. "Interview with Iranian President Mohammad Khatami," CNN, Jan. 7, 1998, http://www.cnn.com/WORLD/9801/07/iran/interview.html.

7. Khamenei's statements are quoted from Foreign Broadcast Information Service translations in Rouhollah Ramazani, "Iran and the United States: 'Islamic Realism'?," in *The Middle East from the Iran-Contra Affair to the Intifada*, ed. Robert Freedman (Syracuse: Syracuse University Press, 1990), 176.

8. Ibid., 167–70 and 173–74.

9. "Address by Hojjat-ul-Islam Seyed Ali Khamenei, President of the Islamic Republic of Iran."

10. Quoted from *Tehran Times*, Oct. 20, 1987, in Ramazani, "Iran and the United States."

11. Ibid. After pointing out that "there are conditions where our ties with the United States could be normalized," Khamenei went on to explain that "the phrase 'neither East nor West' does not mean not having friendly ties with the East or West. It can be interpreted as not accepting domination from the East or West."

12. See, esp., Karim Sadjadpour, *Reading Khamenei: The World View of Iran's Most Powerful Leader* (Washington, D.C.: Carnegie Endowment for International Peace, 2009), and Ray Takeyh, *Guardians of the Revolution*, 162–63, and "Domestic Politics Color Iran's Susceptibility to Western Courtship."

13. Rafsanjani recounts his impressions in his first set of memoirs, which have not been translated into English.

14. Quoted in Ramazani, "Iran and the United States," 173.

15. This point has been made to us by several of Rafsanjani's former foreign policy advisers.

16. *Pariah State.*

17. Giandomenico Picco, *Man without a Gun: One Diplomat's Secret Struggle to Free the Hostages, Fight Terrorism, and End a War* (New York: Crown, 1999), 99–229.

18. *Pariah State.*

19. Picco, *Man without a Gun*, 7.

20. *U.S. Actions Regarding Iranian and Other Bosnian Arms Transfers to the Bosnian Army, 1994–1995*, Report of the Select Committee on Intelligence, United States Senate, together with additional views, Nov. 1996.

21. Former Rafsanjani advisers have told us that Rafsanjani took the decision.

22. James Risen and Doyle McManus, "U.S. OKd Iran Arms for Bosnia, Offi-

cials Say," *Los Angeles Times*, April 5, 1996. For good examples of U.S. press coverage as the story unfolded, see Tim Weiner and Raymond Bonner, "Gun-Running in the Balkans: CIA and Diplomats Collide," *New York Times*, May 29, 1996, and Walter Pincus and David Ottoway, "Hill Panels May Enter Controversy over CIA Action on Croatia Envoy," *Washington Post*, June 2, 1996.

23. E.g., Takeyh, *Guardians of the Revolution*, 3–5, 119, 125–28, 164–77.

24. "Interview with Iranian President Mohammad Khatami."

25. "Interview—Kamal Kharrazi: Directing Iran's Foreign Policy for a New and More Open Government," *Los Angeles Times*, Sept. 28, 1997, http://articles .latimes.com/1997/sep/28/opinion/op-37059/2.

26. This is reflected in Secretary of State Madeleine Albright's June 1998 address to the Asia Society in New York; see U.S. Department of State, Speech of Secretary of State Madeleine K. Albright, 1998 Asia Society Dinner, June 17, 1998, http://usembassy-israel.org.il/publish/press/state/archive/1998/june /sd1618.htm. Kharrazi delivered a sharply critical response three months later; see "Remarks by H. E. Dr. Kamal Kharrazi," Asia Society, New York, Sept. 28, 1998, http://asiasociety.org/policy/strategic-challenges/us -asia/remarks-he-dr-kamal-kharrazi.

27. Crist, *The Twilight War*, 399–406, and Richard Clarke and Steven Simon, "Bombs That Would Backfire," *New York Times*, April 16, 2006, http://www .nytimes.com/2006/04/16/opinion/16clarke.html.

28. See Gareth Porter, "Khobar Towers Investigation: How a Saudi Deception Protected Osama bin Laden," IPS; part 1, "Al Qaeda Excluded from Suspects List," June 22, 2009; part 2, "Saudi Account of Khobar Bore Telltale Signs of Fraud," June 23, 2009; part 3, "U.S. Officials Leaked a False Story Blaming Iran," June 24, 2009; part 4, "FBI Ignored Compelling Evidence of bin Laden Role," June 25, 2009; and part 5, "Freeh Became 'Defence Lawyer' for Saudis on Khobar," June 26, 2009. On Freeh's later advocacy for the MEK, see Scott Shane, "For Obscure Iranian Exile Group, Broad Support in U.S.," *New York Times*, Nov. 26, 2011, http://www.nytimes.com/2011/11/27/us/ politics/lobbying-support-for-iranian-exile-group-crosses-party-lines.html ?_r=1&pagewanted=all; Michael Isikoff, "Ex-US Officials Investigated over Speeches to Iranian Dissident Group on Terror List," MSNBC, March 16, 2012, http://openchannel.msnbc.msn.com/_news/2012/03/16/10710422-ex -us-officials-investigated-over-speeches-to-iranian-dissident-group-on-ter ror-list#.T2M5DSm9kJY.twitter; Scott Shane, "U.S. Supporters of Iranian Group Face Scrutiny," *New York Times*, March 13, 2012, http://www.nytimes .com/2012/03/13/us/us-supporters-of-iranian-group-mek-face-scrutiny .html; and Hamed Aleaziz, "Romney Adviser Blasts Government Investigation, Says Bring It On," *Mother Jones*, April 2, 2012, http://www.motherjones .com/mojo/2012/03/romney-advisor-blasts-government-investigation-says -bring-it.

29. John Demiszewski, "Saudis Find No Foreign Role in Blast," *Los Angeles Times*, May 23, 1998. (Nayif became crown prince of Saudi Arabia in Oct. 2011.)

30. Warren Christopher, interview transcript for *Iran and the West*, archived at Liddel Hart Center for Military Archives, King's College, London, and "Perry: U.S. Eyed Iran Attack after Bombing," UPI, June 6, 2007, http://www.upi.com/Business_News/Security-Industry/2007/06/06/Perry-US-eyed-Iran-attack-after-bombing/UPI-70451181161509/.

31. "Message to President Khatami from President Clinton," undated, c. June 1999, http://www.gwu.edu/~nsarchiv/NSAEBB/NSAEBB318/doc02.pdf.

32. See "Iran: Fact and Fiction," CNN, Dec. 8, 2007, http://transcripts.cnn.com/TRANSCRIPTS/0712/08/siu.01.html.

33. "Iranian Response to Clinton Letter," undated, early Sept. 1999, http://www.gwu.edu/~nsarchiv/NSAEBB/NSAEBB318/doc03.pdf. Without quoting it, Crist mischaracterizes it as "typically Persian. While the Iranian government denied any involvement, the message added that no such action would happen again." See *The Twilight War*, 413. It is hard to understand how a serious scholar could so grossly misinterpret a document written in perfectly clear English.

34. U.S. Department of State, Secretary of State Madeleine K. Albright, Remarks before the American-Iranian Council, March 17, 2000, http://asiasociety.org/policy/strategic-challenges/us-asia/us-iran-relations.

35. Rafsanjani experienced a humiliating political defeat in that year's parliamentary elections. His allies were routed; Rafsanjani himself could barely win a seat (he was declared the winner only after a recount), which he relinquished before the next Majles was installed.

36. As noted, the fact that U.S. and Iranian officials held talks and cooperated in 2001 and 2002 and Hillary Mann Leverett's participation in these meetings are well documented in the public record; see the sources cited in ch. 2, n. 28.

37. M. Javad Zarif, "A Neighbor's Vision of the New Iraq," *New York Times*, May 10, 2003, http://www.zarif.net/Articles/A%20Neighbor<#213>s%20Vision%20of%20the%20New%20Iraq.htm.

38. Officials present for a National Security Council meeting on post-Saddam Iraq convened in the White House Situation Room in May 2003 told us that Bush's initial reaction to the proposal was positive.

39. Dafna Linzer, "Al-Qaeda Suspects Color White House Debate over Iran," *Washington Post*, Feb. 10, 2007.

40. http://media.washingtonpost.com/wp-srv/world/documents/us_iran_road map.pdf.

41. E.g., neither Clinton's 1999 message to Khatami about the Khobar Towers bombing nor the Iranian response was signed or presented on official, "letterhead" stationery.

42. See Michael Rubin, "The Guldimann Memorandum: The Iranian 'Roadmap' Wasn't a Roadmap and Wasn't Iranian," *Weekly Standard*, Oct. 22,

2007; Steven Rosen, "Did Iran Offer a 'Grand Bargain' in 2003?," *American Thinker*, Nov. 16, 2008; and Lee Smith, "Iran's Man in Washington, *Tablet*, Feb. 9, 2010. For a rejoinder, see Flynt Leverett and Hillary Mann Leverett, "Explaining the Concept of 'Lies' to Jeffrey Goldberg (and Lee Smith)," *Race for Iran*, Feb. 13, 2010, http://www.raceforiran.com/explaining-the-concept -of-%E2%80%9Clies%E2%80%9D-to-jeffrey-goldberg-and-lee-smith. Some neoconservatives and pro-Israel advocates, such as Patrick Clawson, even claimed that the Swiss ambassador, Tim Guldimann, had been recalled from Iran and ultimately dismissed from the Swiss Foreign Ministry for his "misconduct." In fact, Guldimann cut short his assignment in Tehran not long after the Roadmap was transmitted because his wife was diagnosed with cancer and returned to Europe for treatment. After a three-year sab-batical, he returned to service in 2007 as head of the OSCE mission to Kosovo, with ambassadorial rank. Since 2010, he has been Switzerland's ambassador to Germany.

43. Numerous Iranian officials have also privately confirmed the Roadmap's validity.

44. Iran was also concerned to deflect mounting international pressure over its nuclear activities.

45. This reading of Tehran's approach is attested by two of its former nuclear negotiators. See "Sakhnan Hojjatoleslam Doktor Hassan Rohani dar Jame'e-ye Ada-ye Shura-ye Ali-ye Enqelab-e Farhangi" (Speech of Hojjatoleslam Dr. Hassan Rohani to Members of the Supreme Council of the Cultural Revolu-tion), *Rahbord*, Sept. 30, 2005; an English translation, "Beyond the Challenges Facing Iran and the IAEA Concerning the Nuclear Dossier," is available as FBIS-IAP20060223336001. See also Mousavian, "Iran's Nuclear Diplomacy" and *Iran-Europe Relations: Challenges and Opportunities* (Oxford: Routledge, 2008), 156–63.

46. *Statement by the Iranian Government and Visiting EU Foreign Ministers*, Oct. 21, 2003.

47. *Iran-EU Agreement on Nuclear Programme*, Nov. 14, 2004. Because this accord was concluded in the French capital, it is often called the Paris Agreement.

48. Mousavian, *Iran-Europe Relations*, 163–82.

49. "Proposal Presented by Iran in the Meeting of the Steering Committee, Paris," March 23, 2005, http://www.armscontrol.org/pdf/20050323_Iran_ Proposal_Steering_Cmte.pdf.

50. "Proposal by Iran Presented to the Meeting of the Steering Committee, London," April 29, 2005, http://www.armscontrol.org/pdf/20050429_Iran_ Proposal_Steering_Cmte.pdf. Crist overlooks these Iranian proposals in his cursory treatment of Tehran's nuclear negotiations with the EU3 during 2003–05, noting only Iran's "refusal to consider" a much delayed and sub-stantively inadequate European offer; see *The Twilight War*, 490.

51. Mousavian, "Iran's Nuclear Diplomacy."

52. Besides Hassan Rohani, the secretary-general of the Supreme National Security Council and chief nuclear negotiator under Khatami, other nuclear negotiators during Khatami's presidency—e.g., Seyed Hossein Mousavian and Sirius Nasseri—started their careers as Rafsanjani protégés.

53. "Communication Dated 1 August 2005 Received from the Permanent Mission of the Islamic Republic of Iran to the Agency," International Atomic Energy Agency Information Circular (INFCIRC/648), Aug. 1, 2005, http://www.iaea.org/Publications/Documents/Infcircs/2005/infcirc648.pdf. Crist incorrectly states that Ahmadinejad ordered the restarting of Iran's enrichment program after assuming the presidency; see *The Twilight War*, 500.

54. The proposal—entitled *Framework for a Long-Term Agreement*—was registered with the International Atomic Energy Agency on Aug. 5, 2005, http://www.iaea.org/Publications/Documents/Infcircs/Numbers/nr651-700.shtml. For a discussion, see Mousavian, *Iran-Europe Relations*, 182–85.

55. "Communication Dated 12 September 2005 from the Permanent Mission of the Islamic Republic of Iran to the Agency," International Atomic Energy Agency Information Circular (INFCIRC/657), Sept. 15, 2005, http://www.iaea.org/Publications/Documents/Infcircs/2005/infcirc657.pdf.

56. "Communication Dated 3 January 2006 from the Permanent Mission of the Islamic Republic of Iran to the Agency," Report of the Director General (GOV/INF/2006/1), Jan. 3, 2006, http://www.iranwatch.org/IAEAgovdocs/iran-iaea-resumption-010306.pdf.

57. "Interview with Mohamed ElBaradei: Egypt's Military Leadership Is Reacting Too Slowly," *Spiegel International*, April 19, 2011, http://www.spiegel.de/international/world/spiegel-interview-with-mohamed-elbaradei-egypt-s-military-leadership-is-reacting-too-slowly-a-757786.html.

58. Such a conclusion was reached not only by "hardliners," but also by reformists; see Rohani, "Beyond the Challenges Facing Iran and the IAEA Concerning the Nuclear Dossier." Subsequent European policy—cooperating with Washington to impose sanctions, rolling back previously established economic ties, and getting ever more exercised over human rights issues—has further buttressed this Iranian view.

59. Mousavian, *Iran-Europe Relations*, 185–90.

60. An Iranian scholar and analyst well connected to policy-making circles writes, "In terms of the nature of issues and geography, the new geopolitical developments that emanated from the 2003 Iraq crisis, Iran has become the main hub of political-security affairs in the region." Moreover, "with the rise to power of the Shiite factor in Iraq and the region, Iran became capable of powerfully affecting the region's political dynamics." This meant that Iran's regional role was "becoming more significant" precisely in "the areas and issues which have turned into key concerns of the international community." See Barzegar, "Iran, the Middle East, and International Security," *Ortadoğu Etütleri* 1, no. 1 (July 2009), 34–36.

61. Lionel Beehner, "Russia's Nuclear Deal with Iran," Council on Foreign Relations, Feb. 28, 2006, http://www.cfr.org/iran/russias-nuclear-deal-iran/p9985.

62. See, e.g., the letter of Iranian foreign minister Manouchehr Mottaki to Secretary-General Ban Ki-moon of the United Nations, dated March 24, 2008; http://www.iran-un.org/documents/sg/articles/letter%20to%20SG%2025%20March%202008.pdf. See also Mottaki's letter to Ban Ki-moon, dated Feb. 27, 2008, the bulk of which was published in "Mottaki Sends Letter to UN Chief, Member States," Islamic Republic News Agency (IRNA), Feb. 28, 2008, http://www.campaigniran.org/casmii/index.php?q=node/4189.

63. The phrase "comprehensive framework" is used in the May 2008 letter of Iranian foreign minister Manouchehr Mottaki to Secretary-General Ban Ki-moon of the United Nations, which was published as "Mottaki's Letter to UN Chief on Iran's Proposed Security and Nuclear Package," *Tehran Times*, May 13, 2008, http://old.tehrantimes.com/Index_view.asp?code=169162.

64. Likewise, Barzegar writes that "negotiating on several disparate fronts is not in Iran's or the region's interests, nor will it lead to a lasting settlement. The single most effective route is to accept the aforesaid mutual areas of concern as a comprehensive package, which would afford Iran strategic parity in the course of negotiations. Only then will Iran feel confident enough to make genuine concessions and acquire the assurances it has long sought." See "Iran's Foreign Policy after Saddam," 183.

65. Britain, France, and Germany describe this follow-on framework as the "EU3+3," as a reminder of the EU3's original role.

66. *Elements of a Proposal to Iran*, June 1, 2006, http://www.consilium.europa.eu/ueDocs/cms_Data/docs/pressdata/en/reports/90569.pdf.

67. European diplomats involved in discussions over the 2006 package say they recognized that removing security issues would make it a "nonstarter" for Iran but calculated that it was more important to get the United States into the process than to get the substance "right." In retrospect, some of them acknowledge this may have been a "mistake."

68. Islamic Republic of Iran's Response to the Package Presented on June 6, 2006, http://www.isis-online.org/publications/iran/iranresponse.pdf.

69. United Nations Security Council Resolution 1696, S/RES/1696 (2006), July 31, 2006, http://daccess-dds-ny.un.org/doc/UNDOC/GEN/N06/450/22/PDF/N0645022.pdf?OpenElement.

70. Specifically, Tehran insisted that the P5+1 explicitly recognize Iran's rights under article 4 of the NPT; the P5+1 proposal cited only Iran's obligations under article 1 and article 2.

71. E.g., Nick Burns—Rice's point man on Iran policy as undersecretary of state for political affairs—claims that the Bush administration accepted a Solana-proposed deal whereby Tehran would renew suspension of fuel cycle activities and Washington would support a "time-out" on new sanctions. Burns

says that plans were laid for Larijani to travel to New York to meet with Rice during the United Nations General Assembly in September 2006, where they would announce the Solana-brokered arrangement. In the end, Larijani did not come. Iran claims the United States did not issue visas for all members of Larijani's delegation; Burns says that, in fact, all the visas were issued. Whatever the reality is about the visas, there was a larger problem: even if Larijani had been willing to entertain the possibility of another temporary suspension of Iran's fuel cycle activities—something that has never been confirmed on the Iranian side—neither Khamenei nor Ahmadinejad was willing to go along. For Burns's account, see *Iran and the West*, part 3, *Nuclear Confrontation*.

72. United Nations Security Council Resolution 1737, S/RES/1737, Dec. 27, 2006, http://daccess-dds-ny.un.org/doc/UNDOC/GEN/N06/681/42/PDF/N0668142.pdf?OpenElement; United Nations Security Council Resolution 1747, S/RES/1747, March 24, 2007, http://daccess-dds-ny.un.org/doc/UNDOC/GEN/N07/281/40/PDF/N0728140.pdf?OpenElement; and United Nations Security Council Resolution 1835, S/RES/1835, Sept. 27, 2008, http://daccess-dds-ny.un.org/doc/UNDOC/GEN/N08/525/12/PDF/N0852512.pdf?OpenElement.

73. "Mottaki's Letter to UN Chief on Iran's Proposed Security and Nuclear Package."

74. *P5+1 Updated Incentives Package*, June 17, 2008, http://merln.ndu.edu/archivepdf/iran/State/105992.pdf.

75. Hillary Mann Leverett's Iranian interlocutors frequently claimed that a statement by President Bush expressing a desire to resolve Washington's differences with the Islamic Republic in an atmosphere of "mutual respect" would have a profoundly positive impact in Tehran.

76. "Obama Al-Arabiya Interview: Full Text," *Huffington Post*, Jan. 26, 2009, and http://www.youtube.com/watch?v=HO_lLttxxrs.

77. "Videotaped Message by the President in Celebration of Nowruz," March 19, 2009, http://www.whitehouse.gov/the_press_office/Videotaped-Remarks-by-The-President-in-Celebration-of-Nowruz/ and http://www.whitehouse.gov/Nowruz/.

78. "OSC: Khamenei's Speech Replying to Obama."

79. Sadjadpour, "The Sources of Soviet Iranian Conduct"; see also Trita Parsi, *A Single Roll of the Dice: Obama's Diplomacy With Iran* (New Haven: Yale University Press, 2012).

80. Kenneth Pollack and Ray Takeyh, "Doubling Down on Iran," *Washington Quarterly* 34, no. 4 (Fall 2011), 8.

81. "Supreme Leader's Speech to Government Officials."

82. Pollack and Takeyh, "Doubling Down on Iran," 9.

83. "Supreme Leader's Speech to Government Officials."

Part Two: The Islamic Republic as Legitimate State

PROLOGUE

1. David Brooks, "Fragile at the Core," *New York Times*, June 18, 2009, http://www.nytimes.com/2009/06/19/opinion/19brooks.html.

2. See "Ahmadinedschads Sieg: Die amerikaner müssen klare Angebote auf den Tisch legen," Flynt Leverett interview in *Spiegel Online*, June 13, 2009, http://www.spiegel.de/politik/ausland/0,1518,630331,00.html; "The Election in Iran: 'Extraordinary Amount of Wishful Thinking' by US," *Spiegel Online*, June 15, 2009, http://www.spiegel.de/international/world/0,1518,630552,00.html; Flynt Leverett and Hillary Mann Leverett, "Ahmadinejad Won. Get Over It," *Politico*, June 15, 2009, http://www.politico.com/news/stories/0609/23745.html; Flynt Leverett, Hillary Mann Leverett, and Seyed Mohammad Marandi, "Will Iran Be Obama's Iraq?," *Politico*, June 24, 2009, http://www.politico.com/news/stories/0609/24099.html; and Flynt Leverett and Hillary Mann Leverett, "Another Revolution in Iran? Not Likely," *New York Times*, Jan. 6, 2010, http://www.nytimes.com/2010/01/06/opinion/06leverett.html?pagewanted=all.

3. We discuss these polls and the conduct of the June 2009 presidential election in ch. 6.

4. Leverett and Leverett, "Another Revolution in Iran? Not Likely," and Abbas Milani, "The State of the Opposition Is Strong: A Response to the Most Infuriating Op-Ed of the New Year," *New Republic*, January 8, 2010, http://www.tnr.com/article/world/the-state-the-opposition-strong. Even as real-world events validated our analysis, few of our critics showed themselves willing to reconsider their views. Dan Drezner was a gracious exception; see "Your Humble Blogger Was So Wrong," *Foreign Policy*, Aug. 30, 2010, http://drezner.foreignpolicy.com/posts/2010/08/30/your_humble_blogger_was_so_wrong. After hundreds of thousands turned out to celebrate, not protest, the Iranian Revolution's anniversary in February 2010, the political blogger Andrew Sullivan, one of our higher-profile critics, grudgingly acknowledged that we had raised legitimate points about the Greens' weakness—but he charged that we had done so with unseemly "glee." See Sullivan, "Not Going Away," *Atlantic*, Feb. 13, 2010, http://www.theatlantic.com/daily-dish/archive/2010/02/-not-going-away/190424/.

5. Flynt Leverett and Hillary Mann Leverett, "Obama Is Helping Iran," *Foreign Policy*, Feb. 23, 2011, http://www.foreignpolicy.com/articles/2011/02/23/obama_is_helping_iran.

6. See Becky Lee Katz and Ramin Mostaghim, "Iran: Merchants Continue to Protest Government's Proposed Tax Hike," *Los Angeles Times*, July 11, 2010; Michael Ledeen, "Iran Heats Up: The Bazaar Strikes Back," *Pajamas Media*, July 8, 2010, http://pjmedia.com/michaelledeen/2010/07/08/iran-heats-up-the-bazaar-strikes-back/?singlepage=true; and Nazila Fathi, "Strike at Bazaar Spreads beyond Tehran," *New York Times*, July 15, 2010.

7. See, e.g., "Iran's Supreme Leader Tells Ahmadinejad: Accept Minister or Quit," *Guardian*, May 5, 2011; Najmeh Bozorgmehr, "Infighting Undermines Ahmadi-Nejad," *Financial Times*, May 9, 2011; and "Iran: Growing Divisions within the Political Elite" (interview with Robin Wright), ABC, May 14, 2011, http://www.abc.net.au/radionational/programs/saturdayextra /iran-growing-divisions-within-the-political-elite/2950896.

8. Reza Marashi, "The Conservative Rise and the Potential Fall of the Presidency," *Tehran Bureau*, Oct. 17, 2011; Robert Worth, "Iran's Power Struggle Goes beyond Personalities to Future of Presidency Itself," *New York Times*, Oct. 26, 2011; Reza Marashi and Sahar Namazikhah, "Khamenei's Power Consolidation Gambit," *Al Jazeera*, Nov. 11, 2011; Mike Shuster, "In Iran, Secret Plans to Abolish the Presidency?," NPR, Nov. 21, 2011; Neil MacFarquhar, "Elections in Iran Favor Ayatollah's Allies, Dealing Blow to President and His Office," *New York Times*, March 4, 2012; Bernard Gwertzman, "Crisis-Managing the U.S.-Iran Relationship" (interview with Gary Sick), *Council on Foreign Relations*, March 6, 2012; Reza Pakravan, "The End of Iranian Democracy," *Fletcher Forum of World Affairs*, March 23, 2012; and Yasmin Alem, "Is the Islamic Republic of Iran on its Last Elected President?," *Al-Monitor*, Aug. 7, 2012. For further discussion, see Flynt Leverett, Hillary Mann Leverett, and Seyed Mohammad Marandi, "Under the Threat of War, Iranians Affirm Their Support for the Islamic Republic, *Race for Iran*, March 18, 2012, http://www.raceforiran.com/under-the-threat-of-war-iranians -affirm-their-support-for-the-islamic-republic.

9. On neoconservatism's liberal roots, see Tod Lindberg, "Neoconservatism's Liberal Legacy," *Policy Review*, Oct. 1, 2004, and Zhiyuan Cui, "The Bush Doctrine and Neoconservatism: A Chinese Perspective," *Harvard International Law Journal* 46, no. 2 (Summer 2005). For an application of the thesis of Iran's ineluctable transformation into a Western-style secular democracy, see Fakhreddin Azimi, *The Quest for Democracy in Iran: A Century of Struggle Against Authoritarian Rule* (Cambridge, Mass.: Harvard University Press, 2008).

10. E-mail messages shared with the authors.

11. The quote is from "Letter for Tomorrow," an open letter published by Khatami in May 2004.

12. E-mail message received by the authors.

4: RELIGION, REVOLUTION, AND THE ROOTS OF LEGITIMACY

1. Mohsen Sazegara, in *The Man Who Changed the World*; see also "The Khomeini Era Begins," *Time*, Feb. 12, 1979, and Sadeq Tabatabai, in *The Man Who Changed the World*.

2. *Islamic Government*.

3. Hamid Algar, the Berkeley professor who was Khomeini's English-language

translator, notes that this remark was "misinterpreted as a sign of gross insensitivity. On the contrary, it was an indication of a deep inner calm." See "I Knew Khomeini," Al Jazeera, Jan. 23, 2009, http://www.youtube.com/watch?v=PEThWydE0Ok&feature=endscreen&NR=1.

4. V. S. Naipaul, *Among the Believers: An Islamic Journey* (New York: Random House, 1981), 3–83.

5. Kissinger, *Years of Upheaval* (New York: Simon and Schuster, 1982), 670–71.

6. "Interview with Hillary Clinton," ABC News, Sept. 19, 2010, http://abcnews .go.com/ThisWeek/secretary-clinton-expresses-concern-growing-military -influence-iran/story?id=11674543.

7. Hillary Clinton, "Interview with Michel Ghandour of Al Hurra," U.S. Department of State, Feb. 14, 2011, http://www.state.gov/secretary/rm/2011 /02/156571.htm.

8. Graham Fuller, *The Future of Political Islam* (New York: Palgrave Macmillan, 2003), xi.

9. See, e.g., Theda Skocpol, *States and Social Revolutions: A Comparative Analysis of France, Russia, and China* (Cambridge: Cambridge University Press, 1979); Ted Gurr, *Why Men Rebel* (Princeton: Princeton University Press, 1970); and Timur Kuran, "Sparks and Prairie Fires: A Theory of Unanticipated Political Revolution," *Public Choice* 61, no. 1 (April 1989).

10. See, e.g., Jack Goldstone, "Ideology, Cultural Frameworks, and the Process of Revolution," *Theory and Society* 20, no. 4 (Aug. 1991). Somewhat exceptionally, Timur Kuran acknowledges the role of revolutionary leaders not just in molding popular preferences about postrevolutionary politics but also in fostering perceptions that established regimes are vulnerable; see "Sparks and Prairie Fires."

11. Skocpol, *States and Social Revolutions*.

12. Skocpol, "Rentier State and Shi'a Islam in the Iranian Revolution," *Theory and Society* 11, no. 3 (May 1982), 270; rpt. as ch. 11 in Skocpol, *Social Revolution in the Modern World* (Cambridge: Cambridge University Press, 1994). For a thoughtful critique of structuralist accounts of the revolution, see Charles Kurzman, *The Unthinkable Revolution in Iran* (Cambridge: Harvard University Press, 2004).

13. Said Arjomand, "Iran's Islamic Revolution in Comparative Perspective," *World Politics* 38, no. 3 (April 1986), 387.

14. The number of revolutionary casualties is controversial. The Islamic Republic's constitution claims "more than 60,000 martyrs" and "100,000 wounded"; to our knowledge, these figures have never been documented. Emadeddin Baghi, a dissident historian who used to work at the Martyr's Foundation (*Bonyad Shahid*, established to identify those killed during the revolution), holds that, from June 1963 (when Khomeini was arrested, prior to his exile) until February 11, 1979, 3,164 people were killed protesting against the shah; 2,781 died between October 1977 and February 1979. In

The Unthinkable Revolution in Iran, Kurzman argues that the count is lower. Kurzman's argument, however, is based on a single source—*Laleh'ha-ye Enqelab: Yadnameh-e Shahada* ("Tulips of the Revolution: Remembering the Martyrs"), published in the revolution's immediate aftermath and not intended as a final accounting of casualties from Tehran, much less all Iran—and on a 1982 University of Tehran master's thesis that examines records from Behesht-e Zahra and the Tehran coroner. (We thank Professor Kurzman for providing us a copy of this thesis, by Sohbatollah Amira'i.) After reviewing the estimates, we consider Baghi's the lowest plausible figure; the actual count is probably higher—thus, our formulation that "literally thousands of Iranians" were killed between late 1977 and the beginning of 1979.

15. Hamid Algar also makes this point in his introduction to *Constitution of the Islamic Republic of Iran*, trans. Hamid Algar (Berkeley: Mizan Press, 1980), 13.

16. Farhang Rajaee, *Islamism and Modernism: The Changing Discourse in Iran* (Austin: University of Texas Press, 2007), 6.

17. E-mail message received by the authors.

18. Foucault, "Teheran: La fede contro lo Scia," *Corriere della sera*, Oct. 8, 1978. An English translation, "Tehran: Faith against the Shah," is in Janet Afary and Kevin Anderson, *Foucault and the Iranian Revolution: Gender and the Seductions of Islamism* (Chicago: University of Chicago Press, 2005), Kindle ed.; the quote is on 201.

19. Quoted in Mohsen Milani, *The Making of Iran's Islamic Revolution: From Monarchy to Islamic Republic*, 2nd ed. (Boulder: Westview, 1994), 14.

20. Lance Morrow, "The Dynamics of Revolution," *Time*, March 12, 1979.

21. Skocpol, "Rentier State and Shi'a Islam in the Iranian Revolution," 267–68.

22. Max Weber, *Theory of Social and Economic Organization*, trans. A. M. Henderson and Talcott Parsons (New York: Free Press, 1947), 328.

23. In Farsi, *nehzat-e azadi-ye iran*, sometimes translated "Freedom Movement of Iran."

24. Foucault, "L'Iran ai military, ultima carta dello Scia: Sfida all'opposizione," *Corriere della sera*, Nov. 7, 1979. An English translation, "The Challenge to the Opposition," is in Afary and Anderson, *Foucault and the Iranian Revolution*; the quote is on 214.

25. Bazargan, *Shura-ye Enqelab va Dowlat-e Movaqat* [The Revolutionary Council and the Provisional Government] (Tehran: Nehzat-e Azadi-ye Iran, 1983), 21–23, as translated by Kurzman in *The Unthinkable Revolution in Iran*, 3.

26. "Why and How Bazargan Became Prime Minister," Islamic Revolution Document Center, http://www.irdc.ir/en/content/6785/default.aspx.

27. Quoted in "Why and How Bazargan Became Prime Minister." We have edited the translation slightly.

28. In Farsi, *shura-ye enqelab-e eslami.*

29. "Formation of the Council of the Islamic Revolution," in *Islam and Revolution*, 247.

30. This point was made, close to the actual events, by Marvin Zonis; see "Iran: A Theory of Revolution from Accounts of the Revolution," *World Politics* 35, no. 4 (July 1983), 592.

31. Augustus Richard Norton, "A Few Comments after a Long Hiatus, Beginning with Iran," *From the Field*, Jan. 18, 2010, http://bostonuniversity .blogspot.com. Norton was criticizing our op-ed "Another Revolution in Iran? Not Likely."

32. Foucault, "A quoi rêvent les iraniens?," *Le nouvel observateur*, Oct. 16, 1978. An English translation, "What Are the Iranians Dreaming About?," is in Afary and Anderson, *Foucault and the Iranian Revolution*; the quote is on 205.

33. In Farsi, *melli-mazhabi*; see Houchang Chehabi, *Iranian Politics and Religious Modernism: The Liberation Movement of Iran under the Shah and Khomeini* (Ithaca: Cornell University Press, 1990), 26.

34. See *Iran and the West*, part 1, *The Man Who Changed the World*, and Kasra Naji, *Ahmadinejad: The Secret History of Iran's Radical Leader* (Berkeley: University of California Press, 2008). On the Tudeh, see Ervand Abrahamian, *Iran between Two Revolutions* (Princeton: Princeton University Press, 1982).

35. On the MEK's emergence out of the Liberation Movement and its subsequent evolution, see Rajaee, *Islamism and Modernism*, 143–46.

36. "Address at Bihisht-I Zahra," in *Islam and Revolution*, 259.

37. In Farsi, *dah-e fajr.*

38. Khomeini's letter appointing Bazargan is available in English translation in "Why and How Bazargan Became Prime Minister" and in the original Farsi, http://www.irdc.ir/fa/content/5556/default.aspx.

39. For a discussion, see Charles Hill, *Trial of a Thousand Years: Islamism and World Order* (Stanford: Hoover Institution, 2011), 30–31.

40. Electronic communication with the authors.

41. We are grateful to Emile Nakhleh for this aphorism, which works in both Arabic and Farsi.

42. Rajaee, *Islamism and Modernism*, 14.

43. See, e.g., Bernard Lewis, *What Went Wrong? The Clash between Islam and Modernity in the Middle East* (Oxford: Oxford University Press, 2002); Reza Aslan, *No God but God: The Origins, Evolution, and Future of Islam* (New York: Random House, 2005); Nicholas Kristof, "Looking for Islam's Luthers," *New York Times*, Oct. 15, 2006; and Benny Morris, "The Islamic Reformation," *National Interest*, April 5, 2011.

44. Reza Aslan, "Democracy of Believers," *Prospect* (June 2005).

45. Thus, Foucault wrote that the revolution "did not signify a shrinking back in the face of modernization by extremely retrograde elements, but the

rejection, by a whole culture and a whole people, of a *modernization* that is itself an *archaism*." See "Le Shah a cent ans de retard," *Corriere della sera*, Oct. 1, 1978. An English translation, "The Shah Is a Hundred Years behind the Times," is in Afary and Anderson, *Foucault and the Iranian Revolution*; the quote is on 195. For further discussion, see Rajae, *Islamism and Modernism*, 195. John Calvert notes that "Islamists" do not apply the term to themselves, for in their view they are not pursuing a new agenda requiring a new name but rather working to restore authentic belief and practice; see *Sayyid Qutb and the Origins of Radical Islamism* (New York: Hurst/Columbia University Press), 293.

46. *Islamic Government*.

47. Ibid.

48. "In Commemoration of the First Martyrs of the Revolution," in *Islam and Revolution*, 226–27.

49. *Islamic Government*.

50. "Formation of the Council of the Islamic Revolution."

51. Ali Allawi, *The Crisis of Islamic Civilization* (New Haven: Yale University Press, 2009), 256.

52. The quotes, from Sayyid Qutb, are in William Shepard, *Sayyid Qutb and Islamic Activism: A Translation and Critical Analysis of Social Justice in Islam* (Leiden: E. J. Brill, 1996), 112–14.

53. See, i.a., Hamid Dabashi, "Early Propagation of *Wilayat al-faqih* and Mulla Ahmad Naraqi," in *Expectations of the Millennium: Shi'ism in History*, ed. Seyyed Hossein Nasr et al. (Albany: State University of New York Press, 1989), and Hossein Modarressi, "The Just Ruler of the Guardian Jurist: An Attempt to Link Two Different Shi'ite Concepts," *Journal of the American Oriental Society* 111, no. 3 (July–September 1991). See also Abbas Amanat, "From *ijtihad* to *wilayat-i faqih*: The Evolving of the Shi'ite Legal Authority to Political Power," *Logos* 2, no. 3 (Summer 2003); a slightly revised version of this essay appeared in *Shari'a: Islamic Law in the Contemporary Context*, ed. Abbas Amanat and Frank Griffel (Stanford: Stanford University Press, 2007) and in Abbas Amanat, *Apocaplytic Islam and Iranian Shi'ism* (London: I. B. Tauris, 2009). For representative statements by neoconservative writers, see Reuel Marc Gerecht, *The Islamic Paradox: Shi'ite Clerics, Sunni Fundamentalists, and the Coming of Arab Democracy* (Washington, D.C.: American Enterprise Institute, 2004); and Michael Rubin, "Iranian Strategy in Iraq," lecture at the University of Haifa, March 13, 2007, http://www.aei .org/speech/foreign-and-defense-policy/regional/middle-east-and-north -africa/iranian-strategy-in-iraq/.

54. Joseph Schacht holds that the *bab* ("gate" or "door") of ijtihad closed in the Sunni world by the tenth century; see *An Introduction to Islamic Law* (Oxford: Oxford University Press, 1964), 70–71. Wael Hallaq argues that controversy over the issue did not start among Sunni scholars until the

twelfth century and that serious decline in the practice of ijtihad came only after the sixteenth century; see "Was the Gate of ijtihad Closed?," *International Journal of Middle East Studies* 16, no. 1 (March 1984). Besides embracing ijtihad, Shi'a Muslims differ from Sunnis in accepting authenticated sayings of the Twelve Imams as legal sources.

55. For a thoroughly sourced review, see Abdulaziz Abdulhussein Sachedina, *The Just Ruler in Shiite Islam: The Comprehensive Authority of the Jurist in Imamite Jurisprudence* (Oxford: Oxford University Press, 1988).

56. In Farsi, *zil ol ilah*.

57. See also Shahrough Akhavi, "The Ideology and Praxis of Shi'ism in the Iranian Revolution," *Comparative Studies in Society and History* 25, no. 2 (April 1983), 206.

58. Abbas Milani, e.g., describes early-twentieth-century constitutionalists as "quietist" in "The New Democrats: An Intellectual History of the Green Wave," *New Republic*, July 15, 2009, http://www.tnr.com/article/the-new-democrats ?page=0,1. This, too, is a gross misreading, for constitutionalists advocated a strong supervisory (*nezarat*) role for the clergy, to ensure that laws and policies were consistent with Islam.

59. *Islamic Government.*

60. Ibid.

61. Ibid.

62. Ibid.

63. Ibid. Khomeini notes that, while "the just *faqih* has the same authority that [the Prophet Muhammad] and the Imams had, do not imagine that the status of the *faqih* is identical to that of the Imams and the Prophet. For here we are not speaking of status, but rather of function . . . [which] does not earn anyone extraordinary status or raise him above the level of common humanity."

64. Hill, *Trial of a Thousand Years*, 129. In contrast to Hill's hackneyed (and inaccurate) reading, Vali Nasr writes that "Sistani's ability to exert such influence [in post-Saddam Iraq and in the wider Shi'a world] began with his record of never having entangled himself in Iranian politics. He had profound theological and political differences with his fellow clerics who were ruling Iran, but he never tried to promote a rivalry between Najaf and Qom. He rose above disagreements between Muhammad Husayn Fadlallah [in Lebanon] and Iran's clerical leaders; he said nothing about confrontations between reformists and conservatives in Qom, even after the reformist Ayatollah Hossein Ali Montazeri sought to associate himself with Sistani." See *The Shi'a Revival: How Conflicts Within Islam Will Shape the Future* (New York: Norton, 2006), 173–74.

65. It was published in *Kayhan* on April 28 and 29, 1979.

66. See, e.g., Asghar Schirazi, *The Constitution of Iran: Politics and the State in the Islamic Republic*, trans. John O'Kane (London: I. B. Tauris, 1998).

67. This point has been acknowledged even by an expatriate scholar sympathetic to the dissident Abdolkarim Soroush; see Behrooz Ghamari-Tabrizi, *Islam and Dissent in Postrevolutionary Islam: Abdolkarim Soroush, Religious Politics, and Democratic Reform* (London: I. B. Tauris, 2008).

68. In Farsi, *majles-e barresi-ye naha'i-ye qanun-e asasi-e jomhuri-ye eslami-ye iran*, often mistranslated as Assembly of Experts.

69. In Farsi, *khatt-e imam*.

70. The Assembly of Experts' deliberations are available (in Farsi) at http://www .princeton.edu/irandataportal/constitution/.

71. See, e.g., Said Amir Arjomand, *The Turban for the Crown: The Islamic Revolution in Iran* (New York: Oxford University Press, 1988), 103, 107.

72. In Farsi, *majles-e shura-ye melli* and *majles-e shura-ye eslami*, respectively.

73. In Farsi, *shura-ye neghaban*.

74. Determining a law's compatibility with Islam requires a majority vote of the six fuqaha on the council; determining a bill's compatibility with the constitution requires a majority vote of all members.

75. The terms *rahbar-e enqelab* and *vali-ye faqih* are used almost interchangeably.

76. Bani-Sadr was impeached by the Majles and removed from office in June 1981.

77. See, e.g., Shaul Bakhash, *The Reign of the Ayatollahs: Iran and the Islamic Revolution*, rev. ed. (New York: Basic, 1990), 223.

78. The Imam had always allowed clerics to stand for the Majles; with so many high-ranking revolutionary politicians having been assassinated by the MEK, he judged that the Islamic Republic needed a cleric, not a second-rate politician, as its president.

79. In Farsi, *shura-ye baznegari-ye qanun-e asasi*.

80. Khomeini named then president Khamenei as its first chairman. After Khamenei became leader, he named Rafsanjani, his presidential successor, as its second chairman. Rafsanjani retained the position after his presidency ended in 1997.

81. The Assembly of Experts (*majles-e khobregan*) should not be confused with the body that prepared the original constitution, which is also commonly rendered in English as Assembly of Experts.

82. E.g., newspaper accounts of the opening of the first postrevolutionary Majles in 1980 refer to Khamenei as an ayatollah.

83. Electronic communication with the authors.

84. Published in MERIP Reports, no. 98 (July–Aug. 1981). See also Jahangir Amuzegar, "The Iranian Economy before and after the Revolution," *Middle East Journal* 46, no. 3 (Summer 1992); Hossein Askari, "The Iranian Economy, Part 1: Iran's Slide to the Bottom," *Asia Times*, Sept. 14–15, 2010, and "Iran's Economy, Part 2: Ahmadinejad Shuns a Brighter Future," *Asia Times*, Sept. 15–16, 2010; and Steve Hanke, "Iran's Death Spiral," *Global Asia* (Oct. 2009).

85. See, i.a., Central Intelligence Agency (CIA), *World Factbook*; International Monetary Fund (IMF), *World Economic Outlook*; and World Bank, *World Development Indicators*.

86. See Javier Blas, "High Oil Prices Shield Iran from Sanctions," *Financial Times*, April 17, 2012.

87. Ladane Nasseri, "Iran's Non-Oil Exports Rose 28% to $43.7 Billion Last Year," Bloomberg, April 2, 2012, http://www.bloomberg.com/news/2012-04 -02/iran-s-non-oil-exports-rose-28-to-43-7-billion-last-year.html.

88. See CIA, *World Factbook*, and IMF, *World Economic Outlook*.

89. See also Djavad Salehi-Isfahani, "Oil Wealth and Economic Growth in Iran" in *Contemporary Iran: Economy, Society, Politics*, ed. Ali Gheissari (New York: Oxford University Press, 2009), 3–4, 13–22.

90. United Nations Development Programme, "Islamic Republic of Iran," in United Nations Development Programme, *Human Development Report 2011* (New York: United Nations Development Programme, 2011).

91. World Bank, "Iran—Country Brief," April 2012, (http://web.worldbank.org /WBSITE/EXTERNAL/COUNTRIES/MENAEXT/IRANEXTN/0, ,menuPK:312966~pagePK:141132~piPK:141107~theSitePK:312943,00.html).

92. Ann Puderbaugh, "Iran's Health Houses Provide Model for Mississippi Delta," *Global Health Matters* [National Institutes of Health] 8, no. 6 (Nov.–Dec. 2009); Bob Drogin, "Illness Is Their Common Enemy," *Los Angeles Times*, Jan. 25, 2010; "US Looks to Iran for Rural Health Care Model," MSNBC, June 29, 2010, http://article.wn.com/view/2010/06/29/US_looks_to _Iran_for_rural_health_care_model/; and Suzy Hansen, "What Can Mississippi Learn from Iran?" *New York Times Magazine*, July 27, 2012.

93. World Bank, "Iran."

94. The overall literacy rate for adults (defined as people over the age of fifteen) in the Islamic Republic today is roughly 80 percent. The rate is 85 percent for men and 75 percent for women—up from only 25 percent in 1976.

95. In 1978–79, the last academic year that commenced under the old regime, a total of 175,685 students were enrolled in tertiary schools in Iran. By 1999–2000, that figure had grown to more than 1.3 million; today, more than 2 million students are pursuing higher education in the Islamic Republic.

96. E-mail message received by the authors.

97. United Nations Development Programme, "Islamic Republic of Iran."

98. Zakkiyah Wahhab, "Universities in Iran Put Limits on Women's Options," *New York Times*, Aug. 20, 2012.

99. Cara Parks, "Once upon a Time in Tehran," *Foreign Policy*, Feb. 15, 2012, http://www.foreignpolicy.com/articles/2012/02/15/once_upon_a_time_in _tehran.

100. Michael Theodoulou, "First Muslim Women Conquer Mount Everest," *Christian Science Monitor*, June 1, 2005.

101. Beheshteh Olang et al., "Breastfeeding in Iran: Prevalence, Duration, and

Current Recommendations," *International Breastfeeding Journal* 4, no. 8 (Aug. 2009), and Mitra Zareai, "Creating a Breastfeeding Culture: A Comparison of Breastfeeding Practices in Iran and Australia," *Breastfeeding Review* 15, no. 2 (2007).

102. Nazila Fathi, "Iran Fights Scourge of Addiction in Plain View, Stressing Treatment," *New York Times*, June 27, 2008; "United Nations: Iran a Model of Drug Addiction Treatment," *TrèsSugar*, June 29, 2008, http://www .tressugar.com/United-Nations-Iran-Model-Drug-Addiction-Treatment -1743165; Tina Rosenberg, "An Enlightened Exchange in Iran," *New York Times*, Nov. 29, 2010; Francis Harrison, "Iran's Sex-Change Operations," BBC, Jan. 5, 2005; and Vanessa Barford, "Iran's 'Diagnosed Transsexuals,'" BBC, Feb. 25, 2008.

103. "Iran Showing Fastest Scientific Growth of Any Country," *New Scientist*, Feb. 18, 2010.

5: A LEADER AND THREE PRESIDENTS

1. Contrary to Western stereotypes, Khomeini was relatively progressive in his views on cultural issues; see Mehdi Moslem, *Factional Politics in Post-Khomeini Iran* (Syracuse: Syracuse University Press, 2002), 76–77.

2. In Farsi, *jonbesh-e eslahat.*

3. Naji, *Ahmadinejad,* 4–5.

4. On Ahmadinejad's wartime service in the Basij and other aspects of his early career, see "Interview" [with Mojtaba Samareh-Hahsemi, senior adviser to President Ahmadinejad], *Financial Times*, May 30, 2008, http:// www.ft.com/intl/cms/s/0/3c04bcbc-2d9e-11dd-b92a-000077b07658.html #axzz1vgV4dT73.

5. Naji, *Ahmadinejad,* 36–41.

6. *Osulgarayan,* literally meaning "those who adhere to or advocate fundamental principles."

7. James Reynolds, "Profile: Iran's 'Unremarkable' Supreme Leader Ayatollah Khamenei," BBC News, Aug. 4, 2011, http://www.bbc.co.uk/news/world -middle-east-14362281, and Houshang Asadi, "With Mr. Khamenei in the Shah's Dungeon," *Rooz*, Feb. 17, 2008, http://www.roozonline.com/persian /news/newsitem/article/with-mr-khamenei-in-the-shahs-dungeon.html.

8. The critical segment of this footage is included in *The Pariah State.* Less than a month after becoming leader, Khamenei said in a speech that he had not wanted even to be a member of a leadership council, a prospect seriously discussed in the last days and hours of Khomeini's life, and that he had prayed that he would not be involved in leadership in any way if it would damage his status in the hereafter; see Seyed Mohammad Marandi, "Ayatollah Khamenei and a Principled Foreign Policy," paper presented to an international conference, *Renovation and Intellectual Ijtihad in Imam*

Khamenei, Beirut, Lebanon, June 6–7, 2011, http://conflictsforum.org/2011/ayatollah-khamenei-and-a-principled-foreign-policy/.

9. The phrase, *eltezam-e amali*, comes from the Islamic Republic's electoral law.

10. On the left-right divide on economics, see Moslem, *Factional Politics in Post-Khomeini Iran*, 47–67; on the parliamentary debates and disputes between the Majles and the Guardian Council during this period, see Baktiari, *Parliamentary Politics in Revolutionary Iran*.

11. Formally, the IRP was dissolved because it had fulfilled its original purpose of defeating opposition to velayat-e faqih.

12. In Farsi, *jame'e-ye rohaniyat-e mobarez* and *majma'e rohaniyun-e mobarez*, respectively. *Mobarez* is a Farsi word referring to struggle; in this context, its translation as "combatant" is somewhat misleading. In an Iranian context, it is meant to evoke revolutionary descriptions of Islam as *maktab-e mobarez*, the "ideology of struggle."

13. IRNA, May 10, 2005. Five years earlier, Khamenei had made a similar observation in his first Friday prayer sermon after the May 2000 Majles elections.

14. Even before the revolution, Rafsanjani had acquired a reputation as someone who knew how to work the system to benefit his own economic interests. An official who served in the shah's last government has recounted how, as a young technocrat charged with reviewing Iran's trade policies, he launched an initiative to remove official subsidies for pistachio exports. He was soon visited by Rafsanjani, who—notwithstanding his high-profile support for the exiled Khomeini, which had led to his being imprisoned multiple times by the shah's security apparatus—insisted that the subsidies be restored, asking the "young man" on the other side of the desk if he really knew what he was doing. The official stood by his decision, and Rafsanjani left. Before the day ended, Rafsanjani had gotten to the young technocrat's superiors, who reinstated the subsidies.

15. In Farsi, *rast-e modern* and *rast-e sonnati*, respectively. In some English-language commentary, the modern right is described as "pragmatic conservatism"; see, e.g., Buchta, *Who Rules Iran?* Ali Gheissari and Vali Nasr describe the modern right simply as "moderates" or "pragmatists"; see *Democracy in Iran: History and the Quest for Liberty* (New York: Oxford University Press, 2006), 100–101.

16. For a discussion, see Salehi-Isfahani, "Oil Wealth and Economic Growth."

17. Bunny Noorayni, "Statoil Admits Iran Bribe," Bloomberg, Oct. 13, 2006, http://www.bloomberg.com/apps/news?pid=newsarchive&sid=aH7AcF9j_pn0&refer=europe.

18. In a four-man field, Rafsanjani's principal opponent was a conservative (Ahmad Tavvakoli); the other two candidates were also from the right side of the political spectrum.

19. The phrase "revolutionaries-turned-reformers" is from Mehran Kamrava,

Iran's Intellectual Revolution (Cambridge: Cambridge University Press, 2008), 123.

20. For a discussion, see, i.a., Daniel Brumberg, *Reinventing Khomeini: The Struggle for Reform in Iran* (Chicago: University of Chicago Press, 2001), 185–217, and Kamrava, *Iran's Intellectual Revolution*, 120–32.

21. On Ganji's career and thought, see, i.a., his *Road to Democracy in Iran*, trans. Abbas Milani with a foreword by Joshua Cohen and Abbas Milani (Cambridge: MIT Press for *Boston Review*, 2008); see also Kamrava, *Iran's Intellectual Revolution*, 206–9. On Hajjarian, see Rajae, *Islamism and Modernism*, 231–35, and Kamrava, *Iran's Intellectual Revolution*, 141–42 and 147. On Kadivar, see his "Velayat-e Faqih va Mardomsalari" [Velayat-e Faqih and Democracy], www.kadivar.com, and "*Wilayat-e faqih* and Democracy," in *Islam, the State, and Political Authority: Medieval Issues and Modern Concerns*, ed. Asma Afsaruddin (New York: Palgrave Macmillan, 2011); see also Rajae, *Islamism and Modernism*, 214–21, and Kamrava, *Iran's Intellectual Revolution*, 161–67. On Soroush, see *Democracy in Islam: Essential Writings of Abdolkarim Soroush*, trans. and ed. Mahmoud Sadri and Ahmad Sadri (New York: Oxford University Press, 2000); see also Robin Wright, *The Last Great Revolution: Turmoil and Transformation in Iran* (New York: Random House, 2000), 32–76; Rajae, *Islamism and Modernism*, 225–31; Kamrava, *Iran's Intellectual Revolution*, 155–61; and Ghamari-Tabrizi, *Islam and Dissent in Postrevolutionary Iran*. On Yazdi, see "Solution: Constitution without Velayat-e Faqih," interview with Ebrahim Yazdi, *Rooz*, June 29, 2008, http://www.roozonline.com/english/news3/newsitem/archive/2008 /june/29/article/solution-constitution-without-velayat-e-faqih.html.

22. Personal communications from Iranian scholars with access to the highest quality polling data from the 1997 campaign, produced by Islamic Republic of Iran Broadcasting (IRIB). Interestingly, both Chinese and Western diplomats serving in Tehran during the 1997 election say that Rafsanjani was actually quietly supportive of Khatami's campaign; for a more detailed exposition of this argument, see Gheissari and Nasr, *Democracy in Iran*, 131.

23. The "chain murders" were exposed in 1998 by journalists Emadeddin Baghi and Akbar Ganji, writing in a reformist newspaper founded by Saeed Hajjarian. In 1999, the government arrested and prepared to prosecute at least eighteen Information Ministry and Intelligence Ministry officials for their alleged involvement in the murders. The most senior official died in custody before standing trial. Three others were convicted and sentenced to death; their sentences were later commuted to life imprisonment. Nine officials were convicted and sentenced to prison terms of varying duration; five others were acquitted. See "Iranian Killers Spared Death Penalty," BBC News, Jan. 29, 2003, http://news.bbc.co.uk/2/hi/middle_east/2704023.stm.

24. See, e.g., Anoush Ehteshami and Mahjoob Zweiri, *Iran and the Rise of Its*

Neoconservatives: The Politics of Tehran's Silent Revolution (London: I. B. Tauris, 2007).

25. Personal communications with the authors.

26. The phrase is taken from Walter Posch, *Only Personal? The Larijani Affair Revisited*, Policy Brief 3 (Durham: Centre for Iranian Studies, Durham University, Nov. 2007).

27. In Farsi, *jame'e-ye eslami-ye mohandesin*.

28. See, e.g., Robin Wright, "Will Iran's 'Kennedys' Challenge Ahmadinejad?," *Time*, Aug. 17, 2009.

29. In this regard, it is striking how many older conservatives Larijani was able to recruit for the list of candidates associated with him in the 2008 Majles elections.

30. Personal communication with the authors.

31. In Farsi, *jamiyat-e isargaran-e enqilab-e eslami*. For a discussion, see Bill Samii, "Iran: A Rising Star in Party Politics," *Radio Free Europe/Radio Liberty*, Nov. 7, 2005, and "Association of the Devotees of the Islamic Revolution," *Iran Data Portal*, http://www.princeton.edu/irandataportal/parties/isargaran/.

32. Naji, *Ahmadinejad*, 46–47.

33. In Farsi, *e'telaf-e abadgaran-e iran-e eslami*.

34. Within the majority *osulgara* bloc, holding 190–200 of the parliamentary seats, Abadgaran had roughly 90–100 seats; the others were held by a cadre of older, traditional conservatives.

35. See, e.g., "From Brothels to 'Brother Bush': Campaigns of Iran's Hopefuls," *Middle East Online*, May 10, 2005, http://www.middle-east-online.com/english/?id=13456.

36. Marc Gasiorowski, "Viewpoint: The Causes and Consequences of Iran's June 2005 Presidential Election," *Strategic Insight* 4, no. 8 (Aug. 2005).

37. Personal communications with the authors.

38. See Gasiorowski, "Viewpoint." Before the election, Gasiorowski had predicted a Rafsanjani victory; see "Iran on the Eve of the Presidential Election," presentation at the Woodrow Wilson Center, Washington, D.C., May 23, 2005, http://www.wilsoncenter.org/sites/default/files/MarkGasiorowskiSummary.pdf.

6: A CONTROVERSIAL ELECTION

1. See Heideh Farmani and Farhad Pouladi, "Ahmadinejad Heading for Victory in Iran Polls," Agence France-Presse, June 11, 2009.

2. See, e.g., Nazila Fathi, "Support for Moderate a Challenge to Iran's Leader," *New York Times*, May 26, 2009; Scott Peterson, "In Iran, Ahmadinejad Opponent Sees Surge of Enthusiasm," *Christian Science Monitor*, June 6, 2009; and Roger Cohen, "Iran Awakens Yet Again," *New York Times*, June 11, 2009.

3. See Howard LaFranchi, "Wildcard in Iran Election: Obama," *Christian Science Monitor,* June 11, 2009, and Michael Slackman, "Hopeful Signs for U.S. in Lebanon Vote," *New York Times,* June 8, 2011; see also Paul Raushenbush, "The Obama Effect in Iran and Lebanon: Role Model Instead of Strong Man," *Huffington Post,* June 8, 2011, http://www.huffingtonpost.com/paul -raushenbush/the-obama-effect-in-iran_b_212399.html, and Simon Tisdall, "Lebanon Feels the Obama Effect," *Guardian,* June 8, 2009.

4. See Athena Jones, "Obama Administration Has Eye on Iran," MSNBC, June 12, 2009, http://firstread.msnbc.msn.com/_news/2009/06/12/4429059 -obama-administration-has-eye-on-iran?lite.

5. See Suzanne Maloney, "An Absurd Outcome," *Daily Beast,* June 13, 2009, http://www.thedailybeast.com/articles/2009/06/13/an-absurd-outcome .html, and "Reacting to Iran's Disputed Presidential Outcome," *Brookings Institution,* June 14, 2009, http://www.brookings.edu/research/opinions /2009/06/14-iran-election-maloney. See also Trita Parsi and Karim Sadjadpour, quoted in "Instant View: Iran's Election Result Staggers Analysts," Reuters, June 13, 2009; Michael Ledeen, "Faster, Please! The Iranian Circus III," *Pajamas Media,* June 13, 2009; Gary Sick, "Iran's Political Coup," *Gary's Choices,* June 13, 2009, http://garysick.tumblr.com/post/123070238/irans -political-coup; Trita Parsi and Robin Wright, "Iran's Presidential Election," *Diane Rehm Show,* June 15, 2009, http://thedianerehmshow.org/shows/2009 -06-15/irans-presidential-election; Reza Aslan, "Iran's Military Coup," *Daily Beast,* June 15, 2009, http://www.thedailybeast.com/articles/2009/06 /15/irans-military-coup.html; Barbara Slavin, "Analysis: Iran's Regime Likely Shaken for Good," *Washington Times,* June 16, 2009; and Farideh Farhi, "On Miscalculating an Election," Social Science Research Council, June 18, 2009, http://www.ssrc.org/features/pages/social-scientists-comment -on-irans-post-election-conflict/683/685/, and "Iran's Clash of Titans May Not Resolve Itself Soon" (interview with Bernard Gwertzman), Council on Foreign Relations, June 22, 2009, http://www.cfr.org/iran/irans-clash-titans -may-not-resolve-itself-soon/p19679.

6. Ali Ansari et al., *Preliminary Analysis of the Voting Figures in Iran's 2009 Presidential Election,* Programme Paper, Chatham House and the Institute of Iranian Studies, University of St. Andrews, June 21, 2009, http://www .chathamhouse.org/sites/default/files/public/Research/Middle%20East /iranelection0609.pdf.

7. *Daily Show with Jon Stewart,* June 15, 2009, http://www.thedailyshow.com/ watch/mon-june-15-2009/irandecision-2009—sham—wow.

8. Roger Cohen, "Iran's Day of Anguish," *New York Times,* June 14, 2009, and "Iran's Exiles," *New York Times,* March 22, 2010.

9. Discussions with members of President Ahmadinejad's staff, including senior adviser Mojtaba Samareh-Hashemi.

10. Naji, *Ahmadinejad,* 213–22 and 224–26.

11. In 2006, fifty prominent economists wrote an open letter to Ahmadinejad criticizing his government's economic policies; see "Open Letter of Economists to the President," *Economic New Agency*, July 2, 2006. The Majles Research Center also issued reports criticizing Ahmadinejad's economic approach. For a discussion, see Naji, *Ahmadinejad*, 229–35.

12. For details, see Ehteshami and Zweiri, *Iran and the Rise of Its Neoconservatives*, 65–69 and 77–79.

13. In Farsi, *jebhe-ye mottahed-e osulgarayan* and *e'telaf-e faragir-e osulgarayan*, respectively; for discussion, see Walter Posch, *Prospects for Iran's 2009 Presidential Elections*, Middle East Institute Policy Brief 24 (Washington, D.C.: Middle East Institute, June 2009), 5–6.

14. "Tehran Mayor in Davos to Seek $4 Billion for Construction Work," *Tehran Times*, Jan. 27, 2008, http://old.tehrantimes.com/index_View.asp?code=162036.

15. Personal communications with the authors.

16. Posch, *Prospects for Iran's 2009 Presidential Elections*.

17. In Farsi, *e'temad-e melli*.

18. Personal communications with the authors.

19. See the presentation by Steven Kull in "What Does the Iranian Public Really Think?," Panel 1, New America Foundation, Washington, D.C., Feb. 3, 2010, http://www.raceforiran.com/live-stream-what-does-the-iranian-public-really-think.

20. For a discussion, see Steven Kull et al., "An Analysis of Multiple Polls of the Iranian Public: The June 12 Election, The Perceived Legitimacy of the Regime, and the Nature of the Opposition," WorldPublicOpinion.org, Feb. 3, 2010, http://www.worldpublicopinion.org/pipa/pdf/feb10/IranElection_Feb10_rpt.pdf. For links to the data sets, see Kull, "An Analysis of Multiple Polls," and "Analysis of Multiple Polls Finds Little Evidence Iranian Public Finds Government Illegitimate," WorldPublicOpinion.org, Feb. 3, 2010, http://worldpublicopinion.org/pipa/articles/brmiddleeastnafricara/652.php?lb=brme&pnt=652&nid=&id=.

21. International Peace Institute with Charney Research, *Iran: Public Opinion on Foreign, Nuclear and Domestic Issues*, Dec. 8, 2010, http://www.ipinst.org/events/details/256-Iran,%20Lebanon,%20Israelis%20and%20Palestinians-%20New%20IPI%20Opinion%20Polls.html.

22. Personal communications with the authors from advisers to both Mousavi and former president Khatami.

23. Mousavi's wife, artist and academic Zahra Rehnavard, was the first spouse to play a publicly prominent role in an Iranian presidential campaign; Western coverage made much of her participation, reinforcing the image of Mousavi's candidacy as the rebirth of the reform movement.

24. Indeed, a media adviser to one of Ahmadinejad's principlist rivals—who considered challenging the incumbent but ultimately stayed out—told us

that polls commissioned by his boss before the June 2009 election showed that Mousavi did not have the "capacity" to win.

25. For a video, with English-language voice-over, see http://www.youtube.com /watch?v=9DNmR15Lui8. According to a classified U.S. embassy cable published by WikiLeaks, Mousavi advisers told a Voice of America Farsi-language broadcaster that the debates "may have been a mistake"; see London 1423, June 16, 2009, http://www.cablegatesearch.net/cable.php ?id=09LONDON1423.

26. See, e.g., Parsi, *A Single Roll of the Dice*, 85.

27. Mousavi won a majority of the vote in forty-six districts in ten provinces; overall, though, he was bested by Ahmadinejad in twenty-nine of thirty-one provinces.

28. For a more detailed discussion, see Kull, "An Analysis of Multiple Polls of the Iranian Public," and Kull in "What Does the Iranian Public Really Think?"

29. Karroubi and Rezae continued to score in the single digits. For discussion, see Kull, "An Analysis of Multiple Polls of the Iranian Public," and Kull in "What Does the Iranian Public Really Think?"

30. See, e.g., Jon Cohen, "About Those Iran Polls," *Washington Post*, June 15, 2009. See also Hooman Majd's comments in "Iranian Election Results," *Charlie Rose*, June 15, 2009, http://www.charlierose.com/view/inter-view/10385 (Flynt Leverett also appeared).

31. For further discussion, see Kull, "An Analysis of Multiple Polls of the Iranian Public," and Kull in "What Does the Iranian Public Really Think?"

32. Even Hooman Majd—a relative of former president Khatami and one of the few U.S.-based Iranian expatriates, writes with exceptional insight and honesty about life in the Islamic Republic—fell into this trap. In "What Does the Iranian Public Really Think?," he argued that no one should believe any poll conducted in Iran, because "Iranians are famous for not telling the truth to strangers."

33. Besides his own (methodologically flawed) polls, Mousavi had access to polls conducted by the Ministry of Interior. We have not seen them and cannot evaluate their credibility. However, at least one analyst claiming familiarity with them says that, through their last running close to election day, they suggested that Mousavi could at least force Ahmadinejad into a runoff. Following the election, some Mousavi supporters privately hypothesized that the ministry may have slanted the poll results in order to keep Mousavi from dropping out and thereby damaging the election's credibility internationally and perhaps even domestically. Again, we have no basis for evaluating such a surmise.

34. "Iran's Rafsanjani Writes Open Letter to Khamenei over President's 'Accusations,'" *BBC Monitoring International Reports*, June 9, 2009.

35. London 1423.

36. "Mousavi Letter to Iran's Supreme Leader," BBC, June 14, 2009, http://news .bbc.co.uk/2/hi/8099876.stm. Mousavi also charged that Ahmadinejad's administration had engaged in "extensive utilization of government facilities" for its "propaganda," through "trips of official authorities and ministers"—a complaint that has been heard in every Iranian election involving an incumbent president (and that is hardly unique to Iran).

37. These are the "representatives" to which Mousavi referred in his June 11 letter to Khamenei; see "Mousavi Letter to Iran's Supreme Leader." No candidate has ever sent observers to every polling station; typically, though, the more serious candidates send observers to most of them.

38. We have examined the identification cards (*shenasnameh* in Farsi) of several Iranians kind enough to let us inspect them and to describe the voting process to us. This description is essentially identical to that provided in the most thorough study of the election undertaken outside of Iran, by Eric Brill, an American lawyer who is former editor of the *Harvard Civil Rights–Civil Liberties Law Review*. Brill's monograph, *Did Mahmoud Ahmadinejad Steal the 2009 Iran Election?*, was originally published in Flynt Leverett and Hillary Mann Leverett, "Persistent (and Game-Changing) Myths: Iran's 2009 Presidential Election, One Year Later," *Race for Iran*, June 11, 2010, http://www.raceforiran.com/persistent-and-game-changing-myths-iran %E2%80%99s-2009-presidential-election-one-year-later. It is available at http://www.raceforiran.com/wp-content/uploads/2010/06/IranArticle -060110.pdf.

39. This description is drawn from discussions with Iranians who have been involved in the observation process; it is also identical to the description offered in Brill, *Did Mahmoud Ahmadinejad Steal the 2009 Iran Election?*

40. An English translation of Mousavi's June 14 letter to the Guardian Council may be found at http://www.scribd.com/doc/16415619/Mousavis-Letter-to -Guardian-Council-for-Nullification-of-the-Election-Results20090614, and of his June 28 letter in "Mousavi Remains Defiant," *Tehran Bureau*, June 28, 2009, http://www.pbs.org/wgbh/pages/frontline/tehranbureau/2009 /06/mousavi-remains-defiant.html.

41. "Full Text of Guardian Council Report on Iran Presidential Election," BBC Monitoring Middle East, July 18, 2009, http://www.iranaffairs.com/files/ document.pdf (henceforth referred to as Guardian Council report).

42. Ansari, *Preliminary Analysis of the Voting Figures in Iran's 2009 Presidential Election*.

43. See, e.g., Nate Silver, "Worst. Damage Control. Ever," FiveThirtyEight, June 21, 2009, http://www.fivethirtyeight.com/2009/06/worst-damage-control-ever.html.

44. The rule is different for elections to the Assembly of Experts, the Majles, and municipal councils. As the Guardian Council itself explained, "With regard to these three elections, voters who have voted in a certain area in the first

round of the election can only take part in the second round of the election in the same area where they have cast their votes in the first round"; see Guardian Council report.

45. Ibid. Additionally, the Guardian Council points out that, in some districts, the criterion for estimating the number of eligible voters was Iran's most recent census, taken in 2006, while, in others, estimates had simply been carried over from the previous presidential election. Neither was likely to yield a wholly accurate baseline.

46. See Ansari in "Post-Election Iran 2009: Special Coverage, Show 1, Part 2," *Press TV*, http://www.youtube.com/watch?v=awuQ0w_mAqw; see also Seyed Mohammad Marandi's refutation of Ansari's claims on the same program.

47. E.g., Shemiranat, a north Tehran suburb that, by the official results, was perhaps the most pro-Mousavi quarter in Iran.

48. Guardian Council report. The law governing the 2009 presidential election specifies that candidates should present documentation on their observers at least five days before election day.

49. Ibid.

50. Brill, *Did Mahmoud Ahmadinejad Steal the 2009 Iran Election?*

51. Guardian Council report; for a further discussion, see Brill, *Did Mahmoud Ahmadinejad Steal the 2009 Iran Election?* Based on its own investigation, the council concluded that there may have been stations where "candidates' representatives, although aware of the time of voting, turned up to carry out their duties one or two hours after voting had started. It is clear that, under such circumstances, the election could not be delayed and people could not be forced to wait due to the fact that the representatives turned up late."

52. Guardian Council report and *Did Ahmadinejad Steal the 2009 Iran Election?*

53. *Did Ahmadinejad Steal the 2009 Iran Election?*

54. The Mousavi campaign also forwarded to the Guardian Council a number of additional complaints about vote counting that were not highlighted in the candidate's formal letters. According to the Guardian Council, on election day Mousavi's campaign identified seven polling stations where, it claimed, ballot boxes had been improperly handled. The council concluded that the claims were "unsubstantiated," noting that "on election day and amongst the unexpected crowd of people in polling stations and in the presence of Guardian Council observers and candidates' representatives, it is not possible" to move ballot boxes into unidentified locations and tamper with them.

55. E.g., Scott Lucas, "The Latest from Iran (22 June): Rumbling On," *Enduring America*, June 22, 2010, http://enduringamerica.com/2010/06/22/the-latest-from-iran-22-june-rumbling-on/#comments, and Ali Ansari, *Crisis of Authority: Iran's 2009 Presidential Election* (London: Chatham House, 2010), 5–6. In response, Brill notes that "one who claims electoral fraud is expected

to specify who, what, where, when—not merely allege that many wrongs were done to many people in many places at many times, and then insist that the government prove that none of these wrongs was done to anyone, anywhere, at any time." See *Did Ahmadinejad Steal the 2009 Election?*, 13. Brill goes on to note that candidates advancing allegations of fraud "must examine the available information and specify improprieties so that their charges can be investigated. At which polling stations was Mousavi's registered observer barred from watching the ballot-box sealing, or turned away entirely, or ejected or obstructed after he arrived? At which polling stations did Mousavi's representative refuse to approve the count because he believed it was incorrect or had witnessed fraud? Which mobile polling stations were Mousavi's designated observers not allowed to accompany? If Mousavi's complaints are valid, he must have all of this information readily available."

56. Karroubi also boycotted, while Rezae sent observers.

57. Guardian Council report. Of course, one could choose simply to disbelieve the council's findings; this is the approach taken in Farhad Khosrokhavar and Marie Ladier-Fouladi, *The 2009 Presidential Election in Iran: Fair or Foul?*, EUI Working Paper (Florence, Italy: Robert Schuman Centre for Advanced Studies, European University Institute, June 2012). But, as noted in the text, neither Mousavi nor anyone connected with his campaign ever took public issue with any of the council's specific conclusions.

58. See, eg., Gary Sick, "Iranian Opinion and the June Election," *Gary's Choices*, Sept. 20, 2009, http://garysick.tumblr.com/post/192851571/iranian-opinion -and-the-june-election.

59. See Ansari et al., *Preliminary Analysis of the Voting Figures in Iran's 2009 Presidential Election*, and Dubai 0249, June 15, 2009, http://wikileaks.org/ cable/2009/06/09RPODUBAI249.html.

60. See Ansari et al., *Preliminary Analysis of the Voting Figures in Iran's 2009 Presidential Election*; Juan Cole, "Iran's Stolen Election," *Informed Comment*, June 13, 2009, http://www.juancole.com/2009/06/stealing-iranian-election .html; and Khosrokhavar and Ladier-Fouladi, *The 2009 Presidential Election in Iran: Fair or Foul?*

61. This point is made in Reza Esfandiari and Yousef Bozorgmehr, "A Rejoinder to the Chatham House Report on Iran's 2009 Presidential Election Offering a New Analysis of the Results," in "Persistent (and Game-Changing) Myths."

62. Sadjadpour, "Q&A: Was the Iranian Election Rigged?," CNN, June 15, 2009, http://articles.cnn.com/2009-06-15/world/iran.elections.qa_1_amir-taheri -votes-cast-presidential-elections/2?_s=PM:WORLD, and Dubai 0249.

63. In 2009, his margins of victory in Ardabil and East Azerbaijan were smaller, and, as noted in the text, he narrowly lost in West Azerbaijan.

64. Esfandiari and Bozorgmehr, "A Rejoinder to the Chatham House Report," 22.

65. Ansari, *Crisis of Authority: Iran's 2009 Presidential Election* (London: Chatham House, 2010).

66. See, e.g., London 1423 and London 1442, June 18, 2009, http://www.cable gatesearch.net/cable.php?id=09LONDON1442.

67. Ali Gheissari and Vali Nasr, "The Conservative Consolidation in Iran," *Survival* 47, no. 2 (Summer 2005), 180–81; Takeyh, *Guardians of the Revolution*, 227; and Elliot Hen-Tov and Nathan Gonzalez, "The Myth of Post-Khomeini Iran: Praetorianism 2.0," *Washington Quarterly* 34, no. 1 (Winter 2011).

68. Gary Sick, "Iran's Dangerous Power Vacuum," *Daily Beast*, Nov. 26, 2009, http://www.thedailybeast.com/articles/2009/11/26/irans-dangerous-power -vacuum.html, and Glenn Kessler, "Clinton Says U.S. Fears Iran Is Becoming a Military Dictatorship," *Washington Post*, Feb. 15, 2010.

69. The Guards' new mission also meant the government would not decommission sizable cadres of war veterans at a time when the economy was ill-positioned to absorb them into the labor force.

70. Khatam ol Anbia, which would later be subjected to unilateral U.S. sanctions and multilateral sanctions by the United Nations Security Council.

71. See the sources cited in Hen-Tov and Gonzalez, "The Myth of Post-Khomeini Iran," 58, fn. 25.

72. Ali Alfoneh, "The Revolutionary Guards' Role in Iranian Politics," *Middle East Forum* 15, no. 4 (Fall 2008).

73. "Supreme Leader Khamenei's Friday Address Following the Presidential Election," *Informed Comment*, June 19, 2009, http://www.juancole. com/2009/06/supreme-leader-khameneis-friday-address.html and http:// www.youtube.com/watch?v=hLiBp8qxuMA.

74. Kull, "An Analysis of Multiple Polls of the Iranian Public," and International Peace Institute/Charney Research, *Iran*.

75. Jahangir Salehain, "A Step Too Far," *Tehran Bureau*, March 25, 2010.

76. Cameron Abdi, "Neda Lives," *Foreign Policy*, June 14, 2010, http://www.for eignpolicy.com/articles/2010/06/14/neda_lives?page=full.

77. Sue Pleming, "U.S. State Department Speaks to Twitter over Iran," Reuters, June 16, 2009.

78. Thomas Friedman, "The Virtual Mosque," *New York Times*, June 17, 2009, http://www.nytimes.com/2009/06/17/opinion/17friedman.html. For a critical review, see Evgeny Morozov, *The Net Delusion: The Dark Side of Internet Freedom* (New York: PublicAffairs, 2011), 1–19.

79. Mike Musgrove, "Twitter Is a Player in Iran's Drama," *Washington Post*, June 17, 2009, http://www.washingtonpost.com/wp-dyn/content/article /2009/06/16/AR2009061603391.html.

80. Golnarz Esfandiari, "The Twitter Devolution," *Foreign Policy*, June 7, 2010, http://www.foreignpolicy.com/articles/2010/06/07/the_twitter_revolution_ that_wasnt.

81. Steve Cemons, "Dying in Tehran" and "Foreign Embassies in Iran Taking in

Injured?," *Washington Note*, June 20, 2009, http://www.thewashingtonnote
.com/archives/2009/06/dying_in_tehran/ and http://www.thewashingtonnote
.com/archives/2009/06/foreign_embassi/.

82. "The FP Interview: Mohsen Makhmalbaf," *Foreign Policy*, June 18, 2009, http://
www.foreignpolicy.com/articles/2009/06/17/the_fp_interview_mohsen
_makhmalbaf, and Mousavi, Jan. 1, 2010, statement published in Kaleme.

83. For a discussion of the sources and a critical evaluation of Western journalists' misreporting on crowd size, see Flynt Leverett and Hillary Mann Leverett, "Leveretts Respond to Their Critics," *Race for Iran*, Jan. 7, 2010, http://
www.raceforiran.com/leveretts-respond-to-critics.

84. For a discussion, with links to the relevant documents, see "The Green
Movement Is Not the Future of Iran," *Race for Iran*, June 21, 2010, http://
www.raceforiran.com/the-green-movement-is-not-the-future-of-iran.

85. Robin Wright, "Abdolkarim Soroush on the Goals of Iran's Green Movement," *Huffington Post*, Jan. 7, 2010, http://www.huffingtonpost.com/robin
-wright/abdolkarim-soroush-on-the_b_414882.html.

86. See Slavin, "Dawn of a New Iran," *Washington Note*, Feb. 3, 2010, http://
www.thewashingtonnote.com/archives/2010/02/barbara_slavin/, and Wright,
"Abdolkarim Soroush on the Goals of Iran's Green Movement."

87. Leverett and Leverett, "Another Revolution in Iran."

88. See Reza Aslan in "Tensions Arise Anew around Iran's Nuclear, Political
Goals," PBS *NewsHour*, Feb. 11, 2010, http://www.pbs.org/newshour/bb/
politics/jan-june10/iran2_02-11.html (Flynt Leverett also appeared). See
also Aslan, "The Green Movement Is Alive and Well," in Nader Hashemi
and Danny Postol, eds., *The People Reloaded: The Green Movement and the
Struggle for Iran's Future* (Brooklyn: Melville House, 2010).

89. Borzou Daragahi on France 24, Feb. 11, 2010; see Flynt Leverett and Hillary
Mann Leverett, "Misreading Iranian Politics in Washington," *Race for
Iran*, Feb. 12, 2010, http://www.raceforiran.com/misreading-iranian-politics
-in-washington.

90. Michael Crowley, "Iran Contrarians," *New Republic*, Feb. 26, 2010.

91. On this point, too, Mousavi's standing was harmed by Mohsen Makhmalbaf's sensationalist accounts purporting to describe the leader's "private life."
See Makhmalbaf, "Secrets of Khamenei's Private Life, Part 1—His Interests," Dec. 29, 2009, http://homylafayette.blogspot.com/2009/12/makhmalbaf
-secrets-khameneis-life.html; "Part 2—His Entourage and Household Operations," Dec. 30, 2009, http://homylafayette.blogspot.com/2009/12/makhmal
baf-secrets-of-khameneis-life.html; and "Part 3—His Wealth," Jan. 1, 2010,
http://homylafayette.blogspot.com/2010/01/makhmalbaf-secrets-of
-khameneis-life.html.

92. See, e.g., London 1423. A European diplomat in Tehran at the time told us
that Rafsanjani fell four votes short in this effort.

93. Leverett, Leverett, and Marandi, "Will Iran Be Obama's Iraq?"

94. "Assembly of Experts Expresses Strong Support for Leader's Guildelines," *Tehran Times*, June 21, 2009, http://old.tehrantimes.com/index_View.asp?code=197201.

95. "Reliance on Leader Essential for Maintaining Unity: Rafsanjani," *Tehran Times*, Feb. 24, 2010, http://old.tehrantimes.com/index_View.asp?code=197201.

96. http://khordaad88.com/?p=1408#more-1408. We have modified the translation of the quoted passage.

97. Gary Sick, "Assassination in Tehran," *Gary's Choices*, Jan. 12, 2010, http://garysick.tumblr.com/post/331348272/assassination-in-tehran.

98. Hashemi and Postol, "Introduction," in Hashemi and Postol, *The People Reloaded*, xv.

99. Nasser Karimi, "Kahrizak Prison, Holding Iranian Protestors, Ordered Closed after Abuses," Associated Press, July 28, 2009; "Death Penalty for Iran Jail Abuse," BBC, June 30, 2010; and "Three Iranian Judicial Officials Suspended over Kahrizak," *Tehran Times*, Aug. 23, 2010.

100. Amnesty International, "Post-Election Iran Violations among Worst in 20 Years," Dec. 10, 2009, http://www.amnesty.org/en/news-and-updates/report/post-election-iran-violations-among-worst-20-years-20091210.

101. See Amnesty International, "Post-Election Iran Violations among Worst in 20 Years," and Human Rights Watch, "Iran," in *World Report 2011* (New York: Human Rights Watch, 2011).

102. Khamenei pardoned eighty-one people in connection with the first anniversary of the 2009 election; see "Iran Pardons, Commutes Sentences for Dozens of Detainees," CNN, June 3, 2010. In 2011, he pardoned another seventy people during the Muslim month of Ramadan; see Ramin Mostaghim, "Iran Pardons Some Activists in 2009 Election Protests," *Los Angeles Times*, Aug. 28, 2011.

103. "Urban Riots: The Battle for the Streets," *Guardian*, Aug. 9, 2011.

104. "The Criminals Who Shame Our Nation," *Daily Telegraph*, Aug. 9, 2011.

105. "Cameron Riot Statement in Full," *politics.co.uk*, Aug. 9, 2011, http://www.politics.co.uk/comment-analysis/2011/08/09/cameron-riot-statement-in-full.

106. IPI/Charney, *Iran*.

107. "Obama Vows Toughest Sanctions Yet on Iran," CBS News, Oct. 13, 2011.

108. Hooman Majd, "Think Again: Iran's Green Movement," *Foreign Policy*, Jan. 6, 2010, and Hamid Dabashi, *Iran, the Green Movement, and the USA: The Fox and the Paradox* (London: Zed Books, 2010), 101–102.

109. "Mir-Hossein Mousavi's 18th Statement," *khordaad88.com* [from Kaleme], June 15, 2010, http://khordaad88.com/?p=1691#more-1691.

110. Thomas Erdbrink, "Iran's Mousavi Issues Charter, Seeks Radical Reforms on Clerical Rule," *Washington Post*, June 16, 2010.

111. To the consternation of American neoconservatives and other Western

observers, current Iranian initiatives in this area have elicited strong praise from the IMF.

Part Three: The Islamic Republic as American Target

PROLOGUE

1. On the U.S. sanctions in place against the Islamic Republic and on the Iran-related secondary sanctions authorized under U.S. law, see *U.S.-Iranian Relations: An Analytic Compendium of U.S. Policies, Laws, and Regulations* (Washington, D.C.: February 2011, http://www.acus.org/files/publication_pdfs/403/Feb11_ACUS_IranCompendium.pdf), 13–44, 73–165.
2. Victoria Nuland, "U.S. Launches Virtual Embassy Tehran," U.S. Department of State, Dec. 6, 2011, http://blogs.state.gov/index.php/site/entry/virtual_embassy_tehran.
3. United Nations Conference on Trade and Development, *World Investment Report, 2012* (New York: United Nations, 2011), 171.
4. *The World Factbook*, https://www.cia.gov/library/publications/the-world-factbook/rankorder/2187rank.html.
5. *World Economic Outlook, April 2012* (Washington, D.C.: International Monetary Fund, 2012) and Ladane Nasseri and Dana El Baltaji, "Iran's Economy to Shrink on Tighter Sanctions, World Bank Says," Bloomberg, June 12, 2012, http://www.bloomberg.com/news/2012-06-12/iran-s-economy-to-shrink-on-tighter-sanctions-world-bank-says.html.
6. Henny Sender, "Iran Accepts Renminbi for Crude Oil," *Financial Times*, May 7, 2012.
7. For a provocative analysis, see Neelam Deo and Akshay Mathur, "BRICS 'Hostage' to West over Iran Sanctions, Need Financial Institutions," *Financial Times*, June 27, 2012.
8. U.S. Department of Defense, "Remarks by Secretary of Defense Leon E. Panetta at the Saban Center," Dec. 2, 1011, http://www.defense.gov/transcripts/transcript.aspx?transcriptid=4937.

7: MYTHS AND MYTHMAKERS

1. See Michael Hunt, *Ideology and U.S. Foreign Policy* (New Haven: Yale University Press, 1987); Stefan Halper and Jonathan Clarke, *The Silence of the Rational Center: Why American Foreign Policy Is Failing* (New York: Basic, 2007), 2–10, 21–48, and Michael Desch, "America's Liberal Illiberalism: The Ideological Origins of Overreaction in U.S. Foreign Policy," *International Security* 32, no. 3 (Winter 2007–08).
2. See Chaim Kaufmann, "Threat Inflation and the Failure of the Market of Ideas: The Selling of the Iraq War," *International Security* 29, no. 1 (Summer

2004), and Russell Burgos, "Origins of Regime Change: 'Ideapolitik' on the Long Road to Baghdad, 1993–2000," *Security Studies* 17, no. 2 (April 2008).

3. See Uday Singh Mehta, *Liberalism and Empire: A Study in Nineteenth-Century Liberal Thought* (Chicago: University of Chicago Press, 1999); Jennifer Pitts, *Turn to Empire* (Princeton: Princeton University Press, 2006); and Hunt, *Ideology and U.S. Foreign Policy*, 19–91.

4. From the introduction to Mill's 1859 essay *On Liberty*.

5. Weber used the phrase in his 1919 lecture "Politics as a Vocation."

6. Edward Said, *Orientalism* (New York: Random House, 1978).

7. See Douglas Little, *American Orientalism: The United States and the Middle East since 1945*, 3rd ed. (Chapel Hill: University of North Carolina Press, 2008), 9–42.

8. Cyrus Ghani, *Iran and the Rise of Reza Shah: From Qajar Collapse to Pahlavi Power* (London: I. B. Tauris, 1998), 21–63.

9. Even since the United States became a net oil importer in the 1970s, Middle Eastern supplies have never satisfied a high percentage of its oil demand; see "Consumer's Guide to Energy—U.S. Dependence on Foreign Oil Sources," July 28, 2011, http://www.energy.org/cat00040918cmp00003628.html.

10. On Persian Gulf hydrocarbons and America's post–World War II strategic position, see, esp., Doug Stokes and Sam Raphael, *Global Energy Security and American Hegemony* (Baltimore: Johns Hopkins University Press, 2010), 1–53.

11. Said, "Islam Through Western Eyes," *Nation*, April 26, 1980.

12. Linda Witt, "Can the Shah of Iran Survive? A U.S. Expert Has an Answer and Some Surprising Reasons," *People*, Nov. 28, 1978.

13. Edward Said, *Covering Islam: How the Media and the Experts Determine How We See the World* (New York: Random House, 1981).

14. John Mearsheimer, "Hans Morgenthau and the Iraq War: Realism Versus Neo-Conservatism," www.opendemocracy.net, May 19, 2005; see also Brian Schmidt and Michael Williams, "The Bush Doctrine and the Iraq War: Neo-conservatism versus Realism," *Security Studies* 17, no. 2 (April 2008).

15. On Cold War neoconservatism, see John Ehrman, *The Rise of Neoconservatism: Intellectuals and Foreign Affairs, 1946-1994* (New Haven: Yale University Press, 1996); Jacob Heilbrun, *They Knew They Were Right: The Rise of the Neocons* (New York: Random House, 2008), 23–199; and Justin Vaïsse, *Neoconservatism: A Biography of a Movement*, trans. Arthur Goldhammer (Cambridge: Belknap/Harvard University Press, 2010), 21–208.

16. Michael Ledeen, "Let's Talk with Iran Now," *New York Times*, July 19, 1988.

17. Norman Podhoretz, *World War IV: The Long Struggle against Islamofascism* (New York: Doubleday, 2007).

18. See *A Clean Break: A New Strategy for Securing the Realm* (Jerusalem: Institute for Advanced Strategic and Political Studies, 1996) and Project for a New American Century, "Letter to President Clinton on Iraq," Jan. 26, 1998, http://www.newamericancentury.org/iraqclintonletter.htm.

19. See, e.g., Michael Ledeen, "Time to Focus on Iran: The Mother of Modern Terrorism," address to the Jewish Institute for National Security Affairs, Nov. 30, 2003, and *The Iranian Time Bomb: The Mullah Zealots' Quest for Destruction* (New York: St. Martin's, 2007).

20. Eliot Cohen, "World War IV: Let's Call This Conflict What It Is," *Wall Street Journal*, Nov. 20, 2001.

21. See, e.g., "Iran's Supreme Leader Dead," *Pajamas Media*, Jan. 4, 2007, and "Khamenei Said to Be in Coma," *Pajamas Media*, Oct. 13, 2009.

22. Charles Krauthammer, "Obama Misses the Point in Iran Response," *Washington Post*, June 19, 2009; David Brooks and Gail Collins, "The Insanity on and in Iran," *New York Times*, June 24, 2009; and Robert Kagan, "How Obama Can Reverse Iran's Dangerous Course," *Washington Post*, Jan. 27, 2010, and "Seizing the Moment for Reform in Iran," National Public Radio, Jan. 27, 2010.

23. See Michael Ledeen, "Iran with the Bomb or Bomb Iran: The Need for Regime Change," *Encyclopedia Britannica*, Oct. 9, 2007, http://www.britannica.com /blogs/2007/10/the-islamic-threat-and-the-need-for-regime-change-in-iran, and "Iran: Engagement or Regime Change?"

24. See, e.g., Bret Stephens, "Seven Myths about Iran," *Wall Street Journal*, Feb. 2, 2010; Reuel Marc Gerecht, "Should Israel Bomb Iran?," *Weekly Standard*, July 26, 2011; Jamie Fly and Gary Schmitt, "The Case for Regime Change in Iran," *Foreign Affairs*, Jan. 17, 2012; and Niall Ferguson, "Israel and Iran on the Eve of Destruction in a New Six-Day War," *Newsweek*, Feb. 6, 2012.

25. Richard Haass, "Enough Is Enough," *Newsweek*, Jan. 21, 2010, http://www .thedailybeast.com/newsweek/2010/01/21/enough-is-enough.html; for a discussion, see Flynt Leverett and Hillary Mann Leverett, "Richard Haass's 'Enough Is Enough': Where Have We Heard That Before?," *Race for Iran*, Jan. 26, 2010, http://www.raceforiran.com/richard-haasss-%E2%80%9Cenough -is-enough%E2%80%9D-where-have-we-heard-that-before.

26. On post–Cold War neoconservatism, see Stefan Halper and Jonathan Clarke, *America Alone: The Neoconservatives and the Global Order* (Cambridge: Cambridge University Press, 2005); Jacob Heilbrun, *They Knew They Were Right*, 199–280; and Vaïsse, *Neoconservatism*, 220–70. For a further critical discussion of neoconservative views on the Islamic Republic, see Adib-Moghaddam, *Iran in World Politics*, 123–54.

27. See also Halper and Clarke, *America Alone*.

28. Reuel Marc Gerecht, "The Last Orientalist," *Weekly Standard*, June 5, 2006.

29. Heilbrun, *They Knew They Were Right*, 115, 123, 139–40. For an account of Lewis's career by one of his doctoral students, see Martin Kramer, "Bernard Lewis," *Encyclopedia of Historians and Historical Writing* (London: Fitzroy Dearborn, 1999), 719–20.

30. Bernard Lewis, "Communism and Islam," *International Affairs* 30, no. 1 (Jan. 1954).

31. Ibid.

32. Bernard Lewis, "The Roots of Muslim Rage," *Atlantic Monthly*, Sept. 1990, 60.

33. Bernard Lewis, "Islamic Revolution," *New York Review of Books*, Jan. 21, 1988.

34. Bernard Lewis, "Islam and Liberal Democracy," *Atlantic*, Feb. 1993.

35. Lewis, "August 22."

36. Fouad Ajami, *The Foreigner's Gift: The Americans, the Arabs, and the Iraqis in Iraq* (New York: Free Press, 2006).

37. Fouad Ajami, "A History Writ in Oil" [review of James Bill, *The Eagle and the Lion: The Tragedy of American-Iranian Relations*], *New York Times*, May 8, 1988.

38. Fouad Ajami, "Iran: The Impossible Revolution," *Foreign Affairs* 67, no. 2 (Winter 1988), 144.

39. Fouad Ajami, "A Revolution Still," *U.S. News and World Report*, May 7, 2000, and "Iran Must Finally Pay a Price," *Wall Street Journal*, May 5, 2008.

40. Ajami, "Iran Must Finally Pay a Price."

41. www.campus-watch.org.

42. www.defenddemocracy.org.

43. Letter from Senators Robert Menendez and Mark Kirk to Treasury Secretary Timothy Geithner, Jan. 19, 2012, http://www.foreignpolicy.com/files/fp_uploaded_documents/120119_Menendez-Kirk%20Letter%20to%20SEC-TREAS%20on%20CBI%20Implementation%20Rules.pdf.

44. Mearsheimer, "Imperial by Design."

45. Stephen Walt, "What Intervention in Libya Tells Us about the Neocon-Liberal Alliance," *Foreign Policy*, March 21, 2011, http://walt.foreignpolicy.com/posts/2011/03/21/what_intervention_in_libya_tells_us_about_the_neocon_liberal_alliance.

46. For an emblematic statement, see Richard Holbrooke, "Authentically Liberal," *Foreign Affairs*, July–Aug. 2006. For a discussion, see Vaïsse, *Neoconservatism*, 208–19.

47. Burgos, "Origins of Regime Change."

48. Ari Berman, "The Strategic Class," *Nation*, Aug. 29, 2005.

49. Kenneth Pollack, *The Threatening Storm: The Case for Invading Iraq* (New York: Random House, 2002).

50. "An Hour with Thomas Friedman of the *New York Times*," *Charlie Rose*, May 30, 2003, http://www.charlierose.com/view/interview/1947.

51. Tony Judt, "Bush's Useful Idiots," *London Review of Books* 28, no. 18 (Sept. 2006), http://www.lrb.co.uk/v28/n18/tony-judt/bushs-useful-idiots.

52. Anne-Marie Slaughter, "Iran Symposium," *Dissent* (Winter 2007), 95.

53. Suzanne Maloney, "Diplomatic Strategies for Dealing with Iran: How Tehran Might Respond," in James Miller et al., eds., *Iran: Assessing U.S. Policy Options* (Washington, D.C.: Center for a New American Security, 2008).

54. Susan Rice, "We Need a Real Iran Policy," *Washington Post*, Dec. 30, 2004, and Samantha Power, "Rethinking Iran," *Time*, Jan. 17, 2008; see also Slaughter, "Iran Symposium," 96.

55. Leslie Gelb and Jeanne-Paloma Zelmati, "Mission Unaccomplished," *Democracy: A Journal of Ideas* (Summer 2009).

56. *Meeting the Challenge: Stopping the Clock* (Washington, D.C.: Bipartisan Policy Center, 2012).

57. http://www.unitedagainstnucleariran.com/about/mission and http://www.unitedagainstnucleariran.com/about/coalition.

58. http://www.unitedagainstnucleariran.com/about/mission.

59. "Cracks in Iran's Clique," *New York Times*, Sept. 22, 2009.

60. John Mearsheimer and Stephen Walt, *The Israel Lobby and U.S. Foreign Policy* (New York: Farrar, Straus and Giroux, 2007), 112.

61. Hillary Mann Leverett worked at AIPAC as an intern in the summer of 1986.

62. Mearsheimer and Walt, *The Israel Lobby and U.S. Foreign Policy*, 23–48, 150–67, and 168–69.

63. Tom Ricks, in "Counterinsurgency Operations in Iraq," Johns Hopkins University School of Advanced International Studies, March 5, 2010, http://www.c-spanarchives.org/program/ID/220600.

64. On the rhetoric, see Haggai Ram, *Iranophobia: The Logic of an Israeli Obsession* (Stanford: Stanford University Press, 2009).

65. "Israeli Official Doubts Iran Would Nuke His Country," *USA Today*, Feb. 26, 2010.

66. Jeffrey Goldberg, "The Point of No Return," *Atlantic*, Sept. 2010.

67. Ronen Bergmann, "Will Israel Attack Iran?," *New York Times Magazine*, Jan. 25, 2012.

68. In May 2010, retired Israeli military officers, diplomats, and intelligence officials conducted a war game that assumed Iran had acquired nuclear weapons capability; participants later told Western reporters that such a capability does not pose an "existential threat" but "would blunt Israel's military autonomy." See Dan Williams, "Israel Plays Wargame Assuming Iran Has Nuclear Bomb," Reuters, May 17, 2010.

69. E.g., H.R. 1905, The Iran Threat Reductions Act, http://fcnl.org/issues/iran/hr1905ans.pdf, esp. sec. 601(c).

70. See, i.a., AIPAC, "Talks Must Quickly Lead to Iranian Enrichment Suspension," May 2, 2012, http://www.aipac.org/~/media/Publications/Policy%20and%20Politics/AIPAC%20Analyses/Issue%20Memos/2012/05/AIPACMemoIranTalks.pdf, and "Iranian Nuclear Weapons Capability: Unacceptable," March 3, 2012, http://www.aipac.org/~/media/Publications/Policy%20and%20Politics/AIPAC%20Analyses/Issue%20Memos/2012/03/IranTimelineweb.pdf.

71. AIPAC laid out its basic game plan in April 1995, in its "Comprehensive U.S. Sanctions against Iran: A Plan for Action"; see Mearsheimer and Walt, *The Israel Lobby and U.S. Foreign Policy*, 288.

72. Ibid., 288–89, and Robert Dreyfuss, "AIPAC from the Inside, Part I: Isolating Iran," *Tehran Bureau*, June 11, 2011, http://www.pbs.org/wgbh/pages/

frontline/tehranbureau/2011/06/aipac-from-the-inside-1-isolating-iran .html.

73. AIPAC, "Talks Must Quickly Lead to Iranian Enrichment Suspension" and "More Pressure Needed as Iran Advances Nuclear Program," Dec. 8, 2010, http://www.aipac.org/~/media/Publications/Policy%20and%20Politics/ AIPAC%20Analyses/Issue%20Memos/2010/12/AIPAC_Memo_Mounting_ Pressure_Needed_as_Iran_Advances_Nuclear_Program.pdf.

74. See Mearsheimer and Walt, *The Israel Lobby and U.S. Foreign Policy*, 233–43, 255–62, and 291–98, and Robert Dreyfuss, "AIPAC from the Inside, Part II: Wrangling Over Regime Change," *Tehran Bureau*, June 11, 2011, http://www.pbs.org/wgbh/pages/frontline/tehranbureau/2012/05/news -iaea-and-iran-reach-agreement-senate-approves-tougher-sanctions.html.

75. There is wide recognition in Israel's national security establishment that its options for attacking Iranian nuclear targets unilaterally are of doubtful efficacy, esp. compared with American options; see Goldberg, "The Point of No Return."

76. Mearsheimer and Walt, *The Israel Lobby and U.S. Foreign Policy*, 300–303; Steve Clemons, "Cheney Attempting to Constrain Bush's Choices on Iran Conflict," *Washington Note*, May 24, 2007, http://www.thewashingtonnote .com/archives/002145.php; Joe Klein, "Cheney's Iran Fantasy," *Time*, May 25, 2007; and George W. Bush, *Decision Points* (New York: Crown, 2010), 415–20. After Bush's decision, the Olmert government considered a unilateral strike, but Bush reportedly told Olmert he would not support it; see Jonathan Steele, "Israel Asked US for Green Light to Bomb Nuclear Sites in Iran," *Guardian*, Sept. 25, 2008, and David E. Sanger, "U.S. Rejected Aid for Israeli Raid on Iranian Nuclear Site," *New York Times*, Jan. 10, 2009.

77. Flynt Leverett and Hillary Mann Leverett, "Who Will Be Blamed for a U.S. Attack on Iran?," *Race for Iran*, July 11, 2010, http://www.raceforiran.com /who-will-be-blamed-for-a-u-s-attack-on-iran.

78. See, e.g., David Harris, "Jimmy Carter Does It Again," *Huffington Post*, Jan. 30, 2012, http://www.huffingtonpost.com/david-harris/jimmy-carter-iran _b_1240788.html.

79. The phrase was coined by Alan Dershowitz in "Obama's Legacy and the Iranian Bomb," *Wall Street Journal*, March 23, 2010.

80. Cited in Leverett and Leverett, "Who Will Be Blamed for a U.S. Attack on Iran?"

81. Harris, "Jimmy Carter Does It Again."

82. "ADL's Foxman: Obama Has 'Improved,' but Iran Threat 'Serious,'" *Newsmax*, Feb. 9, 2012.

83. http://www.youtube.com/watch?v=Du1ixVZ6bqg.

84. http://www.youtube.com/watch?v=rDpLTRjiHUU&feature=fvst.

85. http://www.adl.org/main_International_Affairs/iranian_threat_faq.htm.

86. http://www.jinsa.org/about; see also Jason Vest, "The Men from JINSA and CSP," *Nation*, Sept. 2, 2002.

87. The most notable example of widely respected scholarship on Iran published by WINEP is Buchta, *Who Rules Iran?* For discussion, see Mearsheimer and Walt, *The Israel Lobby and U.S. Foreign Policy*, 175–78. Hillary Mann Leverett worked at WINEP as an intern for two summers in the late 1980s, as a fellow in the summer of 1991, and as a terrorism fellow during the mid-1990s.

88. Connie Bruck, "The Influencer," *New Yorker*, May 10, 2010.

89. See, e.g., Kenneth Pollack, *Persian Puzzle: The Conflict between Iran and America* (New York: Random House, 2004); "A Vote of No Confidence," *National Interest*, June 15, 2009; and *Which Path to Persia? Options for a New American Strategy toward Iran* (Washington, D.C.: Brookings, 2009).

90. Dennis Ross, *Acting with Caution: Middle East Policy Planning for the Second Reagan Administration*, Policy Paper 1 (Washington, D.C.: Washington Institute for Near East Policy, 1985).

91. On WINEP's first such exercise, in 1988, see David B. Ottaway, "Mideast Institute's Experts and Ideas Ascendant," *Washington Post*, March 24, 1989. The assessment is affirmed by reviewing how many of the participants in subsequent study groups went on to occupy executive branch positions dealing with national security and foreign policy. Flynt Leverett participated in the 2004 presidential study group.

92. Public Affairs Alliance of Iranian Americans, "PAAIA Releases 2011 National Survey of Iranian Americans," Dec. 7, 2011, http://www.paaia.org /CMS/paaia-releases-2011-national-survey-of-iranian-americans.aspx.

93. See Connie Bruck, "Exiles," *New Yorker*, March 6, 2006.

94. Michael Ledeen, "Why in the World Would We Want to Support the MEK?," *National Review Online*, Jan. 21, 2011; Danielle Pletka, "Lobbying for Terrorists, More on the MEK," American Enterprise Institute, July 6, 2012, http:// www.aei.org/article/foreign-and-defense-policy/terrorism/lobbying-for -terrorists-more-on-the-mek/, and Michael Rubin, "What's Behind the Campaign to Delist the Mujahedin Al-Khalq Organization?," *Commentary*, Feb. 24, 2011, http://www.commentarymagazine.com/2011/02/24/whats-behind -the-campaign-to-delist-the-mujahedin-al-khalq-organization/.

95. See Max Boot, "How to Handle Iran," *Los Angeles Times*, Oct. 25, 2006; Daniel Pipes and Patrick Clawson, "A Terrorist U.S. Ally," *New York Post*, May 20, 2003; and Pipes, "Washington Puzzles Over the Muhajedeen-e Khalq," Aug. 17, 2003, with updates, http://www.danielpipes.org/blog/2003 /08/washington-puzzles-over-the-mujahedeen-e.

96. http://www.foxnews.com/story/0,2933,300239,00.html.

97. http://www.iranpolicy.org/index.php.

98. Flynt Leverett and Hillary Mann Leverett, "With 'Engagement' Failing, Washington Voices Urge Obama to Embrace the MEK and Remove Its Terrorist Designation," *Race for Iran*, Jan. 23, 2011, http://www.raceforiran.com/with-%E2%80%9Cengagement%E2%80%9D-failing-washington-voices-urge-obama-to-embrace-the-mek-and-remove-its-terrorist-designation; "White House Support for Middle East 'Uprisings' Depends on How and Whether They Can Be Used against Iran," *Race for Iran*, Feb. 19, 2011, http://www.raceforiran.com/white-house-support-for-middle-east-%E2%80%98uprisings%E2%80%99-depends-on-how-and-whether-they-can-be-used-against-iran; and "Obama Adviser Lee Hamilton Joins Call to De-List the MEK," *Race for Iran*, Feb. 22, 2011, http://www.raceforiran.com/obama-adviser-lee-hamilton-joins-call-to-de-list-the-mek. See also Hamed Aleaziz, "Romney Adviser Blasts Government Investigation, Says Bring It On," *Mother Jones*, April 2, 2012, and http://www.executiveaction.com/services. On Iranian American financial support for these lobbying efforts, see Kevin Bogardus, "Federal Investigation of Iran Dissident Group Bypasses K Street Firms," *The Hill*, March 20, 2012, and Daniel Larison, "The Greed, Cluelessness, and Poor Judgment of the MEK's American Advocates," *American Conservative*, July 8, 2012. Some of the individuals named in the text are reportedly under investigation by the Treasury Department to determine if they received money either directly or indirectly from the MEK; as of July 2012, no charges have been brought against anyone. See Shane, "U.S. Supporters of Iranian Group Face Scrutiny"; Isikoff, "Ex-US Officials Investigated over Speeches to Iranian Dissident Group on Terror List"; and Aleaziz, "Romney Adviser Blasts Government Investigation."

99. Edmund Berger, "Soros and the State Department: Moving Iran Toward the Open Society," *Foreign Policy Journal*, May 14, 2011, http://www.foreignpolicyjournal.com/2011/05/14/soros-and-the-state-department-moving-iran-towards-the-open-society/; on the Rockefeller Brothers Fund see n. 109 below.

100. Dabashi, *Iran, the Green Movement, and the USA*, 100–101.

101. See, e.g., Karim Sadjadpour, "Why Iran '09 Could Be Like Florida '00," *Foreign Policy*, June 10, 2009; Ashley Fantz, "Moussavi: Painter, Architect and Possibly Iran's Next President," CNN, June 11, 2009; the sources cited in chapter 6, notes 5, 84, and 88; and Hashemi and Postol, *The People Reloaded*.

102. Pollack and Takeyh, "Doubling Down on Iran."

103. David Ignatius describes Sadjadpour as "an Iran expert . . . whose views are closely studied at the Obama White House"; see "How to Sink Iran's Regime? Sanctions, Not Bombs," *Washington Post*, March 9, 2012. See also Jordan Michael Smith, "Inside Obama's Iran Policy Shop," *World Politics Review*, Oct. 28, 2009.

104. See Jeanene Harlick, "Square Peg," *San Francisco Chronicle*, Nov. 11, 2005, http://www.sfgate.com/cgi-bin/article.cgi?f=/c/a/2005/11/11/PNGVAFIL7Q1.DTL&ao=all.

105. Abbas Milani, Michael McFaul, and Larry Diamond, *Beyond Incrementalism: A New Strategy for Dealing with Iran* (Stanford: Hoover Institution, 2005).

106. Shirin Ebadi and Muhammad Sahimi, "The Follies of Bush's Iran Policy," *New York Times*, May 30, 2007; see also Eli Lake, "Ganji Says Iran Dissidents Will Spurn U.S. Funds," *New York Sun*, July 14, 2006.

107. Eli Lake, "Iran Launches a Crackdown on Democracy Activists," *New York Sun*, March 14, 2006, and Steve Weissman, "Iran: Nonviolence 101," *Truthout*, June 21, 2009, http://archive.truthout.org/062109Y.

108. http://www.niacouncil.org/site/PageServer?pagename=About_parsi; http://www.niacouncil.org/site/PageServer?pagename=About_index; http://www.niacouncil.org/site/PageServer?pagename=About_faq; Trita Parsi, "Make Them Wait," *Foreign Policy*, July 30, 2009, http://www.foreignpolicy.com/articles/2009/07/30/make_them_wait; and http://www.niacouncil.org/site/PageServer?pagename=Policy_us_iran_relations.

109. http://www.niacouncil.org/site/PageServer?pagename=About_myths_facts.

110. Ansari, *Crisis of Authority*, xii.

111. See James Peck, *Ideal Illusions: How the U.S. Government Co-opted Human Rights* (New York: Metropolitan Books, 2010).

8: IRAN AND AMERICA'S IMPERIAL TURN

1. "Shields, Brooks on Iowa Debate, 'Rattling Sabers' over Iran, Iraq War's Legacy," PBS *NewsHour*, Dec. 16, 2011, http://www.pbs.org/newshour/bb/politics/july-dec11/shieldsbrooks_12-16.html.

2. Ferguson, "Israel and Iran on the Eve of Destruction in a New Six-Day War."

3. For a discussion reflecting a range of political perspectives, see Hunt, *Ideology and U.S. Foreign Policy*, 19–91, 125–35; Robert Kagan, *A Dangerous Nation: America's Foreign Policy from Its Earliest Days to the Dawn of the Twentieth Century* (New York: Random House, 2006); and Michael Lind, *The American Way of Strategy: U.S. Foreign Policy and the American Way of Life* (New York: Oxford University Press, 2006), 3–78.

4. For a discussion, see Christopher Layne, *The Peace of Illusions: American Grand Strategy from 1940 to the Present* (Ithaca: Cornell University Press, 2006), 3–5, 7, 29–36, and 118–35, and Desch, "America's Liberal Illiberalism."

5. X [George Kennan], "The Sources of Soviet Conduct," *Foreign Affairs* 25, no. 4 (July 1947).

6. NSC-68, "United States Objectives and Programs for National Security," Report to the President Pursuant to the President's Directive of January 31, 1950 [Top Secret], April 14, 1950.

7. John Lewis Gaddis has summarized the differences between Kennan's original concept and the strategy laid out in NSC-68 as a clash between "strongpoint defense" and global "perimeter defense"; see *Strategies of Containment: A Critical Appraisal of Postwar American National Security Policy* (New York: Oxford University Press, 1982), 57–58.

8. For a powerful and insightful elaboration of this argument, see Andrew Bacevich, *Washington Rules: America's Path to Permanent War* (New York: Metropolitan Books, 2010).

9. See Raymond Aron, *La république imperiale: Les États-Unis dans le monde* (Paris: Calmann-Lévy, 1973), available as *The Imperial Republic: The United States and the World, 1945–1973* (New Brunswick: Transaction, 2009).

10. See Shoon Murray, *Anchors against Change: American Opinion Leaders' Beliefs after the Cold War* (Ann Arbor: University of Michigan Press, 2002).

11. See, i.a., John Lewis Gaddis, *The United States and the Origins of the Cold War, 1941–1947* (New York: Columbia University Press, 1972), 309–12, and *Strategies of Containment*, 30–31; Bruce Kuniholm, *The Origins of the Cold War in the Near East: Great Power Conflict and Diplomacy in Iran, Turkey, and Greece* (Princeton: Princeton University Press, 1980), 130–398; Kuross Samii, *Involvement by Invitation: American Strategies of Containment in Iran* (State College: Pennsylvania State University Press, 1987); and Rashid Khalidi, *Sowing Crisis: The Cold War and American Dominance in the Middle East* (Boston: Beacon, 2009), 40–62.

12. More generally, for the first three decades of the Cold War, the United States operated in the Middle East in a manner that, as Andrew Bacevich notes, "minimized overt U.S. military involvement"; *The New American Militarism: How Americans Are Seduced by War* (New York: Oxford University Press, 2005), 180. For a more detailed discussion, see Khalidi, *Sowing Crisis*, 6–16, 107–11.

13. See W. Taylor Fain, *American Ascendance and British Retreat in the Persian Gulf Region* (New York: Palgrave Macmillan, 2008), and Kinzer, *All the Shah's Men*.

14. Anthony Cordesman, *Saudi Arabia Enters the Twenty-first Century*. Vol. 1: *The Political, Foreign Policy, Economic, and Energy Dimensions* (Westport: Praeger, 2003), 110–11, and Roham Alvandi, "Nixon, Kissinger, and the Shah: The Origins of Iranian Primacy in the Persian Gulf," *Diplomatic History* 36, no. 2 (April 2012).

15. Andrew Scott Cooper, *The Oil Kings: How the U.S., Iran, and Saudi Arabia Changed the Balance of Power in the Middle East* (New York: Simon and Schuster, 2011).

16. National Security Decision Directive, "U.S. Policy toward Iran," Top Secret, June 17, 1985, http://www.gwu.edu/~nsarchiv/NSAEBB/NSAEBB210/17-Draft%20NSDD%20on%20Iran%206-17-85%20(IC%2001217).pdf.

17. Richard Haass, "The George H. W. Bush Administration," in *The Iran Primer*, ed. Robin Wright (Washington, D.C.: United States Institute of Peace, 2010).

18. Brent Scowcroft, interview transcript for *Iran and the West*, archived at Liddel Hart Center for Military Archives, King's College, London.

19. Personal communications with the authors in 2006 and 2007.

20. In August 1992, Baker abandoned Foggy Bottom to become White House chief of staff, in a desperate move to shore up the president's chances.

21. Haass, "The George H. W. Bush Administration"; see also Haass's segments in *The Pariah State*.

22. See Scowcroft's segments in *The Pariah State*.

23. Personal communications with the authors in 2006 and 2007.

24. See George Bush and Brent Scowcroft, *A World Transformed* (New York: Vintage), 432–33.

25. Chas Freeman, "Excerpts from a Talk at the Institute for Defense Analyses," Nov. 10, 2004; rpt. in Chas Freeman, *America's Misadventures in the Middle East* (Charlottesville: Just World Books, 2010).

26. Andrew Bacevich, *American Empire: The Realities and Consequences of U.S. Diplomacy* (Cambridge: Harvard University Press, 2002).

27. Martin Indyk, *Innocent Abroad: An Intimate Account of American Peace Diplomacy in the Middle East* (New York: Simon and Schuster, 2009), 31.

28. Ibid., 43.

29. Martin Indyk, "The Clinton Administration's Approach to the Middle East," speech to the Washington Institute for Near East Policy, May 18, 1993, http://www.washingtoninstitute.org/policy-analysis/view/the-clinton-administrations-approach-to-the-middle-east.

30. See Burgos, "Origins of Regime Change."

31. Indyk, "The Clinton Administration's Approach to the Middle East."

32. Anthony Lake, "Confronting Backlash States," *Foreign Affairs* 73, no. 2 (March–April 1994).

33. Indyk, *Innocent Abroad*, 168.

34. Aaron David Miller, *The Much Too Promised Land: America's Elusive Search for Arab-Israeli Peace* (New York: Bantam, 2008).

35. Indyk, *Innocent Abroad*, 32. Remarkably, Indyk went on to assert that "the Bush administration had tried a benign approach, offering to reward constructive behavior by indicating to the Iranians that, in the words of President Bush, 'good will begets good will.' But the Iranians had spurned this offer."

36. Dennis Ross, *The Missing Peace: The Inside Story of the Fight for Middle East Peace* (New York: Farrar, Straus and Giroux, 2004), 6–7.

37. Indyk, *Innocent Abroad*, 217.

38. See, e.g., Pollack, *The Persian Puzzle*, 244–342, and Bruce Riedel, "The Clinton Administration," in Wright, ed., *The Iran Primer*.

39. James Mann, *The Vulcans: The History of Bush's War Cabinet* (New York: Viking, 2004).

40. For a discussion, see Flynt Leverett, "Illusion and Reality," *American Prospect*, Sept. 2006.

41. See, e.g., "Interview with Secretary of State Condoleezza Rice," *Financial Times*, April 20, 2007.

42. See Seymour Hersh, "The Iran Plans," *New Yorker*, April 17, 2006, and "The Bush Administration's Operations in Iran," *New Yorker*, July 7, 2008.

43. *The Iraq Study Group Report: The Way Forward—a New Approach* (New York: Vintage, 2006), 36, and "Bush Vows New Approach on Iraq, Plans Speech," Reuters, Dec. 8, 2006.

44. Dick Cheney, with Liz Cheney, *In My Time: A Personal and Political Memoir* (New York: Threshold, 2011), and Jonathan Steele, "Israel Asked US for Green Light to Bomb Nuclear Sites in Iran," *Guardian*, Sept. 26, 2008.

45. National Intelligence Council, *Iran: Nuclear Intentions and Capabilities*, National Intelligence Estimate, Nov. 2007, http://www.dni.gov/press_releases/20071203_release.pdf.

46. Bush, *Decision Points*, 419.

47. U.S. Department of Defense, "Speech, as Delivered by Secretary of Defense Robert M. Gates, West Point, NY, Friday, February 25, 2011," http://www.defense.gov/speeches/speech.aspx?speechid=1539.

48. As noted (see ch. 3), the administration made one more pro forma foray into nuclear diplomacy with Iran in June 2008, when William Burns—who had taken over from Nick Burns as undersecretary of state for political affairs—was allowed to sit in but not participate in a P5+1 meeting with an Iranian delegation.

49. See, e.g., *The Iraq Study Group Report*.

50. On Israeli, Saudi, British, and French perspectives, see Parsi, *A Single Roll of the Dice*, ch. 2.

51. See Mark Mazzetti, "U.S. Is Said to Expand Secret Actions in Mideast," *New York Times*, May 24, 2010, and Flynt Leverett and Hillary Mann Leverett, "Obama Steps Up America's Covert War against Iran," *Race for Iran*, May 25, 2010, http://www.raceforiran.com/obama-steps-up-america%E2%80%99s-covert-war-against-iran.

52. Parsi asserts that the administration designated PJAK as a positive "signal" to Iran and chastises Tehran for not appreciating it; see *A Single Roll of the Dice*, 42. However, he cites no source for the claim. By contrast, U.S. intelligence officials have told us that PJAK was designated as a gesture to Turkey.

53. See also Flynt Leverett and Hillary Mann Leverett, "U.S. Reverses Course and Designates Anti-Iranian Jundallah as a Terrorist Organization," *Race for Iran*, Nov. 3, 2010, http://www.raceforiran.com/u-s-reverses-course-and

-designates-anti-iranian-jundallah-as-a-foreign-terrorist-organzation; Mark Perry, "False Flag," *Foreign Policy*, Jan. 13, 2012, http://www.foreign policy.com/articles/2012/01/13/false_flag; and Flynt Leverett and Hillary Mann Leverett, "Who's Running Covert Ops against Iran? The Obama Administration Protests Too Little," *Race for Iran*, Jan. 13, 2012, http://www .raceforiran.com/who%E2%80%99s-running-covert-ops-against-iran-the -obama-administration-protests-too-little.

54. Flynt Leverett and Hillary Mann Leverett, "Have We Already Lost Iran?," *New York Times*, May 29, 2009, http://www.nytimes.com/2009/05/24/opinion /24leverett.html?pagewanted=all.

55. Roger Cohen, "The Making of an Iran Policy," *New York Times Magazine*, July 30, 2009.

56. See Flynt Leverett and Hillary Mann Leverett, "WikiLeaks and Iran—Take I: Obama's Legacy Will Be Change You Can't Rely On," *Race for Iran*, Nov. 29, 2010, http://www.raceforiran.com/wikileaks-and-iran%E2%80%94take -i-obama%E2%80%99s-legacy-will-be-change-you-cant-rely-on.

57. Ibid.

58. See Reza Marashi, "WikiLeaks: U.S.-Iran Relations 'Now What' Moment?," *Huffington Post*, Nov. 30, 2010, http://www.huffingtonpost.com/reza-marashi /wikileaks-usiran-relation_b_789673.html, and remarks by Vali Nasr on "The Real Story of Iran," *Fareed Zakaria GPS*, Jan. 8, 2012, http://transcripts .cnn.com/TRANSCRIPTS/1201/08/fzgps.01.html (Hillary Mann Leverett also appeared on this panel).

59. Jack Fairweather and Anton LaGuardia, "Chalabi Stands By Faulty Intelligence That Toppled Saddam's Regime," *Telegraph*, Feb. 19, 2004.

60. For a detailed discussion, see Flynt Leverett and Hillary Mann Leverett, "Listening Posts on Iran Produce Same Sorts of Bad Intel as Iraqi Defectors," *Race for Iran*, Dec. 9, 2010, http://www.raceforiran.com/listening-posts-on -iran-produce-same-sort-of-bad-intel-as-iraqi-defectors.

61. Smith, "Inside Obama's Iran Policy Shop," and Ignatius, "How to Sink Iran's Regime?" Under the Obama administration, Kahlili serves as a consultant to the Defense Department and the FBI.

62. Leverett and Leverett, "WikiLeaks and Iran—Take I."

63. Parsi, *A Single Roll of the Dice*, 147–50.

64. See Olivier Meier, "Iran and Foreign Enrichment: A Troubled Model," *Arms Control Today* (Jan.–Feb. 2006).

65. Leverett and Leverett, "WikiLeaks and Iran—Take I."

66. Parsi, *A Single Roll of the Dice*, 164.

67. See David Albright, quoted in Glenn Kessler, "Analysis: Iranian Plan Will Put Nation a Step Closer to Having Material for Bomb," *Washington Post*, Feb. 9, 2010, and Indira Lakshmanan and Viola Gienger, "Iran's Nuclear Breakthrough Called 'Hype' by US as Crude Oil Price Gains," Bloomberg, Feb. 16, 2012.

68. Personal communications with the authors.

69. For a discussion and a link to the letter, see Flynt Leverett and Hillary Mann Leverett, "President Obama Should Be Honest about the Iran-Turkey-Brazil Nuclear Deal," *Race for Iran*, May 27, 2010, http://www.raceforiran.com/president-obama-should-be-honest-about-the-iran-turkey-brazil-nuclear-deal. Turkish diplomats say that Obama's letter to Erdoğan was virtually identical.

70. "Text of the Iran-Brazil-Turkey Deal," *Guardian*, May 17, 2010, http://www.guardian.co.uk/world/julian-borger-global-security-blog/2010/may/17/iran-brazil-turkey-nuclear.

71. Janine Zakaria, "Spat over Iran May Further Strain Relations between Allies U.S., Turkey," *Washington Post*, May 24, 2010.

72. "Giving Diplomacy a Chance," *International Herald Tribune*, May 26, 2010, http://www.nytimes.com/2010/05/27/opinion/27iht-eddavutoglu.html.

73. For a discussion, see "President Obama Should Be Honest about the Iran-Turkey-Brazil Nuclear Deal" and Laura Rozen, "Obama Administration Dismisses Leak of Obama Letter on Fuel Deal," *Politico*, May 28, 2010, http://www.politico.com/blogs/laurarozen/0510/Obama_admin_dismisses_leak_of_Obama_letter_on_Iran_fuel_deal.html.

74. See Flynt Leverett and Hillary Mann Leverett, "Baradei Supports the Iran-Turkey-Brazil Nuclear Deal, Warns against Sanctions and Military Strikes," *Race for Iran*, June 2, 2010, http://www.raceforiran.com/baradei-supports-the-iran-turkey-brazil-nuclear-deal-warns-against-sanctions-and-military-strikes.

75. See Flynt Leverett and Hillary Mann Leverett, "Understanding (and Appreciating) Brazil's Vote against New Iran Sanctions," *Race for Iran*, June 10, 2010, http://www.raceforiran.com/understanding-and-appreciating-brazil%e2%80%99s-vote-against-new-iran-sanctions.

76. Celso Amorim, "Let's Hear from the New Kids on the Block," *New York Times*, June 14, 2010, http://www.nytimes.com/2010/06/15/opinion/15iht-edamorim.html. Some senior Iranian officials we spoke to were also puzzled by the administration's categorical rejection of the Tehran Declaration; at least one, however, predicted privately at the time the declaration was announced that Washington would not accept it.

77. Links to the Iranian PowerPoint presentation (in three parts) are available in Scott Peterson, "Iran Makes Its Nuclear Case—With PowerPoint," *Christian Science Monitor*, July 9, 2012.

78. Michael Massing, "The War Expert: Wrong, Wrong, Wrong Again. But the Media Still Want Ken Pollack," *Columbia Journalism Review* (Nov.–Dec. 2007) and Glenn Greenwald, "Lessons Not Learned," *Salon*, March 20, 2008 and "War Advocates Like Anne-Marie Slaughter Demand That You Forget the Past," *Salon*, March 21, 2008.

9: THE ROAD TO TEHRAN

1. Chen Jian, *China's Road to the Korean War: The Making of the Sino-American Confrontation* (New York: Columbia University Press, 1994), 50.

2. Kennan, "The Sources of Soviet Conduct."

3. For discussions, see Jian, *China's Road to the Korean War*, 18–21, and James Peck, *Washington's China: The National Security World, the Cold War, and the Origins of Globalism* (Amherst: University of Massachusetts Press, 2006).

4. By 1948, even Kennan argued in a State Department paper that the CCP had propagandistically appropriated "the sentiment of nationalism (anti-imperialism)" and "the urge toward reform and order" to rally popular support but was itself already being brought "under Kremlin control." See PPS/39, "To Review and Define United States Policy toward China," Sept. 15, 1948, http://www.russilwvong.com/future/kennan/pps39.html. This memorandum was subsequently circulated within the executive branch as NSC-34.

5. For a discussion, see Ronald Steel, *Walter Lippmann and the American Century* (New York: Random House, 1981), 466.

6. "Address to the Preparatory Meeting of the New Political Consultative Conference," June 15, 1949, in *Collected Works of Mao Tsetung*, vol. 4.

7. Jian, *China's Road to the Korean War*.

8. On Japan and America's post–World War II grand strategy in Asia, see Robert Gilpin, "The Rise of American Hegemony," in Patrick Karl O'Brien and Armand Cleese, eds., *Two Hegemonies: Britain, 1841–1914, and the United States, 1941–2001* (Aldershot: Ashgate, 2001).

9. This point is brilliantly made in Peck, *Washington's China*.

10. See Acheson, "New Era in Asia," March 15, 1950, in *Vital Speeches of the Day* 16 (April 1, 1950), 355.

11. See Rusk, "Chinese-American Friendship: Peiping Regime Is Not Chinese," May 18, 1951, in *Department of State Bulletin*, May 28, 1951.

12. Peck, *Washington's China*, 6–7, 48–82.

13. Quoted in Peck, *Washington's China*, 5.

14. On this point, see, esp., Leslie Gelb and Richard Betts, *The Irony of Vietnam: The System Worked* (Washington, D.C.: Brookings, 1979).

15. See E. J. Kahn, *The China Hands: America's Foreign Service Officers and What Befell Them* (New York: Viking, 1975).

16. Flynt Leverett and Hillary Mann Leverett, "What We Really Wanted to Tell You about Iran," *New York Times*, Dec. 22, 2006, http://www.nytimes.com/2006/12/22/opinion/22precede.html.

17. "America and Iran's Green Movement: The Iran Debate in America," *Economist*, March 2, 2010, http://rss.economist.com/blogs/democracyinamerica/2010/03/america_and_irans_green_movement.

18. In a 1957 article, then senator John Kennedy argued that "the fragmentation of authority within the Soviet orbit" meant that the American posture

toward the People's Republic was "probably too rigid." See Kennedy, "A Democrat Looks at Foreign Policy," *Foreign Affairs* 36, no. 1 (Oct. 1957).

19. Richard Reeves, *President Kennedy: Profile of Power* (New York: Simon and Schuster, 1993), 29–33.

20. Stewart Alsop, "The Madness of Mao Tse-tung," *Saturday Evening Post*, Oct. 26, 1963.

21. Jeffrey Goldberg, "Obama to Iran and Israel: 'As President of the United States, I Don't Bluff,'" *Atlantic*, March 2, 2012, http://www.theatlantic.com/international/archive/2012/03/obama-to-iran-and-israel-as-president-of-the-united-states-i-dont-bluff/253875/; Gordon Chang, "JFK, China, and the Bomb," *Journal of American History* 74, no. 4 (March 1988); and William Burr and Jeffrey T. Richelson, "Whether to 'Strangle the Baby in the Cradle': The United States and the Chinese Nuclear Program, 1960–64," *International Security* 25, no. 3 (Winter 2000–01).

22. For further discussion, see Chang, "JFK, China, and the Bomb," and Burr and Richelson, "Whether to 'Strangle the Baby in the Cradle.'"

23. Henry Kissinger, *On China* (New York: Penguin, 2011), 199.

24. Kissinger, *Diplomacy* (New York: Simon and Schuster, 1994), 703–4.

25. Ibid, 705.

26. As Kissinger later put it, realigning relations with the People's Republic would allow the United States "to regain the diplomatic initiative while the war in Vietnam was still in progress" (*Diplomacy*, 713).

27. We are grateful to Chas Freeman for this point.

28. Kissinger observes, "The United States remained essential to international stability, but it would not be able to sustain the freewheeling interventionism that had brought over 500,000 Americans into Indochina without a strategy for victory. The survival of mankind ultimately depended on the relationship of the two superpowers, but the peace of the world depended on whether America could distinguish between those responsibilities in which its role was merely helpful and those to which it was indispensable, and whether it could sustain the latter without tearing itself apart." See *Diplomacy*, 707.

29. Charles Freeman, "The Process of Rapprochement: Achievements and Problems," in *Sino-American Normalization and Its Policy Implications*, ed. Gene Hsiao and Michael Witunski (New York: Praeger, 1983), 8.

30. Kissinger, *On China*, 214.

31. Kissinger, *Diplomacy*, 720–21.

32. Ibid., 720.

33. See *U.S. Foreign Policy for the 1970s: A New Strategy of Peace*, First Annual Report to the Congress on United States Foreign Policy for the 1970s (Washington, D.C.: Government Printing Office, February 19, 1970), 119.

34. Goldberg, "Obama to Iran and Israel."

35. Quoted in Kissinger, *On China*, 233. While Nixon kept the Warsaw channel

open, he did not rely on it as a major forum for Sino-American rapprochement and did not let disturbances in that channel deter him from pursuing his ultimate goal. Charles Freeman recounts how, after Nixon approved a resumption of the ambassadorial talks in Warsaw, the first meeting, scheduled for February 1969, "was abruptly canceled by the Chinese. . . . While expressing disappointment, the new administration pledged 'new initiatives to re-establish more normal relations with Communist China.'" See Freeman, "The Process of Rapprochement," 3.

36. Kissinger, *Diplomacy*, 722–23.
37. Freeman, "The Process of Rapprochement," 10.
38. Kissinger, *Diplomacy*, 722, 726, 727–28.
39. Quoted in Kissinger, *On China*, 215.
40. Freeman, "The Process of Rapprochement," 3, and Tim Weiner, *Legacy of Ashes: The History of the CIA* (New York: Random House, 2007), 349–50.
41. *U.S. Foreign Policy for the 1970s*, 140–42.
42. Kissinger, *Diplomacy*, 723–24, and *On China*, 210–20.
43. See, i.a., Henry Kissinger, *White House Years* (Boston: Little, Brown, 1979), 762–63, and Yukinori Komine, *Secrecy in US Foreign Policy: Nixon, Kissinger and the Rapprochement with China* (Aldershot: Ashgate, 2008).
44. Kissinger, *On China*, 216.
45. For representative statements, see Flynt Leverett, *U.S.-Iran Relations: Looking Back, Looking Ahead*, Emirates Lecture Series (Abu Dhabi: Emirates Center for Strategic Study and Research, 2003); Flynt Leverett, *Dealing with Tehran: Evaluating U.S. Diplomatic Options toward Iran* (New York: Century Foundation, 2006); Flynt Leverett, "All or Nothing: The Case for a U.S.-Iranian 'Grand Bargain,'" Statement to the Subcommittee on National Security and Foreign Affairs, Committee on Government Oversight and Reform, U.S. House of Representatives, Nov. 7, 2007, http://democrats.oversight.house.gov/images/stories/subcommittees/NS_Subcommittee/11.7.07_Iran_II/Flynt_Leverett_Testimony.pdf; Flynt Leverett and Hillary Mann Leverett, "The Grand Bargain," *Washington Monthly*, Aug.–Oct. 2008, http://www.washingtonmonthly.com/features/2008/0808.leverett.html; and Leverett and Leverett, "The United States, the Islamic Republic of Iran, and the Middle East's New 'Cold War.'"
46. These would include the Subsidiary Arrangements General Part "Code 3.1," dealing with the provision of design information about new nuclear facilities to the IAEA.

ACKNOWLEDGMENTS

We have accumulated many debts while writing *Going to Tehran*. We are grateful for the support we have received as faculty members at Penn State's School of International Affairs and Dickinson School of Law (Flynt) and American University's School of International Service (Hillary). In particular, we thank Philip McConnaughay, dean of Penn State's School of International Affairs (SIA) and Dickinson School of Law; Amy Gaudion, assistant dean; Tiyanjana Maluwa, director of SIA; Shoon Murray, director of the U.S. Foreign Policy Program at American University's School of International Service (SIS); and Robert Pastor of the SIS faculty. We are especially appreciative of our students at AU and Penn State; throughout the writing of this book, they have helped us sharpen our thinking about Iran, its foreign policy and domestic politics, and U.S.-Iranian relations—and about how best to present our ideas. During 2010–11, while in the early stages of writing, we were senior fellows at Yale University's Jackson Institute for Global Affairs; we are grateful to our Yale students, undergraduate and graduate, for the same reasons. Among our students, Adam Pourahmadi (American University), Jan Burnett (Penn State), and Elham Sadri (Penn State) provided research assistance, for which we thank them.

Hillary inaugurated our engagement with Iran and the many problems and possibilities in U.S.-Iranian relations. During 2001–03, she was one of a handful of U.S. officials authorized to have discussions with Iranian counterparts about Afghanistan and Al-Qa'ida, first as political adviser to the U.S. Mission to the United Nations in New York and, after 9/11, as director for Iran and Afghanistan affairs at the National Security Council. She admires the Iranian diplomats who engaged in these discussions; they worked to advance Iranian interests through better relations with the United States and risked their careers to do so—not because someone in Tehran was going to turn on them but because past experience told them that Washington was unlikely to reciprocate Iranian good faith. Since leaving government service, we have been able to expand our contacts with Iranian officials, former officials, scholars, and others. The comments, observations, and experiences they shared with us have enriched our knowledge and appreciation of the Islamic Republic enormously and are, in many respects, the foundation for this book. This book is unique largely because we have listened to and taken seriously the perspectives of Iranians who support the Islamic Republic. We thank all those Iranians, from senior officials and high-level politicians to scholars and students, who have helped us understand their country better.

We are deeply grateful to colleagues and friends who read the manuscript and offered suggestions and criticism that made this an infinitely better book than it would have been otherwise. At the University of Tehran, Seyed Mohammad Marandi commented closely on the manuscript; we thank him not only for that but for the innumerable insights he has provided us over several years of friendship and collegial interaction. We also thank Ebrahim Mohseni, now Seyed Mohammad's faculty colleague at the University of Tehran, for reading and commenting on the manuscript. We first got to know Ebrahim while Flynt was a member of his doctoral dissertation committee at the University of Maryland's School of Public Policy; we just hope he learned even half as much from us as we have learned from him. In China, Hua Liming—a former ambassador of the People's Republic in Tehran, now a senior fellow at the China Institute of International Studies—and Wu Bingbing at Peking University offered invaluable insights. Here in the United States, Andrew Bacevich, Paul Pillar, Cyrus Safdari, and Stephen Walt read, and commented extensively on, various drafts. All have been prescient and courageous contributors to the debate over America's role in the world; we aspire to meet the intellectual and moral standards they set in their work. While we could not take every suggestion they made, the book is vastly better because of their feedback.

Early versions of analyses and arguments developed in the book were aired in presentations (some individual, some joint) at American University, Harvard University, the University of Maryland's School of Public Policy, the Massachusetts Institute of Technology, New York University, the Norwegian Institute for International Affairs, Peking University, Penn State's Dickinson School of Law, the U.S. Army War College, and Yale University. We appreciate the comments and feedback we received from participants in these events. Over the last several years, the chance to take part in gatherings organized by the Conflicts Forum in Beirut has added immeasurably to our thinking about the Islamic Republic and its place in a changing Middle East. (Hillary is pleased to serve on the forum's board.) We thank Alastair Crooke, the forum's founder, as well as his partner, Aisling Byrne, for the opportunities and support they have extended to us while we were writing *Going to Tehran.* More recently, one of the greatest stimuli for our work has been our association with Peking University's School of International Studies, where we are visiting scholars. Our gratitude to Wang Jisi, dean of the school, for making such a great opportunity available to us and (again) to Wu Bingbing for being such a wonderful friend and colleague.

We extend boundless thanks to our publisher, Sara Bershtel, who took what we thought was a good idea and showed us how to turn it into a book worth reading. We are also beholden to Craig Seligman for his exemplary editing, to Roslyn Schloss for copyediting that was both meticulous and artful, and to our literary agent, Andrew Stuart, who was so instrumental in getting this project off the ground.

Finally, we offer a special word of love and gratitude to our beautiful children. You teach us each day that the struggle to live a life with dignity and to manage conflict is profound at any age and in every culture. You inspire us as we hope to inspire you. We dedicate this book to you with the wish that you might live in a world with a bit less "hatred and vainglory."

INDEX